Reviving the Invisible Hand

Reviving the Invisible Hand

THE CASE FOR CLASSICAL LIBERALISM
IN THE TWENTY-FIRST CENTURY

Deepak Lal

PRINCETON UNIVERSITY PRESS   PRINCETON AND OXFORD

Library of Congress Cataloging-in-Publication Data

Lal, Deepak.
    Reviving the invisible hand : the case for classical liberalism in the
twenty-first century / Deepak Lal.
        p. cm.
    Includes bibliographical references and index.
    ISBN-13: 978-0-691-12591-6 (hardcover : alk.paper)
    ISBN-10: 0-691-12591-0 (hardcover : alk.paper)
    1. Liberalism.   2. Capitalism.   3. Globalization.   I. Title.
    JC574.L35 2006
    320.51'2—dc22   2005030009

British Library Cataloging-in-Publication Data is available

This book has been composed in Goudy

Printed on acid-free paper. ∞

pup.princeton.edu

Printed in the United States of America

3 5 7 9 10 8 6 4 2

In Memory of Classical Liberal Friends I Miss

Peter Bauer, Gottfried Haberler,
Keith Joseph, and Shirley Letwin

Contents

Preface

In the early 1980s, when developing countries were clamoring for a new international economic order (NIEO), I wrote a small book (*The Poverty of "Development Economics"*)[1] questioning the *Dirigiste Dogma* which lay behind these demands and which were aided and abetted by the then fashionable theories of "development economics." This was surprisingly well received and I hope had some influence in persuading many of the harm that the Dirigiste Dogma had caused the world's poor.[2]

The Dirigiste Dogma encompassed a set of interrelated beliefs: First, that the price mechanism or the working of a market economy needs to be supplanted (and not merely supplemented) by various methods of direct government control to promote economic development. Second, that orthodox price theory (microeconomic) is of minor concern for the design of public policies. Instead, governments should attach prime attention to macroeconomic accounting aggregates to chart and implement a "strategy" for rapid and equitable growth. Third, that the classical liberal case for free trade is invalid for developing countries and government restrictions of international trade and payments are necessary for economic development. Finally, to alleviate poverty and improve domestic income distribution, massive and continuing government intervention is required to redistribute assets and manipulate the returns to different types of labor and capital through pervasive price and wage controls. *The Poverty of Development Economics*, whilst accepting the objective of poverty redressing growth, showed how these dirigiste panaceas were the problem rather than the solution. By the mid-1980s there was general acceptance of this growing critique of the Dirigiste Dogma.

The subsequent Age of Reform, encompassing both the Third and Second Worlds, seemed to presage a new era with the acceptance of the so-called Washington Consensus, as more and more countries—most notably China and India—liberalized their economies and joined the bandwagon of globalization. But, the dirigiste impulse does not die. It has now transmuted itself into a *new dirigisme*, which as in the past is being supported by various members of the clerisy. Though *The Poverty of "Development Economics"* has gone through a number of editions in which I have tried to keep it up to date with various addendum, in many ways it is out of date. For the new dirigisme, though motivated by the same collectivist impulse, has changed its stance since the demise of the countries of "really existing socialism." It now claims to be providing a Third Way, to create "capitalism with a human face." It no longer wishes to supplant the price mechanism through central planning but seeks to regulate the workings of the market economy to overcome purported "market failures" and to subserve various "moral" and "social" objectives.

Many of the protesters marching through the streets of Seattle or Genoa or meeting annually in Porto Allegro against the perceived ills of globalization and what they call "neo-liberalism"[3] are echoing this "new dirigisme." Its passions arise from various moral as well as factual claims, but even more so because it is not globalization per se, but the globalizing of capitalism to which they object. For capitalism, that midwife of modernity, has been under attack ever since it arose in the High Middle Ages in Western Europe.

A few years ago I began a project on "globalization and order" to counter this new dirigisme. Its aim was to show that these claims were either false, atavistic, or based on the half-baked culturally specific values of what remains at heart Western Christendom. It also sought to show the link between empires and globalization. Many readers of this original manuscript—in particular David Henderson and Angus Maddison—persuaded me that it should be turned into two complementary books: one on empires, the other on the current debates on development. This is the second of these books, the first being a book called *In Praise of Empires* (Lal 2004a). There is inevitably some overlap in the two books. *The Case for Classical Liberalism* provides the detailed argument in favor of the classical liberal case for capitalism and its globalization. The other book, *In Praise of Empires*, deals in part with an important lacunae within the classical liberal case for globalization, namely its eschewing of power politics in the belief that the international global order required for an international liberal economic order would emerge as a spontaneous byproduct of limited government and unilateral free trade promoted at home. The two books are thus complementary. *In Praise of Empires* deals with the international political aspects, *The Case for Classical Liberalism* with the international economic aspects of the globalization of capitalism. Both seek to set contemporary debates within a broad cross-cultural and historical context.

As with *The Poverty of "Development Economics,"* this book is meant for the general reader. I have thus tried to spell out various economic frameworks which will appear tedious or simplistic to the cognoscenti but which are necessary if the interested layperson is to understand the issues underlying ongoing public debates on globalization. Also, as understanding and countering the new dirigisme involves questions of values, this book, unlike *The Poverty of "Development Economics,"* is broader in scope, dealing not only with narrower issues of technocratic economics but also with questions concerning politics and culture: questions I have been concerned with over the last decade. For these reasons it also draws on my book *The Political Economy of Poverty, Equity and Growth—A Comparative Study* (written with Hla Myint) concerning the political, as well as my recent book *Unintended Consequences—The Impact of Factor Endowments, Culture and Politics on Long Run Economic Performance,* concerning the cultural aspects of development. But as with *The Poverty of "Development Economics,"* I do not go into the various scholarly disputes and fine qualifications which are appropriate for a scholarly treatise, but would be mere pedantry in a work that is addressed to those more concerned with getting to the heart of the matter in various debates on development than with intellectual pyrotechnics and scholarly exegesis—though the notes and references provide some guidance to general readers with such interests. As stated in the 1985 preface to *The Poverty of "Development Economics,"* "these debates deal with ideas which have public consequences. One essential function of scholarship, in my view, must be to make these ideas accessible to the general public, so they can judge what is at stake." Moreover, this book defending global capitalism is written from the classical liberal viewpoint. It provides a more robust case for economic liberalism, based on evidence and argument, than many recent defenders of globalization seem willing to make, as they remain partly infected with the new dirigisme with which I take issue in this book. If as a result this book, like *The Poverty of "Development Economics,"* "reads more like a pamphlet than a conventional work of scholarship, so be it. For as Keynes wrote in his memoir of Alfred Marshall: "Economists must leave to Adam Smith alone the glory of the Quarto, must pluck the day, fling pamphlets into the wind, write always *sub species temporis,* and achieve immortality by accident, if at all" (Lal 2000, p. xviii).

I am grateful to Surjit Bhalla, Harold Demsetz, Stanley Engerman, David Henderson, Mats Lundahl, Angus Maddison, and Razeen Sally for comments on a draft of the original manuscript on "globalization and order" of which some of this book formed a part, and to the referees of Princeton University Press for incisive comments on the manuscript of this book which have greatly helped in its improvement. Finally, thanks are due to Chris DeMuth and Nick Eberstadt at the American Enterprise Institute for inviting me to give the 2002 Wendt lecture on "In Defense of Empires" which presented some of the arguments of this and the complementary book on *In Praise of Empires.*

In the cacophony of outpourings on globalization by sundry sociologists, philosophers, and political scientists as well as some economists, the classical liberal viewpoint from which this book is written has often been obscured if not misrepresented. In restating that case, which I believe remains powerful for bringing modernity and the prosperity it engenders to the world, I trust the shades of my late classical liberal friends to whom the book is dedicated will be assuaged by seeing that classical liberals have not laid down their arms.

D. Lal
Los Angeles and London

Reviving the Invisible Hand

Introduction

This is a book about an ancient process (globalization) and a modern set of economic institutions (capitalism) which are transforming the world. It is best to begin with the new.

The Origins of "Capitalism"

Both economic historians (like Richard Tawney) and sociologists (like Max Weber) have identified the distinctive institutions of capitalism as the midwife of modernity, culminating in the rolling Industrial Revolution. Economists (like Sir John Hicks), however, preferred to talk of the rise of the market economy as the distinctive feature of modernity, in part because of the Marxian connotations of the word "capitalism" and the sundry and unnecessary intellectual baggage it thereby carries. All are agreed that the rise of the West from among a host of (probably richer) ancient Eurasian agrarian civilizations was associated with the rise of capitalism. There are continuing disputes about the nature and timing of this Great Divergence in the relative fortunes of the Eurasian civilizations (see chapter 1).

What Is Capitalism?

But what is capitalism? As the French economic historian Jean Baechler has cogently argued in his important book *The Origins of Capitalism*, neither Marx's nor Weber's outline of the distinctive features of capitalism allows us to differentiate its essence from the various cited features as they are to be found throughout human history and in many different cultures. For Marx, capitalism was "defined as the conjunction of capitalist ownership of the means of production with the wage laborer who has neither hearth or home."[1] But as Baechler shows, while this might have been true of the full-blown

1

industrial capitalism that was in full flower in Victorian England when Marx was writing, capitalism itself predates this phenomenon.

Nor is capitalism to be identified with markets, profit seeking, banking, bills of exchange, and business firms, for instance. For these are all found in ancient civilizations. Thus

> in ancient Mesopotamia there was the *Karum* . . . entrepots and commercial houses where importers, exporters, provisioners, and bankers all conducted their affairs. Occasionally these houses functioned as commercial tribunals . . . the Assyrian tablets dating from the 20th and 19th centuries B.C. [from] Cappadocia . . . reveal a complete commercial network run by genuine capitalists. In spite of state control, or at least state interference, the *Karum* had their own commercial activities and developed a series of institutions within which capitalist activity, as defined by Max Weber, took place. Banks undertook and granted loans; large warehouses brought together the merchandise of groups of merchants; bank accounts were opened where most of the operations were made by multilateral balancing of accounts. . . . By the beginning of the second millennium, at Ur and then at Larsa, capitalism seems to be entirely free of state control. Private entrepreneurs had replaced the temple and palace as disbursers of loans at interest (33 percent per annum); they made advances to wholesale merchants and directed the copper imports. . . . [By] the sixth to fourth century B.C. . . . in Nippur and Babylon firms were created through the association of capitalists. They took in money deposits, issued cheques, made loans at interest, and most importantly, participated directly in economic changes by investing in numerous agricultural and industrial enterprises. (Baechler 1975, pp. 37–8)

Similar examples can be multiplied from all the ancient agrarian civilizations.

But these agrarian civilizations looked upon these merchant capitalists as, at best, a necessary evil, as commercial activities were universally held in low esteem. Being intermediaries in the economic process, the merchants produced nothing in a tangible way, and were looked upon as parasites who were satisfying the demands of a tiny urban elite by transferring the rural surplus produced by those who wielded the plough to feed the warriors and priests in the towns. Devoted primarily to profit they became immensely rich, but their wealth was not matched by social acceptance or political power. It was only in the western part of Eurasia in the High Middle Ages that this changed, and the capitalists were eventually able to create an economy where their unceasing search for profit became not only acceptable but the norm. Thus, capitalism as an economic system came about when the merchant and the entrepreneur finally were given social acceptance and protection from the predation of the state.

Who Were the Capitalists?

Before I come to my story of how and why this happened in the western edge of Eurasia, we also need to ask: who were these merchants and why were they universally despised in the ancient agrarian civilizations? The answers are also relevant in explaining the ongoing cultural hatred of capitalism and in particular of its supreme embodiment—the United States of America.

The first point worth noting is that these merchant capitalists were a minority in agrarian economies. Their calling necessarily involved assuming risks and valuing novelty, behavioral characteristics that were not common among the settled agrarian communities, who over the centuries would have learned and adapted to the cyclical risks associated with variations in the climate and other quirks of nature. This learned behavior was fixed through social custom (see chapter 6). Novelty seeking and risk-taking behavior could have endangered these socially accepted ways of making a living. But these are precisely the behavioral attributes that successful capitalists need. This became clear when I was interviewing the aged founder of one of India's leading industrial conglomerates in the late 1960s. He had just chosen his successor from among his heirs to run his business when he died. I asked him how he had made the choice. He told me (probably apocryphally) that a few years before he had given each of his possible successors a large sum of money to set up their own businesses. Nearly all of them made some sort of go of this opportunity, except one grandson who after a year came to see him, crestfallen, saying that he had unfortunately lost all that he had been given on a speculative overseas venture. The old man decided that he was the suitable heir to take over his business!

There is now growing evidence that the behavioral traits which predispose some of us to risky and novelty-seeking behavior have a genetic basis. A recent book, *American Mania*, by a colleague, Peter Whybrow, director of UCLA's Neuropsychiatric Institute, summarizes this evidence. He begins by noting that human migration is one major form of risky and novelty-seeking behavior. Only a few of our species left their ancestral home in the African savannahs and began that long walk to the ends of the earth which allowed homo sapiens to colonize the world. Who were these earliest migrants? It turns out they had a particular genetic profile. They had a higher percentage of an exploratory and novelty-seeking gene than those remaining behind. As novelty seeking and risk taking "are . . . behaviors essential to exploration and migration . . . this should be reflected in a distribution pattern of the relevant allele [the D4-7 allele gene] that is similar to the ancient migratory paths of our species."[2] How do we know this? The geneticist Luigi Luca Cavali-Sforza of Stanford University and his colleagues have provided a genetic mapping of the geographical dispersal of homo sapiens from their original home in

3

Africa.[3] Subsequently, Dr. Chauseng Chen of the University of California, Irvine,[4] found that a coherent pattern emerges from this mapping "where those who stayed close to their original homeland have a higher percentage of the common D4-4 allele in the population and a lower prevalence of the exploratory and novelty-seeking D4-7 allele."[5]

Thus in Africa, from where humans began their worldwide migratory dispersal between ten and twenty thousand years ago, those remaining behind who constitute Africa's current population have "a far higher percentage (between 60 and 80 percent) of the [non-migrant version of the D4 gene] D4-4, compared with those who continued the initial migrant expansion of our species across the Asian continent." Within Africa the Bantu, who have migrated the farthest, have a majority of the migratory D4-7 allele gene. In Asia, those Chinese who migrated from the mainland and Taiwan to South East Asia have a "greater percentage of D4-7 allele in the population than the aboriginal population of Taiwan who stayed behind." As our human ancestors crossed the land bridges linking Asia to the Americas in the Ice Age, we should expect that those who walked farthest down the South American peninsula would have had the migratory gene. This turns out to be so, as "those who pushed into the Southern Hemisphere, the Colombians and members of the Karitiana, Surul, and the Ticuna tribes—carry a *preponderance* of the [migratory] D4-7 allele."[6] By contrast, in Japan the frequency of the migratory gene is very low and in parts of East Asia does not exist at all.

This "migration" gene, as we may call it, is also found in those who evince the most extreme form of risk-taking and novelty-seeking behavior to which the gene predisposes its bearers: addictive behavior which often descends into manic depression (bipolarity).[7] Risk taking and novelty seeking are of course also the hallmarks of the merchant and the entrepreneur. For both migrants and entrepreneurs are "mavericks . . . who run at the edge of the human herd. Migrants are a self-selected band of seekers—those of adventurous and curious mind—who in their restless approach to life lie at the extreme of the bell-shaped curve of behavioral distribution." So the migrant gene will be rare. As even during the great disruptions of human history caused by the four horsemen of the Apocalypse "for every two individuals who sought their salvation in migrant flight, ninety-eight remained behind to accept what fate would bring."[8]

It seems likely, therefore, that the capitalists of yore carried this rare migrant gene like their cousins who migrated from the homeland. It would explain why immigrant communities have often produced the merchants and entrepreneurs in so many countries, and why America with three centuries of continuing and substantial immigration would have a higher proportion of the migratory gene in its population, which by predisposing its bearers toward novelty seeking and risk taking would make it the capitalist country par excellence.

But novelty seekers do not make good farmers. Having over the centuries honed agricultural techniques to the natural variations of soil and place and the rhythms of the climate, the ancient sedentary agrarian civilizations of Eurasia would take a dim view of the novelty seekers and risk takers—the merchants and entrepreneurs in their midst. Though the commerce and trade these capitalists undertook would remain a necessary part of the economy, it would not command social approbation. The periodic raids on its merchants' wealth by the predatory state would not have been unpopular in these ancient agrarian civilizations. Thus, though these maverick capitalists existed in all the ancient Eurasian civilizations, it was only in one that they came to be given their head, and their novelty-seeking and risk-taking behavior eventually came to be the economic norm. This marked the emergence of capitalism which led to the Great Divergence between the West and the Rest.

The Great Divergence

My own story of this Rise of the West is contained in my book *Unintended Consequences* based on my Ohlin lectures. Part of this story is summarized in chapter 6. It contends that the Great Divergence was due to a legal revolution in the eleventh century due to Pope Gregory VII, who in 1075 put the church above the state and through the resulting church-state created the whole legal and administrative infrastructure required by a full-fledged market economy. Many of the specific institutions of capitalism, as we have seen, predate this papal revolution. But they were insecure and most often based on the trust engendered within the extended families of traders and merchants.[9] Furthermore, they did not have the legal protection of the state, which more often than not looked upon them as milch cows for their own predatory purposes. The eleventh-century papal revolution, by creating the church-state, provided a legal bulwark and administrative system whose reach, unlike most of the political states, covered the whole of Western Christendom. It allowed the novelty-seeking and risk-taking capitalists with the migratory gene to securely pursue their enterprise over a larger space and with myriads of strangers. It is thus, in my view, properly looked upon as initiating that capitalism which has changed the world.

This dating of the Great Divergence to the eleventh century also fortunately meshes with the quantitative evidence Angus Maddison has laboriously assembled for the world economy since the beginning of the Christian era. Hicks's identification of the rise of the market economy with the medieval European city-states, where the movement from a revenue to a market economy became manifest, also fits into this time frame. For, although merchants and markets (in the form of "fairs" and shopkeepers) have been ubiquitous in all the Eurasian agrarian civilizations for millennia, it was only when the peculiar needs of a mercantile economy, "the need for protection of property and the need for the protection of contract" were systematically met in a political system that the market economy could take off. These needs were best met in states where "the rulers are themselves merchants or are deeply involved in trade themselves."[10] The city-states of medieval Europe were trading states par excellence and were the seedbeds for the rise of the market economy.

"By the end of the fifteenth century," Joseph Schumpeter in his *History of Economic Analysis* tells us, "most of the phenomena we are in the habit of associating with that vague word Capitalism had put in their appearance, including big business, stock and commodity speculation and 'high finance' to all of which much people reacted much as we do ourselves." Adding in a footnote, "owing to the importance of the financial complement of capitalist production and trade, the development of the law and the practice of negotiable paper and of 'created' deposits afford perhaps the best indication we can have for the rise of capitalism."[11] But these institutions, which Schumpeter rightly notes were in full flower by the late fifteenth century, did not arise spontaneously. As Harold Berman shows in his important book *Law and Revolution*, they were the result of the papal legal revolution of Pope Gregory VII of 1075 when he proclaimed: "Let the terrestrial kingdom serve—or be the slave of—the celestial,"[12] which inaugurated the church-state.

Berman has shown how the whole Western legal tradition derives from the development of both canon and secular law during the eleventh to thirteenth centuries under the aegis of the Roman church. For the rise of the market economy the most important was the development of the "law of the merchant"—the *lex mercatoria*. "The church-state set an example for the city-state, and church law set an example for city law and for commercial law."[13] Berman lists many of the features that we currently associate with the modern institutional infrastructure for trade and commerce as having arisen in these three centuries of the High Middle Ages. They include:

> the invention of the negotiability of bills of exchange and promissory notes; the invention of the mortgage of movables (chattel mortgage); the development of a bankruptcy law which took into account the existence of a sophisticated system of commercial credit; the development of the bill of lading and other transportation documents . . . the invention of the bottomry loan; . . . the replacement of the more individualistic Graeco-Roman concept of partnership (societas) by a more collectivist concept in which there was joint ownership, the property was at the disposition of the partnership as a unit, and the rights and obligations of one partner survived the death of the other; the development of the joint venture (commenda) as a kind of joint-stock company, with the liability of each investor limited to the amount of his investment; the invention of trademarks and patents; the floating of public loans secured by bonds and other securities; the development of deposit banking.[14]

In short, all the essential legal infrastructure for a modern commercial and industrial economy: the institutions of capitalism!

It was during this time that the Roman church formed into a church-state, a law-state that also "developed the governmental institutions and the bureaucratic apparatus needed to make this legal system work: a professional judiciary, a treasury, a chancery. This was the first modern system of government and law. It was eventually emulated by the secular polities that took form in the succeeding generations"[15] in Western Europe. This was the Great Divergence which led the West to outpace and eventually overtake its other Eurasian peers in generating modern intensive economic growth. It was only with the progress of globalization under the British Empire in the nineteenth century that these institutions of capitalism came to be transferred—however haltingly—to the rest of the world, while the current period of globalization can be seen as the latest phase in completing this globalizing of capitalism.

Changing Material and Cosmological Beliefs

The rise of capitalism also involved changes in the *material* beliefs (how best to make a living) of the West. These were succinctly summarized by Tawney, by contrasting the attitudes to the material environment—of a pre-industrial agrarian economy shared by all the ancient Eurasian civilizations and the new attitudes generated by capitalism: "between the conception of society as a community of unequal classes with varying functions, organized for a common end, and that which regards it as a mechanism adjusting itself through the play of economic motives to the supply of economic needs; between the idea that a man must not take advantage of his neighbour's necessity, and the doctrine that 'man's self-love is God's providence'; between the attitude which appeals to a religious standard to repress economic appetites, and that which regards expediency as the final criterion."[16] It is the atavistic pre-modern attitudes which have carried over to our day and are still being used to question the moral basis of capitalism (chapter 6).

I have argued in *Unintended Consequences* that in the High Middle Ages there was also a change in what I have called the *cosmological* beliefs of the West. Cosmological beliefs concern the world view of a civilization: how people should live. They provide its moral anchor. They are transmitted through the socialization processes in childhood by harnessing the powerful emotions of shame and guilt. Most Eurasian civilizations were shame-based and had similar family values, for agrarian civilizations required stable settled families to operate their settled agriculture. To maintain this stability all these cultures sought to limit the common human but ephemeral passion of love as the basis of marriage. Their values were communalist. It was the first papal revolution of Gregory the Great in the sixth century which changed these hitherto communalist values to the individualist ones which have come to characterize and

7

distinguish the West from the Rest. This papal revolution, by promoting love as the basis of marriage and advocating the independence of the young, led to the rise of individualism in the West. But to curb the dissolution of family bonds and the resulting instability in family formation this would have caused, the Church created a fierce guilt culture in the Middle Ages. In this guilt culture, sex was sinful and the marriage bond—albeit based on love—was sacrosanct. They thus put a lid on the human passions which their individualism had unleashed. But, once the Christian God lost his universal sanctity in the West with the Darwinian revolution, this theological underpinning of the traditional Eurasian family values was removed and the West gradually reverted to the family values of its nomadic hunter-gatherer ancestors. These traditional and common Eurasian values in the domestic domain have been further undermined in our own day by the technological advances in contraception which have allowed sex to be separated from procreation, and to the rise of feminism.

Though for contingent reasons (see chapter 6) these changes in the material and cosmological beliefs of the West were conjoined, there is no necessary connection between the two. One of the major conclusions of *Unintended Consequences* was that for the Rest it is possible to accept the material beliefs of the West which have led to the rise of capitalism without accepting its cosmological beliefs. Much of the opposition to globalization in the Rest is due to its belief that embracing global capitalism will also lead to losing its soul. But as the examples of Japan, and increasingly China and India show, acceptance of the West's material beliefs by joining the global capitalist bandwagon need not entail abandoning their own ancient cosmological beliefs—their own special morality. The opposition to globalization in the countries of Islam for instance is based on the erroneous belief that adopting Western capitalism will also mean adopting Western ways of living, particularly in the domestic domain. They are against globalization and not necessarily against capitalism.

By contrast, the many Western anti-globalizers marching through the streets of Porto Allegre are not against globalization per se, but against globalizing capitalism. It is capitalism they hate for many of the same atavistic reasons it has been under attack since the Middle Ages. In addition, the erosion of the cultural constraints on capitalist activity promoted through the guilt culture the Christian church created in the Middle Ages, the unbridled individualism which was unleashed, has been castigated on moral grounds. But, with most of the Western critics subscribing to the same individualism whose fruits they criticize, they too have erroneously linked the material and cosmological beliefs of the West. They are against capitalism—the material beliefs of the West—when it is the cosmological beliefs—the unbridled individualism of which they themselves are the products—which should be their real target.

Globalization

Unlike the modernity of capitalism, globalization is an ancient cyclical phenomenon that has been associated with the rise and fall of empires. For the essence of globalization is the creation of a common economic space amongst hitherto loosely linked or autarkic regions. The Pax generated by empires has provided this common economic space and led to those gains from trade emphasized by Adam Smith and thereby to what can be labeled Smithian intensive growth.[17] Thus, the Graeco-Roman empires linked the areas around the Mediterranean, the Abbasid empire of the Arabs linked the worlds of the Mediterranean and the Indian Ocean, the Mongol empire linked China and Central Asia with the Near East, the various Indian empires created a common economic space in the subcontinent, while the expanding Chinese Empire linked the economic spaces of the Yellow River with those of the Yangtze. But, until the creation of the British Empire in the eighteenth and nineteenth centuries, the imperial sway was usually limited to particular regions, and the resulting economic integration was not truly global. The first truly global empire was that of the British, and it was the nineteenth century which saw the emergence of the first truly global economy—the first liberal international economic order (LIEO).

Till the emergence of the British Empire the other ancient empires were agrarian organic economies, which were dependent upon the products of land. As this was fixed and subject to diminishing returns, the Smithian impulse from greater economic integration petered out. So, each of the empires had its economic climacteric, as with stagnant technology and the binding land constraint, they could not generate what I have labeled Promethean growth—which depends upon converting an economy based on the energy derived from the products of limited land to one which uses the unlimited energy provided by fossil fuels. Thereafter they were in a "high level equilibrium trap" with only extensive growth occurring—with output keeping pace with population growth and per capita income stagnating. We have no quantitative evidence for all the ancient empires, but heroic attempts have been made to piece together the per capita incomes and population of the three major empires at the beginning of the Christian era (India, China, and Rome) and are summarized in table I.1.

India, which had reached its climacteric after it was united under the imperial Mauryas in the third century B.C., was by the beginning of the Christian era probably the richest and most populous. Thereafter, its per capita income fluctuated around this "high level equilibrium" for the next two millennia (till the late nineteenth century). Population and the standard of living fell in the long periods (sometimes centuries) during which the country was engulfed by wars against invaders or else between feuding Indian chieftains trying to establish another pan Indian empire.[18]

9

TABLE I.1
GDP and Population for Ancient Powers, 0 AD

	GDP (in million of 1990 US$)	Population (in 000s)	GDP per capita
Roman Empire	20961	55000	381
China	26820	59600	450
India-1	33750	75000	450
India-2	55146	100000	551

Sources: Maddison, Angus. (2001). Tables B-21, p. 264, B-18, p. 261, B-10, p. 241 for China and India-1; Goldsmith, R.W. (1984) Sept. for the Roman Empire (tons of gold converted into US$ at the average 1990 price); Lal, Deepak (1989) for India-2 (1965 $ converted into 1990 $ using GDP deflator).

The Chinese saw their efflorescence under the Sung in the eleventh century. This was based on the linking of the river valleys of the Yellow and Yangtze rivers, an agricultural revolution in wet rice technology, and the linking of the rural economy through a national hierarchy of markets. Above all there were remarkable scientific and technological advances, so much so that China had developed all the ingredients necessary for an Industrial Revolution.[19] But, because of "the closing of the Chinese mind,"[20] the incipient industrial revolution never occurred. There was no Promethean intensive growth and per capita income stagnated. China then experienced extensive growth into the modern period, with output rising with population at 0.4–0.5 percent per year over these four centuries. It too had reached a high-level equilibrium trap, but at a higher per capita income than India's.

The third of our ancient civilizations, Rome, reached its climacteric in the reign of Augustus (29 B.C.–A.D.14), who replaced the Republic with the Principate. The figures shown in table I.1 are Raymond Goldsmith's estimates for A.D. 14, the date of Augustus's death. They probably represent the per capita income level when the Roman Empire reached its high-level equilibrium trap.[21] Nevertheless, until the expansion of the United States and Russia in the mid-nineteenth century, it was the largest political, economic, and monetary unit in the Western world. Its population and national product too were not surpassed by any Western economy until the nineteenth century. It was the largest Western economic unit for nearly a millennium.[22]

But, unlike the Chinese, the Roman Empire declined, and despite various attempts no one since has succeeded in establishing imperial hegemony over Western Europe. The causes of the decline of the Roman Empire were ultimately economic.[23] The extension of the empire to its natural boundary meant that the average costs of maintaining the empire were rising and thus the sustainable rents it could garner were declining. As the treasures looted in the previous wars of conquests and the steady supply of slaves dried up—with the empire having absorbed most of the civilized Western world—foreign plunder no longer offered an independent source of revenue. As the past "rents" acquired during the empire's growth had been in part committed to a vast expansion of what we would today call a welfare state—which could not be cut without causing domestic disorder—and with no expansion of the domestic tax base, the empire faced an endemic fiscal crisis. It tried to close the "deficit" by levying the inflation tax through debasement of the currency. But this was not enough, and the state had to raise the burden of taxation above the sustainable rate, as toward the middle of the fourth century this "tax pressure grew heavier . . . the tendency to evasion—illegal or legitimate—on the part of high officials and large landowners was increased."[24]

The endemic fiscal crisis also led to the problem of maintaining the old military organization, as the "scarcity of means . . . did not allow a satisfactory treatment of the men in military service, the area of recruiting was enlarged just in time to prevent the legions being filled with the poor and desperate. . . . In this way, for budgetary reasons the sword passed in the early Empire from the hands of the Italici into those of provincials and from them, in the late Empire, into the hands of the barbarians . . . who served in autonomous military formations under their own chieftains . . . this system . . . turned out to be less costly than to equip anew, and to maintain, regular troops."[25] But these fiscal exigencies which led the empire to let the barbarians inside the gates sealed its doom.

This vicious circle, whereby the creation of "politically determined entitlements to income" leads to an endemic fiscal crisis, was to be observed later in the post-Renaissance mercantilist states of Europe and in our own times in the neo-mercantilist states of the Third and Second Worlds.[26] Three alternative outcomes ensued from these historical fiscal crises of the state: reform and economic liberalization to recover the tax base (as in England in the eighteenth and nineteenth centuries, and much of the Third World since the 1980s); revolution (as in France in 1789, and in much of the Second World in 1989); or collapse of the state (as in Rome and in many post-independent African countries).

The Chinese and Indian imperial states survived these endemic fiscal problems which led to the periodic overthrow of a dynasty till another competitor was able to recreate the empire. By contrast, the decline of the various gunpowder European empires created after the Renaissance merely reflected the changing balance of economic and military power in their metropole's struggle for the mastery of Europe, for these empires were an overseas extension of this struggle.

But, before the revolution in administration of the sixteenth century and the growing monetization of the economy, the power of any state to tax was very limited compared to modern states. Thus, Goldsmith notes of the Roman Empire that, reflecting its economically liberal policies, very close to those which would later be called "laissez faire," but also due to limitations of an as yet only partly monetized economy, the share of the expenditures of central and local governments in the early Roman empire was very low, probably not above 3 percent for the imperial government and on the order of 5 percent for all government units. This is not only far below the figures to which we have become accustomed since World War I in developed countries, but also below those in less developed countries, where the share of public expenditure in 1960 averaged 8 percent, a ratio similar to that in England in 1688 and in the United States and in France in 1820.[27]

The decline of empires was followed by both domestic disorder and a disintegration of the enlarged economic spaces they had created.[28] Thus, the Roman Empire had through its Pax brought unprecedented prosperity to the inhabitants of the Mediterranean littoral for nearly a millennium. With its demise, the ensuing disorder and the destruction of the imperial economic space led to a marked fall in the standards of living of the common people inhabiting the fallen empire. Thus, as Finer notes:

> If a peasant family in Gaul, or Spain, or northern Italy had been able to foresee the misery and exploitation that was to befall his grandchildren and their grandchildren, on and on and on for the next 500 years, he would have been singularly spiritless—and witless too—if he had not rushed to the aid of the empire. And even then the kingdoms that did finally emerge after the year 1000 were poverty stricken dung heaps compared with Rome. Not till the full Renaissance in the sixteenth century did Europeans begin to think of themselves as in any ways comparable to Rome, and not till the "Augustan Age" of the eighteenth century did they regard their civilization as its equal.[29]

Similarly, the periodic collapse of Chinese empires has led to periods of warlords and widespread disorder, until the Mandate of Heaven was passed on to another imperial dynasty which restored order. The Chinese have therefore always placed a very high value on the order provided by their successive empires. In our own times, the death of the nineteenth-century liberal economic order (LIEO) built by Pax Britannia on the fields of Flanders led to nearly half a century of economic disintegration and disorder, because the British were unable and the Americans were unwilling to maintain an imperial global Pax (see chapter 1).

After the fall of Rome, the "poverty stricken dung heaps" of a politically disunited Europe began their slow ascent. It was the great legal revolution of Pope Gregory VII in the eleventh century,[30] with the creation of a transnational legal and commercial infrastructure for the market economy (see chapter 6), which eventually led to the European miracle. The other great agrarian civilizations—China and India—did not suffer any absolute

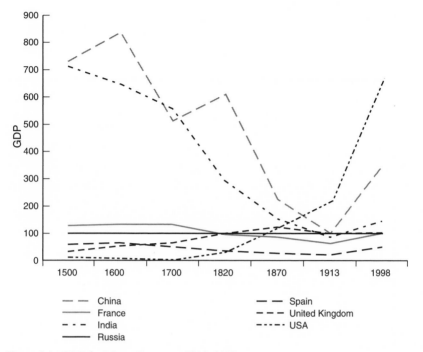

Figure I.1: GDP for Major Countries 1500–1998.

economic decline. But with the Great Divergence accompanying the slowly rolling Industrial Revolution, they were slipping relatively to the countries of the West. This can be seen from table I.2, and figure I.1, which normalizes the relative GDPs of India and China and the major Western countries around Russia (with a value of 100) from 1500 to 2000.

These ancient civilizations, and other parts of what is today called the Third World, were to experience the full force of the rising economic and military strength of the European gunpowder empires after the voyages of discovery in the sixteenth century. After the period of direct and indirect Western imperialism in the nineteenth century, it has taken nearly a century and a half for the ancient civilizations of India and China to come to terms with the West—by recognizing that they can modernize without Westernizing (chapter 6). Since the 1980s they have joined the globalization bandwagon with impressive gains in their standards of living, including of their poor (chapters 5 and 6).

Furthermore, since the nineteenth century, the mutual gains from globalization have greatly expanded. Before the nineteenth century LIEO fostered by the British, primitive methods of transportation, limited economic integration. The British LIEO, coinciding with the Industrial Revolution and

13

TABLE I.2

GDP, GDP Per Capita and Population for Major Countries, 1500–2000 (Million 1990 International $)

					Country				
Year	China	France	India	Netherlands	Russia(1)	Spain	United Kindom	USA	Germany
	GDP (million 1990 International $)								
1500	61,800	10,912	60,500	716	8,475	4,744	2,815	800	0
1600	96,000	15,559	74,250	2,052	11,447	7,416	6,007	600	0
1700	82,800	21,180	90,750	4,009	16,222	7,893	10,709	527	0
1820	228,600	38,434	111,417	4,288	37,710	12,975	36,232	12,548	0
1870	189,740	72,100	134,882	9,952	83,646	22,295	100,179	98,374	71429
1913	241,344	144,489	204,241	24,955	232,351	45,686	224,618	517,383	237,332
1998	3,873,352	1,150,080	1,702,712	317,517	1,132,432	560,138	1,108,568	7,394,598	1,460,069
	GDP per capita (1990 International $)								
1500	600	727	550	754	500	698	714	400	0
1600	600	841	550	1,368	553	900	974	400	0
1700	600	986	550	2,110	611	900	1,250	527	0
1820	600	1,230	533	1,821	689	1,063	1,707	1,257	0
1870	530	1,876	533	2,753	943	1,376	3,191	2,445	1,821
1913	552	3,485	673	4,049	1,488	2,255	4,921	5,301	3,648
1998	3,117	19,558	1,746	20,224	3,893	14,227	18,714	27,331	17,799
	World Population for Major Countries (in 000s)								
1500	103,000	15,000	110,000	950	16,950	6,800	3,942	2,000	0
1600	160,000	18,500	135,000	1,500	20,700	8,240	6,170	1,500	0
1700	138,000	21,471	165,000	1,900	26,550	8,770	8,565	1,000	0
1820	381,000	31,246	209,000	2,355	54,765	12,203	21,226	9,981	0
1870	189,740	72,100	134,882	41,814	83,646	22,295	100,179	98,374	39231
1913	437,140	41,463	303,700	6,164	156,192	20,263	45,649	97,606	65,058
1998	1,242,700	58,805	975,000	15,700	290,866	39,371	59,237	270,561	82,029

Source: Maddison, Angus (2001), Tables B-21, p. 264, B-18, p. 261, B-10, p. 241.
(1) refers to the former USSR area

its invention of the steam engine, led through the development of the railways, the steamship, and the telegraph, to a substantial fall in global transport costs. This had important implications for the extent of economic integration that could be achieved as compared with other past empires. The goods which were traded along the new channels created by past agrarian empires had to be of high value, because of the high costs of transport and communications. These "non-competing" goods—"luxury" goods (like Chinese porcelain or Dacca muslins) or more generally consumed primary products (like spices, tea, tobacco, coffee)—were not usually produced in the areas to which they were trans-shipped. Much domestic production in the areas linked by an empire would, therefore, not have been affected by the new imports. The main growth effects would come through the spread of knowledge and technology and the monetary effects of settling the trade balances between the newly linked regions.

The nineteenth-century LIEO for the first time saw domestic production being affected by a convergence in the domestic and foreign prices for the mass of goods consumed. It led to specialization along lines of comparative advantage and "Smithian" growth. The distinctive nineteenth-century pattern of trade arose, where the "North"—mainly Western Europe—specialized in the new industrial products and experienced Promethean intensive growth, while the "South"—which included the current Third World and the areas of "new" settlement in the Americas and Australasia—specialized in primary products and experienced Smithian intensive growth. This "colonial" international division of labor has been the target of economic nationalists in the South ever since, and was discussed in detail in *The Poverty of "Development Economics."* As we document in chapter 1, this nineteenth-century pattern of trade generated spectacular Smithian intensive growth in the South.

In the current phase of globalization, this process has gone even further with the fragmentation of production processes, so that countries and regions specialize not in "cars" or "shoes" but in the components that make up these products. The convergence of domestic and foreign prices of competing traded goods leads to countries specializing in producing and exporting the goods which use more of their abundant factors of production and importing those using more of those which are scarce. This leads to income-distribution effects with, ceteris paribus, the returns to the country's abundant factor rising relatively to that of the scarce. Thus, in a country with a lot of labor and little capital, opening up trade in competing goods will raise wages relative to profits. In the nineteenth century and current periods of globalization, these distributional effects have led to resistance to globalization from the scarce factors being hurt by the opening up of trade. They have sought to use the political process to protect their incomes. We examine these distributional effects in chapters 2 and 3. With the revolution in information technology, various services that were locally provided, as they could not be traded, are now being traded internationally and being produced where the costs are the lowest. Thus, many workers in service industries whose wages were protected by distance—being set by local demand and supply—find that the IT revolution's banishment of distance has made them compete with workers in a global labor market. The international "outsourcing" of services has added to the atavistic fear of foreign trade and globalization.

The backlash that has arisen against both the nineteenth century and current periods of globalization has led the critics to articulate alternative panaceas. In the nineteenth century, with the rise of socialist thought, the alternative was a planned collectivist economy in contrast to the market-based economy promoted by the British LIEO. This continued to carry resonance in much of the Third World in the post–Second World War era. My *The Poverty of "Development Economics"* was a critique of the *Dirigiste Dogma* on which it was based. But, since the collapse of the Second World with its countries of "really existing socialism," this support for the suppression of the market is no longer plausible. So the critics of global capitalism have now taken a different tack, which can be called the *New Dirigisme:* to create "capitalism with a human face"—a "third way" between capitalism and socialism. This New Dirigisme is based partly on economic arguments (see chapters 3, 4, 5) but more on ethical, cultural, and environmental claims (see chapters 6, 7, 8). The major purpose of this book is to argue against this New Dirigisme, and also to question the route the current imperial power—the United States—has taken in not wholeheartedly supporting the twin principles of laissez faire and unilateral free trade (correctly upheld by its British predecessor), but instead creating a whole host of international agencies to promote its LIEO. These international institutions, I will argue, no longer serve their initial purpose and are proving to be counterproductive in globalizing capitalism (see chapters 3, 4, 5). But before that we need to see how we got to where we are today.

1

Liberal International Economic Orders

Writing of the twilight of the Edwardian era which marked the high water-mark of Pax Britannia, John Maynard Keynes wrote in his great book on *The Economic Consequences of the Peace*:

> What an extraordinary episode in the economic progress of man that age which came to an end in August 1914! The greater part of the population, it is true, worked hard and lived at a low standard of comfort, yet were, to all appearances, reasonably contented with this lot. But escape was possible, for any man of capacity or character at all exceeding the average, into the middle and upper classes, for whom life offered, at a low cost and with the least trouble, conveniences, comforts, and amenities beyond the compass of the richest and most powerful monarchs of other ages. The inhabitant of London could order by telephone, sipping his morning tea in bed, the various products of the whole earth, in such quantity as he might see fit, and reasonably expect their early delivery upon his doorstep; he could at the same moment and by the same means adventure his wealth in the natural resources and new enterprises of any quarter of the world, and share, without exertion or even trouble, in their prospective fruits and advantages; or he could decide to couple the security of his fortunes with the good faith of the townspeople of any substantial municipality in any continent that fancy or imagination might recommend. He could secure forthwith, if he wished it, cheap and comfortable means of transit to any country or climate without passport or other formality, could despatch his servant to the neighboring office of a bank for such supply of the precious metals as might seem convenient, and could then proceed abroad to foreign quarters, without knowledge of their religion, language or customs, bearing coined wealth upon his person, and would consider himself greatly

17

aggrieved and much surprised at the least interference. But, most important of all, he regarded this state of affairs as normal, certain and permanent, except in the direction of further improvement, and any deviation from it as aberrant, scandalous, and avoidable.[1]

A modern Keynes surveying the contemporary world from New York or London or Tokyo or Seoul or Hong Kong or Singapore and increasingly from Shanghai and Bombay would have been able to make the same claims (at least before September 11th), except for the freedom to travel without passports. For, with the rise of the welfare state, which creates property rights in citizenship, immigration controls have now become ubiquitous. What both would be describing are the fruits of globalizing capitalism by two liberal international economic orders (LIEOs): the nineteenth-century one promoted by Pax Britannia, and the contemporary one promoted by Pax Americana. But these two periods of globalization were sandwiched between a near half-century of global disorder: with two World Wars, a Great Depression, and the battles against two illiberal creeds—Fascism and Communism.

If Rip van Winkle had gone to sleep at the end of about 1870 and woken up in the last few years, he would find that little has changed in the world economy. He would note the various technological advances in transportation and communications (airlines, telephones, and the Internet), which have further reduced the costs of international trade and commerce and led to the progressive integration of the world economy which was well under way when he went to sleep. The terrible events of the twentieth century would form no part of Rip van Winkle's memory. Nor would the various and varying fads in economic policy—both national and international—during this century make any sense, for example, exchange controls, the use of quotas rather than tariffs as instruments of protection, centralized planning and associated controls on production and distribution, and restrictions on the free flow of capital.

Having read his de Tocqueville he would also not be surprised that the United States and Russia had become Great Powers in the middle part of the twentieth century, nor that it took the United States nearly a century to become the predominant power, just as it took Britain nearly a century from the mid-eighteenth century conflict with France till the end of the Napoleonic Wars to achieve its brief relative predominance. His reading of de Tocqueville would also allow him to see a natural progression from the rise of Great Britain—which was in a sense the victory of an aristocratic oligarchy over the divine right of kings—to that of the United States, which is a victory of Demos over aristocracy. Whether this is an unmixed blessing is open to question. In a sense, it would appear that the world had really just picked up where he had gone to sleep.

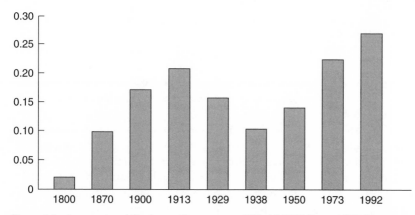

Figure 1.1: International Trade as a Percentage of World GDP Since 1800. Exports plus imports divided by output. Source: Estevadeordal, Frantz, and Taylor (2003).

This rise and fall and rise of a liberal economic order over the last two hundred years is depicted in figures 1.1 and 1.2, which show the trends in the share of international trade and international investment in world income (GDP) over this period.[2] But, how did these two LIEOs arise, and why did the nineteenth-century LIEO break down, and is the same fate awaiting the current LIEO? These are some of the questions I will be trying to answer in this chapter and the rest of this book.

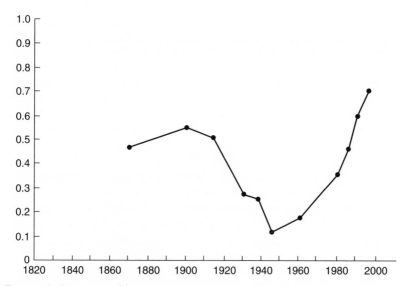

Figure 1.2: International Investments as a Fraction of World GDP Since 1870. Source: Obstfeld and Taylor (2003).

Mercantilism

Both LIEOs arose from previous periods which can be characterized as mercantilist and neo-mercantilist. The insights of the great historian of mercantilism, Eli Hecksher, provide the reasons for both the rise and fall of mercantilism in Europe from the seventeenth to nineteenth centuries.[3]

Hecksher argued that the mercantilist system arose as the Renaissance princes sought to consolidate the weak states they had inherited or acquired from the ruins of the Roman Empire. These were states encompassing numerous feuding and disorderly groups which the new Renaissance princes sought to curb, to create a nation. The purpose was to achieve "unification and power," making the "State's purposes decisive in a uniform economic sphere and to make all economic activity subservient to considerations corresponding to the requirements of the State." The mercantilist policies—with their industrial regulations, state-created monopolies, import and export restrictions, price controls—were partly motivated by the objective of granting royal favors in exchange for revenue to meet the chronic fiscal crisis of the state—a problem shared by many countries of the contemporary Third World, as we shall see. Another objective was to extend the span of government control over the economy to facilitate its integration.

But, as Hecksher showed, this attempt to extend the span of government control to create order only bred disorder. As economic controls became onerous, economic agents attempted to escape them through various forms of avoidance and evasion. By the eighteenth century this dirigisme bred corruption, rent seeking, tax evasion, and illegal activities in underground (or "black") economies. The most serious consequence for the state was that this avoidance and evasion eroded its fiscal base, and led to the prospect of an unMarxian withering away of the state. It was this dire prospect which prompted economic liberalization to restore the fiscal base and thence government control over what had become ungovernable economies. In France this changeover could only come about through a revolution. For, it occurred because the king had to call the "Etats General" in order to deal with a severe fiscal crisis.[4]

Following the Glorious Revolution of 1688, the British had created a fiscal-military state, which provided the "gentlemanly capitalism"[5] emerging in the eighteenth century the sinews to extend the geographical scope of British trade and commerce by "the sustained use of force, backed up by skillful deployment of diplomacy in order to make and to retain economic gains at the expense of their major rivals—Spain, Portugal, and above all the Netherlands and France. Merchants pressed for safe and unimpeded access to the consumers and sources of supply of all other European powers and their colonies in the Americas, Africa, and Asia as well as for entree to the Mughal and Chinese empires in the East."[6] The eighteenth century thus saw Britain both industrializing and engaged in continual wars with its continental rivals, which by the time of Waterloo had left it with the largest global empire seen to that date.

Adam Smith and the classical liberals had maintained that this early British imperialism did not make much of a difference to Britain's industrialization. Some economic historians have even tried to provide a counterfactual with "an international economic order, operating between 1688 and 1815 under competitive conditions, virtually free from governmental interference with trade and untroubled warfare." But O'Brien rightly argued this is wholly unrealistic. It was the establishment of British ascendancy and in particular of the Royal Navy, as a result of this century-long internecine warfare with its continental rivals, which created the international order in which the benign Smithian processes of free trade and commerce could operate.[7] It is, as I would argue, a similar failing of modern-day classical liberals to see that for the benign Smithian processes to work in a global economy, a similar global order is needed. For their hope that adherence to free trade and laissez faire is sufficient to lead to a spontaneous global order—which explains their opposition to empires—is likely to be belied in the real and dangerous world of power politics.[8]

But this continual mercantilist warfare was expensive. It was financed in large part by the expansion of the public debt, and its transformation into tradable "promises" of the government by the Financial Revolution accompanying the Glorious Revolution. By the 1820s, the "state's funded debt amounted to more than twice the national income—a ratio remarkable for the period and astonishing even by the standards of profligate borrowing displayed by many governments of the 20th century."[9] To service the interest on this debt, taxation had to rise from 3–4 percent in the reign of James II—the last Stuart king—to nearly 43 percent of national income by the 1820s. This rise in taxation led to all the evasions and avoidances described by Hecksher. But, as O'Brien notes, "somehow an aristocratic and unrepresentative regime, serviced by an ostensibly incompetent and corrupt administration, managed to appropriate what was by European standards, a remarkable share of national income from a people depicted by some historians as ungovernable."[10] Once the expensively acquired empire was relatively secure after Waterloo, Victorian statesmen embraced economic liberalism, and rolled back the state, so that they were able to defend Britain and its empire with a share of national income no higher than what it was in the time of James II.

The ensuing nineteenth-century Age of Reform was motivated less by the writings of Adam Smith than the desire of governments to regain their fiscal bases which had been destroyed by the unintended consequences of mercantilism. The results were spectacular. As Hecksher noted, the new-found economic liberalism achieved the goal sought by mercantilism:

21

Great power for the state, the perpetual and fruitless goal of mercantilist endeavour, was translated into fact in the 19th century. In many respects this was the work of laissez faire, even though the conscious efforts of the latter tended in an entirely different direction. . . . The result was attained primarily by limiting the functions of the State, which task laissez faire carried through radically. The maladjustment between ends and means was one of the typical features of mercantilism, but it disappeared once the aims were considerably limited. In laissez faire they consisted, indeed, only in certain elementary and unavoidable functions of foreign policy, defense, legislation, and the administration of justice, nicknamed by Carlyle "Anarchy plus the Constable." Disobedience and arbitrariness, unpunished infringements of the law, smuggling and embezzlement flourished particularly under a very extensive state administration and in periods of continually changing ordinances and interference with the course of economic life. It was because the regime de l'ordre bore this impress that disorder was one of its characteristic features.[11]

The Nineteenth-Century LIEO

The nineteenth-century LIEO was created under British leadership after its repeal of the Corn Laws in 1846 (see chapter 3). Within the half century thereafter, there was virtually free mobility of commodities, capital, and labor. This marked the beginning of the first true era of globalization. For the first time in history, economies were truly linked together through international trade in commodities which were produced both at home and abroad. Previously, with the extension of an empire and its protection of long-distance trade, most of the commodities that were traded through long-distance trade were goods that were not produced in each of the trading regions (they were noncompeting goods). This meant that domestic prices and thence the returns to the domestic factors of production (land, labor, and capital) of domestically produced goods were determined solely by local domestic demand and supply conditions. This was largely because the high costs of transportation made most goods, except nonbulky high-value goods, into "nontraded" goods.[12]

Import restrictions and prohibitive tariffs are also equivalent to "transport costs" insofar as they convert domestic goods, whose prices would be set by international prices if they could be freely imported and exported, into "nontraded" goods. Thus, wheat from the prairies would not be imported into, say, England if the costs of shipping it from the United States to England was greater than the difference in the prices of wheat in the low-cost (United States) and high-cost (England) countries. Equivalently, if the cost of shipping fell so that the import price of wheat (including transport costs—the cif price as it is called) was less than the domestic price of wheat in England, there would still be no trade in wheat if England put on a tariff which was equal to the difference between the cif and domestic English price. Wheat, though "tradable"—because transport costs were low enough to allow imports to compete with domestic production—would have been converted into a "nontraded" good. This distinction between *nontraded* goods (created by either high transport costs or trade restrictions) whose domestic prices are set by domestic demand and supply, and *traded* goods whose prices are set by international prices is crucial, not just in identifying when globalization began but in its effects on the distribution of income, and as we shall see in the ongoing debates about exchange rates and capital flows (chapter 4).

Before 1820, most goods in most countries were nontraded due both to high costs of international transport and the import restrictions of the mercantilist era. This meant that there was not much convergence in the prices of most commodities produced in different parts of the world. The nineteenth century saw a dramatic reduction in both transport costs and tariffs. Both were associated with developments in the country that was to promote a liberal international economic order—Great Britain. The dramatic fall in transport costs was associated with the use of the steam engine—the hallmark of the Industrial Revolution—in lowering the costs of sea transport with the development of the steamship, and land transport with the spread of the railways, and the fall in the costs of communication with the development of the telegraph. Many previously nontraded goods, including those produced well inside the hinterland, now became traded, as the costs of transporting them from their place of production to the intercontinental place of import fell dramatically. This decline in natural barriers to trade was matched by that in the artificial barriers created by the various restrictions on foreign trade of the mercantilist period.

Elementary Trade Theory

It is the conversion of an economy in which most goods are nontraded into one in which most are traded that leads to the famous gains from trade which Adam Smith eulogized and Ricardo (in his famous numerical example of the gains from trade based on comparative advantage) formalized.[13] The convergence in the prices of commodities that are traded leads each of the trading countries to specialize in the goods in which they have a *comparative* advantage, even though one country might have an *absolute* advantage in producing both goods. The resulting reallocation of production in the trading countries allows them to raise their respective national incomes through both the "consumption gain" of obtaining goods at lower prices and the "production gain" through specialization in producing the export good, and using the cheaper "technology" provided by foreign trade of transforming domestic resources into the good that was previously produced at home and is now imported.

23

The major amendment to Ricardo's theory of comparative advantage and the gains from trade was provided by the Swedish economists Eli Hecksher and Bertil Ohlin. Ricardo had assumed that goods were produced by labor alone. The technology for producing the two commodities (wine and cloth) in England and Portugal differed (in his numerical example). But, as he shows, even though one country's labor productivity was higher than the others in producing *both* goods, it could gain by trading with the other country by specializing in the good where it had the higher *relative* productivity and hence comparative advantage.

Hecksher and Ohlin amended two of Ricardo's unrealistic assumptions. They argued that goods were not produced merely by labor alone, but also by other factors of production, namely capital and land. Moreover, given that technology can be imitated and thus be diffused, it was implausible to assume that countries used different technologies to produce goods. They argued that instead of differences in technology it was differences in the *relative endowment* of different factors of production (the ratio of labor to capital—abstracting for the moment from land) which determined a country's comparative advantage. Thus, a country with relatively abundant labor but scarce capital would have relatively lower costs of labor (wages)—and higher costs of capital (rentals)—than a country with more abundant capital and scarce labor. Its costs of production of labor-intensive goods would thus be relatively lower than those of capital intensive goods, compared with the capital abundant country. With the opening up of foreign trade and the conversion of the previously nontraded into traded goods, the labor abundant country, which has a comparative advantage in producing the good using its abundant factor, would specialize in labor intensive goods, exporting them and importing the capital intensive good from the capital abundant country. As in Ricardo's model, this would again lead to "consumption" and "production" gains from trade for each country.

Furthermore, there will also be "dynamic" indirect gains, which have been emphasized since Adam Smith. These consist of the transfer of foreign technology which increases domestic productivity. Also, by promoting competition, less productive firms are forced to contract and more productive firms to expand, thus increasing the industry's overall productivity.[14] These "improvements in the processes of production"[15] will raise a country's productivity. Thus, both the "static" gains from the reallocation of existing resources as well as the "dynamic" gains from raising productivity will increase the economy's rate of growth. The case for free trade is therefore simple and powerful. In its static version it states that free trade is in the interest of each country because it expands its feasible set of consumption possibilities, by providing, in effect, an indirect technology for transforming domestic resources into the goods and services that yield current and future utility to consumers. The dynamic version incorporates investment in line with a country's comparative advantage, which minimizes the present value of the resource costs of its future demand. There is considerable empirical validation for these claims from the historical record.[16]

But, there may be a fly in this ointment, as was shown in a famous extension of the Hecksher-Ohlin model by Paul Samuelson and Wolfgang Stolper (which bears their name as the Stolper-Samuelson theorem). National income in *both* countries will be higher when most goods have been converted from nontraded into traded goods, but what will happen to the incomes of the two factors of production—labor and capital (abstracting from land for simplicity)? As the relatively labor-abundant country shifts production into its labor-intensive industries with the opening up of foreign trade, the demand for labor will go up and ipso facto that for capital will decline, raising the real wage and reducing the rental rate (return to capital). Hence the Stolper-Samuelson theorem: with the opening up of trade, the return to the abundant factor of production will rise and that of the scarce one will fall. It is these *income distribution* effects of the opening up of trade which effect the politics of free trade, as the scarce factor whose income suffers a relative decline will try to reverse this by using the political process to provide it protection in the form of a tariff. But whether the polity *should* give in to these sectional pressures is a different matter. The distribution of income in any growing and hence changing economy will be altering for all sorts of reasons. To prevent these distributional shifts is to eschew change and thence growth. In offsetting these pressures for protection, the current climate of opinion— *ideas*—as well as the relative political strength of those gaining and losing from protection—*interests*—will determine the final outcome.

Furthermore, as international trade theorists have argued since Adam Smith, a country will benefit from removing its own tariffs and import restrictions even if all its trading partners maintain theirs. For as long as the domestic prices of goods in our country under autarky differ from those at which they can be imported and exported under free trade, the country will be able to obtain the gains from trade both by obtaining imported goods at a lower cost than they are produced at home (the consumption gain) and by specializing in producing and exporting those goods in which it has a comparative advantage and importing the others (the production gain), irrespective of the tariffs applied by their trading partners. For these trade restrictions only damage the protectionist country's welfare, and it would be senseless not to improve one's own welfare just because someone else is damaging theirs. There is no point throwing rocks into one's own harbor just because others are throwing rocks into theirs. Hence, there is an incontrovertible case for every country to *unilaterally* adopt free trade, irrespective of the protectionist policies of other countries—with one exception.

Suppose that a country is the only producer (a monopolist) of some good—say, oil. The price at which it can sell its good will then depend upon the amount of the good it puts on the market, unlike the market for a competitive good produced by many producers where the producers cannot influence the price at which they sell their good. The monopolist can raise the price of his good and thus his revenues by restricting supply of the good: the maximum revenue being obtained where the marginal cost of producing the good equals the marginal revenue from selling it. Now, suppose that, though the country is the only producer of the good, so it is a monopolist in *world* markets, there are many producers of the good *within* the country. They will then be competing against each other and the price and quantity of the good they will be willing to sell will be the competitive price and quantity. If, however, they could all band together to become a monopolist, they could raise the total revenue from their sales. Hence, it is in the country's interest that its many competitive producers behave as if they were a single monopolist when they are exporting the good to world markets. This can be achieved if the government levies an export tax on the producers so that they are forced to raise their prices in world markets. This raising of the export price will then allow the country to garner the monopoly profits from its exports. It will in the process have improved its *terms of trade* (the relative price of its exports to its imports). The same argument applies if a country which is a large importer in the world markets (so it has monopsony power) can reduce the price at which foreigners sell it its imports by putting on an import tariff. This is the so-called *terms of trade* or *optimal tariff* argument for protection. It allows countries which are "large," in the sense of being a major producer of the goods it exports or consumer of goods it imports, to garner a larger share of the cosmopolitan gains from trade for itself by turning the terms of trade in its favor through export/import taxes.[17]

But, even a "large" country which tries to turn the terms of trade in its favor by levying the "optimal tariff" has to forbear because of the danger of retaliation by other "large" countries. For, if they follow the example of the country initiating this departure from free trade, a trade war would ensue, in which, at the end of the day, the country beginning it could be worse off than if it had not attempted to exploit its monopoly/ monopsony power and maintained free trade.[18] Thus, though, as we shall see (see chapter 2), this optimal tariff argument remains the only theoretically valid argument for protection, its practical relevance is extremely limited. It is by and large a theoretical curiousum.[19]

In nineteenth-century Britain both ideas and interests conjoined to make it accept unilateral free trade as its trade policy after the repeal of the Corn Laws in 1846. For, though Robert Torrens first stated the terms of trade argument in the debates over the Corn Laws, Prime Minister Robert Peel and his associates would have no truck with it. In this Peel was right, for as Irwin (1988) has shown, Britain possessed much less monopoly power than Torrens and a number of contemporary economic historians (e.g., McCloskey 1980) have claimed. The British thereafter, despite pressures in the backlash against globalization at the end of the nineteenth century, largely maintained free trade until the Great Depression in 1931.

The United States by contrast (as we shall see) has from its inception never accepted the economically correct principle of a unilateral move to free trade. It has believed in *reciprocity*: it would only cut its tariffs in exchange for cuts by its trading partners. The underlying assumption is the erroneous one that trade like disarmament is a zero sum game—one should only disarm simultaneously with one's opponents.[20]

Pillars of the British LIEO

There were three pillars on which the nineteenth-century LIEO promoted by the British was based—free trade, the gold standard, and international property rights. We discuss each in turn and how they were undermined.

Free Trade. Apart from the reasons for Britain's adoption of free trade and laissez faire cited by Hecksher, it was also in the interests of labor and capital (the relatively abundant factors in the British economy by the beginning of the nineteenth century) to combine against the scarce factor land, which alone benefited from protection. As, by the late eighteenth century, Britain was ceasing to be primarily an agricultural economy,[21] the interests gaining from free trade carried a greater weight than the landed interest, which with the repeal of the corn laws acquiesced in its relative decline. But, in addition, intellectual reasons changed the climate of opinion from the previous support for mercantilism to that for classical liberalism and free trade.[22] Ideas and interests were thus equally important in changing the "material beliefs"[23] of Britain. But how did this change in material beliefs spread to the rest of the world?

The British example of the *unilateral* adoption of free trade was not followed by other countries. In France, Napoleon III, who had come to power in a coup d'etat in 1851, decided to befriend Britain, partly to gain political status and diplomatic respect.[24] Also there was a strong current of opinion seeking to reverse traditional French protectionism and embrace economic liberalism. The economist Michel Chevalier persuaded the emperor that a trade treaty with Britain would be desirable, as under the new constitution, although the legislature had to approve any domestic law, the emperor had the exclusive right to sign foreign treaties which had the force of law. Having failed to convince the legislature—because of domestic vested interests—to reform tariff policy, Napoleon was persuaded that a treaty with Britain was the only way to introduce the economic liberalism he sought. Chevalier used the good offices of his friend Richard Cobden to persuade William Gladstone of the desirability of such a treaty, because the policy of unilateral trade liberalization

27

followed by Britain was not viable in the face of domestic protectionist pressures in France. Thus was the Cobden-Chevalier treaty of 1860 born. An essential feature of the treaty was the *most favored nation (MFN) clause*—whereby any tariff concessions given in bilateral agreements with one trading partner were automatically extended to all the trading partners of both. As Britain, having unilaterally adopted free trade, had no tariffs to bargain with other protectionist countries, it was left to the French to sign a string of treaties with other European countries—all embodying the MFN clause. Subsequently this network of trade treaties, each embodying the MFN principle, led to a general reduction of tariffs and to virtual free trade in Europe during the 1860s and 1870s.[25] But with (what was called) the "Great Depression" of the 1870s, both the intellectual and domestic political climate changed and the era of creeping protectionism began, leading ultimately to the destruction of the LIEO with the onset of the First World War.

Most of the remaining tariffs in the second half of nineteenth century, as Williamson (2003) has shown, were motivated not by a protectionist impulse but by the exigencies of obtaining revenue. He argues that even in the United States and Germany, where the ideas of Alexander Hamilton and Fredrich List were influential in advocating a tariff to protect "infant industries," the real motive was to obtain revenue.[26] Also, in both cases, as the resulting unified economic areas were large, it was hoped that the common external tariffs of the respective unions would also improve their terms of trade vis-a-vis Britain, on the lines of the optimum tariff argument outlined above.

After 1865, the growing integration of the Atlantic economy led to the convergence of commodity prices and the prices of factor of production (land, labor, and capital) as the Hecksher-Ohlin model would predict.[27] This meant that, in relatively land-scarce and labor-abundant Europe, wages would rise and land rents fall, while in the relatively land-abundant and labor-scarce United States the converse would happen, with land rents rising and wages falling. As capital was also relatively scarce in the United States and Germany till the late nineteenth century (in contrast with Britain), the interests of both capital and labor would be in favor of protection in the United States and those of land and capital in Germany, following these effects of globalization on income distribution.

These predictions are borne out by the political history of these two countries.[28] In the United States, the landed interest, which was particularly dominant in the Southern plantation economies, could be expected to be in favor of free trade, whereas the interests of the growing industrial labor force and capitalists on the eastern seaboard of the North would be in protection. The Civil War led to the victory of the North, and protection. The ensuing agrarian discontent coalesced into the Populist movement which among other demands also wanted free trade.[29] But by the end of the century the United States was becoming a relatively capital-abundant country and, with a lag, this led American business leaders to see foreign trade not as a threat but as an asset. Both Theodore Roosevelt and Woodrow Wilson emphasized tariff reform, which Wilson actually delivered.

In Germany, the "grain invasion" from the New World threatened the owners of the scarce factors in the country—land and capital. They combined in the so-called marriage of iron and rye which introduced protection, while "German labor strongly and consistently endorsed free trade,"[30] choosing to fight a class war by embracing socialism. By 1890, however, as Germany's rising wealth turned it into a relatively capital-abundant country, this marriage of "iron and rye" began to fray. Thus began a move toward the low tariffs advocated by labor, which were introduced after the Reichstag elections of 1912.

Britain alone among the relatively land-scarce, labor-abundant European countries did not turn to protection in the later part of the nineteenth century. This was because it was also capital-abundant relative to land, and the combined forces of labor and capital had defeated the protectionist interests of land at the time of the Corn Laws. By the time of the European "grain invasion," the share of agriculture in British employment was low enough that it did not have enough political voice to get protection.

But there was another consequence of the nineteenth-century globalization in Britain. Williamson[31] has estimated that between 1827 and 1871, the relative wage of unskilled to skilled workers fell from 0.34 to 0.29.[32] In the subsequent thirty years this was reversed, with the ratio rising from 0.29 in 1871 to 0.39 in 1901. The 1870s also saw the rise and acceptance of trade unions for skilled workers.[33] The fall in their wages relative to the unskilled was sought to be countered by trying to exert monopoly power through combination.

So what explains this switch in trends in the unskilled—skilled wage differential which led to the rise of the British trade union movement? Jones and Engerman (1996) provide an explanation in terms of the Hecksher-Ohlin model. The skilled labor was mainly employed in the export industry dominated by textiles during this century. During this whole period, the relative price of textiles was falling (in part because of the growth of competitors in Germany, the United States, India, and Japan), but the extent of technical progress (rate of productivity increase) was much greater in the first than in the second period. In the first period to 1871, the productivity increase in textiles relative to the rest of the economy was greater than the relative price fall, hence the factor used intensively in the production of textiles—skilled labor—would have seen its wages rise relative to the other sectors employing unskilled labor. In the second period there was no relative increase in the productivity of textiles but there was a relative price fall, which would have lowered the skilled wage relative to that of unskilled labor. Given the prevailing combination of ideas and interest still supporting free trade, trade unions of the skilled arose to raise the price of their labor.

This anti-liberal development, along with the rise of protectionist coalitions in the United States and Germany, began the gradual process whereby economic liberalism was gradually displaced by the creeping Dirigiste Dogma.[34] Ideas, like those of Torrens and Mill on the optimum tariff argument, and Hamilton and List on the infant industry argument for protection buttressed the play of interests in promoting the creeping protectionism and dirigisme which undermined the nineteenth-century LIEO. It was not till the refurbishing of the argument in favor of free trade (by decoupling it from that for laissez faire—see chapter 3) with the development of the modern theory of trade and welfare in the 1960s that the infant industry argument was finally laid to rest—at least among most economists! Various other arguments for protection were shown to be based on what came to be called "domestic distortions" in the working of the price mechanism, for which the appropriate remedy was not protection but some combination of domestic taxes and subsidies. The "terms of trade" argument remained as the only valid argument circumscribing the classical case for free trade.

The Gold Standard. The gold standard was the second pillar of the nineteenth-century LIEO. It became the international monetary system from about 1870 largely because Britain, the leading economic, political, and commercial power, was on the gold standard. Britain itself had moved from the bimetallic standards which had been common in most of Europe and the United States to a de facto gold standard as a result of the accidental fixing of too low a gold price for silver by Sir Isaac Newton—the master of the mint— in 1717. As a result all the silver coinage, however debased, disappeared from circulation. Given Britain's preeminence in trade and capital flows, most countries chose to adopt Britain's monetary practice. This was a case of the incentive of emulation of the successful. "Out of these autonomous decisions of national governments an international system of fixed exchange rates was born."[35]

There was, however, an Achilles heel in the gold standard—and which bedevils its modern-day equivalent: currency boards. This was the danger posed by the rise of fractional reserve banking, whereby banks only kept a fraction of the reserves that would be needed to fully back the deposits they held, the rest being lent out to borrowers at positive rates of interest. Financing these loans (which were the relatively *illiquid* assets of such banks) with deposits (which were their *liquid* liabilities) exposed the system to bank runs. To stop such runs, the central bank needed to act as lender of last resort by granting unlimited credit to the banks in trouble. But this could imply that it had to extend credit beyond the limits consistent with the rules of the gold standard. The expedient used was to break the gold standard rules in the short run while adhering to them in the long run. This was credible because, unlike today, domestic politics—before the advent of mass suffrage and the rise of labor parties and the welfare state—did not require the Central Bank to take account of any other domestic economic goals apart from maintaining monetary stability, with full convertibility at the fixed exchange rate being assured in the long run. This credibility meant that the system was bolstered by stabilizing capital inflows when the currency was weak during a panic, as foreign investors hoped to gain from the eventual strengthening of the currency that they fully expected the Central Bank to ensure. As Eichengreen puts it: "central banks possessed the capacity to violate the rules of the game in the short run because there was no question about obeying them in the long run" (1996, p. 32).

With the rise of Demos, the domestic political feature that had underpinned the gold standard disappeared and doomed the system. In addition, there was the deflationary bias of a system in which the world's money supply was rigidly tied to a slowly and randomly expanding gold supply at a time when output was rising much faster. This led to the Great Depression of the 1870s.[36] The rise of trade unions and the inflexibility they introduced into industrial labor markets did not permit the flexibility of money wages and prices on which adjustments to economic shocks were predicated under the gold standard. This doomed it after the series of serious shocks that the international economy suffered in the interwar period.

International Property Rights. A third pillar of the LIEO maintained by Pax Brittania was the transnational legal system created for the protection of property rights, in particular of "foreigners." This, as Lipson in his magisterial study *Standing Guard* shows, was due to the commercial treaties signed by European states in the mid-nineteenth century. These treaties provided rules for protecting international property rights which "hardened into general principles of international law" (1985, p. 8).[37] These international standards built on the system of commercial law that had been created as a result of Pope Gregory VII's papal revolution in the eleventh century, which established the church-state, and a common commercial law for Christendom.[38] The treaties of Westphalia (1648) and Paris (1763) further strengthened the economic rights of foreigners and their property abroad. The nineteenth century saw a culmination of this process with the security of foreign persons and their property guaranteed by every European state, by the United States soon after its independence, and by the new Latin American states after their wars of independence. Crucial in understanding this extension of the international rule of law is that it covered what was previously Christendom in Europe and in the New World, and it continued the role of the medieval Catholic Church in providing the first "international" legal system.

As legal systems are in part derived from people's material beliefs, as I have denoted them in my *Unintended Consequences*, it is not surprising that this common international standard was readily adopted in the lands where

31

the people shared this common Judaeo-Christian heritage and the material beliefs associated with Pope Gregory VII's legal papal revolution. Matters were very different when it came to the areas with very different material beliefs in the Middle East, and in Asia and Africa. Even there, the principle of reciprocity which had partly led the European states of the Middle Ages to accede to various international standards was also behind the acceptance by the Ottoman Empire of various "capitulation" treaties dating back to the 1500s. Through these treaties the Ottomans granted commercial privileges to the states of Christendom and in return Muslim merchants and other subjects of the Porte received protection for their goods and persons abroad. The Ottoman treaty of 1540 had the principle of reciprocal protection directly written into it.

With its growing economic strength in the nineteenth century, and worried about Russian expansion in the Eastern Mediterranean, Britain and Turkey signed the Anglo-Turkish convention in 1838, which effectively opened up the Ottoman Empire to European trade and investment. With the growing enfeeblement of the Ottomans, in time new arrangements arose concerning disputes with foreigners whereby "international property rights were effectively guaranteed by the extra territorial application of European and American laws."[39]

Moreover, the European powers under British leadership found that, to expand trade and investment in parts of the world where the European material beliefs were alien, they had to create systems of foreign concessions and extraterritorial laws as in the treaty ports of the Far East. Where, as in Africa, political arrangements were fragile, the creation of political and legal structures which would serve commercial expansion led to difficult choices for the Victorians in integrating the agricultural periphery with the dynamic industrialism of the Center.[40] "Their policies naturally aimed at a vast, global extension of commerce. At the same time, they tried to limit the direct imposition of political and military controls, which were expensive and difficult to manage."[41, 42]

Pax Britannia and Economic Development

These three pillars of the nineteenth-century LIEO allowed the worldwide expansion of trade and commerce. The legal framework was an integral element of Pax Britannica. Together with the economic integration through free trade and an international payments system based in the City of London, it allowed the Empire to fulfill a:

> wider mission which can be summarized as the *world's first comprehensive development programme*. After 1815, Britain aimed to put in place a set of like

minded allies who would cooperate in keeping the world safe from what Canning called the "youthful and stirring nations," such as the United States, which proclaimed the virtues of republican democracy, and from a "league of worn out governments" in Europe whose future lay too obviously in the past. Britain offered an alternative vision of a liberal international order bound together by mutual interest in commercial progress and underpinned by a respect for property, credit and responsible government, preferably of the kind found at home.[43]

And compared with the previous millennia, the results were stupendous. It was at the height of this nineteenth-century LIEO from 1850 to 1914 that many parts of the Third World for the first time experienced intensive growth for a sustained period. Lloyd Reynolds in his survey of the economic histories of forty-one developing countries dated the turning points when developing countries entered the era of *intensive* growth (with a sustained rise in per capita incomes), as compared with the ubiquitous *extensive* growth of the past (when output growth just kept up with that of population) as shown in table 1.1.

TABLE 1.1
A Turning Point Chronology

1840	Chile	1900	Cuba
1850	Brazil	1910	Korea
1850	Malaysia	1920	Morocco
1850	Thailand	1925	Venezuela
1860	Argentina	1925	Zambia
1870	Burma	1947	India
1876	Mexico	1947	Pakistan
1880	Algeria	1949	China
1880	Japan	1950	Iran
1880	Peru	1950	Iraq
1880	Sri Lanka	1950	Turkey
1885	Colombia	1952	Egypt
1985	Taiwan	1965	Indonesia
1895	Ghana	–	Afghanistan
1895	Ivory Coast	–	Bangladesh
1895	Nigeria	–	Ethiopia
1895	Kenya	–	Mozambique
1900	Uganda	–	Nepal
1900	Zimbabwe	–	Sudan
1900	Tanzania	–	Zaire
1900	Phillippines		

Source: Reynolds (1985), table 1, p. 958.

Maddison sums up the achievements of this period as follows:

> From 1870 to 1913 world per capita GDP rose 1.3 percent p.a. compared with 0.5 percent in 1820–70 and 0.07 percent in 1700–1820. The acceleration was due to more rapid technological progress, and the diffusionist forces unleashed by the liberal economic order of which the United Kingdom was the main architect. It was not a process of global equalization, but there were significant income gains in all parts of the world. Australia and the United States reached higher levels than the United Kingdom by 1913. Growth was faster than in the United Kingdom in most of Western and Eastern Europe, in Ireland, in all the Western Offshoots, in Latin America and Japan. In India, other Asia (except China) and Africa, the advances were much more modest, but per capita income rose more than a quarter between 1870 to 1913. (Maddison 2001, p. 100)

There is, however, a view associated with the French economic historian Paul Bairoch, picked up by the global historian Fernand Braudel, and later by the "dependencia" theorist Andre Gunder Frank that these beneficial development effects of the British Empire on the Third World are an illusion. Bairoch[44] suggested that, in terms of relative income per head, China in 1800 was well ahead of Western Europe; Japan and the rest of Asia were only lower than Western Europe by 5 percent; Latin America was well ahead of North America; and Africa was about two-thirds of the West European level. This leant support to his long maintained thesis that the Third World had been impoverished by the West through imperialist exploitation.[45] But as Chesnais (1987) noted, he was fabricating ammunition for his hypothesis. As Maddison observes, Bairoch never documented his highly improbable scenario for Asia, Latin America, or Africa: "His figures for these areas were essentially guess estimates."[46] Pomeranz (2000) in his detailed study of China also cautiously supports Bairoch. But, as I and others have argued, his evidence is not persuasive.[47] Gunder Frank also accepts Bairoch's position and states "that around 1800 Europe and the United States, after long lagging behind, suddenly caught up and then overtook Asia economically and politically."[48]

By contrast, in his detailed and careful study piecing together long-term estimates of world GDP and population, Maddison (2001) conclusively shows that the so-called Great Divergence, which led one small part of the Eurasian continent to begin a process that slowly but certainly led it to forge ahead of the other Eurasian civilizations, began in the eleventh century. This date also fits my argument in *Unintended Consequences*, that it was the change in the material beliefs of the West inaugurated by the second of two papal revolutions which led slowly but certainly to the Great Divergence. Maddison finds that "Western Europe overtook China (the leading Asian economy) in per capita performance in the 14th century. Thereafter China and most of the rest of Asia were more or less stagnant in per capita terms until the second half of the 20th century" (p. 44). He rightly concludes "in view of the laborious efforts

I have made to accumulate quantitative evidence of this topic, I now conclude that Bairoch and his epogini are quite wrong" (p. 47).

Nor does my detailed study in *The Hindu Equilibrium* of the impact of the British Raj on the nineteenth-century Indian economy—when it followed the twin metropolitan policies of free trade and laissez faire—bear out the nationalist and Marxist thesis of the colonial exploitation of the subcontinent.[49] The most radical change introduced by the Raj was the establishment of an institutional—particularly legal and economic—framework, through which an escape from the ancient equilibrium into the modern world by labor-intensive industrialization was possible. But this movement into a new era was rather half-hearted, and its effects very thinly spread over the vast subcontinent.

Nevertheless, despite nationalist cant, up until the First World War, the Indian response to the new opportunities for industrialization was impressive. Under the nineteenth-century regime of free trade and laissez faire, Indian enterprise and capital were able to turn the tables on Lancashire and set up a thriving and efficient modern textile industry. Similarly, plantations and a number of other industries including steel were begun. Indian industrialization thus began well before that of most other developing countries. Its industrial performance in the free trade era was well above the world average, and better than nearly all other countries except Japan. India also succeeded in raising the rate of growth of its manufactured exports, and thus became a modern exporter of manufactures rather than of traditional handicrafts as it had been in the past.

It was the combination of protective labor legislation (instigated at the behest of a coalition of protectionist Lancashire interests and well-meaning humanitarian pressure groups) and discriminating protection through revenue tariffs (instituted essentially on grounds of fiscal expediency) during the last phase of the Raj, which set in motion those trends toward an inward-looking, import-substituting, capital-intensive form of industrialization whose apotheosis was reached in the 1950s and 1960s. This did immense damage to India's laboring poor, and it is only with the partial reversal and move back to the free trade and laissez faire policies of the Raj, after the economic crisis of 1991, that India is once again picking up where it left off in the late nineteenth century. The attendant marked improvement in its economic performance has begun to redress its ancient mass poverty.

In sub-Saharan Africa, the ending of the slave trade—enforced by the British Navy—ended the domination of quasi-feudal warrior elites whose power rested on weapons and cattle, and revenues on the capture and sale of slaves. This allowed the peasants to exploit the new opportunities provided by the export markets of the new LIEO.[50] The ensuing rise in their income gave them political power as well as the means to purchase guns to enforce it. The traditional warrior elites tried to ally themselves with the rising peasantry, while others tried without much success to exploit the new trading opportunities with slave-worked plantations. In many places they were replaced by merchant princes or local oligarchies of traders who worked out assignments of monopoly trading rights within specified territorial boundaries with neighbors. It has even been claimed by some scholars that, with the fall in commodity prices in the depression after 1873, it was the European and some Africans' resentment of these arrangements that "led to armed conflict, growing exclusionism, and ultimately the scramble for European colonies in Africa."[51]

Colonialism, in effect, empowered the mass of peasants with relatively abundant land and labor at the expense of those with scarce capital (largely in the form of cattle). Jean Copans (1980) has argued that in this early phase of the colonial economic system, the access to world markets "made the former slave a free and independent agricultural producer."[52] Where there were white settler communities, as in the Kenyan highlands, the Europeans sought to set up subsidized plantations and used various means to coerce African labor to work on them. But they never succeeded in undermining African peasant production.[53] Thus, with the exception of the predatory Belgian regime in the Congo, colonialism (despite Marxist and nationalist historiography) greatly benefited the African masses. It was with independence, partly caused by the inherent racism of the European colonial powers and their settler progeny (with the Portuguese being a notable exception), that the colonial institutional framework which had brought prosperity to the African masses was gradually undermined by predatory nationalist elites, and Africa gradually descended into that "heart of darkness" which in the imperial period had largely been confined to the Congo.

The End of the First LIEO

The nineteenth-century LIEO did not last. It was undermined first by a creeping and then a galloping dirigisme in much of the twentieth century. Why?

The Rise of Collectivism

The missing answer is provided in part by the conservative British philosopher Michael Oakeshott. He makes a crucial distinction between two major strands of Western thought on the state: the state viewed as a *civil* association, or alternatively as an *enterprise* association. The former view goes back to ancient Greece, the latter has its roots in the Judaeo-Christian tradition. The view of the state as a civil association sees it as a custodian of laws that do not seek to impose any preferred pattern of ends (including abstractions such as "social welfare" or fundamental "rights"), but which merely facilitates individuals to pursue their own ends. The enterprise view by contrast sees the state as the manager of an enterprise seeking to use the law for its own substantive purposes, and in particular for the legislation of morality. The classical liberalism of Smith and Hume entails the former, whereas the major secular embodiment of society viewed as an enterprise association is socialism, with its moral aim of using the state's power to equalize people.

Oakeshott distinguishes three versions of the collectivist morality that the state viewed as an enterprise association has sought to enforce. The first was a religious version epitomized by Calvinist Geneva and in our own day by Khomeni's Iran. The second is a productivist vision seeking to promote "nation building," which was the enterprise undertaken by the Renaissance princes and the leaders of most ex-imperial states. The third is the distributivist version with its aim of promoting some form of egalitarianism. Both the secular "enterprise" visions involve dirigisme.

Oakeshott (1993) notes that as in many other pre-industrial societies, modern Europe inherited a "morality of communal ties" from the Middle Ages. This was gradually superseded from the sixteenth century by a morality of individuality.[54] This individualist morality was fostered by the gradual breakdown of the mediaeval order which allowed a growing number of people to escape from the "corporate and communal organization" of medieval life. But this dissolution of communal ties also bred what Oakeshott terms the "anti-individual," who was unwilling or unable to make his own choices. Some were resigned to their fate, but in others it provoked "envy, jealousy and resentment. And in these emotions a new disposition was generated: the impulse to escape from the predicament by imposing it upon all mankind" (p. 24). This the anti-individual sought to do through two means. The first was to look to the government to "protect him from the necessity of being an individual" (p. 25). A large number of government activities epitomized by the Elizabethan Poor Law were devoted from the sixteenth century onward "to the protection of those who, by circumstance or temperament, were unable to look after themselves in this world of crumbling communal ties" (p. 25).

The anti-individual, second, sought to escape his "feeling of guilt and inadequacy which his inability to embrace the morality of individuality provoked" (p. 25), by calling forth a "morality of collectivism," where "'security' is preferred to 'liberty,' 'solidarity' to 'enterprise' and 'equality' to 'self-determination'" (p. 27). Both the individualist and collectivist moralities were different modifications of the earlier communal morality, but with the collectivist morality in addition being a reaction against the morality of individualism.

This collectivist morality inevitably supported the view of the state as an enterprise association. While this view dates back to antiquity, few if any pre-modern states were able to be "enterprising," as their resources were barely sufficient to undertake the basic tasks of government: law and order and external defense. This changed with the creation of centralized "nation-states" by the Renaissance princes and the subsequent Administrative Revolution, as Hicks[55] has labeled the gradual expansion of the tax base and thus the span of control of the government over its subjects' lives. Governments now had the power to look upon their activities as an enterprise.

The period of economic liberalism during the nineteenth century's great Age of Reform was short-lived in part due to the rise of another substantive purpose that most European states came to adopt: the egalitarian ideal promulgated by the Enlightenment. Governments in many developing countries also came to espouse this ideal of socialism. The apotheosis of this version of the state viewed as an enterprise association were the communist countries claiming to establish the socialist ideal of equalizing people. The collapse of their economies under similar but even more severe strains than those that beset less collectivist neo-mercantilist Third World economies is now history, though I cannot help remarking on the irony that it took two hundred years for 1989 to undo what 1789 had wrought!

Interwar Turmoil

The First World War marked the end of this nineteenth-century LIEO. By the late nineteenth century, the United States was by far the dominant economic power. As I argue in *In Praise of Empires,* an international hegemon is needed to provide the international public good of international peace on which global trade and commerce depend. Contrary to the presumption of classical liberals that, in a free trading world linked by a myriad mutually beneficial ties arising from global commerce and mutually beneficial capital flows, a spontaneous international order would arise to maintain the peace, or else a concert of powers would succeed in doing so, in practice through much of human history it is empires that have provided this essential public good through their Pax. The British did so through their direct and indirect empire policed by the Royal Navy for most of the nineteenth century after Waterloo. But, by the end of the century, British economic dominance and with it its complementary military power was slipping with the rise of the United States and Germany. If the United States had joined Britain in creating a joint Anglo-American imperium, the various international alarums and the rise of the two illiberal creeds of Fascism and Communism could perhaps have been averted.

But after the First World War, the United States under Wilson first sought to create an idealistic international moral order of sovereign nation-states policed by the League of Nations through sanctions. Their abject failure showed that the peace could not be maintained through these means. The flawed Versailles treaty—much as Keynes had predicted in his *The Economic Consequences of the Peace*—led to increasing political and economic disorder in Europe. The British were too weak to stem it. The Americans, after Wilson failed to secure ratification of his beloved League of Nations, though able were unwilling to bear the burden of maintaining a global Pax. They retreated into isolationism. Worse, during the Great Depression—which was in part caused by its faulty monetary policy and retreat into protectionism[56]—the United States failed to do what Britain in the depression of the 1870s had done: maintain open markets for trade and finance.[57] The interwar Smoot-Hawley tariff and the blue-sky laws (which banned U.S. banks from lending to foreign governments) in effect ended the LIEO.

Much worse, the turmoil of the interwar period also unraveled that complex web of international law and practice the British had woven in the nineteenth century to protect foreign capital. From the start of the First World War till 1929 (when international capital markets effectively closed down), the United States was the largest lender, with U.S. foreign investments increasing sixfold in the period, so that by 1929 the U.S. stock of foreign investment equaled that of Britain. But the weakening of British hegemony meant that the enforcement of the international rules created in the nineteenth century became problematic. As Lipson notes,

> Before the war, the United States had assumed responsibility for enforcing property rules only in Latin America. Elsewhere, sanctions were either British or collective. Now, however, Europe was weak and divided, and Britain was unable to act alone. The most obvious solution was condominium between the two largest investors, the United States and Great Britain. Yet President Wilson's defeat excluded that hypothetical solution. Even though U.S. economic interests continued to expand, the state flatly refused to assume commensurate political and military responsibilities outside the Western hemisphere. That refusal and Britain's shrunken power diminished the capacity of advanced capitalist states to enforce traditional property rules.[58]

Moreover, even if Wilson had not had a stroke, it is doubtful that he would have enforced international property rights, given his sympathies with socialism, ambivalence toward the Mexican and Russian revolutions,[59] and his promotion of national self-determination. For it was the Mexican and Russian revolutions and the explicit introduction of statist policies by Attaturk in Turkey—the successor state to the Ottoman Empire extinguished at Versailles—which led to the questioning of the legitimacy of these rules. Subsequently, there was a worldwide erosion of public acceptance of the sanctity of private property rights when faced with social policies designed to promote the nationalist weal.

Even though the United States after the Second World War, chastened by the global disorder its interwar isolationism had caused, sought a partial restoration of these nineteenth-century international rules, it did not extend them to the newly decolonized Third World, which experienced an explosion of economic nationalism. The "embedded liberalism" (coined by John Ruggie 1983 and adopted by Eichengreen 1996, p. 4, and which is just another label for democratic socialism) promoted by both Wilson and then Roosevelt within the United States, also meant that the sanctity of property rights which the classical liberals had always sought to further, no longer had much resonance in the domestic politics of either the United States or the United Kingdom. With anti-imperialist moralism becoming a part of U.S. foreign policy after Wilson, attempts to protect property rights, like the ill-fated Suez adventure of the British and the French in 1956 to prevent Nasser's nationalization of the Suez Canal, were scuttled by the United States. There was no way in which anyone could thereafter stand against the new nation-states' assertion of their rights of national sovereignty against any purported international property rights. There was no bulwark against this disintegration of the international legal order. Most developing countries' governments (and many European ones too), being both nationalist and dirigiste, sought to regulate, tax, or nationalize particular foreign investments on the grounds of national social utility rather than any particular antagonism to private property. This made it difficult for the United States to identify expropriation of foreign capital with a socialist ideology, as demonstrated by its acquiescence with the nationalization of foreign oil companies in the 1960s and early 1970s by right-wing governments in the Middle East. This still casts a long shadow.

U.S. political elites realized during the Second World War that they had to take over from the British as the new imperial power, and in *In Praise of Empires* I show how gradually they have fulfilled that ambition. But, this was hidden from the populace. It is Osama bin Laden's supreme though ironic achievement that he may have succeeded in finally bringing popular support for this enterprise. The most overt attempt at succeeding the British was in the attempt to recreate a new LIEO under Pax Americana.

Recreating a New LIEO

After the Second World War, at Bretton Woods, the United States tried to resurrect the economic pillars on which the nineteenth-century LIEO had been built—free trade, the gold standard, and free capital mobility. But, whereas the British Empire had fostered these by example, treaties, and direct and indirect imperialism, the United States instead created transnational institutions—the GATT followed by the WTO, the IMF, and the World Bank. These will be dealt with in greater detail in the following chapters, but a few points can be made in this more general narrative.

Trade

Rather than following the correct British policy of adopting unilateral free trade and then allowing its hegemony to spread the norm, the United States has chosen the extremely acrimonious route of multilateral and more recently bilateral negotiations to reduce trade barriers. This is due to the fact that, unlike the British who have correctly seen free trade as a non–zero sum game and since the repeal of the Corn Laws adhered to it and its close cousin laissez faire[60] throughout the nineteenth century—despite various attempts by politicians like Joseph Chamberlain to stir the pot by demanding protection in the name of "fair trade"—the Americans have never accepted the classical liberal case for free trade. They have always looked upon trade as a zero sum game. They have been protectionist. Only for a relatively brief period (from 1846 to 1861) was there a relatively liberal trade policy, and even then the average ad valorem tariff on the fifty-one most imported categories of goods was 27 percent.[61] The original intellectual justification for protectionism was provided by Hamilton's flawed argument for "infant industry" protection.[62] But once U.S. industry had caught up with and even overtaken European industry by 1890, this argument was no longer persuasive, and the United States argued for the principle of reciprocity as the central principle of its trade policy. In his 1901 message to Congress, Theodore Roosevelt said: "Reciprocity must be treated as the handmaiden of Protection. Our first duty is to see that the protection granted by the tariff in every case where it is needed is maintained, and reciprocity be sought so far as it can be safely done without injury to our home industries."[63]

This principle of reciprocity has been the central tenet of U.S. trade policy ever since, and the twentieth-century hegemon has sought to achieve free trade through reciprocal concessions in GATT and the WTO. But as the anti-globalization riots from Seattle onward demonstrate, by perpetuating the myth that trade is a zero sum game, and that removing tariffs can only be done on the basis of reciprocity, the United States has ensured that various protectionist lobbies have been given various handles in the name of "fair trade."

Exchange Rates

The attempt to resurrect something similar to the gold standard (based on a quasi-fixed exchange rate system policed by the IMF) foundered on its basic premise that, while freeing trade and maintaining convertibility on the current account (covering mainly trade in goods and services), the capital account (covering capital flows) could be controlled and managed by distinguishing between long-term (good) and short-term (bad) capital flows (see chapter 4). The freeing of trade made these capital controls ineffective.

Capital could be moved through the process of "leads and lags" in the current account. The gradual and long drawn move to floating exchange rates eliminated the need for the policeman of the Bretton Woods system—the IMF. It has since sought various changing roles, as we shall see (chapter 4). This new international monetary system, which has been dubbed a "non-system,"[64] however, has the advantage of being decentralized. It does not require the international cooperation of a quasi-fixed exchange rate system with its potential for international discord.

Development

The World Bank was to be the instrument to channel capital for development to the Third World. Since their interwar defaults and the passage of the U.S. blue-sky laws—which forbade U.S. financial intermediaries from holding foreign government bonds[65]—they had been denied access to world capital markets. The World Bank, or International Bank for Reconstruction and Development (IBRD) as its initial and still major component is called, was set up as a financial intermediary to fill this lacunae. Its intergovernmental ownership and guarantees allowed it to borrow at preferential rates in developed-country markets and lend the money at near commercial interest rates to the Third World. For those countries deemed too poor to borrow at these rates, a soft loan window—the IDA—was established with money subscribed by Western governments.

The financial intermediation role of the bank was soon overtaken by its role as a multilateral foreign aid agency, in part to play its role in the Cold War: both by tying the "non-aligned" to the free world, and by promoting economic development. These developed-country governments had also established their own bilateral foreign aid programs, designed more for the competition for political influence in the Third World during the Cold War than to serve their professed aim of alleviating world poverty.

As nearly all of these capital flows were mediated through multilateral or bilateral governmental channels, the access of developing countries to world capital markets was necessarily politicized. This was in stark contrast to the nineteenth-century pattern when private capital flowed from Europe to the rest of the world on market principles. Politically mediated "foreign aid" also sought to create another international development program. This was analogous to the program the British had promoted in the nineteenth century through the propagation and enforcement of rules concerning international property rights, and through direct and indirect imperialism. But, as these routes were eschewed by Pax Americana, the only available instrument was the use of "conditionality" tied to these aid flows to change state behavior for the promotion of the appropriate development policies in the Third World.

But, as with sanctions to serve foreign policy goals, this ever more stringent "conditionality" has been unsuccessful.[66] So the current development "mantra" is that "good governance is all." But, now the stark choice which faces the successors of Wilsonian idealism in foreign policy also faces them in international economic policy: can the order required for prosperity be promoted except through direct or indirect imperialism? My answer is provided in *In Praise of Empires*.

From Plan to Market

The interwar breakdown of the nineteenth-century international trading and payment systems, which had transmitted the growth impulse around the world, led the Third World to follow the Second World of the Communists to turn inward.[67] This was ironic, as the partial restoration of the LIEO under U.S. aegis did lead to a reduction in trade barriers, and within the developed world (grouped together in the Organization for Economic Cooperation and Development, OECD) to a removal of the restrictions on capital flows and the exchange controls which had become ubiquitous in the interwar period. This led to a boom in world trade and income growth. The Third World, still traumatized by its interwar experience and aided and abetted by the seemingly new "development economics," did not emulate the developed countries in liberalizing their controls on foreign trade and payments. A few small countries around the Pacific Rim, the so-called Gang of Four (South Korea, Taiwan, Hong Kong, and Singapore), bucked this trend and found that even a partial opening up of their economies allowed them to participate in the global boom which has been called the postwar Golden Age. Their spectacular success in raising their growth rates through following "outward-looking policies"[68] finally had some effect in persuading other developing countries, first haltingly and more recently in a flood, to switch from their inward-to outward-looking policies. But the real turning point for the Third World came with the OPEC coup of 1973 and its unintended consequences.

In 1973, OPEC (the Organization of Petroleum Exporting Countries) raised oil prices threefold. This brought the postwar Golden Age to an end. It also saw the emergence of demands by the Third World for a New International Order (NIEO), in which their presumed "commodity power" would be used to redistribute income from rich to poor countries. Not having participated in the Golden Age boom, most developing countries, caught in the time warp of their import substitution strategies, did not reap its full benefits, claiming and getting their right to special privileges and exceptions in the emerging global free trade regime. The NIEO was their final attempt to replace this liberal trading order by one that was politically managed.

But within a decade the wind had gone from their sails. The supposed commodity power wielded by OPEC proved to be illusory. As market-oriented economists had predicted, any attempt by a cartel to artificially raise the price of its product would eventually come unstuck.[69] For such a price rise would, first, induce a search for substitutes which would reduce the demand for the product, and second, lead to a search for alternative sources of supply. Both occurred. Various members of the cartel also succumbed to the temptation of increasing their share of the rationed output at the expense of the other members. Within a decade the oil price was no longer headline news. After the failure of another brief attempt at rigging it in the late 1970s, it has continued to decline in real terms till recently.[70] This effectively killed the illiberal dream of the NIEO. GATT has now successfully transformed itself into the WTO after its latest Uruguay round, and developing countries are now its most loyal supporters.

In the monetary sphere, the IMF was created to supervise the new gold exchange rate system based on the adjustable peg. It replaced the nineteenth-century gold standard which, as the events of the interwar period had so painfully shown, could lead to mass unemployment because of rigidities in domestic labor markets. The socialist "enterprise" association viewpoint which had triumphed in much of the West, in the form of social democracy, supported Keynesian prescriptions of aggregate demand management to maintain "full employment." Exchange rate changes were then deemed to be necessary when a country could only cut its real wages to achieve this target through a devaluation. The only country not permitted this "luxury" was the United States—because it formed the base of the gold exchange standard through its fixed parity with gold.

One consequence of the OPEC coup was to raise the costs of an essential input in all non–oil producing countries. The partial monetary accommodation of this relative price rise led to a rise in the general price levels of most countries. With the United States already suffering from the inflationary excesses associated with financing the Vietnam War, this further push to the inflationary process (and the accompanying stagnation in output) made the U.S. balance of payments unviable. A devaluation was required to realign its domestic with the international price level. This was achieved by President Nixon's closing of the gold window, which in turn inflicted the coup de grace to the gold exchange standard. The subsequent period has seen the institution of a worldwide free-floating exchange rate regime among the major economic powers, which has made it unnecessary to use dirigiste means to manage the balance of payments. This was the first benefit from the OPEC coup.

It also undermined the original mandate of the IMF, which has since, like Pirandello's *Six Characters in Search of an Author*, been looking around for a play. It has skillfully found a role in the ongoing adjustments from the plan to market underway in both the Third and Second worlds. But this has a natural limit. The IMF's future cannot be bright, particularly (as we see in chapter 4) in light of its most recent actions in South East Asia.

The second benefit from the OPEC coup was that the ensuing stagflation exposed the fallacies of Keynesian macroeconomics. Gradually, all Western governments realized that full employment could no longer be maintained by expanding nominal demand. The classical prescriptions of sound money and deregulated labor markets (along with other supply-side measures) were the only way to deal with stagflation.

The third consequence, and the most momentous for the Third World, arose from the disposition of their newfound oil wealth by the sparsely populated countries of the Middle East. The OPEC coup set in motion a chain of events which would dramatically change the postwar politicization of the disposition of international capital noted above. The OPEC countries could not domestically absorb the large surpluses derived from the oil price rise. They had to place them abroad. As Third World capital markets were underdeveloped, this in effect meant the West. But having obtained their newfound wealth through a political coup, the OPEC countries were fearful of placing it within reach of government whose citizens they had robbed. It could be confiscated—a not unreasonable fear, as shown by the subsequent sequestration of Iranian assets by President Carter. So they placed their money in the offshore branches of the money center banks (the so-called Eurocurrency market).

These offshore banks of the Eurodollar market had developed outside the jurisdiction and reach of their parent monetary authorities and governments in the 1960s. Their origins lay in the British government's restrictions on British banks financing trade among countries outside the sterling area in order to protect the value of sterling. The banks avoided these capital controls by offering dollar loans against the dollar deposits they had from foreign depositors. The offshore branches of the money center banks thus created the Eurodollar market, which was free of government control. This market was given a fillip when, after the Cuban missile crisis, Russian banks afraid their American accounts would be frozen, shifted their dollar reserves to London. But it was the ballooning U.S. deficits during the Vietnam War which led to a massive rise in dollar deposits outside the United States—a problem made worse by the various measures (like the interest equalization tax on purchases by Americans of foreign securities) to stem the outflow of dollars—which brought the Eurodollar market to maturity.[71] By the time of the OPEC coup there was thus in the Eurodollar market a legal means for capital to flow free of any national regulation. The newfound wealth of the OPEC countries found a natural home in these offshore institutions which would not be subject to political pressure.

The consequent explosion in the liquidity of these Western offshore branches led them to a frantic scramble to on-lend this money. This recycling of the OPEC surpluses was also pressed by their governments. They were concerned by the worldwide deflationary consequences of an increase in the worldwide savings propensity, caused by the transfer of income from countries with relatively low to those with high savings propensities, entailed by the OPEC coup. There were many eager borrowers in the Third World, in particular in the "inward-looking" countries of Latin America. Thus the seeds of the debt crisis were sown.

This bank lending to the Third World was based on variable interest rates linked to LIBOR (the London Inter Bank Offer Rate). When, in the late 1970s, the United States and subsequently much of Europe adopted sound money policies to deal with the stagflation that had plagued them since the OPEC coup, world interest rates and the cost of servicing debt rose dramatically. As most of the Third World borrowers—mainly in Latin America but not in East Asia—had borrowed to deal with their longstanding fiscal deficits, they now found themselves unable to service their foreign debts. Starting with Mexico, many in effect defaulted on their obligations. They were forced to recognize—as had the mercantilist states in the past—that the only way to restore their diminished control over the economy was through economic liberalization. Thus began the long, drawn-out process of reform whereby dirigiste "inward-looking" regimes are gradually being replaced by more market-friendly "outward-looking" ones all over the globe.

Economic liberalization has also provided many developing countries a newfound access to direct foreign and portfolio investments. For them this is a more desirable form of borrowing than bank borrowing at variable interest rates, because the associated currency and income risks are shared with the foreign investors. More sustainable forms of capital flows are thus now available to developing countries willing to change their nationalist attitudes to multinationals.[72] These market-based capital flows now dwarf the politicized flows from bilateral and multilateral agencies—whether they be IBRD loans or various forms of foreign aid. The future of this politicized part of the world capital market is increasingly in jeopardy.[73]

Finally, the stagflation resulting from the OPEC coup also led to the replacement of demand management by supply-side policies in most developed countries. Beginning with the Thatcherite revolution in the United Kingdom, the worldwide movement toward privatization and deregulation is reversing nearly century-old trends and the habits and intellectual beliefs they had engendered. With the spectacular collapse of the Communist economic system,[74] dirigisme for the first time in a century is seemingly in worldwide retreat. The most spectacular reversals in policies are those of China in the early 1980s and India's in 1991—both after endemic economic crises which were in large part the consequence of their past dirigisme. Thus, apart from Africa and the Middle East, most of the Third and Second World has now embarked on the modernization offered by globalization.

But, there is nevertheless growing discontent with globalization. A large part, as we shall see, is based on questions of morality (see chapters 6 and 7), but there are also many professed economic sources of discontent, concerning foreign trade, international capital flows, and questions relating to inequality and poverty. Some have expressed legitimate fears that current trends and policies in these areas may yet lead to the unraveling of the current LIEO. We turn to examining these in the following chapters.

2

From *Laissez Faire* to the *Dirigiste Dogma*

The twin pillars of the domestic policy of the British Imperium were the classical liberal policies of "laissez faire" and unilateral free trade. For the classical liberals, Adam Smith and David Hume, these were in the country's national interest, and though free trade would help in promoting understanding between states, they did not believe (as some of their later acolytes like Richard Cobden) that this would lead to international peace. To maintain international order, a balance of power through a network of alliances and treaties is needed.[1] We have seen that the new imperial power—the United States—has instead sought to achieve global free trade through reciprocity, and since the New Deal in the Great Depression, it has also eschewed laissez faire. It has however gradually built up its imperium, though only recently has it begun to use its unprecedented economic and military power to maintain international order. In the following three chapters, dealing with the current discontents with globalization under the U.S. imperium, I want to show that, while most of this discontent is based on simple economic fallacies and invalid empirical assumptions, it has been allowed currency in large part because the United States has eschewed the twin economic principles which underpinned the nineteenth-century LIEO. But what are these principles?

Classical Liberalism and Laissez Faire

Laissez Faire

The laissez faire doctrine has been caricatured as "the night watchman state," as assuming "a harmony of interests," and as assuming utility-maximizing

48

rational actors. But all these are alien to the thought of the fathers of classical liberalism—Hume and Smith.[2] They do not look upon man as a rational utility maximizer with perfect knowledge. Hume talks of the "imperfections and narrow limits of human understanding" and that "reason is, and ought only to be the slave of the passions and can never pretend to any office other than to serve and obey them."[3] Their central claim is that, a free market economy, by promoting the division of labor, and by coordinating the division of knowledge (which necessarily exists in any society) through the price mechanism can goad individuals to become more rational. The specialization that then ensues allows a better allocation of a society's resources and leads to greater national wealth. But, the free market is not considered to be one which has perfect competition as defined by modern-day economists.

Moreover, instead of there being a harmony of interests, a legal framework is needed to mediate between clashing interests and reconcile individual self-interest with the public good. Classical liberals strongly believe in "liberty under the law" and therefore a *qualified*, not an absolutist *laissez faire*.[4] This "liberty under the law" is moreover based on a procedural view of justice, where the latter, as Adam Smith put it, is "but a negative virtue, and merely hinders us from hurting our neighbors."[5] The law must be nondiscriminatory, applying to everyone without regard to particular circumstances. This rules out "positive" notions of justice, for instance of the distributive sort, in part because then the law would be based on the discretion of fallible and most likely corrupt men, to discriminate against some in favor of others.

Thus, the nature of the government is crucial in recommending policy. The great classical liberals from Hume to Smith to Mill were aware of this. If, as I have argued elsewhere,[6] most states are predatory—even democratic ones, where the predators are the median voter and successful pressure groups— concerned more with net revenue maximization than with social welfare maximization, then *normative* analysis based on postulating that the government consists of Platonic Guardians can go horribly wrong.

For the essential problem of political economy is to devise ways in which the state will provide the essential public goods at least cost from taxes. This was clearly recognized by the Classics, whose recommendation of laissez faire was based on a realistic assessment of the nature of governments. The classical policy prescriptions have been caricatured "by Carlisle's phrase anarchy plus the constable, or by LaSalle's simile of the night watchman."[7] But as Robbins (1976) and Myint (1948) have noted, this is a calumny. The classical liberals were not hostile to the state, nor did they believe that governments had only a minor role in economic life. Their view of the state was positive, and as Robbins indicates, Adam Smith's famous statement of the three functions of the state, viz., (i) to protect society from foreign invaders, and (ii) every member, as far as feasible, from oppression and injustice by other

49

members of society, and (iii) provide and maintain various public works and public institutions which provided public goods,[8] is almost identical with Keynes's famous formulation in *The End of Laissez Faire*: "the important thing for government is not to do things which individuals are doing already, but to do those things which at present are not done at all."[9] The ensuing principles of economic liberalism were clearly set out in Mill's *Principles*, and their clearest modern reformulation is set forth in Hayek's *The Constitution of Liberty*. In fact, the current "Washington Consensus" on economic policy is essentially a classical liberal policy package.[10]

However, from Smith to Hayek to Friedman, classical liberals have maintained that "equality" comes into conflict with "liberty," and a true "liberal is not an egalitarian" (Hayek 1960, p. 402). For, as Nozick demonstrated brilliantly with his Wilt Chamberlain example, "no end-state state principle or distributional patterned principle can be continuously realized without continuous interference with people's lives [as any patterned distribution can be upset by people's voluntary actions in exchange]. . . . The socialist society would have to forbid capitalist acts between consenting adults."[11]

Classical liberals have, however, always advocated public transfers if private transfers are unavailable or insufficient to help the "deserving poor,"[12] and also, since Mill, the public *financing* but not *provision* of merit goods, such as health and education for those unable to afford them. Just as in the case of the economic package, the social package promoted by social democrats is increasingly coming to resemble these classical liberal prescriptions, except for merit goods. Thus, eschewing egalitarianism in taxation—in practice if not in rhetoric—and by attempting to reform welfare states to confine the benefits to the "deserving poor," both the New Democrats under President Clinton in the United States and New Labor under Prime Minister Blair in the United Kingdom, are closer to the classical liberal viewpoint than they imagine.

Conservatism

Classical liberalism must also be distinguished from conservatism, though both share some common features. Thus, Hayek, in his magisterial restatement of classical liberal principles in *The Constitution of Liberty*, ended the book with a postscript titled "Why I am not a Conservative."[13]

Hayek distinguishes three points on which classical liberals and conservatives differ. "One of the fundamental traits of the conservative attitude is a fear of change, a timid distrust of the new as such, while the [classical] liberal position is based on courage and confidence, on a preparedness to let change run its course even if we cannot predict where it will lead."[14] This conservative attitude to change is linked, says Hayek, "to two other characteristics of conservatism: its fondness for authority and its lack of understanding of economic forces."[15] These lead conservatives to have strong moral convictions but no political principles which allow them to work with people with different moral values. "The most conspicuous attribute of [classical] liberalism that distinguishes it as much from conservatism as from socialism is the view that moral beliefs concerning matters of conduct which do not directly interfere with the protected sphere of other persons do not justify coercion."[16] Also linked to this fear of the new, says Hayek, "is its propensity to reject well-substantiated new knowledge because it dislikes some of the consequences which seem to follow from it—or, to put it bluntly, its obscurantism,"[17] as well as "its hostility to internationalism and its proneness to a strident nationalism."[18]

The major votaries of classical liberalism today are American conservatives. For, as Hayek noted: "It is the doctrine on which the American system of government is based."[19] But, contemporary American conservatism is a novel brew which, Micklethwait and Wooldridge rightly note, is a mixture of the individualism of classical liberalism and "ubertraditionalism."[20] It represents adherence to the bourgeois organization of society epitomized by that much-maligned word, "Victorian": with its faith in individualism, capitalism, progress, and virtue. Having been silenced by the seemingly endless march of "embedded liberalism" since the New Deal, American conservatism has since the late 1960s regrouped, and under Presidents Reagan and George W. Bush created a new powerful political movement. Thus, apart from the brief period of Margaret Thatcher's ascendancy in Britain,[21] it is only in the United States that the classical liberal tradition continues to have political force.

The End of Laissez Faire

The principles of classical liberalism and laissez faire did not survive the trauma of the First World War, which brought the first LIEO to an end. It was the rise of the "enterprise" voice of socialism and rampant nationalism toward the end of the nineteenth century which led to "the end of laissez faire"—as Keynes called his influential pamphlet. The process began in Europe with Bismarck's social insurance scheme in Germany and the liberal welfare reforms instituted by the Liberal party under Lloyd George in Britain in 1906–14. Following the Great Depression it spread to the United States through Roosevelt's New Deal. The resulting "embedded liberalism,"[22] as it has been called, but which is more appropriately termed "social democratic" became the dominant ideology, not least because of the scribbling of economists. Consequently, by the time of the Second World War the classical liberalism of the nineteenth century was replaced by the Dirigiste Dogma.

51

Poverty and Industrialization in Nineteenth-Century Britain

The role of the historians, novelists, and various diverse social activists was crucial in changing the climate of opinion in England. For nearly a century, English history was dominated by "the Whig interpretation of history" of which Macaulay's *History of England* was the crowning achievement. As Hayek notes: "its beneficial effect in creating the essentially liberal atmosphere of the nineteenth century is beyond doubt and was certainly not due to any misrepresentation of the facts."[23] But this was political and constitutional history. As the socialist impulse gathered momentum in the second half of the nineteenth century, prompted by the Romantic revolt against the Enlightenment and the view of many sensitive souls that the emerging industrial society was dehumanizing,[24] historical interest shifted to social and economic history. The social surveys of poverty by Booth and Rowntree, the writings of Henry Mayhew, and above all of Engels gave rise to a popular perception that the new capitalist industrial society had accentuated rather than relieved poverty.

The ensuing century-old debate, about the effects of the Industrial Revolution on the standard of living of workers, rumbles on to our day. But, we can now reach at least some firm conclusions. Nicholas Craft has both summarized the debate and offered the best statistical evidence on which to judge it. He shows that till about 1820 there was only very low growth in output per head, but subsequently it rose. Personal consumption per head grew more slowly than output per head between 1770 and 1820, as increasing shares of output were taken by investment and government expenditure. After 1820, consumption per head in real terms grew in line with the growth of output per head. "The best guess available indicates that in the long run at least growth of real earnings for workers as a whole moved in line with growth of national output per head. Models which postulate a massive shift of income distribution against workers do not seem appropriate."[25] But till 1820, though workers as a whole saw their per capita consumption grow there were many who saw it fall, and whether "there were more gainers than losers in the working classes in 1830 is still contentious."[26] Thus it would seem incontrovertible that over the long haul the Industrial Revolution in Britain and the globalization that accompanied it did raise workers' standard of living.

But, it was a slow and drawn-out process. It is worth stating the likely reason, as it has echoes in contemporary debates about the effects of globalization on the wages of the unskilled in developed countries, particularly the United States. Sir John Hicks maintained that the defining feature of the Industrial Revolution was a large substitution of fixed for circulating capital in the production process.[27] This is best illustrated by the industry which was at the heart of the early Industrial Revolution—textiles. In the old handicraft mode for producing textiles, production was organized through the "putting out system" where traders advanced loans and inputs to the handicraft workers to produce textiles in their homesteads, which they then bought and sold in the wider marketplace. The capital of the traders in this system was their circulating capital. But with the development of the textile mill and its more mechanized means of producing textiles replacing the "putting out" system, the machinery in the mills represented larger concentrations of fixed capital than in the handlooms of the "putting out" system. This new mill technology was more efficient as it used less capital and labor per unit of production than the old handicraft technology. This meant that for a given rate of capital accumulation the composition of capital shifted over time from circulating to fixed capital. During this transition the demand for labor—which was higher for the circulating than fixed capital component of the rising aggregate capital stock—would not increase as fast and could even fall (as Ricardo showed in his famous chapter "On Machinery" in the last edition of his *Principles*), as compared with the case when the growth of the capital stock was in circulating capital. Thus, wages would not grow, and could even fall, until the substitution of fixed for circulating capital was complete. Once the transition was over, and all the labor in textiles was using the more productive technology, there would be (as there was) a secular rise in wages. This is what seems to have happened in the long nineteenth century in Britain.

Also, whereas in the "putting out" system, labor was largely casual and rootless, in the mills the labor force had to be permanent. The high fixed cost of the machines meant that producers could not afford to leave them unutilized and needed a permanent labor force to man them. Having acquired firm-specific skills, this permanent labor force would be in a position of bilateral monopoly with their employers. With the factory floor also facilitating permanent relationships with their peers, "class consciousness" and combinations to use the strike weapon (to get a larger share of the joint returns to the deployment of their acquired skills on the fixed capital in the factory) would develop. Trade unions would then emerge naturally from this process.

"Manna from Heaven" Distributivism

Apart from the change in the climate of opinion engendered by the historians, novelists, and activists in nineteenth-century Britain, there was also a gradual shift in academic opinion from the classical liberalism of Smith and Hume to the various dirigiste panaceas which came to dominate economic policy in the twentieth century. The turning point came with John Stuart Mill. Though his *Principles* is by and large a codification of the policy prescriptions of classical liberalism, he also began what Hayek has called the "manna from heaven" presumptions of contemporary distributive theories.

All the classical nineteenth-century thinkers, including Marx, considered production and distribution to be inseparable parts of a single economic system. Mill demurred. He wrote: "The laws and conditions of the production of wealth, partake of the characters of physical truth. There is nothing optional, or arbitrary in them. . . . It is not so with the distribution of wealth. This is a matter of human institutions solely. The things once there, mankind, individually or collectively, can do with them as they like. They can place them at the disposal of whomsoever they please and on whatever terms."[28] This is in contradiction to the truth known to all classical economists (including Marx) that, though there may be a choice between economic systems,[29] "we do not have the freedom to mix the productive arrangements of one system with the distributive arrangements of another."[30] This is a truth that modern-day economists are painfully rediscovering after a century-long detour.

The new institutional economics (including the economics of organization, transactions costs, and imperfect information) shows that "one of the main pillars of Walrasian neo-classical economics—the separability of equity and efficiency—breaks down when transactions costs and imperfect information are important; the terms and conditions of contracts in various transactions, which directly affect the efficiency of resource allocation, now crucially depend on ownership structures and property relations."[31] Thus, the growth and productivity outcomes of particular institutional forms cannot be separated from their system of property rights (and the distribution of income streams flowing from them). We cannot, as in the welfare economics initiated by Pigou's *Economics of Welfare*, devise a *Pareto-efficient* productive structure—in the sense that with given resources and available technology, no individual can be made better off without making someone else worse off—and then implement the social welfare–maximizing distribution of national income to yield a full "welfare optimum," the *Pareto optimum*—even if this is done through lump-sum taxes and subsidies.

For there is another truth well known to the classics but obscured by Mill which mitigates against these socialist panaceas—namely that politics and economics cannot be separated. The classical economists, including Marx, were quite happy to apply their methods to both politics and economics. But James Mill's *Essay on Government* had no successor till the modern writings of the "new" political economists.[32] This was because his son John Stuart Mill insisted that Bentham's and his father's utilitarian techniques were only applicable to economics.[33] The polity was subsumed, largely for technical reasons, into a committee of Platonic Guardians charged with maximizing a social welfare function subject to the usual technological and resource constraints. As part of this exercise, the optimal trade-off between equity and efficiency would emerge. This way of thinking reached its apotheosis in what is currently touted as providing the "grammar for arguments" about public policy, namely public economics. As two distinguished purveyors of its methods state in an introduction to a book commending the application of optimal tax theory to developing countries, the theory postulates that "the government has coherent, unified and largely benevolent objectives, captured in the social welfare function, and we search for ways in which the tools available to it can be used to improve the measure of welfare."[34] It does not take even the most casual empiricism to recognize that such a theory must be irrelevant, as most polities do not even come close to these assumptions about their character. Yet, the various socialist panaceas supported by the still entrenched *Dirigiste* Dogma are based implicitly on this assumption.[35]

I have grave doubts about the utility for public policy of "public economics." For, in a world where politicians are not Platonic Guardians, it clouds what would be "optimal" from what is reasonable to expect or hope for. The basis for this theory comes from the well-known Arrow-Debreu fundamental theorems of welfare economics, which theorists assert provide the justification for the superiority of a market economy and thereby laissez faire.[36] If one or the other conditions for the existence of the Utopian state of perfect competition are not met, there is "market failure" and thence a prima facie case for government intervention. This justification for "dirigisme" has always seemed bizarre to me.[37] To compare "competition" in any actual market economy with an unattainable ideal is a form of "nirvana economics."[38] For it is child's play to show that because of incomplete markets, external effects, and the existence of public goods, "market failure" defined as deviations from a perfectly competitive norm is ubiquitous. But the corollary that this then justifies massive corrective public action is highly dubious.

Thus, Stiglitz's[39] claim that neoclassical public economics allows optimal tax-subsidy interventions to be derived to make Pareto improvements is belied by the qualifications that he and Greenwald have to make. Thus, on political economy they state in a footnote: "It might be noted that we ignore any discussion of the political processes by which the tax-subsidy schemes described below might be effected. Critics may claim that as a result we have not really shown that a Pareto improvement is actually possible."[40] Quite.

While on their claim "that there exist Pareto-improving government interventions . . . [and] that the kind of intervention required can be simply related to certain parameters that, in principle are observable" (p. 231), they are forced to concede in their concluding comments: "We have considered relatively simple models, in which there is usually a single distortion . . . Though the basic qualitative proposition, that markets are constrained Pareto efficient, would obviously remain in a more general formulation, the simplicity of the policy prescriptions would disappear. Does this make our analysis of little policy relevance? The same objection can, of course, be raised against standard optimal tax theory. (Some critics might say, so much the worse for both)" (p. 258). Quite!

Competition and Monopoly

The trouble with this whole mode of policy analysis lies not only in its neglect of political economy but also in its deviation from the classical liberal concept of competition. As Blaug (1987) notes, there is a "subtle but nevertheless unmistakable difference in the conception of "competition" before and after the "marginal revolution." The modern concept of perfect competition, conceived as a market structure in which all producers are price takers and face perfectly elastic curves for their outputs, was born with Cournot in 1838 and is foreign to the classical conception of competition as a process of rivalry in the search for unrealized profit opportunities, whose outcome is uniformity in both the rate of return on capital invested and the prices of identical goods and services but not because producers are incapable of making prices. In other words, despite a steady tendency throughout the history of economic thought to place the accent on the end-state of competitive equilibrium rather than the process of disequilibrium adjustments leading up to it, this emphasis became remorseless after 1870 or thereabouts, whereas the much looser conception of "free competition" with free but not instantaneous entry to industries is in evidence in the work of Smith, Ricardo, Mill, Marx, and of course Marshall and modern Austrians. For that reason, if for no other, it can be misleading to label classical economics as a species of general equilibrium theory except in the innocuous sense of an awareness that "everything depends on everything else."[41]

From Adam Smith onward, classical liberals also recognized that deviations from free competition (like monopoly) ultimately depend upon government actions which prevent potential rivals from competing. By contrast, the theoretical model, as Demsetz notes: "*assumes* that monopoly power exists, it does not explain *how* monopoly power is exercised and maintained. . . . [N]o good explanation is provided for how present and potential rivals are kept from competing without some governmentally provided restrictions on competitive activities."[42] For we now know from the theory of "contestable markets"[43] that, even with economies of scale and scope which limit the number of firms that can service a particular market, as long as potential rivals can contest the "monopoly," the single eventual incumbent's pricing and output policies need not diverge from those under competition. The only rents such a "monopolist" can acquire are the sunk costs of firm-specific assets essential for production. Thus, antitrust regulations designed to increase competition are unnecessary. Worse, there is evidence of monopolistic capture of regulatory agencies by the companies being regulated.[44] Hence, there is a clear danger that such regulations, instead of promoting competition, will create government-mediated barriers to entry which nurture monopolies.

The dynamic efficiency of capitalism, as Joseph Schumpeter emphasized in his magisterial book *Capitalism, Socialism and Democracy,* does not only depend upon the *imitative* output competition emphasized by perfect competition. In this form of competition, each producer in an industry imitates the products of its competitors and hence the competition is between identical products produced by a large number of producers. Rather, the essence of capitalism Schumpeter notes is the process of creative destruction involving *innovative* competition. He writes:

> In capitalist reality as distinguished from its textbook picture, it is not that kind of [imitative] competition which counts but the competition from the new commodity, the new technology, the new source of supply, the new type of organization—competition which commands a decisive cost or quality advantage and which strikes not at the margins of the profits and the outputs of the existing firms but at their foundations and their very lives. This kind of competition is as much more effective than the other as a bombardment is in a comparison with forcing a door, and so much more important that it becomes a matter of comparative indifference whether competition in the ordinary [imitative] sense functions more or less promptly; the powerful lever that in the long run expands output and brings down prices is in any case made of other stuff. It is hardly necessary to point out that [innovative] competition . . . acts not only when in being but also when it is merely an ever-present threat. It disciplines before it attacks . . . In many cases, though not all, this will in the long run enforce behavior very similar to the perfectly competitive pattern.[45]

This is as spare and incisive a description of the capitalist process and its dynamics as can be found. It gives the lie to all the dirigiste panaceas being touted by the New Dirigisme based on a myriad of "market failures" within the perfect competition model and the accompanying call for the regulation of a market economy. Thus, for the innovative competition which lies at the heart of the capitalist process, efficiency does not require a large number of firms. Most innovations partake of a race in which the winner takes all. As Demsetz notes: "the competitive intensity of [such] a contest is not always increased by adding more contestants."[46] Patents and other devices to prevent imitative competition allow the winners in innovative competition to secure a big payoff for their innovative effort. This shows that in a dynamic market economy there may be many dimensions of competition, with some of them being inversely related—for example imitative competition requires a large number of firms, while innovative competition requires a small number. Moreover, as the different dimensions of competition relevant for the efficient functioning of a dynamic economy are incommensurable, there can be no single measure of competitiveness (such as market concentration) to judge the efficiency of an actual market economy.

Nor will the "rate of return" or "price cap" regulatory formulae necessarily ensure competition in the large. For, with economies of scale, prices can no longer equal marginal costs and there cannot be perfect competition. Competition will not be merely imitative but have some of the elements of a contest in which some agents will lose and others win. It would be inappropriate to judge the intensity of competition of such a contest by the *ex post* rate of return of the winner. For, as Demsetz notes, "if one were to gauge competitive intensity by the rate of return on investment made by winners in a lottery game, the rate of return would be quite high, but a negative return is obtained if the calculation includes the wagers made by losers."[47] So, if one were to use the rate of return criterion to judge the competitiveness of a particular industry, ideally the calculation should include the costs incurred by those who competed to become incumbents but lost. If, moreover, incumbency depends on government favors, then the "rent seeking" costs of all the contestants associated with competing for political favor would also have to be included. This inclusive rate of return need not be above some competitive norm. But, in practice, it will be impossible to calculate.

But what about natural monopolies? Surely, once a firm acquires one, it will, *faut mieux* exploit its monopoly power, and hence such natural monopolies will require some form of regulation. Most infrastructural services like roads, rail, electricity, and water have elements of natural monopoly. This was the justification used in the past for their nationalization. But, with growing fiscal constraints and the well-known inefficiencies associated with public enterprises, there is a welcome global move toward their privatization. Will this not inevitably lead to natural monopolies being used by private producers to exploit consumers? Hence, should these utilities not be regulated?

The UCLA Industrial Organization school has provided a distinctive and important answer to this question, which unfortunately is not as well known as the various dirigiste regulatory regimes currently being touted by mainstream theorists. The basic idea has been labeled "competition for the field" by Harold Demsetz, following a distinction due to Edwin Chadwick in the nineteenth century between it and "competition within the field."

"Competition for the field" differs from the later development of the notion of "contestability," insofar as the latter is concerned with competition between an existing incumbent and potential entrants to the natural monopoly. By contrast, "competition for the field," as its name suggests, is concerned with the competition for becoming an incumbent in the first place. This has important consequences for the configuration of prices and output and thence the competitive efficiency of the economy. In the theory of contestable markets it has been shown that, in equilibrium, the only rents the incumbent of a natural monopoly can acquire are the incumbent's sunk costs which a new entrant would have to incur in moving in and out of the monopoly. If an outsider can enter and exit a market without incurring any transition costs, the natural monopoly would be perfectly contestable and, despite economies of scale and scope, the incumbent insider would not be able to garner any rents.

But, as in many natural monopolies there will be substantial transition costs; insiders will usually be able to extract them as rents from consumers.[48]

The situation is very different from the viewpoint of competition for the field. Here the competition takes place *before* production begins. Would-be natural monopolists would compete for the right to serve the market at the lowest cost, adopting the best technology. In this competition for the field, as Demsetz showed in his famous essay, "Why regulate utilities?" the potential rents of the natural monopoly would be competed away with the best bid amongst the rivals to become the incumbent being accepted by the community. Thereafter, there would be a distinction between insiders and outsiders, and substantial transition costs for the latter—in sharp contrast with the conclusions of contestability theory. For, without these entry barriers, the successful incumbent may not realize the potential cost reductions associated with scale economies. The frequency of competition for the field, or equivalently the length of a franchise to the natural monopoly, will depend upon the particular supply and demand conditions for the output of the natural monopoly.[49] But what cannot be laid down is some ideal form of contract. For, given the ubiquitousness of imperfect information and the associated uncertainty, agents can only search for the best available mutually advantageous contract. In Hayek's felicitous phrase, the market is par excellence "a discovery process."[50]

The Rise of "Embedded Liberalism" in the United States

Why did the United States, the capitalist economy par excellence, pioneer antitrust legislation in the late nineteenth century? The answer lies in its history. Schumpeter noted:

> [I]n the Anglo-American world monopoly has been cursed and associated with functionless exploitation ever since, in the sixteenth and seventeenth centuries, it was English administrative practice to create monopoly positions in large numbers which, on the one hand, answered fairly well to the theoretical pattern of monopolist behavior and, on the other hand, fully justified the wave of indignation that impressed even the great Elizabeth. Nothing is so retentive as a nation's memory. . . . That practice made the English-speaking public so monopoly-conscious that it acquired a habit of attributing to that sinister power practically everything it disliked about business. To the typical liberal bourgeois in particular, monopoly became the father of almost all abuses—in fact, it became his pet bogey. Adam Smith, thinking primarily of monopolies of the Tudor and Stuart type, frowned on them in awful dignity . . . And in this country [the U.S.] monopoly is being made synonymous with any large- scale business.[51]

The American founding fathers had imbued this attitude from their country of origin.

In a perceptive essay, L. M. Hacker has argued that the anti-capitalist bias emerged in the United States and was amplified by its historians because of a political debate going back to its foundation between the Hamiltonians and Jeffersonians. The former were for a strong interventionist central government, the latter for a weak central government and little or no state intervention. The differences were not based on economic arguments but on moral and political issues. The Jeffersonians believed that a working federation based on states' rights would have emerged but for the Hamiltonian federalists who "won the day, partly by duress and fraud, and the consequences were dire. The establishment of a Supreme Court to override the legislative will and the acceptance of the idea of implied powers in the central government were some of the political results."

Jeffersonian ideas became prominent among historians in the twentieth century. They saw "Jefferson as the champion of natural rights (for natural today read 'human'); Jefferson as the spokesman for equalitarianism; Jefferson as the foe of an established church; Jefferson, notably, who sought to challenge 'monopoly'—this is the advocate whose words (not deeds) are being invoked. . . . [T]he broad implications of Jefferson's attack on "monopoly" [were that] only in the wide diffusion of property ownership (i.e., wealth) could social stability and economic progress be found."[52]

The third historical strand was associated with Andrew Jackson. Jacksonianism was also leveling like Jeffersonianism. Jackson "sought to speak for the common man, notably challenging the power of the central government . . . Jackson raised the cry of "monopoly" and was successful" (p. 84). After the Civil War, organized farmers took up the anti-capitalist cause by challenging the new industrialists, demanding "Peoples' Land, People's Money and People's Transportation." Their cause became "a moral crusade—they were the victims of those same monopolies against whom Jefferson and Jackson had inveighed."

The opponents of these populist groups were the Hamiltonians, Whigs, and Radical Republicans. They sought "the intervention of government to secure monetary stability and economic progress. A protective tariff system, a national banking program, government support of railroads, homesteads for farmers, easy immigration."[53]

The anti-capitalist bias of American historians was set by Charles Beard in his influential *The Rise of American Civilization*. He "took over the agrarian prejudices of his own Indiana boyhood to the capitalist processes. Late in life he found a remote and mechanical justification for his dislikes. He never showed an interest in these capitalist processes as such or in their economic consequences; but he rejected both for moral rather than for class, ideological, or dialectical reasons."[54]

It was Franklin Roosevelt's genius to knit these various strands together to create the "embedded liberalism" which has remained the dominant economic ideology in the United States Hacker argues:

Franklin D. Roosevelt assumed the mantle of Jefferson and Jackson as a leveler and defender of human rights. That is to say socially and morally, his identifications were with Jeffersonianism; but not politically. For Roosevelt called upon state interventionism on a grand scale to achieve his intention: the Big State, which Jefferson and Jackson had feared and fought, was his creation. But, because he talked the language of Jefferson, his defenders have turned on the economic ideas of the anti-Roosevelt forces. Capitalism is stagnant and dominated by monopolists; without state intervention the business cycle cannot be resolved, social injustices ameliorated, real wages increased. Once again the anti-capitalism of the New Dealers is political and moral; for certainly no case has been made out against capitalism as such.[55]

As such it is the moral critique of capitalism, best epitomized by the hugely influential book *The Robber Barons* by Matthew Josephson, which continues to resonate in America. Its anti-capitalist attitudes being summarized as: "(1) that great fortunes in America were built up by fraud; (2) that the country's natural resources were looted in the process; and (3) that the social consequences of private ownership and wealth were unhappy—in creating classes, in subordinating agriculture, in building slums, etc."[56] These attitudes are still prevalent in the United States, not least in its academies. I deal with this moral repugnance for capitalism in chapter 6. For today, it is the basic reason for the rise of the New Dirigisme.[57]

3

The Changing Fortunes of Free Trade

The shift in economists' views from the virtues of laissez faire toward dirigisme was mirrored in the numerous arguments they developed against free trade. So, by the end of the Second World War, not only the case for laissez faire but also free trade seemed to have been completely undermined. Planning in its various forms became the vogue among both economists and governments, particularly in the Third World. But, in the 1960s when I was becoming an economist, a backlash against this dirigisme began. It has been labeled the neoclassical resurgence in development economics.[1] One of its centers was the group around Ian Little and Maurice Scott at Nuffield College, Oxford. I formed part of this group. At the same time, Max Corden had joined the college as the Reader in International Economics at Oxford. He was to produce a magisterial work *Trade Policy and Economic Welfare (TPW)* which provided a comprehensive statement of the new theory of trade and welfare which the neoclassical resurgents were validating in their empirical studies of numerous developing countries.[2]

The Rise, Fall, and Rise of Free Trade

Corden began TPW with a historical overview of the longstanding debate about protection and free trade. He distinguished three stages of thought. The *first*, which I would label the "classical liberal" phase, covered the nineteenth century when "the case for free trade was developed simultaneously with the case for laissez faire. Indeed, the case for free trade was really a special case of the argument for laissez faire."[3]

The *second* stage, which I would label "collectivist"—for reasons to be set out below—covered most of the early part of the twentieth century till the end of the Second World War, during which numerous exceptions to laissez faire were adumbrated and "the arguments for protection emerged pari passu with the qualifications to the case for laissez faire, and since there are numerous qualifications to the latter, there are also numerous arguments for protection" (Corden 1997, p. 3).

In the *third* phase beginning in the late 1950s with the work of Meade (1955), Bhagwati and Ramaswami (1963), and Johnson (1965), which I would call "social democratic"—and what is now called "embedded liberalism"—the link between the case for free trade and the case for laissez faire was broken. The theory of "domestic distortions" evolved as the contemporary theory of trade and welfare. It was clearly and ably expounded in TPW. It showed that apart from the optimum tariff argument, where a country with monopoly or monopsony power in foreign trade could successfully turn the terms of trade in its favor,[4] all other arguments were second best, in the sense that there were superior tax-subsidy instruments compared with the tariff to deal with the "domestic distortion" in the working of the price mechanism which provided the prima facie case for protection. Thus, while departures from laissez faire were required to implement the appropriate tax-subsidy measures to deal with the domestic distortion, departures from free trade were not.

But I would argue, using the famous diagram from TPW (see the appendix to this chapter), that logically there should now be a *fourth* stage, where along with the case for free trade that for laissez faire is also restored.

The basic reason concerns what Anne Krueger has termed "rent seeking." This can be best seen in the economic costs of the most common form of protection in the Third World: import quotas. Thus, suppose the import quota is imposed to protect domestic producers of cloth. Say this quota is for importing 100,000 units of cloth. As the imports of cloth are thereby restricted below the level they would have been under free trade, the domestic price of cloth will rise above its import price. Suppose the domestic price rises from the free trade import price of $10 to $15 per unit of cloth. But who gets the quota? As was common in import quota regimes, the government authorizes its officials to issue licenses for importing quantities of cloth summing up to the total amount of 100,000 units. Anyone who gets a license can import a unit of cloth for $10 (the import price) and sell it for $15 (the domestic price), making a handsome profit of $5 per unit of cloth for merely getting an import license. This is the "rent" per unit of cloth from the quota, the total rents associated with the import quota of 100,000 units of cloth being $500,000. These are the quota rents to be shared among all those lucky enough to receive an import license. As these become government licenses to print money, there will be many "rent seekers" wishing to acquire them. They will use their own resources—time spent queuing for licenses, money spent on covert or overt bribery—to get these licenses. Competing against each other, these rent seekers would be willing to spend as much as the "rents" on offer. For it would be worth spending $1 of one's own resources, at the margin, to gain $1 of rents. Thus, the total amount of their own resources rent seekers will be willing to spend to get the licenses for importing 100,000 units of cloth will be the total rents available of $500,000. But, as far as the overall economy is concerned, this rent-seeking expenditure is totally unproductive. It is equivalent to dumping these resources into the sea. This social cost of rent seeking will outweigh any conceivable gain from the protection offered to producers (see appendix).

Such rent seeking is widely documented and took many forms. Thus for example in Ghana, Douglas Rimmer reports that "the granting of import licenses became a notorious arena for the appropriation of administratively generated rents. Kept women could be kept by the issuance of licenses, so that aspirants to this status paraded themselves for libidinal pleasures in return for favors."[5]

This rent seeking argument seemed to put a final nail in the coffin for arguments for protection to deal with domestic distortions in the working of the price mechanism. It left domestic subsidies as the favored way of dealing with such distortions. Thus, in the previous example, a production subsidy of $5 per unit of cloth would have the same effect on the profitability of domestic production as the import quota (or tariff). For a tariff which raises the domestic price of an imported good is equivalent to a production subsidy to domestic producers financed by a tax on consumers of that good. This was the third stage in the argument of TPW which de-linked the case for free trade from that for laissez faire.

But suppose there is no domestic distortion. Producers nevertheless know that the government is in the subsidy game. They are likely to lobby for a subsidy claiming a domestic distortion when in fact none exists, a fact which is virtually impossible for governments to verify. If successful in their *subsidy seeking*, the producers will be able to get producer "rents" and, as in the case of the license holders of import quotas, will be willing to spend a sum equivalent to the "rents" on offer from their own resources in this directly unproductive activity. This is again a total social loss. Thus, even if there are domestic distortions which could in principle have justified a production subsidy, once the government is seen to be in the subsidy game, a whole host of subsidy seekers will arise to garner rents through the political process, even when there are no domestic distortions in the workings of their industries. So, even if there are presumed to be domestic distortions it may be best to do nothing, that is maintain both laissez faire and free trade.

U.S. Economic Policy

The United States, though giving rhetorical support to both free trade and laissez faire as the desirable policies for economic policy around the world, nevertheless has not adopted them consistently in its own domestic policies. The departure is more marked in the expansion of government beyond the laissez faire principle. For, as regards free trade, the United States basic instincts have been protectionist (chapter 1), and it is its movement to relatively free trade in the post–second World War period that is exceptional. We need to briefly examine why it turned against laissez faire but in favor of free trade.

Dirigisme

Measuring the size of government by the share of general government expenditure in GDP, table 3.1 shows that in the late nineteenth century the United States had a smaller government than the United Kingdom. In the United Kingdom there was a sharp rise in the early years of the twentieth century, continuing into the interwar years, and then another spurt in the post–second World War period. But, in the United States, the share of government expenditure in GDP and thence the size of government remained small till the 1920s. The Great Depression and Roosevelt's New Deal were "the defining moment"[6] for the expansion of government and the abandonment of laissez faire. There had been some extension of government intervention in the late nineteenth century with the passage of antitrust legislation following populist attacks against the "robber barons." But it was Roosevelt's New Deal which led to "an ideological shift—from widespread skepticism about the ability of the central government to improve the functioning of the economy to widespread faith in the competence of government."[7]

Rockoff argues that the Depression in itself could not have been responsible for this shift, as there were earlier crises in the 1830s and 1890s, with severely depressed incomes and high unemployment which did not lead to a dirigiste response. He argues that a change in the dominant ideology among intellectuals and opinion-makers was responsible. As George Stigler[8] was the first to point out, this change in opinion was not based upon any hard empirical evidence. The European move to dirigisme, their construction of the welfare state, and the supposed success of Stalinist planning in transforming an underdeveloped Russia, were the dominant factors in the change of opinion. This process was aided by the development of Keynesian economics and welfare economics, which, as Myint noted, with its: "emphasis on market failures, externalities, and the divergences between social and private costs,

TABLE 3.1
Growth of General Government Expenditure, 1870–1996 (Percent of GDP)

Country	About 1870	1913	1920	1937	1960	1980	1990	1996
France	12.6	17.0	27.6	29.0	34.6	46.1	49.8	55.0
Germany	10.0	14.8	25.0	34.1	32.4	47.9	45.1	49.1
Italy	13.7	17.1	30.1	31.1	30.1	42.1	53.4	52.7
Japan	8.8	8.3	14.8	25.4	17.5	32.0	31.3	35.9
Sweden	5.7	10.4	10.9	16.5	31.0	60.1	59.1	64.2
Switzerland	16.5	14.0	17.0	24.1	17.2	32.8	33.5	39.4
United Kingdom	9.4	12.7	26.2	30.0	32.2	43.0	39.9	43.0
United States	7.3	7.5	12.1	19.7	27.0	31.4	32.8	32.4

Source: Tanzi and Schuknecht (2000), table I.1, pp. 6–7.

has for many decades been a powerful intellectual force behind intervention-ist policies."[9],[10]

Not till the stagflation of the 1970s did opinion shift toward the more skeptical view of government of the nineteenth century. This had been pre-saged by the growing recognition that, because of problems related to infor-mation and incentives, planning and Keynesianism were not the touted panaceas, while the "new" political economy showed how most welfare pro-grams would be captured by the "middle classes." But despite Ronald Reagan's attempt in the United States and Margaret Thatcher's in the United King-dom to "roll back the state," there has been little reduction in the size of gov-ernment in these economies. Milton and Rose Friedman[11] maintain that this is due to the influence of an "iron triangle "of beneficiaries, bureaucrats, and legislators created by the previous periods of government expansion.

Most of the growth of government since the second World War has been due to the expansion of social expenditures. These have taken the form of cash transfers to redistribute income, whereby "limited social safety nets [have been turned] into universal social benefits."[12] But the actual amount of redistribution achieved has been minimal and most of this social expenditure represents fiscal churning.[13] The attendant inefficiencies are compounded by the universal public provision of merit goods (like health and education), rather than these being merely financed for the needy. It is doubtful if, in light of the aging of the population in most developed countries, current publicly funded health and pension benefits are sustainable. They are creating an in-tergenerational war, with the young being taxed to subsidize the old.[14] It re-mains to be seen whether this will lead to another fiscal crisis of the state fol-lowed by liberalization as in the eighteenth and nineteenth centuries.

Even though there are current (2003–04) worries about the burgeoning U.S. fiscal deficit of $475 billion in 2004, as the Chairman of the U.S. Council of Economic Advisers Gregory Mankiw[15] has pointed out, the deficit represents only about 4.2 percent of the $11 trillion U.S. economy and is manageable, being smaller than deficits in six of the last twenty years in the aftermath of recessions. Much more serious is the implicit deficit involved in funding the social security and Medicare entitlements of the retiring baby boomers. It has been estimated[16] that the shortfall between the present value of all the revenue the government can expect to collect in the future and the present value of all its future expenditure commitments, including debt service, is a staggering $44,000bn. This is nearly four times current GDP and swamps the current federal debt of $6,500bn. Like Rome, the current U.S. imperium seems to be on the road to fiscal ruin.

But, to date, the hope of some classical liberals, and fears of social democrats, that an increasingly integrated world economy would erode the tax base for funding government expenditure—as mobile capital and skilled labor moved from high to low tax areas—has not been realized. As table 3.1 shows, there has hardly been any marked fall in the size of government. What globalization has at best succeeded in doing is limiting the further growth of the state.

Free Trade

By contrast, since the second World War the United States has moved from being a protectionist to a largely free trading country. As we have seen, the natural instinct of the United States is protectionist. It was not even eroded when, as it industrialized and accumulated capital and skills in the late nineteenth century, its comparative advantage shifted from land-intensive to capital- and skill-intensive goods. The U.S. Constitution, which grants Congress the power to impose duties and to regulate international commerce, has allowed the interplay of domestic interest groups to be the main determinant of U.S. trade policy. As any trade treaty signed by the executive needs to be ratified by a two-thirds majority in the Senate, the route taken by Louis Napoleon to overcome protectionist pressures in nineteenth-century France was also not open.

There is an important reason why the interests seeking protection (which represent the scarce factors of production) have been more politically successful than the free trading interests (representing the abundant factors). This is the problem of collective action in a democracy addressed by Mancur Olson.[17] He showed that pressure groups representing small numbers are likely to be more successful than larger groups. For, a persistent problem in organizing a pressure group is that of free riders: who will gain from the successful outcome of pressure group activity even if they contribute nothing toward it. The smaller the group, the easier it is to control free riding. Also, the

smaller the group, the larger the share of each member in the collective benefits obtained. By contrast, a pressure group encompassing a larger group will
face the problem of free riding, and the benefits of each member from success
in the group's redistributive activity will be lower. As pressure group activity,
like most politics, is a redistributive activity, the costs of any success by a pressure group's success in raising its members' incomes must come from an implicit tax on other groups in society. The larger the group sharing the costs of
this redistribution, the smaller the cost to any single member. This means
that the benefits to members from organizing large groups as well as the costs
of giving in to the demands of smaller pressure groups are small. Hence, small
groups will be more successful in the redistributive pressure group game than
larger groups. So, the larger consumer groups and exporters (representing the
abundant factor in the economy) will be less successful in organizing themselves than the smaller protectionist groups. U.S. trade policy bears this out.
Moreover, through vote trading by different protectionist lobbies, there is
likely to be a ratcheting up of the average tariff.

The big change in U.S. trade policy came after the recognition that the
disastrous Smoot-Hawley tariff in the interwar years had worsened the Great
Depression. As part of the New Deal, Roosevelt got Congress to enact the
Reciprocal Trade Agreements Act (RTAA) in 1934. This allowed the president to "reduce tariffs in agreements negotiated with other countries, without
the specific approval of Congress. Congress also endorsed the unconditional
most-favored nation (MFN) clause, under which the lower U.S. tariffs negotiated with one country would be automatically extended to other countries."[18] But, this "fast track authority," as it came to be called, had to be re-
newed every three years, for, otherwise, Congress would have lost all control
of trade policy. If the authority was unlimited, a two-thirds majority would
have been required to repeal it, and any president would have vetoed any legislation to strip him of this newly acquired power.

The RTAA had important consequences. It meant that the legislative
logrolling which had raised U.S. tariff levels was short circuited, and as the
president represented a broader constituency than members of Congress, he
could follow the national interest in freeing trade. It also meant that exporters could now organize and lobby for lower foreign tariffs (which benefited them) in exchange for lower domestic tariffs. Finally, the RTAA by-
passed the need for each trade treaty to be ratified by a two-thirds majority in
the Senate, which made it easier to negotiate and enforce trade treaties.

The New Protectionism

But, underlying the RTAA was the principle of reciprocity, which was incor-
porated into the General Agreement of Tariffs and Trade (GATT) after the

second World War. Under the auspices of GATT, eight so-called "trade rounds" to reduce tariffs have been completed, the latest being the Uruguay Round agreement in 1994. Following the conversion of the GATT into the World Trade Organization (WTO), there formed an ongoing round (the Doha round). These multilateral rounds have been remarkably successful in lowering tariffs in OECD countries, particularly in the United States. So, by the end of the millennium, the average U.S. tariff on all imports was 2 percent, on dutiable imports, 5 percent, and over 60 percent of imports were duty-free. These were the lowest trade barriers in U.S. history. But protectionism never dies. Newfangled means in the form of nontariff barriers were adopted. The most notorious were *voluntary export restraints* (VERs), as well as the increasing use of "anti-dumping" laws to prevent so-called unfair trade caused by the subsidies given by foreign governments to their exporters.

Both these are economically stupid policies. In the case of VERs, foreign exporters agree to quota restrictions on how much they will export to the United States. This means that the quota rents (unlike domestic import quotas) accrue to the foreign exporters.[19] VERs tax U.S. consumers and transfer the tax revenue to foreign companies. Moreover, as many VERs are on intermediate products which are major inputs into other industries—like steel in cars—there are further losses of economic efficiency. Thus, the quotas on steel imports introduced in March 2001, while protecting 3,700 jobs in the steel industry, are estimated to have caused the loss of 19,000 to 30,000 jobs in the industries using steel. The cost to steel consumers over five years varied between $6.8 to 14.5 billion, which is about $732,000 per steel job protected.[20]

But the most notorious and longstanding of these VERs is the Multi Fiber Agreement (MFA) to protect the textile and apparel industries in developed countries. It is to be phased out by 2006 under the agreement which concluded the Uruguay round. But it has inflicted grave damage on developing countries, particularly the poorest. For the textile industry is one where most labor-abundant developing countries can acquire the necessary know-how and capital to export successfully.[21] The costs to the developed countries are also high. Thus, estimates of the costs of the MFA to the United States, and hence of the gains from its abolition in terms of the net deadweight losses, are over $9–10 billion a year, of which one study finds over 70 percent is due to the transfer of quota rents to foreigners. The direct cost to consumers of this protection in the United States amounted to over $24 billion in 1990, which is equivalent to a tax of over $260 per U.S. household.[22]

Equally pernicious is the increasing use of the *anti-dumping* escape clause in the GATT codes. This "escape clause" allows countries to impose countervailing duties on imports of goods which have been subsidized by its trading partners. This, again, is a stupid argument. If a foreigner chooses to subsidize the goods which we import, our consumers will get these goods more

69

cheaply than they would otherwise. It would constitute dumping only if the purpose of the subsidies was to temporarily lower prices to drive other producers out of world markets to establish a monopoly, which could then charge the monopoly price. But there has never, to my knowledge, been such a case. In fact, as Irwin notes, in a study of every one of 282 industries involved in every anti-dumping case in the 1980s, it was found that only in 14 percent of the cases could there be even a presumption that because of the concentration of domestic and foreign businesses in the industry such predatory pricing was likely. As he notes of the cases in which anti-dumping cases were upheld: "Were the Bangladesh shop towel producers trying to eliminate their foreign rivals and achieve a monopoly position? Were the flower growers from Colombia doing the same?" The fact that prices differ in different locations does not mean that the motive for the price discrimination is predatory. For there is nothing inherently harmful or anti-competitive about price discrimination. "Price discrimination is an accepted feature of domestic competition. It would be surprising if domestic prices were *exactly* the same as an exporter's home price."[23] The total cost of nontariff barriers, including the costs expended on "rent seeking" by special interests to get protection, is huge. For the United States, Daniel Treffler estimated that in 1983, nontariff barriers on manufactured imports reduced imports by nearly $50 billion, which was 24 percent of U.S. manufacturing imports.

The most pernicious of the barriers to trade exist in *agriculture*, which until the Uruguay round had never been brought within the multilateral bargaining framework. Developed countries have protected farmers through a complex system using tariffs, import quotas, domestic price supports, and export subsidies. Apart from the costs to developed countries, it also does great harm to the poor developing countries with a comparative advantage in producing many agricultural products. Thus, subsidies to U.S. cotton producers allow them to undersell the cotton produced by poor African farmers with inimical effects on their levels of living. The Uruguay Round agreement limited the use of export subsidies and internal price supports by capping them, and then reducing them from a base date. Also it required countries to convert their various nontariff barriers on agricultural products into a single import tariff. Many countries, including developing ones like India, used this as an occasion to ratchet up their implicit tariffs. Thus, the "new" tariffs on agricultural products remain very high. But it is still an achievement to have converted all the various distorting nontariff barriers into one transparent tariff. One of the major tasks of the Doha round, launched in November 2001, is to reduce these agricultural tariffs and export subsidies. But the recent increase in farm subsidies by the United States, the tepid reform of the Common Agricultural Policy by the European Union, as well as the continuing reluctance of Japan to give up on its highly restrictive agricultural trade policy do not augur well for the outcome.

The Rise of Preferential Trading Arrangements

Even more serious is the retreat of the United States from the multilateral system of free trade it sought to establish after the second World War. From the 1980s, largely as a result of frustration at the slow progress in the multilateral processes, it began to move toward bilateral and regional trading arrangements, of which the North America Free Trade Agreement (NAFTA) was the most notable. The Europeans through the European Union (EU) had in effect already created the largest preferential trade bloc in the world.

Preferential trading arrangements (PTAs)[24] or trade blocs can be classified into four categories. In a free trade agreement (FTA), tariffs are reduced against members but maintained against the rest of the world. In a customs union (CU), tariffs of members are eliminated and a common external tariff is applied to nonmembers. A common market (CM) is a customs union which also permits free movements of capital and labor among members. Finally, an economic union is a customs union which also has common economic laws covering things like standards across member countries.

A trade bloc, while creating a larger common economic space for its members by eliminating tariffs between them and thus *creating* trade between them, also involves imposing a common tariff (as in a customs union) or maintaining the individual country's existing tariffs against nonmembers (as in a preferential trading arrangement, PTA). This could lead to trade *diversion* when a member country which was importing a good from the cheapest world source finds that, with the common tariff (in a customs union), this is now more expensive than buying less efficiently produced substitutes from a partner country with which there is free trade. Thus the net effect of the formation of a customs union, or PTA trade bloc, will depend upon whether it is net trade creating or trade diverting.

The negotiating mechanisms underlying the promotion of multilateral free trade under GATT and its successor the WTO are mercantilist. Mercantilists view trade as a war, and the various GATT rounds with their "concessions" to economic virtue are like multilateral disarmament. If in this contest some countries decide to disarm themselves and that on balance does not hurt others (that is, if the arrangements are net trade creating), then the resulting trading bloc is to be blessed. This in essence is the rationale of GATT's article 24 allowing exceptions to its MFN rule and the principle of nondiscrimination—the cornerstone of the multilateral trading system constructed under its auspices since the Second World War.

Most economists agree that the net effects of the two major trading blocs—the EU and NAFTA—are likely to be net trade creating,[25] but others like Mercosur—the customs union among Brazil, Argentina, Uruguay, and Paraguay—have been shown to involve significant losses from trade diversion.

There are a number of worries. First, instead of being building blocs to free trade, PTAs can become stumbling blocs,[26] with the rise of new interest groups created by the trade diversion which accompanies any preferential trading arrangement. They will oppose any further movement to a multilateral trading system. Second, to protect the preferences granted to partners, PTAs set out complex rules of origin to prevent nonmembers shipping goods to partners with high external trade barriers through those with lower ones.[27] For instance, if, say, Canada had a lower tariff than the United States on some good exported from Japan, the Japanese could first export the good to Canada (at the low Canadian tariff) and then ship it at a zero tariff under NAFTA from Canada to the United States (avoiding the higher U.S. tariff). The "rules of origin" try to prevent this. Third, and most seriously, as those excluded from a preferential arrangement form their own preferential arrangements with other groups, these preferential arrangements can multiply, leading to what has been termed a "spaghetti bowl"[28] and the destruction of the multilateral trading system. That this is not an idle fear is borne out by the explosion in these arrangements since the late 1980s. By 2002 "there were over four hundred formed and contemplated, and the number was growing by the week."[29] This is creating a maze whereby two countries form a preferential arrangement "with each having bilateral treaties with other and different countries, the latter in turn bonding with yet others, each in turn having different rules of origin for different sectors" (Bhagwati 2002a, p. 112).

The European Union

How has this come to pass? The trouble began with the formation of the European Common Market. Despite the classical liberal hope that, by creating a larger internal European market and successively lowering external tariffs and quotas, the EU would be a building bloc to global free trade, it has turned out to be an inward-looking protectionist bloc—particularly for agricultural trade. This is because, despite appearances and its stated aim of being an economic project, the EU is and always has been a political one—to create a United States of Europe. The main movers in this project have been the French and the Germans—the former claiming with some justification to be riding the German horse. The aim is to recreate a new Holy Roman Empire. The French and the Germans have tried to do this in the past through force of arms, but with Napoleon's defeat at Waterloo in 1815, and the German defeats in the two twentieth-century World Wars, war is not seen as a feasible route to create this territorial empire. Rather, it is a neo-mercantilist project which is reminiscent of the post-Renaissance European princes who, as Heckscher argued, were motivated by the desire to create nation states out of the varied feuding groups which comprised their patrimony.

This project is, moreover, a top-down project which has tried to suppress normal politics in the member countries to get its various stages ratified. It is a project borne out of the respective weaknesses of the participants and not their strengths. The French, despite their bravado and pride, are a defeated nation. They see the Anglo-Saxons, not least in their language and culture, triumphing worldwide. The French elite—most of whom seem to be associated in one way or another with the Ecole National du Administration (ENA) (and can be properly called ENArques)—has therefore seen the EU as its only hope of global influence in a Europe in which they would jointly exercise hegemony with the Germans.

Germany, because of its World War trauma, has gone along with this illusion, and used the clever ploy of promoting an economic union leading to political union to tie down German nationalism as the best way to tame the passions which have led to two savage European wars. Italy has gone along because it wishes to unload the unending burden of subsidizing its South—the Mezzogiorno—to a larger body of European taxpayers, while the rest of the Mediterranean countries and Ireland have looked upon the subsidies, through the Common Agricultural Policy (CAP) and other regional schemes they have obtained from Europe, as a drunk given free access to a liquor store.

And Britain? In search of a post-Imperial role and identity, a part of its elite—particularly in the Foreign Office—has come to the defeatist conclusion that the only role left for Britain is as a part of "Europe"—the quotation marks emphasizing the artificiality of this project[30]—where its worldly experience would allow it to join France and Germany in running Europe. To another part of the establishment and the general public, the European project was sold as merely a common market which would provide the usual gains from trade in a larger unified economic space. The explicitly political aim of the European partners was said to be just window-dressing. As this lie has been gradually exposed, Europe has become the great dividing line in British politics with the Euro, and now the proposed European Constitution, at its center.

Linking most of these elites also is a barely disguised distaste for the United States and a desire to build a Europe which will be a bulwark against the crass and uncaring attitudes seen to be dominant across the Atlantic. Moreover, for the ENArques—whose connections are Europe-wide—despite the lip service paid to "subsidiarity," it will also be a Europe run by technocrats and not Demos, nor a free market. This is why we see the divide between big and small business in their support for "Europe": with big business—which is more easily able to co-opt regulators to its benefit—being in favor of the regulatory state[31] favored by the technocrats, and small business—more interested in the more level playing field a true free market economy provides—being against.

The turning point in the battle between two ideas, which had jousted in the early years of the EU, came with the Maastricht treaty.[32] The liberal of these ideas held that the economic power of the state must be kept in check. The other was that, if nation-states cannot protect their sovereignty individually, they need to create a supranational authority within which the economic power of the state can be re-established. The Maastricht treaty and now the proposed European constitution are dirigiste charters. Instead of increasing individual economic freedom, they seek to centralize the exercise of political power and to harmonize taxes, labor laws, welfare provision, etc. Moreover, as the antics of the French and Germans in the runup to the Iraq war showed, for these prime movers of the European project, anti-Americanism is a central feature of their desired "Europe." They want to create a United States of Europe in opposition to the United States of America. Though, till recently, the Americans have looked upon the process of European integration as a benign process, the disagreements over the Iraq war seem to at least have opened their eyes. A Franco-German led USE would not be in the interests of the U.S. imperium, and it is hoped that the United States will now change its tune and seek to undermine the project. With the recent enlargement of the EU to take in countries previously behind the Iron Curtain, the potential conflicts of interest between what Donald Rumsfeld called the "new" and "old" Europe have begun to surface, Whilst the rejection of the constitution in the French and Dutch referenda might portend the end of this political project.

But while it was possible to contrast a dirigiste Europe with a liberal United States, in particular regarding trade policy till the 1980s, that is no longer possible. One of the most surprising developments in the last two decades has been that while developing countries which had turned their backs on the postwar liberal international economic order are now rushing to be integrated into the world economy, it is Europe and the United States—the leaders of the postwar free trade movement—who are turning inward. For the EU it has done so essentially to fulfill its political ambitions. But why has the United States?

The United States

Most observers agree that the early 1980s marked the turning point when the United States moved away from the multilateralism it had hitherto pursued through GATT toward what has been called "aggressive unilateralism" and preferential trading arrangements. The U.S. Trade Representative William Brock found that, following the successfully completed Tokyo round, there was opposition from the EU and some major developing countries—India and Brazil—to launch another GATT round. Frustrated by this difficulty, he announced a "two-track" approach where, if multilateral progress toward freeing trade was blocked, the United States would join other like-minded countries in liberalizing trade through preferential arrangements. The unintended consequences of this have been the explosion of PTAs in the 1990s.

But, since the 1970s the United States has also been pursuing aggressive unilateralism to counter what it considers to be unfair trade. With the passage of the notorious Section 301 of the U.S. Trade and Tariff Act of 1974 the United States has sought to bludgeon other governments into actions desired by the U.S. government. This Act, besides allowing the United States to retaliate against violation of its rights under GATT and bilateral treaties, also gives the president the right to act against "unreasonable" trade practices outside these areas. The Act has been amended in 1979, 1984, and 1988, the last adding Super 301 and Special 301, giving the U.S. executive virtually unlimited power to designate anything it dislikes as being "unreasonable." The set of practices that Congress has deemed unreasonable includes barriers to trade in services, persistent denial of worker's rights, export targeting, foreign conditions on U.S. investments, and anti-competitive practices that adversely affect the United States. This Act had led to the privatization of trade policy, as "any industry exporting to foreign markets or competing against imports in the United States [could] get government to act on its behalf."[33] This Act, however, has played itself out. First, the establishment of the WTO's dispute settlement mechanism (see below) means that the United States no longer needs to unilaterally threaten countries not living up to their treaty obligations. Second, because 301 was rightly seen as bullying, the WTO recently ruled that the United States could not use the Act to extract new concessions unilaterally. This has in effect killed Section 301.

But the view that the United States is the only fair trader and that everyone else indulges in unfair trade still thrives. It arose in the 1970s when, as a result of Japan's spectacular economic growth and large bilateral trade deficit with the United States, it was argued that Japan was doing better than the United States because of its unfair trade practices. But this view was based on another economically stupid argument. It is a matter of arithmetic that the two parts of the balance of payments, the current account (consisting of imports and exports of goods and services) and the capital account (consisting of capital inflows and outflows) must cancel out, to give an overall balance in the balance of payments. The bilateral trade deficit with Japan is then the other side of the coin of the positive surplus in the capital account with Japan, as Japanese investors bought more U.S. assets than U.S. investors did Japanese, this inflow being "financed" by a surplus of Japanese exports over its imports. Another way of looking at a country's balance on the current account is given by the difference between domestic savings and investments. If domestic investment is higher than domestic savings, a country must necessarily run a current account deficit, which is financed by a capital account surplus, as foreign savings come into the country and supplement domestic savings to equal the level of investment. Thus, to ask the Japanese (and now the Chinese) to reduce their current account surplus with the United States is equivalent to asking them not to send their savings to the United States, which in turn implies that domestic investment in the United States would be lower. The current account deficit with Japan (and China), rather than being a bane, is a blessing for the United States, as it allows the country to live beyond its means and to have higher investment (which fuels its future growth) than could be financed from its domestic savings.

This ridiculous argument for "fair trade" was then buttressed by many others concerning the unfair social policies relating to the labor and environmental standards of trading partners. These, it is claimed, lead to social dumping. The claims about the unfair *labor standards* of trading partners is an old protectionist argument. By the second half of the nineteenth century India had turned the tables on the Lancashire textile industry.[34] In the 1850s it had established a modern textile industry based on Indian entrepreneurship and capital and foreign technology. It began exporting cotton manufactures to Britain. The Lancashire cotton interests lobbied the British-Indian government to "apply British factory legislation *en bloc* to India so as to neutralize the 'unfair' advantages which the Indian mill industry was enjoying because of large scale employment of child labor and long hours of work."[35] In this agitation they were joined by various well-meaning philanthropists. The result was the introduction in 1881 of the first of the Factories Acts which was to transfer much of the British labor legislation to India. This Act has been aptly described as the result of agitation in the United Kingdom by "ignorant English philanthropists and grasping English manufacturers."[36] As is usual in such alliances, the selfish English protectionist interest was better served by this legislation than the altruism of the philanthropists. The protectionist objective was to raise the effective price of labor, the most abundant factor of production in India, on which the competitiveness of the country's manufactured exports depended. The "rights" granted to Indian labor in 1881 hobbled the Indian textile industry in competing for export, and later domestic markets, with the rising industry of Japan. Lower Indian wages reflected lower efficiency. Whereas the Japanese textile industry was built on using female labor working two shifts a day, the Bombay textile industry was hamstrung by labor laws which forbade such practices.[37] These labor laws have continued to our day and are in part responsible for India's relatively poor industrial performance.

The demand for introducing labor standards in the WTO gives me a great sense of dejàvu, particularly as in the 1970s when, under pressure from labor unions, the U.S. Congress had included in the Trade Act of 1974 a provision requiring the president to raise the subject of "fair labor standards" in the GATT framework. The U.S. administration of President Jimmy Carter duly obliged in October 1979 just before the end of the Tokyo round negotiations. About the same time, the European Commission also suggested that "minimum labor standards" be included in the Lome convention which provided tariff preferences and technical and financial aid to a group of African,

Caribbean, and Pacific countries. While in 1980, as the Multi Fiber Agreement (MFA) which has regulated trade in textiles and clothing came up for renewal, organizations representing entrepreneurs and labor in textiles and clothing industries in America and Western Europe advanced proposals for a "social clause" to be inserted in the MFA.

I wrote a pamphlet[38] countering this variant of the pauper labor argument. The new twist in the "protectionists" case was that rather than claiming like the old pauper labor argument that imports from countries with low wages were inimical to the welfare of the importing countries, it was now being claimed that tariffs (or import controls) were required against imports produced by foreign workers who had been denied their so-called human rights in countries without "minimum labor standards." Protection of imports from poor, low-wage countries was to be instituted to promote the interests of these poor, exploited benighted foreign workers. Fortunately nothing came of this hypocritical drive to legislate a particular morality in the subsequent decade. But with another democratic president in power, and with the fear of "low wage" imports from the developing world being fanned by the stagnation of the wages of the low skilled in the United States and the very high unemployment rates in continental Europe,[39] the same cry for protection on the high-minded grounds of promoting the "human rights" of Third (and now also Second) World workers was once again raised in the 1990s. *Plus ca change!*

But there are two other additional arguments in the protectionist's armory. The first is the argument called "the race to the bottom." It is being argued that buying goods produced by Third World workers with low labor and environmental standards will lead to an erosion of these standards in the First World. For with capital being mobile, home industries unable to compete with low standard imports will locate abroad and/or use the political process to obtain a lowering of the standards in the West. To prevent this "social dumping," protectionist procedures, analogous to the anti-dumping codes which currently allow protection against supposed economic dumping, should be instituted.

The second argument is based on what have been labeled "psychological spillovers."[40] The utility of consumers in the First World is claimed to be affected by the way goods are produced or by their environmental effects in the Third World. This leads to demands for "ethical trade," as in the recent call by the former U.K. secretary of state for international development, Clare Short, as well as various measures being advocated to label goods as having been produced by ethical means (e.g., without cruelty to animals, or by saving the rainforests or not using child labor). An example is the Rugmark label which certifies the rug is not produced by child labor.

On the first of these new arguments I can be brief because of two comprehensive papers surveying the analytical models and the empirical evidence concerning the race to the bottom. One[41] surveys the empirical evidence concerning environmental regulation and industry location within the United States and internationally. It finds little empirical evidence of such a race. The other[42] surveys the various analytical models which have dealt with the theoretical case of a "race to the bottom" in environmental standards. It finds that the case "is mixed at best." There can be no race to the bottom if there are no domestic distortions and no constraints on tax-subsidy instruments. So the relevant question is one of political economy: Why would governments choose to lower standards rather than use more appropriate tax-subsidy measures? But surely, the prior question about the global harmonization of *social* standards is whether there are any such universal standards to be legislated in the first place. We are back in the world of ethics—a subject I take up in chapter 6.

But what of the argument that labor standards are needed to improve the standard of living of workers, both in developed and developing countries? We consider each in turn.

Developed Countries. In developed countries, improved labor standards (e.g., safety and health regulations and various trade union "rights") resulting from social legislation can be looked upon as shifting their comparative advantage away from sectors where such legislation particularly impinges—relative to their competitors. Any resulting reduction in national income is the "price" paid, as it were, for the improved social conditions of the groups affected.

If, in addition, a tariff to impede the entry of goods from countries without similar legislation is imposed, it will inflict further costs in terms of higher prices on users of these goods in the home country, and those resulting from the ensuing prevention of the flow of resources out of these "inefficient" industries into those which are more efficient. And, if the "protection" of these high "social standards" industries is not through domestic tariffs, but by raising the costs of production in foreign countries through the international adoption of minimum labor standards, it would still lead to higher prices paid by domestic users of the product.

Developing Countries. Those motivated by notions of cosmopolitan welfare, however, might still argue that these losses to advanced-country consumers flowing from the international adoption of minimum labor standards would be counterbalanced by the resulting gains in the standard of living of poor countries' workers. At its most naive this argument is based on a non sequitur. For although it may be true that there is a high *correlation* between observable high living standards and the existence of various aspects of the welfare state in many OECD countries, this does not mean either that the latter *cause* the former or that the latter *component* of possibly higher living standards can be acquired without costs.

This view is implicit in an ILO analysis of the likely impact of the ILO's standards concerning trade union "rights" and economic development.[43] The demand for labor depends, in large part, on the availability of the co-operant factors of production, and the wage rate. For any given level of the former, the demand for labor will be greater, the lower the wage rate. In many developing countries the level of the available co-operant factors of production is insufficient to generate sufficient demand for the labor which would be supplied by their burgeoning labor forces at what might be considered a "fair" wage. Any attempt by various combinations of labor or trade unions to raise the wages of their members must reduce the overall demand for labor—thus implying that the rise is at the expense of other workers who would henceforth be unemployed or underemployed. While the "standard of living" of the "labor aristocracy" which had found jobs in the high-wage unionized sector would no doubt be greater, it would be achieved at the expense of its numerically preponderant but unfortunate fellow workers who had not succeeded in gaining entry into this select group. Any argument that the imposition of fair labor standards (including any notion of a global minimum wage) is in the interests of raising the standards of living of the bulk of the labor force in developing countries is thus deeply flawed.

So, too, is the argument that banning child labor will benefit the poor in developing countries.[44] It is poverty which makes many families in developing countries dependent on their laboring children for part of their household income. Thus, it has been found[45] that the incidence of child labor is strongly related to per capita GDP. Once it reaches $5,000, child labor disappears. Moreover, most currently developed countries depended on child labor when they were underdeveloped. The United States only banned child labor in 1938, when its per capita income level was well above the $5,000 threshold. In fact the United States, Canada, and many other developed countries have not signed the ILO's charter laying down minimum ages of work, and Canada still does not prohibit children under thirteen from working at night.[46] The only way to reduce the incidence of child labor is to reduce poverty, which globalizing capitalism (as we shall see in chapter 5) does spectacularly. Rising per capita incomes also lead to the provision of adequate educational opportunities.[47] As only about 5 percent of working children are employed in the export sector, with over 80 percent in agriculture, liberalizing trade in agriculture would lead to a rise in rural incomes and fall in child labor. Thus, in Vietnam, when the government permitted exports of rice leading to a rise in its domestic price and thence a rise in farm incomes, farmers reduced their use of child labor.[48] Moreover, banning child labor in export industries does not necessarily lead to its end. It merely leads to the children ending up in a far worse situation. Thus, an Oxfam study found that, when U.S. retailers sought child-free labels on imported goods, the effect in Bangladesh was that "between 1993 and 1994 around 30,000 of the 50,000 children [mainly girls] working in textile firms . . . were thrown out of factories because suppliers feared losing their [export] business if they kept the children on. But the majority of these children have, because of penury, been forced to turn to prostitution or other industries like welding where conditions pose far greater risks to them."[49]

In fact, the whole notion of "ethical trading" is incoherent and very dangerous. The classical liberal case for free trade depends upon nondiscrimination, including by whom and how goods are produced. In a debate on Australian television with one of the arch purveyors of this notion, Ralph Nader, as he was banging on about how morality must enter into trade, I asked him whether when he went to buy his meat he inquired if the butcher beat his wife. Of course I should have said, to make the point even more pointedly: would it be morally acceptable if racists organized a boycott of shops run by blacks, or if Robert Mugabe—who takes the fundamentalist Christian view about the immorality of homosexuality—should be allowed to ban imports of goods into Zimbabwe made with gay labor! Apart from the fact that most of the morality being espoused to boycott imports from developing countries is *not* universal as claimed but are rather the culture-specific prejudices of the West (see Chapter 6), even within its own ethics these boycotts go against another important Western ideal—nondiscrimination.

Western demands to incorporate these so-called social standards in the WTO are thus rightly seen by developing countries as being just high-minded (and often hypocritical) arguments for protection. As in nineteenth-century India, these Western altruists are only aiding the "grasping" special producer interests, and not the poor and wretched of the Earth in whose name they claim to speak and agitate. This attempt to legislate the West's "habits of the heart" worldwide through the WTO, and the United State's current push for a whole slew of PTAs (with offers recently being made to various states in the Middle East) raises the question of whether the WTO does and should have a future, and whether it still makes sense for an imperial power like the United States to use reciprocity as a means of attaining global free trade.

Another Globalization Backlash?

In answering these questions it is worth emphasizing that despite the economic illogic of the GATT and WTO process—based on looking at trade as a zero sum game—it has been successful in removing the worst forms of protection. The United States led this multilateral process and its domestic politics did not become an impediment. It is since the 1980s that the United States seems to have turned against this process. Why?

The answer lies in developments in the U.S. labor market. From the late-1970s till about 1992 there was a fall in U.S. real wages. Thereafter they have stagnated. The lowest paid male workers have seen their wages fall by about 10 percent between 1977 and 1995. These wage trends in turn have led to an increase in inequality (in family income) since1973, as compared to the positive trends in all these variables in the earlier period—the so-called Golden Age—from the end of the Second World War till the oil price rise in 1973 As the U.S. economy became increasingly integrated into the world economy during the later period, there is a perception that globalization—particularly through trade and overseas investments by multinationals—accounts for these trends.

But the second period has also seen a profound change in the international division of labor. This is the result of the *third industrial revolution* associated with advances in communications through the spread of computers and the development of the Internet. There is a continuing and unsettled debate about the causes of the stagnation in wages of low-skilled workers in the United States (or historically high unemployment rates—which is the other side of the same coin as in Europe). There are some who argue that these trends are due to the integration of low-wage countries like India and China into the global economy.[50] Following from the Samuelson-Stolper theory (outlined in chapter 1), unskilled labor-intensive imports into the United States will hurt the relatively scarce factor of production in the United States, which is now unskilled labor. But, if this trade effect is the cause for these wage trends, then it would have to work through a fall in the domestic relative prices of labor-intensive goods. There seems to be little evidence that this has happened[51]—mainly because various forms of protection have kept up the domestic prices of unskilled labor-intensive goods. For, in the HOS trade model, relative factor prices are determined by relative commodity prices. If the latter do not change, neither can the former. The other cause for the observed wage trends could be technical change. If there has been technical progress in the sectors that use *skilled* labor intensively, then even if commodity prices are unchanged, the real wage of *unskilled* workers must fall. Hence, it has been argued that technological change is the main cause of these trends.[52]

The question whether low-skilled wages are now set by those of Chinese and Indian coolies[53] or are stagnant because of technological changes in the West is unlikely, in my view, to be resolved, because of a massive structural change taking place in the global economy. This is as momentous as the *first Industrial Revolution* we have discussed, which substituted fixed for circulating capital in the processes of production—as the "factory" replaced the "putting out" system. The current structural revolution can be characterized as the replacement of human for fixed capital as epitomized by the communications revolution in the West.

The *second Industrial Revolution* relied on long production lines to manufacture mass consumer goods. It has been called "Fordism" in recognition of the revolution in standardized mass production of consumer durables achieved by Henry Ford. Today much of the consumer goods industry seems to be going "bespoke." It produces differentiated versions of the same good more closely tailored to differing individual tastes. Variety rather than standardization is the name of the game in this "designer" world of commodities in the affluent West. Shifts in its variegated tastes are increasingly reflected in changes in differentiated products to meet this volatile demand. Meanwhile, most heavy industry is moving to the South, as many of the larger Third World countries increasingly have a comparative advantage in its products.

The North is coming to own "virtual factories." This was the name given to his enterprise by a young and very rich entrepreneur I met in California. He is in the business of producing consumer goods. His virtual factory consists of a few bright youngsters sitting in front of computers in San Francisco. They have contacts and communicate electronically with the major stores and designers in the United States, as well as with production facilities strung out all over the Asian Pacific Rim. With the volatile and highly differentiated tastes of consumers, the stores take orders for highly individualized products which are then produced "just in time" by the cheapest facilities the "virtual factory" can find in Asia.[54] The virtual factory provides the "head" for the parts of the "body" scattered all over the developing world.

Moreover, there is a further twist to this emerging international division of labor. In the nineteenth century—North-Western Europe and later North America—specialized in the production of manufactures and experienced Promethean growth. The South—which included most of the postwar developing world as well as land-abundant countries of new settlement like the United States, Argentina, and Australia—specialized in the production of primary commodities and experienced Smithian intensive growth. In the current LIEO there is a three-way international division of labor. The North now specializes in the skill-intensive end of manufactures and services. The labor-abundant countries of Asia, India, and China specialize in unskilled and semiskilled manufacturing and services. Both the North and emerging Asia are experiencing Promethean intensive growth: one based on the inexhaustible supply of new ideas and technology produced by human capital, the other on the relatively unlimited labor and energy available to fuel industrialization. Finally, the land-abundant countries of Latin America and (hopefully) Africa again find that their nineteenth-century pattern of specialization in providing primary products to the burgeoning industries of China and India is once again yielding them spectacular Smithian intensive growth. Thus, the much derided "colonial" pattern of trade is alive and thriving, except it now applies to countries within the Third World!

A new subdivision of the nineteenth-century international division of labor of the North, based on "outsourcing" and "just in time production," reminiscent of the old national "putting out" systems—is emerging. The "design" and "sales" capacities which are human capital intensive are located in "rich" countries. They then have "virtual factories," with their production bases spread across the world, which use modern telecommunications to convert these "designs" into the differentiated "bespoke" consumer goods increasingly demanded by consumers in the West.

One feature of this outsourcing is that the activities outsourced are those facing a higher relative wage for unskilled and semiskilled labor at home than abroad. Thus, the assembly of components or the performance of simple repetitive tasks will move to lower labor cost in developing countries. This is happening in the factories of Southern China and the call centers in India. This outsourcing reduces the demand for unskilled and semiskilled labor in much the same way as if these workers were replaced by automation. Hence, outsourcing has a similar effect in reducing the demand for unskilled relative to skilled labor within an industry as skill-based technological change.[55]

In this brave new world of the virtual factory where most trade is in intermediate goods, instead of being competing explanations for the increased wage differential between unskilled and skilled labor in the North, trade and technology are in fact complementary. The current backlash against the outsourcing of service sector jobs to India and of manufacturing jobs to China is thus doubly misguided. An example should make this clear. When I joined UCLA in 1991, part of the terms I had negotiated included the services of a secretary. Within a few years, as I became familiar with using the computer and the Internet, I felt no need for one. This technological change had made my secretary's job and that of many of her peers redundant. No trade was involved. This technical change naturally raised productivity and no doubt the secretaries retrained and retooled and found other jobs. There was no Luddite call for smashing the computers which had made secretarial jobs redundant. The same increase in Northern productivity results from "outsourcing" service sector jobs to the call centers in India. It is exactly equivalent to the introduction of a new cost-saving technology. Resisting it would be equivalent to the Luddite smashing of computers to preserve secretarial jobs.

Both trade and technology will thus put a premium on skills in the West. A signal for the acquisition of these skills is a widening of skill differentials and the stagnation of the wages of the unskilled, as is evident in the United States. If, as in Europe, the labor market is inflexible, the result will be rising unemployment. But once incentives created to acquire skills lead to the necessary accumulation of human capital, the levels of living of even those on the lowest rung of the current income distribution should rise. This process will take time, however, just as happened to British living standards in the nineteenth century, when the previous major structural change was taking place. It appears from a still unsettled debate that these living standards took a long time to rise as, for instance, the handloom weavers of the old "putting out" system were converted into the factory workers of the modern age.

It was this so-called *social question* which in part led to the unraveling of the nineteenth-century LIEO, as the redistributive and egalitarian politics arising from the rise of Demos undermined that belief in classical liberalism which underlay the intellectual underpinnings of the LIEO. Today there is less danger that the social question in the current phase of globalization will undermine the new LIEO. There are two reasons for this.

First is the differences in the "losers" in the North in the two cases and the mitigating actions they can take to preserve their prosperity. While political action by threatened interest groups seemed inevitable to deal with the distributive consequences of globalization at the end of the nineteenth-century, the situation is much more benign in the current phase of globalization. For, unlike the nineteenth century when the losers—the industrial workers in the United States or United Kingdom or the landowners in Germany—could not acquire the material means to prevent their relative decline, this is not so today in the North. The main losers are the unskilled, and unlike the industrial factory workers of the nineteenth century who could not acquire the physical or financial capital to stem their relative decline in incomes, today's unskilled *can* acquire the necessary human capital to share in the immense gains from globalization of their skilled compatriots in the North. Today, instead of agitation, it is hoped that the unskilled have learned that to preserve their prosperity they need to go to school.

Second, and equally important, as most Northern economies become primarily service economies, many more workers will be working in areas where the products are sheltered from foreign competition as they are "non-traded." A hairdresser in South Central Los Angeles is not going to see his or her rates cut by competition from barbers in Bangkok. However, many of these personal services require not just acquired skills but also personal attributes like tidiness, punctuality, politeness, and trustworthiness. Mothers are hardly likely to employ a member of the so-called "underclass" as a baby sitter or housekeeper even if they were willing to accept the wages of a maid in India. The reform of Western welfare states which have undermined the Victorian personal virtues in the underclass[56] is required to help the potential "losers" from the current processes of globalization.

As the required adjustments to the new international division of labor take place, we would expect that, as in the nineteenth century, there will eventually be a rise in real wages and fall in inequality in the United States. This should ease the domestic pressures that have led to the incoherent trade policy the United States has followed since the 1980s. But what stance should the United States now take as an imperial power trying to maintain global order, and what should be the future role of the WTO?

Adjustment Assistance?

It has been argued that to facilitate the required adjustments in declining in-dustries, the government should provide assistance from public funds to the losers of globalization. For, despite the tangible overall gains in efficiency flow-ing from globalization, to improve the overall welfare of the populace the req-uisite changes in the economy have to be Pareto efficient—in the economist's jargon.[57] Pareto efficiency requires that no individual is worse off while some others are better off as a result of the change. There was an interminable de-bate in the early literature of welfare economics whether this implied that a particular change was Pareto efficient as long as it could be shown that, in prin-ciple, the gains of the winners were sufficient to hypothetically compensate the losers from the change. Some argued that for a net overall welfare gain the compensation could not be hypothetical. It had to be actual. This is, however, an impossible requirement to implement, as it would paralyze all action which leads to change. So applied welfare economists have, by and large, resorted to a two-part strategy to ascertain the desirability of a particular policy or project.[58] First, determine if there is a net gain (measured for instance by the net present value of the project or policy). Second, outline the distributional effects. Then leave it to the authorities to judge whether taking the two together (the effi-ciency and distributional effects) the policy or project is worth undertaking.

Though I did in my misguided youth subscribe to this view, and tried to implement it, for instance in helping to set up a Project Evaluation Unit for the Indian Planning Commission in the early 1970s, I have come to believe that though useful for some large public investment projects, welfare econom-ics is not a useful way of thinking about public policy.[59] This is in part because it partakes of the "nirvana economics" of the perfect competition–market failure paradigm I took issue with in chapter 2. But more importantly, it di-verts attention from the actual workings of a market economy and the classi-cal liberal principle that distributional judgments should not form part of our appraisal of the workings of markets or public policy. This is important when we consider the support provided by many mainstream economists for adjust-ment assistance to those "harmed" by import competition.

On classical liberal principles there is no case of compensation for losses arising in a competitive capitalist economy.[60] The dynamics of such an econ-omy, as Schumpeter emphasized, involves constant economic change embod-ied in new products, new technologies, and new sources of supplies. If those who lose in this competitive process were always to be compensated by the winners, it would attenuate the very process of change. It would for instance require that the inventors and producers of the personal computer (PCs) would have had to compensate all the manual typewriter producers and their users for the creative destruction their product had caused. The dynamic change associated with the IT revolution which has markedly raised productivity would have been slowed and possibly prevented. Or, should those who have bought a share on the stock market, because they expected its price to rise, be compensated for their loss if the share price falls? In any dynamic competitive economy, whose essence is continual change, there will be innumerable losers and winners—most often impossible to identify. But these "losses" are the result of the changing value placed in voluntary exchanges of the "labor" and "capital" specifically owned by the losers in a changing dynamic economy. They are not the same as the involuntary taking of someone's property which constitutes theft. A prescription for winners to always compensate the losers in a competitive economy is one to preserve the status quo and to prevent the economic changes which lead to economic progress. It is the policy of the Luddite. The same arguments apply to the economic changes induced by import competition. Apart from the unemployment insurance provided in most developed countries to deal with transitional unemployment, just as with domestic economic changes which inevitably create winners and losers, there is no case for any other compensation to the losers.

This argument has been fiercely resisted, mainly by lawyers. As the distinguished Chicago University law professor Richard Epstein notes: "The common argument is that economic losses from competition are every bit as real to their victims as those that result from the use of force. If we allow compensation for physical injuries, and injunctions against their future occurrence, then we should do the same for competitive losses, which should be likewise enjoined or compensated."[61] But this claim has been largely rejected in the classical legal tradition by the principle of "harm but not actionable harm." The reason is that, while theft and physical harm are rightly proscribed because to condone them would lead to a Hobbesian state of nature, and an economy of "taking" involving a negative or zero sum game with a fixed or shrinking total economic pie, the competitive process is one of an economy of "making," of expanding the overall pie—a positive sum game.[62] The "losers," by adjusting and adapting to their new changed circumstances in the "making" game, can share in the general prosperity that the positive sum capitalist process engenders, while in the negative or zero sum Hobbesian game they remain just losers. Epstein therefore rightly argues that "there must be no compensation or protection against economic losses sustained through the operation of competitive markets."[63]

Whither the WTO?

In my judgment, the "twin track" policy that the United States has adopted since the 1980s to promote global free trade has now ceased to be useful. The track based on the proliferation of bilateral preferential trade agreements has fatally undermined the multilateral track through the WTO. But, equally, many of the non–trade related demands the United States and the EU made in the multilateral Uruguay round, which were reluctantly agreed to by developing countries, have also fatally undermined the WTO.

The coup de grace was the TRIPS agreement the United States forced through under domestic pressures from Hollywood and pharmaceutical companies. Till then it was axiomatic that the GATT/WTO process only applied to trade in goods and services. By forcing through an agreement on protecting intellectual property rights, the United States has opened the gates for a whole host of other trade-irrelevant areas to be introduced into the WTO, like the various social policies we have discussed. The attraction of the WTO route for the numerous pressure groups pushing for areas extraneous to the cause of spreading free trade is that the WTO provides the weapon of trade sanctions, which many in the West would like to use for the worldwide legislation of Western "habits of the heart." Apart from the economic arguments we have noted against most of these proposed measures extraneous to trade, they are by and large aimed at developing countries—and in particular their poor (see chapter 8).

The TRIPS agreement is particularly heinous. It is well known that giving the inventor a temporary monopoly over the use of his invention through a patent increases the incentives for individuals to invest their time and energy in inventive activity. For, if an invention could be easily copied, the inventor would get nothing for his exertions. He would not invest in inventive activity. Hence a temporary monopoly provided by the patent is required. But while there maybe a case for patents for industrial products because of the large required investments in R & D, does the argument also apply to pure research, books, music, and films? Would this creative activity fall below some socially desirable level in the absence of the monopoly provided by copyright?[64] There was no patent when Pythagoras discovered his theorem or Newton his law of gravity. This did not prevent them from investing the necessary time and resources to make their discoveries. This is because much of basic science is motivated purely by the inquisitive Greek spirit and the lure of fame. To the extent that basic science today requires expensive overhead investment in laboratories and the like, and is a public good, it is usually funded by universities who put the fruits of their research in the public domain. To promote investments in applications of the basic ideas there is still a case for granting a temporary monopoly provided by a patent.

But with TRIPS there has been a rush to patent things and ideas that already exist in developing countries—like various herbs and plants which might have a medicinal purpose. This does not aid the creativity the patent system is supposed to promote. Moreover, as in the early stages of development, the human capital required for R&D is relatively scarce, there is

87

unlikely to be much patented intellectual property produced in developing countries. They are right to complain that, unlike the mutually beneficial tariff reductions, the TRIPS agreement merely transfers income from them to developed-country producers. It has been estimated[65] that once fully implemented, the TRIPS agreement would transfer $5.8 billion to the United States and a further $2.5 billion to other developed countries from developing countries. As the current agitation to get drug companies to sell their AIDS drugs at a discount to developing countries shows, the issue of patents has also become a moral issue agitating many activists. While patents for drugs may be justifiable, is the use of WTO sanctions to protect the "intellectual" property rights of the Rap singer Snoop Dog justifiable too?

Even more serious are the consequences of strengthening the WTO's dispute settlement procedure as part of the Uruguay round agreements. Claud Barfield has argued in an important book that there is now a formidable constitutional flaw in the WTO. This is the imbalance "between [its] consensus-plagued, inefficient rule making procedures and its highly efficient dispute settlement system—an imbalance that creates pressure to 'legislate' new rules through adjudication and thereby flout the mandate that dispute settlement judgments must neither add to nor diminish the rights and obligations of WTO members."[66] As there is no consensus on the many complex regulatory issues that the dispute settlement system will have to address, there is a danger that the highly efficient judicial mechanisms which have in essence created a "world court" on trade-related issues will "'create' law, raising the intractable question of democratic legitimacy" (Barfield 2001, p. 7). Worse, from the viewpoint of developing countries, this "judicialized" WTO dispute settlement, while arguably constraining U.S. aggressive unilateralism, also means that they have to compete with very limited legal resources of their own with the tight public-private partnerships between trade officials and trade lawyers in both the United States and the EU. These "partnerships have the potential to exploit and dominate the highly "judicialized" dispute settlement system and curtail the ability of developing countries to exercise their WTO rights" (p. 76).

This constitutional flaw is aggravated by the demands of a myriad of NGOs seeking to highjack the WTO for their own purposes. They want to use the "trade sanctions," which are a part of the trade dispute systems, to legislate their "habits of the heart." I deal with the claims of these NGOs to represent global civil society in chapter 8. But it should be noted that most of the causes they represent have failed to get democratic assent in the domestic politics of the Northern countries of their origin. So they are now trying to enforce their preferences by taking over international bureaucratic organizations, employing the well-known methods of "entryism" used by Communist cells in the past. In this international bureaucratic arena it is in the interest of some politicians (very often in the social and environmental ministries) to join international NGOs to create new international laws and regulations which increase their power and influence.[67] What they seek is a dirigiste international regulatory regime which they would run. This is a far cry from the free trade and laissez faire Pax Britannia promoted so effectively, and with such benign effects on prosperity during its Imperium.

If the United States genuinely wants to promote global free trade (as it claims it does and as it should as an essential element in maintaining world order), perhaps the time has come to abandon the principle of reciprocity, with its dangerous byways, and instead follow the nineteenth-century British example of unilateral free trade. No other single measure would untangle the mess that U.S. trade policy has got itself into. The WTO having done its job should then be wound up. If others are foolish enough to shoot themselves in the foot, no effort should be expended on preventing them. As in the nineteenth century, it is likely that the current hegemon's unilateral move to free trade would be emulated by most other countries. At present many developing countries like Chile and China have unilaterally reduced their tariffs, but because they are forced by the United States to play the "reciprocity game," they are reluctant to completely disarm and be left with nothing to bargain with the United States and EU.

In fact, as Nicholas Lardy has shown, since adopting its Open Door policy China has undertaken a massive unilateral trade liberalization even before its accession to the WTO (see figure 3.1). "By a number of measures China transformed its economy from one of the most protected to perhaps the most open among emerging market economies."[68] This led to its spectacular export

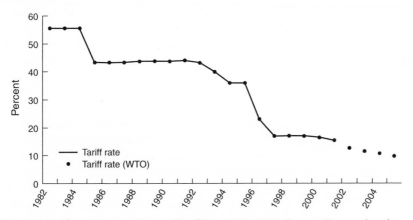

Figure 3.1: China's Average Import Tariff Rate 1982–2005. Source: Figure taken from India's and China's Recent Experience with Reform and Growth, by Wanda S. Tseng and David G. Cowen. Published by Palgrave Macmillan, 2005. Reproduced with permission of Palgrave Macmillan.

and growth performance and has made it the workshop of the world (see chapter 6).

It is truly ironic for the United States, the supposed champion of free trade, to be dabbling with protectionism at a time when an erstwhile Communist country is embracing the correct economic principle of unilateral trade liberalization. By ending the reciprocity game, not only would intellectual honesty be restored to U.S. trade policy, but it would also disarm the numerous special interests feeding at the public trough in this game. It is an open question if U.S. domestic politics will allow this desirable outcome.[69] But at least professional economists like me, who in the past have played the reciprocity game as a "second-best" way of getting to the desirable goals of free trade and laissez faire by cheering the multilateralism of the WTO while denouncing the unilateralism of PTAs, now need to state the intellectually honest case for the unilateral adoption of free trade.[70] Perhaps Keynes's famous dictum about "mad men in authority, who hear voices in the air, are distilling their frenzy from some academic scribbler of a few years back"[71] will then come true.

Appendix

Free Trade and Laissez Faire in Theory

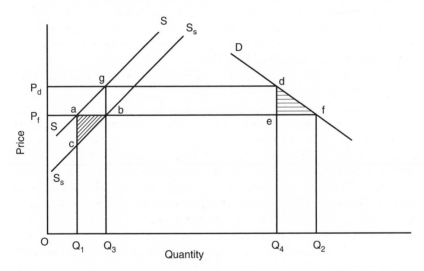

Figure A.1: Analytics of Tariff Protection

Consider figure A.1 based on TPW, which depicts the price and quantity configuration for an importable—say cloth—where DD is the demand and SS the market supply curve.[72] Assume a factor market distortion due to either the wage differential argument of Manoilescu (which states that in many developing countries the industrial wage is above the true social cost of employing labor, and hence industrial producers are at a disadvantage and should be protected), or a market rate of interest above the social opportunity cost of capital, which is the basis of the infant industry argument due to Hamilton and List. The social supply curve, Ss Ss—if there were no factor market distortion—will then lie below the market supply curve SS. With free trade and laissez faire, the good can be imported at the world price, pf, leading to OQ2 of the good being consumed of which OQ1 will be produced domestically, and Q1 Q2 will be imported. But, because of the domestic distortion, domestic import substitute output will be less than the socially optimal level OQ3, on the social supply curve Ss Ss. The first best policy would be a lump-sum subsidy financed by lump-sum taxation (assuming no collection and disbursement costs) to remove the factor market distortion which would lead to the market supply curve SS coinciding with the social supply curve Ss Ss, and producers would produce the optimum quantity OQ3, leading to the net social production gain of the triangle abc. This gain can be derived as follows. With the increase in domestic production by Q1Q3, an equivalent amount of imports will be replaced. This will mean that the economy will have an extra abQ3Q1 of foreign exchange to spend as it will. But from this foreign exchange savings, the social cost of the extra domestic production of cbQ3Q1 needs to be subtracted to give the net gain of abc. Moreover, as *ex hypothesi*, both the taxes and subsidies are lump sum,[73] which are inescapable and cannot be avoided by economic agents altering their otherwise efficient choices, a full efficiency optimum would be achieved.

By contrast, for a tariff which raised the domestic price of the good to pd, to evince the optimal output of OQ3 on the market supply curve SS, there would in addition to the production gain be a "by-product distortion" cost of the net consumer surplus[74] lost of def, as consumption of the good shrinks to OQ4 because of the price rise. This means that total consumer surplus declines by dfQ2Q4, but as the reduction in imports of Q4Q2 leads to a savings in foreign exchange of efQ2Q4, the net loss is only def. The net gain from the tariff will thus be the production gain abc minus the consumption loss def. The size of these triangles depends upon the relevant elasticities of supply and demand, which represent the sensitivity of the quantity consumed or supplied to changes in the price of the good. If with a price rise there is little reduction in the quantity demanded or increase in the quantity supplied, the demand/curve will be inelastic (closer to the vertical in figure 3.1), and the smaller the triangles def and abc. Conversely, with goods with high demand and supply elasticities. So, depending upon the relevant elasticities of demand and supply for the good, there may be no net welfare gain at all from the tariff.

In addition, there would be the continuing distortion of the choice of techniques. As the distortion in the factor market leads to a wage above the true social wage, producers will be choosing techniques of production which are insufficiently labor intensive. The "first best" policy of a wage subsidy lowers the wage faced by producers and allows them to choose the optimal labor-intensive technique. The tariff, however, does not correct this factor price distortion. So, though producers will increase production with the tariff, they will still be using the inappropriate, less labor-intensive technique in the production of the good, as the factor price ratio would still diverge from the socially optimal one.

Furthermore, there would be a "home market" bias. This arises because a tariff on manufactures only protects manufactured import substitutes, and is an implicit tax on other manufactures which are exportable. In fact, as Abba Lerner showed in the 1940s, a tariff by raising the relative price of importables to exportables is equivalent to an export tax. This home market bias is associated with further "by-product" welfare losses associated with the tariff, hence, Corden's famous hierarchy of policies to deal with domestic distortions. For the case we have discussed this would be: first best, a subsidy to the factor to remove the distortion at source; second best, a production subsidy; third best, a tariff cum export subsidy; with the tariff being the worst option.

But, this argument depends upon the subsidies which are superior to the tariff being financed through lump-sum taxes. As these in practice are infeasible (witness the fate of Mrs. Thatcher's famous poll tax in Britain in the late 1980s), any realistic application of the above theory will have to be based upon using "distortionary" taxes (which change the behavior of economic agents), with their own deadweight net consumer surplus triangle losses like def. These consumption losses of the taxes will need to be taken into account in assessing the net welfare effects of the tax cum subsidy alternative to the tariff in dealing with domestic distortions. As a tariff is nothing but a production subsidy to producers financed by a consumption tax on consumers of the protected good, much of trade theory, as Ian Little put it, turns out "to be simply public finance, and [if the unrealistic assumptions of no collection and disbursements costs is removed] indeed to boil down to such mundane matters as administrative costs"[75] If one believes that the government is following the canons of optimal taxation by applying Ramsey taxes based on the inverse elasticity rule of taxing the goods in inelastic demand most highly,[76] then a subsidy financed by suitable rearrangement of these optimal taxes is likely to incur lower welfare costs than those associated with the tariff's implicit tax on the good being protected. I do not want to go into the complexities of these public finance arguments. Suffice it to say that even with distortionary taxation and administrative costs it is likely that the Corden hierarchical ordering of policies would still hold.

But, as the subsequent incorporation of the costs of "rent seeking" and "directly unproductive activities" (DUP)[77] into the theory of trade and welfare shows, this is not the end of the story. Rent seeking is a term coined by Anne Krueger for the competition for licenses in import control regimes, which were ubiquitous in the post–Second World War Third World. Suppose that, instead of imposing a tariff on cloth, the government instead imposes an import quota so that only Q4Q4 of cloth can be imported into the country.

Its net effect will be to raise the domestic price of cloth from the world price of pf to pd. But who gets the quota? Suppose, as was common, the government authorizes some of its officials to issue import licenses for importing quantities of cloth summing to the overall quota of Q3Q4. Anyone who gets a license can import cloth at the world price pf, and sell it in the domestic market at pd, making a handsome profit of bg, for doing nothing but getting a license. This is the rent from the quota. . . . The total rents associated with the quota of Q3Q4 being gdeb. These are the quota rents which anyone lucky enough to get a license will receive. Given this license to print money, there will be many rent seekers. Competing among themselves, they will be willing to spend as much as the rents on offer, that is, gdeb. But this expenditure is socially unproductive, it is a deadweight loss like the consumer surplus loss def. So the total social loss taking account of rent seeking is the whole area gdfb.

Thus, in the presence of "rent seeking" for the quota rents and/or tariff and revenue seeking, the area gdeb would be entirely or partially dissipated in rent seeking or DUP activities. That would outweigh any potential production gain abc. So, irrespective of the public finance argument, there would now be a knock-down argument against protection in favor of the tax-subsidy solution. That is where the argument circa the 1980s seemed to stand.

But once one accepts this rent-seeking-DUP argument, there is still one further consideration to be taken into account. So far we have assumed that the "domestic distortion"—which led to a consideration of the relative net welfare effects of tax-subsidy versus protection to deal with it—was *genuine*. Suppose it was not. But producers know that governments are in the subsidy game. Then they are as likely to lobby for a subsidy claiming a domestic distortion where none in fact exists. If successful, they seek to gain the producer rents of pd gb pf—as the market and social supply curve are in fact the same. In the limit, this area will represent the rent seeking costs associated with this *subsidy seeking*. This is clearly a net welfare loss, as there is, *ex hypothesi*, no social production gain. As in practice it is virtually impossible to determine whether or not there is a domestic distortion, or more importantly the size of the distortion and hence the requisite subsidy, this form of cheating will be difficult to avoid. Alternatively, even if there is a domestic distortion so that Ss Ss lies below SS, producers are likely to dissipate the area pd ga pf in lobbying to get the subsidy—on similar lines to the tariff-seeking argument, which could again outweigh the social production gain abc.[78] This implies that the tax-subsidy solution for dealing with domestic distortions too need not lead to a welfare improvement, and hence the best policy may be to leave well alone—that is laissez faire! Even within the framework of the theory of domestic distortions, therefore, because of these rent seeking considerations the wheel does seem to have come full circle—free trade and laissez faire, as the classical liberals saw so clearly, do hang together.

4

Money and Finance

I went to Latin America for the first time in the early 1980s when I was working as the research administrator at the World Bank. I felt that, like Alice in
Wonderland, I had walked through the looking glass. In Brazil, each morning
I went to a little foreign exchange shop near Copacabana to change my dollars for the day's spending into cruzerios at the unofficial exchange rate. I had
to take a briefcase along to hold the huge wads of notes I got in return for
changing about $20. One afternoon I had to visit the director of the famous
Vargas Institute at about 3 p.m. He ushered me into his office and excused
himself to make an urgent telephone call to his stockbroker. After the
lengthy phone conversation he told me that he had just placed the small
change he had left over from his daily expense account in the overnight
money market at a rate of interest indexed to the nearly 100 percent per day
inflation rate. Failing to do so would mean that the $10 or $20 he had left
over would have been worth nothing by the morning. Moving on to Argentina, I exchanged my dollars for pesos, and was amazed to get 100,000
peso notes that were worth just a few cents. Having looked at the Central
Bank's money supply figures, I saw that the money supply had been increased
by about 80 percent over the previous month. When I asked the governor of
the Central Bank how they could have engineered such a massive increase,
he looked at me as if I was an idiot and said: "We have a printing press." This
was truly a weird and fascinating world.

For, I remembered, from the time I spent working at the Indian Planning Commission in the early 1970s, that there was panic if the annual inflation rate rose anywhere near 15–20 percent, and as for printing money, this
was virtually impossible. When Prime Minister Indira Gandhi declared an

emergency and gave her younger son Sanjay the power to debauch the polity and the economy, he found the former easier than the latter. When he tried to print money for his own purposes, he came up against the brick wall of the South Indian clerks in the Finance Ministry—the high priests of the complex system of financial accounting that the Raj had created and independent India had inherited. He could not increase the money supply by printing money, as he had hoped, without an understanding of these complex rules.

My Latin American experience vividly illustrated two ancient truths: Princes are always short of money, and they will try various ruses to get it. They first try taxation, but when this becomes onerous and tax evasion and avoidance become rife, they switch to borrowing from abroad, which more often than not ultimately leads to the bankruptcy of their lenders[1] and the drying up of foreign credit. They then resort to debasing the currency—gaining seignorage[2] through the inflation tax. Realizing this, the public will try and escape this tax by reducing their holdings of paper money by exchanging it for goods or foreign money. As this flight from paper money shrinks the inflation tax's base, the government has to print more and more money. This eventually leads to hyperinflation, as real money balances start shrinking with the pervasive flight from domestic paper money. What I was observing in dramatic form in my travels in the Latin American Wonderland was the last phase of this process. Also clear was the folly of all those economists who had argued for the irrelevance of inflation, because its costs were merely those of the shoe leather worn out by going to the bank more often. It was claimed that a doubling of the money supply would not affect anything real, as it would be just like exchanging two units of an old currency for one unit of a new one. Money is only a veil, or as economists say, money is neutral. But, in a hyperinflation the veil prevents distinguishing changes in relative prices from those in the price level. A spanner is thrown into the workings of the price mechanism with the attendant inefficiencies. Moreover, the only people left in the inflationary tax net are those without access to domestic money markets who are left with paper money and are unable to switch easily to foreign currencies. They are the poor on low incomes. The inflation tax is highly regressive.

Stable money is thus a public good, and a century-long debate has ensued about the monetary regime best suited to maintain this stability. A linked question concerns the free flow of capital between countries. Finally, monetary instability has been associated with cycles of boom and bust in the real economy. This has led to a continuing divide among those who believe that a capitalist economy is inherently unstable, requiring government intervention for stability, and those who argue that despite manias, panics, and crashes, a capitalist economy is inherently stable, with these unavoidable fluctuations taking place along a rising overall trend of national income. Government intervention to dampen or eliminate the business cycle will be either ineffective or counterproductive. In this chapter we examine these linked questions about the appropriate international monetary and financial architecture for a globalized economy.

International Monetary Regimes

As we saw in chapter 1, since the nineteenth century there have been four international monetary regimes: the gold standard in the second half of the nineteenth century till the First World War, a period of mixed systems during the interwar period, the Bretton Woods gold exchange standard till 1974, and since then a "nonsystem" with various forms of floating exchange rate systems. In understanding these divergent systems and why they changed, it is useful to note the so-called "trilateral dilemma": one can have two but not all three among fixed exchange rates (as in the gold standard, and quasi-fixed rates under Bretton Woods), monetary independence (to tailor domestic monetary policies to deal with domestic booms and slumps), and free international mobility of capital. Thus, under the gold standard there were fixed exchange rates and free mobility of capital, but not monetary independence. Under the quasi-fixed exchange Bretton Woods system of the gold exchange standard, there were fixed exchange rates and monetary independence, but capital controls which restricted movements of short-term capital. In the current floating rate nonsystem there is monetary independence and free mobility of capital, but not fixed exchange rates.

Balance of Payments Adjustments

To see the reasons for the evolution of these international monetary regimes over the last two centuries, and form a judgment on what is likely to be the ideal one for the current period of globalization, it is useful to think in terms of a very simple model of adjustment in an open economy subject to various internal shocks (like the domestic business cycle) and external shocks (like changes in a country's terms of trade and/or volatility in its capital inflows). This is the so-called Australian model named after the country of origin of its twin inventors, the late Professors Salter and Swan.[3]

We consider a "small" country that faces given terms of trade for its imports and exports which it cannot influence as it has no monopoly or monopsony power in any of its import or export markets. It is a "price-taker" in international markets. At these given prices of importables and exportables we can combine the two into a composite *traded* good whose weighting of the two components is provided by the fixed world prices of the two goods. The domestic price of the traded good will then be given by the foreign currency prices of the two component tradables and the nominal exchange rate. Any domestic excess demand or supply of this traded good is met through foreign trade, with excess demand (supply) being met by running a trade deficit (surplus). In addition there is a *nontraded* good, which either because of high transport costs (services like haircuts or real estate) or prohibitive trade taxes does not enter foreign trade. As such, unlike the traded good whose price is set by world prices (the given foreign currency prices converted into domestic prices at the *nominal exchange rate*), the price of the nontraded good must equate domestic demand and supply. Having thus collapsed the economy into two goods, a traded good and a nontraded good, the crucial relative price in the model becomes the relative price of nontraded to traded goods. The *real exchange rate*[4] is defined as the domestic relative price (ratio) of nontraded to traded goods.[5]

Suppose the economy maintains a fixed *nominal* exchange rate. It is initially in internal and external equilibrium, with domestic output equal to expenditure, and with no deficit in the current account of the balance of payments. There is then a large inflow of capital (or foreign exchange earnings from a rise in the price of its commodity exports). This will have two effects. First, it will allow domestic expenditure to exceed output by the amount of the inflow. Second, the country will have to run a current account deficit—with imports exceeding exports—by the same amount to absorb the inflow. Both effects will lead to a real exchange rate appreciation. For, the excess expenditure, now made possible, will raise in some proportion—depending on preferences—the demand for both traded and nontraded goods.

The excess demand for traded goods will be readily met through net imports (imports minus exports) without any change in the domestic price of traded goods. But as the supply of nontraded goods, *ex hypothesi*, is purely domestic, the excess demand for them must raise their relative price. This will induce an increase in their supply and, by lowering the relative price of traded goods, will also lead to a shift in consumption toward traded goods, which will be met by a further increase in net imports. In the new equilibrium, the relative price of nontraded goods (the real exchange rate) will thus be permanently higher. There will be a reduction in the domestic output of traded goods and expansion in that of nontraded goods, and there will be a current account deficit exactly equal to the inflow. Also, the price level will be higher (as the price of nontraded goods has gone up, while that of traded goods is unchanged).

But this latter effect depends crucially upon the assumed fixity of the *nominal* exchange rate. If the latter were flexible, then the required *real* exchange rate appreciation (which is an equilibrium phenomenon and hence unavoidable) could come about with a fall in the domestic price of traded goods through an appreciation of the nominal exchange rate.[6] There would be no need for the price of nontraded goods and hence the general price level to rise. But the relative output effects with a shrinkage of the traded good producing sectors must still occur. These two aspects of what has been called "the Dutch disease,"[7] which have been identified and observed in many countries receiving foreign currency bonanzas or large capital inflows, are different: the shrinkage of the traded goods sector is unavoidable, but not the rise in the price of nontraded goods. This depends upon what policy is followed with respect to the nominal exchange rate. To see the relative merits of *fixed versus flexible nominal* exchange rates[8] in adjusting to volatile capital or commodity markets, consider the case when—for whatever reason—the capital inflow or the foreign exchange bonanza ends. In that case the country will no longer be able to finance the excess of domestic expenditure over output, and of imports over export earnings which the foreign currency inflows had previously allowed. It will have to both cut domestic expenditure and eliminate the current account deficit.

Suppose the country, by deploying suitable monetary and fiscal policies, is willing to *reduce expenditure* so that it equals output. But it maintains a fixed nominal exchange rate. If for whatever reason *the prices of nontraded goods are inflexible downward*, or slow to adjust, then the relative price of nontraded goods (the real exchange rate) will not fall as is needed. This will prevent the required *switch of domestic expenditure* from traded to nontraded goods and thereby the cure for the balance of trade deficit. In such a case, the only way in which the requisite depreciation of the real exchange rate can occur is if the nominal exchange rate is devalued. Without this adjustment, the expenditure reduction required to achieve balance of payments equilibrium must lead to a domestic recession with unemployment.

As in any dynamic economy, the real exchange rate can be expected to be changing continually; there are two considerations in choosing between alternative exchange rate regimes. The first is that, whereas under a fixed exchange rate changes in the real exchange rate would have to come about with movements in the domestic prices of a large number of nontraded goods, under a flexible exchange rate they would come about automatically with changes in the nominal exchange rate. Putting it differently, whereas under a fixed exchange rate the equilibrium configuration of domestic and international prices would have to come about by changing millions of individual wages and prices in terms of domestic currency, only a single change in the nominal exchange rate is required with a flexible exchange rate. A flexible exchange rate also gives a country the freedom to choose its own monetary policy without being concerned about the balance of payments impact. These were the major reasons why two Nobel Prize winners, the classical liberal Milton Friedman and the social planner James Meade, were both early advocates of flexible exchange rates.

Both also realized that a flexible exchange rate system generates and requires speculation about the future value of the nominal exchange rate.

Friedman argued that there was a presumption that such speculation would be stabilizing. For, as all speculation is based upon making guesses about an unknowable future, those whose guesses turn out ex post to be correct will make profits at the expense of the rest. Speculation would only be destabilizing if there were an infinite supply of "suckers" who enter the market each day to be fleeced by the professionals. In other words, profitable speculation can be expected to dampen deviations from the emerging and only slowly recognizable equilibria, but the possibility of destabilizing speculation cannot be ruled out.[9]

The second consideration in choosing an exchange rate regime is that, unlike various intermediate exchange rate regimes like managed floating or an adjustable peg, both a genuinely fixed exchange rate and a freely floating one do not require any discretionary action by the authorities. Their operations and the adjustments they induce are automatic. By contrast, all the intermediate regimes require the authorities to take specific actions. This requires them to make guesses about an unknowable future. Just as the planning syndrome was based on implicitly assuming omniscient planners who could readily acquire the information to devise an optimal plan, those in favor of various intermediate exchange rate regimes implicitly assume that the authorities have the requisite information concerning an irreducibly uncertain future to devise an optimal exchange rate regime. Clearly they do not. Hence, they have no way of knowing either the extent or even the direction of the requisite exchange rate movements in the future. By contrast, in either of the automatic exchange rate systems the authorities can let the myriad of private agents act on their own private information to make their individual gambles about the future, with the assurance that under either regime the requisite balance of payments adjustment will take place automatically. As such, it is not surprising that during the last thirty years the various intermediate regimes—crawling pegs, tablitas, managed floating—have ultimately all come unstuck.

As domestic wage and price adjustments in most economies are sluggish, adherence to a fixed exchange rate can lead to a misalignment of real exchange rates. There is considerable evidence that such misalignment,[10] due to inappropriate nominal exchange rate policies, led to the painful adjustment many Latin American and African countries had to make in dealing with their debt crises in the 1980s.[11] In an increasingly integrated world economy with global capital markets moving huge sums at the press of a button, flexibility of the nominal exchange rate becomes an important means of insulating the economy from the volatility of capital flows and commodity prices. That is why, along with Friedman and Meade, I have favored freely floating exchange rates among the two automatic systems of balance of payments adjustment.

The Evolution of the International Monetary System

We can now examine the prerequisites of the various international monetary regimes, and why they broke down. The *gold standard* was predicated on the flexibility of domestic prices, including wages. This allowed the monetary authorities to be unconcerned about the domestic adjustments required with fixed nominal exchange rates and capital mobility. But, with the rise of trade unions and Demos, money wages became sticky downward. Keynes realized this, and his "General Theory" was based on the realistic assumption that nominal but not real wages were sticky. With these rigidities in domestic wages and thence nontraded good prices, the requisite real exchange rate depreciation could not occur automatically in a fixed exchange rate system. With the resulting fixity of the real exchange rate, the only means to bring the balance of payments into equilibrium was through deflation and the loss of employment and output that entailed. In the interwar period, this led country after country to abandon the gold standard for various forms of flexible exchange rates or exchange controls.

The post–Second World War, *Bretton Woods system* was based on a compromise between the flexible exchange rate system—which the experience of the 1930s led many observers to believe had bred instability and competitive "beggar my neighbor" type devaluations—and the gold standard fixed exchange rate system, which had led to unemployment. The answer was the *gold exchange standard*, whereby the dollar was fixed in terms of gold, and all the other currencies were fixed to the dollar. These fixed exchange rates vis-a-vis the dollar could be changed in consultation with the International Monetary Fund (IMF) if a country was faced with a fundamental disequilibrium in its balance of payments, and as its domestic wages were sticky it needed to devalue the nominal exchange rate to maintain both full employment and balance of payments equilibrium. The Bretton Woods system was thus a quasi-fixed exchange rate system. It, moreover, required short-term capital flows (hot money) to be prohibited. For, otherwise, speculators would be offered a one-way bet whenever a country was seen to be facing a fundamental balance of payments disequilibrium. Speculators betting on the likelihood of a devaluation would sell the currency and make a profit if it occurred, and would not make a loss if it did not, as they could switch back to their base currency at the unchanged rate. This speculative attack could only be prevented if either the country had sufficient foreign exchange reserves to beat off the speculators, or if, because of controls on short-term capital flows, the speculators did not have the means to attack the currency. Thus, the quasi-fixed exchange rate system required controls on short-term capital flows and adequate foreign exchange reserves. It was thus a system which sacrificed full capital mobility but had fixity of exchange rates and domestic monetary independence to manage internal aggregate demand.

101

This system collapsed for three reasons. The first was the need for adequate international reserves to maintain the fixity of the exchange rate, with normal fluctuations in the current account balance. The dollar was the major reserve currency. With the growth of international trade, the only way to increase the international reserves required for transactions purposes was for the United States to run current account deficits financed by printing dollars. Other countries could avoid accumulating dollar reserves—equivalent to unrequited virtually interest-free loans to the United States—by converting their dollars into gold. For the U.S. government was committed to convert its dollars at a fixed price into gold under the rules of the gold exchange standard. Some countries, most notably France and China, did accumulate gold reserves. But as the gold price was fixed, the burst of worldwide inflation in the 1960s led to a depreciation of the real value of these gold reserves. Thus, the opportunity cost of holding gold was rising relative to holding U.S. government debt as reserves. Furthermore, the net additions to the world's supply of gold were lower than the growth of world trade. If countries had converted all their dollars into gold, there would have been a shortage of international liquidity precipitating another depression as in the 1870s. To deal with these twin crises of international liquidity some economists, of whom Sir Roy Harrod of Oxford was the most notable, recommended raising the price of gold in terms of dollars. This would at a stroke raise the dollar value of the world's gold stock and thence international liquidity without relying on the United States printing dollars to cover continuing current account deficits in perpetuity. But this solution was not favored by those who saw it as rewarding the main gold producers at the time: the South Africa of apartheid and the Communist regime in the Soviet Union.

The second reason for the collapse of the Bretton Woods system was that the United States was the only country that could not devalue if faced with a fundamental disequilibrium in its balance of payments. As all the other countries were fixed to the dollar which in turn was fixed to gold, a dollar devaluation could only occur if all the other currencies were revalued, which other countries were loath to do. In the 1960s the United States relied on large-scale deficit financing of the Vietnam War, which led to both domestic inflation and a large current account deficit. The United States could not adjust like other countries faced with a similar problem: namely, by both *reducing* domestic expenditure through monetary and fiscal policies and *switching* it through a devaluation. Thus, both full employment and balance of payments equilibrium would be attained. President Nixon solved this problem by closing the gold window in 1974. The United States would no longer be willing to exchange dollars (at the fixed price) for gold. The dollar's value would be determined relative to others in a free market for currencies. The world moved to the current floating rate system.

The third reason for the collapse of the Bretton Woods system was probably the most fundamental. The quasi-fixed exchange rates on which it was based were predicated on the control of short-term capital flows, without which they would be subject to speculative attack. In the immediate postwar period, exchange controls, which provided the necessary administrative apparatus to enforce controls on capital flows, were ubiquitous. Britain only gave them up when the Thatcher government came to power in 1979. Under the Bretton Woods system the authorities were expected to distinguish between the supposedly benign long-term flows of capital and the wicked short-term flows. The former were to be allowed, the latter banned, as they threatened speculative attacks on the quasi-fixed exchange rate system. But, with the increasing liberalization of world trade and its stupendous growth in the postwar Golden Age, it was increasingly difficult to prevent movements of short-term capital. These could be effected through the "leads and lags" in trade, as exporters underinvoiced their exports and overinvoiced their imports, keeping the difference in whatever foreign currency they chose. But it was the growth of the Eurodollar market that was to be the decisive event which would undermine these capital controls. We have seen how the Eurodollar market arose in the 1950s and 1960s to provide apolitical financial intermediation. OPEC's oil price coup in 1973 greatly augmented the funds flowing through the Eurocurrency market. This growth of the Eurodollar market meant that there was now a wall of footloose capital which no country could control. This was to be the death knell for any quasi-fixed exchange rate system.

Most of the advanced countries of the world have thus moved to a floating rate system, which does not need international reserves. But many countries—mainly in Asia—which still maintain fixed or quasi-fixed exchange rate regimes pegged to the U.S. dollar, are in effect still on a Bretton Woods type dollar standard.

European Monetary Union. Europe has sought to buck this trend toward flexible exchange rates. Through its European Monetary Union (EMU) it has created an irrevocably fixed exchange rate system based on the Euro. What are its prospects?

Since the Second World War the world has effectively been on a dollar standard. A successful Euro could challenge this dominance. For the share of Euroland in global trade and production matches that of the United States, and this could make it attractive as an international store of value and a vehicle currency for international transactions in goods and services, as well as for the dealings of the burgeoning international underground economy.[12]

But would this rivalry with the hitherto dominant dollar be in the global interest? As we have seen, the breakup of the nineteenth-century LIEO was partly caused by the decline of Pax Britannica not being smoothly followed by the rise of Pax Americana. The economically and politically dominant power did not accept its new responsibility till the end of the Second

World War. It is this U.S. hegemony that Europe seeks to challenge. But, apart from the question of the likelihood of success, there is the danger that this attempt might create frictions similar to those which led to the break-down of the nineteenth-century LIEO.

However, if the Euro can successfully challenge the dollar as an international store of value, a larger share of the world's money supply (including reserves) will be held in Euros rather than in dollars. This will provide implicit revenue in the form of seignorage to the European Central Bank.[13] There would also be two global consequences. If there was a large enough shift out of existing U.S. assets and of further flows from the world's savers into the Euro, the current imbalance between savings and investment in the United States would become untenable and its current account deficit unsustainable. A depreciating dollar, rising interest rates, and a collapse of asset prices would follow. This might still come about in the near future as I write (November 2004). The other consequence would be that with the inflows of capital induced by a desire of world investors to diversify their portfolios, ceteris paribus, the Euro would soar. This has happened with the appreciating Euro largely bearing the effect of the dollar's weakness.

But is the Euro likely to replace the dollar as the world's major reserve currency? I conjecture it will not. For the Euro is not perceived, as yet, as being credibly as good as the dollar. This is because, while there is no question in anyone's mind that the dollar, in which the U.S. Treasury's long-term (30-year) bonds are denominated, will still be around when they are redeemed, no one can be as certain of the Euro's survival when the 30-year Euro bonds issued by the ECB come up for redemption.

This lack of credibility about its survival is intimately linked to the way the Euro was set up: by putting the cart of monetary union before the horse of political union. The currency of a genuine political state is credible because the currency's demise would be coterminus with that of the state issuing it—which is unlikely. If not underpinned by a political union, a currency union is only credible if it fulfills the criterion of what economists call an "optimum currency area"—within which exchange rates should be fixed. Europe does not fulfill these conditions. For a monetary union to work it is important that, to deal with the unemployment that asymmetric shocks to different regions in the currency area could cause, there is either wage and price flexibility, or else there should be easy migration—as in the United States—between regions with deficient and excess demand for labor. Neither attribute exists in Europe.[14] Its labor markets are notoriously inflexible, and the major differences in customs and language make labor—except in the top echelons—largely immobile. When coupled with the "stability" pact, countries in Euroland are unable to deal with unemployment either via the exchange rate or expansionary fiscal policy. Nor, as in the genuine federal polity—the United States—are federal fiscal transfers on a requisite scale likely to be forthcoming to offset regional unemployment. Hence, the bulk of respectable mainstream economists see the Euro as a dangerous gamble with a high chance of failure.

International Capital Flows

The case for free international mobility of capital parallels that for free trade in goods and services. There are mutual efficiency gains for both the lenders and borrowers as capital is deployed in the locations and uses with the highest risk-adjusted returns. Capital mobility also allows countries to smooth temporary fluctuations in consumption through international borrowing and lending, and allows countries to diversify risks.

We have seen how, since the Second World War with the elimination of exchange controls and the collapse of the Bretton Woods system, most developed countries gradually have established relatively free capital markets. Many developing countries also gained access to global capital markets after the OPEC coup, and with the progressive liberalization in their economies since the 1980s many have relaxed their controls on capital movements. But a series of financial crises in the 1990s in both developing and developed countries have led many to question the desirability of free capital mobility.[15] This backlash has not so far affected developed countries themselves but has spread among those concerned with developing countries. Is this fear of free capital movements justified, and is there a need for developing countries to maintain (as in China and India) or to reintroduce capital controls (as Malaysia did for a short period)?

Macroeconomic Instability

These questions raise the more fundamental one: whether the debt crises since the 1980s—in particular relating to sovereign debt—are endemic to a liberal order of capital flows, and whether public action can prevent or mitigate them or will it instead exacerbate them? This is the central issue that continues to separate what I would label the "classical liberal" viewpoint from the various "dirigiste" viewpoints. Underlying these differences is another major division about the functioning of both the national and international macroeconomy. The classical liberals believe that a competitive macroeconomy without barriers to adjustment erected by governments will be self-correcting; the dirigistes believe that the inherent instability of the macroeconomy requires public intervention. The irony is that, whereas most governments have now virtually accepted the classical liberal viewpoint as regards the domestic macroeconomy by eschewing the Keynesian interventions commonly accepted in the two postwar decades, they are increasingly recommending various dirigiste means to "control" the international macroeconomy.

Fluctuations in aggregate economic activity are not new. In the past, when most economies were agrarian, these fluctuations were due to annual variations in climate, particularly rainfall. With the advent of industrialization new sources of cyclical variation were introduced, caused both by the variations in investment—depending on the changing "animal spirits" of entrepreneurs—and the short-run stickiness of money wages of industrial labor markets. The business cycle—whose ultimate causes are still disputed—came to characterize industrial economies. With the globalization of the nineteenth century, these booms and slumps in the North also affected the South through the variations in the demand for its primary product exports. The Keynesian revolution held out the hope that activist fiscal policy could control the business cycle. But despite assertions by various politicians (most recently by Gordon Brown, the U.K. Chancellor of the Exchequer in the late 1990s) that they had tamed the business cycle, it quickly taunted them by its reappearance.

Controlling the Business Cycle

What does the historical record show about the nature of the business cycle since the 1870s and the effectiveness of public policy for its control? For the United States, Christina Romer has examined the evidence from 1886 to 1997, and finds that "what has not changed, at least dramatically, between the prewar and postwar eras is the volatility of broad macroeconomic indicators and the average severity of recessions. What has changed between the prewar and postwar eras is the frequency and distribution of recessions. Expansions are noticeably longer after World War II than before World War I, indicating that recessions happen less often today than in the past. Also, recessions while not less severe on average in the postwar era, do appear to be somewhat more clustered in the moderate range."[16] She finds that, whereas the pre–First World War boom–bust cycle was driven by animal spirits and financial panics, the postwar boom and bust cycle has been driven by public policy—largely the Keynesian policies emphasizing discretionary fiscal policy.

This is true for a number of reasons. On the one hand, with the expansion of government, automatic stabilizers have become operative: government revenues move with the cycle, while public expenditures on unemployment and welfare move countercyclically, leading to budget deficits rising automatically in a recession and falling in the boom, while the development of deposit insurance has eliminated the bank runs which caused financial panics. These two developments have increased macroeconomic stability. But, on the other hand, activist stabilization policies have created their own instability. "Recessions have continued in the postwar era because we have created them to reduce inflation. Inflation has been a persistent problem in the postwar era because policy, especially monetary policy, has tended to be overly expansionary. Overly expansionary policy has generated periods of rapid growth in the postwar era that have fueled price increases."[17] It is the active use of monetary policy at the bottom of a recession which, however, has moderated postwar recessions.

In a study of fifteen countries from 1870 to the present, Basu and Taylor (1999) confirm that recent business cycles are no less volatile than they were a century ago. Though the interwar period saw a rise in volatility, this was largely due to the unprecedented Great Depression. Interestingly, they find that fears of the floating exchange regime of the current era of globalization being associated with greater macroeconomic instability are also unfounded. Dividing the period since 1870 by the various international monetary regimes we outlined, they find that volatility increased markedly from the time of the gold standard (1870–1914) to the interwar period (1919–1939). Then in the Bretton Woods period (1945–1971) it fell back to gold standard levels, and has fallen still further in the current period of floating exchange rates.[18] They also confirm that it is the volatility of investment which lies at the heart of the business cycle, and that money matters.

Many of the lessons to be drawn from this historical record seemed to have been learned. By the 1970s it was evident that the Keynesian fiscal policies of the 1960s had failed—first, because the large budget deficits they generated exacerbated the problem of inflation. Furthermore, it was realized that politicians used fiscal policy to generate political "business cycles" to garner votes. Finally, with the lags involved in designing and implementing tax and spending decisions, fiscal policy was recognized as being at best a very blunt and unreliable instrument. The current consensus is that fiscal policy should be concerned with the microeconomy and the financing of public goods. It should aim to balance the budget over the business cycle. Stabilization policy should seek to control the rate of inflation through monetary policy. To prevent the politicization of monetary policy, it should be entrusted to independent central banks. This it is hoped will reduce the policy-induced instability that has been documented for the postwar period.

Despite the numerous schools of macroeconomic thought still using different labels to differentiate their product, it would appear that a classical version of monetarism seems to have won the day.[19] The central recommendation of monetarism is that policy should be based on rules rather than discretion, largely as the information that is required for any discretionary stabilization policy is not available. As Alan Meltzer notes:

> Rules may be adaptive, not fixed, and can adjust in a predictable way to permanent changes in real growth or intermediation. Support for rules is related to five monetarist propositions: (1) neither the central bank nor private forecasters can predict output, employment, inflation or other variables with sufficient accuracy to damp fluctuations on average; (2) lags are not constant; neither

CHAPTER FOUR

government nor private forecasters can distinguish between permanent and transitory disturbances to levels and growth rates until sometime after they occur; (3) the response of particular relative prices to monetary and other impulses in any cycle may differ from previous cycles depending on initial conditions, the nature of shocks and the policy rule that is followed; (4) the private sector damps fluctuations and returns to stability if undisturbed by unanticipated policy impulses; and (5) rules that are easily monitored reduce costs of information.[20]

The Classical Theory of the Business Cycle

This brings back into focus what was until the Keynesian "revolution" the accepted view of the causes of business cycles and how public policy should or should not react in dealing with them. The modern exponent of this classical view of the business cycle, developed most fully by the Austrian economists and the great Swedish economist Knut Wicksell, was Fredrich Hayek. With Keynes he was the leading macroeconomist in the interwar period. It was his work on business cycles (in particular his *Prices of Production* and *Theory of Capital*) which the Nobel committee cited in giving him the prize. At the center of business cycles on this classical and "Austrian" view are interacting movements in business profits, investments, and credit.[21] Recurrent fluctuations in a private enterprise economy are caused by the changing outlook for profits. When it is favorable, investment and production increase, and conversely when it deteriorates. Rising investment fuels growth, which ceteris paribus will produce more profits and further investment. But, the whole process is uncertain, as any act of investment is based on expectations about future relative prices. Every act of investment is thus necessarily a gamble—a hostage to fortune. The expected profit (return) must at least be higher than the opportunity cost of the funds invested. This is given by the rate of interest that prevails in financial markets. The credit and financial markets are therefore crucial in the boom-bust cycle in this classical theory. The Austrians, especially Hayek, emphasized the crucial role of intertemporal prices which link the present with the future, in particular the level and structure of interest rates in the economy. Central to understanding this structure and the false signals from misguided monetary policy was Hayek's notion of "neutral money." Following from the quantity theory of money—which Hayek maintained is broadly valid—he argued that the traditional view that money was neutral as long as the value of money (i.e., the level of prices) was unchanged—for instance with money increasing in proportion to increases in output—was based on assuming an absence of "injection effects," that is, the distortionary effects of how the money supply is increased. If the injection of money is through the credit markets, then even if the total ensuing increase in the money supply is proportionate to the increase in economic activity and hence noninflationary, the changes in *interest rates* induced by the expansion of credit could lead to false signals in the pattern of intertemporal prices and thence to a misallocation of resources.

For changes in the interest rate will have a systematic effect on the pattern of prices which allocate resources among different stages of production. In modern terminology, a fall in the interest rate due to credit expansion will lead to businesses undertaking relatively more capital-intensive investment projects with lower prospective rates of return. The artificially low rate of interest induced by injecting money through credit expansion will also lead to an unsustainable boom as more investment projects are undertaken than can be completed, and as the accompanying resource scarcities emerge the boom will turn into a bust. The economy will only recover once the "malinvestments" are liquidated and resources reallocated in line with intertemporal consumer preferences and resource availabilities.

But, even with appropriate monetary policy, a private capitalist economy will inevitably have booms and busts. Unlike many contemporary theories of the business cycles which believe that shocks of various kinds are the true "causes" of business cycles, this older view sees the business cycle as being an endogenous self-sustaining feature of private capitalist industrial economies.[22] Thus, consider a business expansion fueled by rosy profit expectations, and expressed in rising investment. During this upswing, credit is generally loose given the generally rosy economic environment. During this expansion market rates will stay below what Wicksell labeled the "natural" rate of interest—the expected yield or marginal productivity of investment. Interest rates rise but only slowly as credit expands to finance investment. But, with the expansion, overly optimistic forecasts of future profitability lead to bad investments. At some stage, as demand slackens profits fall, and businesses begin to retrench as excess capacities are revealed. With the ending of the boom, many of the excesses, like the bad debts created with the looseness of credit in the upturn, are revealed. Once the excesses of the boom are worked out of the system, the economy begins to recover.

This seems to be as spare a description of the recent Internet boom and bust as well as of the Japanese slump. Can public policy do anything to alleviate this boom-bust cycle? The simple answer is: very little. If the monetary authorities try to end the boom, they would generate the policy-induced recessions which have characterized much of the postwar era. They can perhaps, as Alan Greenspan at the U.S. Federal Reserve did in the recent U.S. recession, soften the blow by easing monetary policy in the downturn. But, as the basic problem is the bad investments and excess capacity created in the boom, the only solution to this "structural" slump is to allow these distortions to be worked out, so that another period of expansion can begin. As the Japanese example shows, Keynesian policies of running large budget deficits to cure the slump will be at best counter productive.

Does Macro-Instability Matter?

If booms and busts along a rising trend are endemic to the private capitalist economy, and public action is as likely to exacerbate rather than solve the problem, does this unavoidable macroeconomic instability matter? This is an old debate in the economics of developing countries. It was argued by many that, with their integration into the world economy, primary product–producing developing countries would suffer a retardation in their long-term growth rates from the income instability resulting from the fluctuations in their export earnings as the Northern economies waxed and waned. The detailed study of the postwar experience of twenty-one developing countries in Lal and Myint (1996) found that there is no relationship between the volatility of growth rates and their long-term trends. Instability in growth rates does not necessarily lead to poor overall growth performance. Thus Hong Kong has had one of the most volatile of growth rates, while India one of the most stable in the postwar period. Yet this has not prevented Hong Kong from producing one of the most stellar postwar growth records, compared with India, whose low but stable growth rate has been the stability of the comatose.

More recently, my UCLA colleague Aaron Tornell and his associates have looked at the empirical evidence concerning financial crises and growth. Unlike the doomsayers they find "a robust empirical link between higher growth and a propensity for crises" (Ranciere et al. 2003, p. 2).[23] In light of the 1990s financial crises, they consider the safe, stable dirigiste credit path followed by India and the more risky private sector–dominated unstable path followed by Thailand. They conclude : "Thailand has experienced lending booms and crises, while India has pursued a safe growth path for credit. GDP per capita grew by only 99 percent between 1980 and 2001 in India, whereas Thailand's GDP per capita grew by 148 percent, despite having experienced a crisis" (p. 3). Underlying the interventionist view, which has resurfaced with the recent financial crises in emerging markets, is an implicit assumption about the omniscience of the authorities and the myopia of private agents. Any real world economy is likely to be subject to all kinds of unforeseeable changes. In the ancient agrarian economies this uncertainty was largely due to nature, most often the climate. A dynamic capitalist economy is subject to even greater volatility, due to shifting tastes, technologies, and resources. Added to these are the shocks from domestic monetary and fiscal policies. Hence, there will be a constantly shifting notional "equilibrium" of relative prices, including the real exchange rate (the relative price of non-traded to traded goods) as well as portfolio equilibrium in asset markets. These shifting equilibria cannot be predicted with certainty by either Platonic Guardians or market participants. How will market participants react to this irreducible uncertainty? As these unforeseeable shocks lead to fluctuations in income and thence their consumption, private agents will attempt to smooth them through saving and investing when times are good, and running these investments down and dis-saving when times are bad. In the absence of well-developed financial markets this "consumption smoothing" was often done by hoarding precious metals in the form of jewels when incomes were unexpectedly high and selling them when income and consumption unexpectedly fell.

It might be thought that the government acting as the agent of the people could do even better, particularly if financial and insurance markets are underdeveloped, by acting as the custodian of the public interest to perform this consumption smoothing. This was the justification provided for the many schemes to stabilize commodity prices or the incomes of producers of primary products in developing countries. The most famous of these were the various marketing boards that were created to deal with the gyration of prices of primary products in world markets. In these schemes the government bought, say, coffee or cocoa from producers at the average of the world price of the commodity over the price cycle, and then made profits when world prices were high to set off the losses it made when they were lower than the average price it paid its domestic producers. Though fine in principle, these schemes invariably became predatory instruments for taxing domestic producers of primary products rather than stabilizing their incomes. Thus, instead of paying them the average of the world price, the producers were paid a lower price, the difference being pocketed by the predatory state. Innumerable examples of such predatory behavior can be cited (see Lal and Myint 1996), the most notorious being that of Nkrumah's Ghana, where a peasant crop—cocoa— introduced and developed by small farmers was destroyed by the predatory actions of its marketing board.[24] The same story can be told about the natural resource rents from minerals, like oil (e.g., Nigeria)[25] and bauxite (e.g., Jamaica),[26] accruing to the public sector.

In fact, we have a very important study of the coffee boom in East Africa in the 1970s by David Bevan, Paul Collier, and Jan Gunning. During this boom the policies followed by the two major countries benefiting from the boom—Kenya and Tanzania—differed markedly in the deployment of these unexpected rises in the profits of coffee production. In Kenya the rise in profits of coffee production associated with the rise in its world price was allowed to be retained by the peasants; in Tanzania it was in effect taxed away for "public" uses. The outcomes could not have been more different though they are wholly predictable. The private Kenyan producers, seeing a temporary rise in their incomes and profits, saved and invested these temporary windfalls, to be used on a future rainy day to maintain their constant consumption levels, while in Tanzania the taxed profits were wasted on various inefficient public expenditure schemes and to maintain and expand the predatory bureaucracy.

There is further evidence that controverts the implicit assumption underlying dirigiste panaceas about the irrationality and myopia of private agents. As we have seen, in terms of national income accounting, the current account of the balance of payments is equal to the difference between domestic savings and investment. In an open economy the current account will thus reflect the consumption smoothing domestic residents—both private and public—are undertaking in the face of various external and internal shocks to their income streams. The countervailing movements in the country's capital flows, including changes in reserves (which from the balance of payments identity is exactly equal to the country's current account), being the means by which this consumption smoothing is undertaken through international capital markets. Thus, with capital mobility the current account serves as a buffer to smooth consumption when there are shocks to output, investment, and government expenditure.[27] In a study of forty-five developing countries, Ghosh and Ostroy (1995) found that in about two-thirds of their sample countries, private agents were able to fully smooth consumption in the face of shocks. Even more remarkable is a finding by the Reserve Bank of India that a simple "intertemporal consumption optimization" model of India's current account between 1951 and 2002 was "able to explain the direction and turning point of the consumption-smoothing component of the current account balance fairly well. The correlation coefficient between the optimal and actual current account balance is close to one. Thus, fluctuations in the current account balance in India are the outcome of residents trying to smooth their consumption paths when the national cash flow fluctuates. The result is noteworthy, given the restrictions on capital flows and the intermittent external shocks experienced."[28]

Two lessons can be drawn which are relevant for the following discussion of financial crises and capital controls. First, and most important, private agents even in the poorest countries behave like *homo economicus*. They are perfectly able to take care of the volatility in their incomes caused by external or internal shocks. Public action, even if well intentioned, is unnecessary and could be counterproductive. As the instincts of most governments are predatory rather than benevolent, promoting government action to deal with the volatility of national income streams could, as it has, do great damage to the welfare of their citizens—their prey. Second, the Indian example shows the leakiness of even the most draconian capital controls. Unless a country is willing to close its economy to both flows of trade and capital, in the long run it is not feasible to control capital flows.

Financial Crises

We have seen that although there is an emerging consensus—which is broadly classically liberal—on domestic macroeconomic policy, there is a growing divergence of opinion on international macroeconomic policy, particularly on how developing countries should deal with capital flows. These debates have been fueled by the financial and debt crises that have buffeted many developing countries since the 1980s.[29] Many are calling for developing countries to maintain or institute capital controls to prevent financial crises, and others are arguing for a new international financial architecture to manage the international economy. In order to form a judgment on these issues, we briefly outline the essential features of the various debt crises that have plagued the Third and now the Second World since the 1980s.

Three types of capital flows can be distinguished: foreign direct investment, equity investment, foreign bank loans and bonds denominated in foreign currency. These three types of capital flows differ in the sharing between borrowers and lenders of the "income" and "foreign currency" risks associated with international capital flows. The income risk arises when a country has to make a payment to foreign lenders which was reasonable given normal times, but which becomes onerous if domestic incomes fall due to a recession. The foreign currency risk arises when the payment to the lender is fixed in foreign currency, and the borrower's currency depreciates, leading to a rise in the payments on the debt in domestic currency. For direct foreign investment and foreign equity investment these two forms of risks are shared by both borrowers and lenders. Thus, the profits of a multinational company will decline with a recession in the host country, and if the currency depreciates, the foreign currency value of the profits repatriated will also fall. Similarly, foreign equity investors will find the value of their equities fall in a recession, and will also get less for any sales of their equity in foreign currency if the domestic currency depreciates. By contrast, for foreign bank lending and bonds the interest payments are usually denominated in the foreign currency, and are independent of the state of the host country's domestic circumstances. Thus, both the income and foreign currency risks are borne entirely by the borrower. Not surprisingly all the debt crises in the past two decades have been associated with the sudden withdrawal or diminution of bank and bond lending.

Causes

The 1980s debt crises were sovereign debt crises caused by the rise in world interest rates when Paul Volcker tightened U.S. monetary policy to cure the stagflation of the 1970s. Many middle-income countries with endemic fiscal problems had used the ready availability of bank credit from the Euro markets to finance their budget deficits. As many of these syndicated bank loans were at negative real interest rates, this proved to be an irresistible way of dealing with an endemic problem. The borrowings had, however, been made at floating interest rates and were in large part directly or indirectly underwritten by their governments. But, with the rise in world interest rates to historically unprecedented levels, and the deterioration in their terms of trade because of the deflation in the North, these indebted countries needed to raise the fiscal resources and convert them into foreign exchange to finance the large increase in debt service that ensued.

Some countries, mainly in East Asia, managed this transfer problem in textbook fashion. They were helped by the capacity of their economies to convert domestic resources into foreign exchange because of their past outward-oriented policies, and because they had established viable fiscal systems. Many debtors in Latin America and Africa shared neither attribute. The debt crisis created an acute fiscal crisis for these states, most often reflected in acute inflation. Given their past neglect of exports, the only way to obtain the necessary balance of trade surplus was through import compression, which in turn led to domestic recession.

The debt crisis began with the Mexican government's inability to continue debt service in 1982. The crisis was not, as some observers claimed,[30] due to the *inability* of these countries to pay—as witness Mexico's immense oil wealth—but rather to their *unwillingness*. For, sovereign borrowers do not face any legal form of enforcement of claims on them. They will, thus, only continue to service their debt as long as the expected utility from repayment is greater than that from default. This means that they will be unwilling to pay well before they are unable to do so.[31]

A prolonged cat and mouse game was then played between these sovereign borrowers and the money center banks who had lent them the money, with the IMF and the World Bank in the middle. Playing on the historical memories of the bank failures of the 1930s, the debtors and the commercial banks hoped they could force a bailout by Western governments, ideally through the concealed means of intermediation by the international financial institutions. By and large these international institutions held tight and called their bluff. They used the leverage, provided by whatever money they gave the debtors to pass on to the lenders, to get the long overdue structural adjustments needed in the fiscal, exchange rate, and trade policies of the debtor countries. An unintended consequence of the debt crisis was to initiate that process of integration of these hitherto inward-looking economies into the global economy.

By May 1987 the major New York money center banks with high exposure to Third World debt saw the game was up. They set aside larger reserves against their Third World debt. Since then various methods, like swap arrangements to buy back part of the existing debt at close to its value in the secondary market, finally resolved the 1980s debt crisis. Except for Africa. Most of its debt was owed to national governments and international institutions. Much of the money lent was stolen by its predatory elites. There are now various moves being made to write off this debt. Even though this creates problems of moral hazard for the future—as it raises the perception of both the borrowers and lenders that they will be bailed out—given that the sums involved are small, while their continuing burden has done widespread damage to the cause of globalization in the region, it maybe prudent to wipe this slate clean.[32] It will also be a salutary punishment for those bilateral and multilateral "aid" agencies which merely succeeded in channeling Western taxpayers' money to the Swiss bank accounts of Africa's predators.

The more recent financial crises in Brazil and Russia were similar to the 1980s crises caused by inappropriate macroeconomic and structural policies. By contrast, the Asian crises in the 1990s were crises in countries with sound macroeconomic management. These were crises in their domestic banking and financial systems.[33] But, like the 1980s crises, they were also fueled by international bank lending.

Both sets of crises also shared a *second* feature. They have hit countries that have maintained some form of adjustable peg exchange rate, which is subject to speculative attack. It is becoming increasingly clear that, with globalized capital markets, only two exchange rate regimes are viable: a fully floating exchange rate or one rigidly fixed, like the currency board of Hong Kong.[34] However, the collapse of the currency board in Argentina shows that, for countries that do not have flexible domestic wages and prices, fixing the nominal exchange rate can lead to a misalignment of real exchange rates, and then to a prolonged recession which forces the necessary domestic wage-price adjustments. Unlike in the political world of the nineteenth-century gold standard, today, domestic politics will not usually tolerate a prolonged recession. The credibility of the currency board will thus be undermined, as it was in Argentina.[35]

Nor is there much to commend the recent movement in Latin America to replace domestic currencies with the dollar.[36] It is argued that domestic interest rates, even with a currency board, will remain above U.S. levels—because of the residual currency risk of the board's collapse. This unnecessarily raises the cost of borrowing, particularly to the government. Dollarization is recommended to lower interest rates to U.S. levels, and to allow domestic firms and the government to issue long-term international bonds. However, these potential cost savings from dollarization have to be set against the adjustment costs avoided by a flexible exchange rate system in the face of negative shocks that require a real exchange rate adjustment. The higher interest rates associated with a flexible exchange rate regime can be looked upon as an insurance premium that avoids these downside costs—a lesson underscored by Argentina's recent debacle with its currency board. So, apart from the unique case of Hong Kong, it appears that for most countries a flexible exchange rate is best suited to deal with the volatility of globalized capital markets.

A *third* feature common to the Asian crises was that it hit countries which had hitherto successfully followed the so-called "Asian" model of development.[37] Their debt crises exposed a systemic flaw in this model. A central

feature of the "Asian" model, as seen most clearly in South Korea, but pre-
saged by the development of Japan, is a close linkage between the domestic
banking system, industrial enterprises (particularly the biggest ones), and the
government.[38] The fatal danger of this "model" is that by making the banking
system a creature of the government's will, it creates tremendous moral hazard. The banks have no incentive to assess the creditworthiness of their borrowers or the quality of the investments their loans are financing, because
they know that, no matter how risky or overextended their lending, they will
always be bailed out by the government. This can lead in time to a mountain
of bad paper and to the de facto insolvency of a large part of the domestic
banking system—as happened in South Korea and Japan. But, as in the U.S.
savings and loan crisis in the late 1980s, the mess in the domestic banking
system can ultimately be cleared up, as is happening in South Korea and
Thailand as they bounce back after their crises.

A *fourth* factor behind the recent crises was the failure to hedge the foreign currency–denominated borrowing against the risk of devaluation. Businesses and banks had borrowed in dollars and lent in domestic currency for
investments in nontraded goods (especially real estate). When capital inflows
suddenly stopped, requiring a depreciation of the domestic currency, they
faced a balance sheet problem, as the domestic currency costs of servicing
their foreign currency–denominated debt rose without any rise in their domestic currency–denominated income. This spelled immediate bankruptcy.
As most emerging market economies are unable to issue debt denominated in
their own currency (what Ricardo Hausman has labeled "original sin"),[39] the
remedy for these "balance sheet" financial crises is for all foreign currency
debt incurred by residents to be hedged against foreign currency risk. In fact,
with a floating exchange rate, as the exchange rate is expected to fluctuate,
there is a built-in incentive for borrowers to hedge their debt against movements in the exchange rate. The costs of hedging will naturally raise the cost
of foreign borrowing and optimally restrict it given the market's perception of
the riskiness of the borrowing.

A fixed or adjustable peg exchange rate regime, by contrast, is based on
the implicit assurance by the government that the exchange rate will remain
stable so that hedging foreign currency–denominated borrowing is unnecessary. If the exchange rate has remained stable for some period (as it had done
in the Asian countries) this implicit assurance becomes more credible over
time, making it reasonable for the private sector to gamble on the exchange
rate remaining fixed by not hedging their borrowing. Thus, even in this case
of "original sin" I find the case for a floating rate trumps that for a fixed one.
The answer to "original sin" is to promote markets for hedging against foreign
currency if they are absent.

The financial crises of the last two decades have also been partly caused
and exacerbated by a *fifth* feature: international moral hazard. This relates to

the adverse effects of insurance on the behavior of the insured. Thus, for example, people taking out fire insurance could take less care to prevent a fire. All banking systems which have deposit insurance face moral hazard. But it is most acute in countries following the "Asian" model.[40] It has been aggravated by the actions of the IMF and the rise of foreign banks (subject to moral hazard themselves) as major international lenders. As their loans are usually denominated in dollars linked to LIBOR (London Interbank Offering Rate), borrowing countries maintaining a quasi-fixed exchange rate find that, when faced by a shock which requires devaluation, the domestic currency burden of the foreign bank debt rises *pari passu* with the changing exchange rate. If the debt is incurred by the private sector, and is unhedged (as it was in most of the Asian countries), this rising debt burden need pose no problem for the country—as long as when the foreign banks run, the private borrowers can default on their debt.

But now, enter the IMF. Ever since the debt crisis of the 1980s the foreign banks facing a default on their international loans have, in effect, sought an international bailout, by arguing that the resulting threat to their own solvency poses a systemic risk to the world's financial system. The IMF has been more than willing to oblige. For, since the end of the Bretton Woods exchange rate regime which it was set up to manage, the IMF has been like a character in Pirandello's play *Six Characters in Search of an Author*: searching for a possible play. The debt crisis of the 1980s provided one such play, the rocky transition of the Second World from plan to market another, and the Mexican, Asian, Brazilian, and Argentine crises a third. The IMF has increasingly become the international debt collector for the foreign money center banks, as well as an important but resented tool of U.S. foreign policy. It should be shut down.[41]

As regards the "Asian" model, despite appearances to the contrary, it is dead (see chapter 7). Countries are increasingly recognizing that only the derisively labeled "Anglo-Saxon model of capitalism" is viable in the long run. It alone can deliver that unprecedented prosperity offered by a globalized economy to all its participants. Hence, most of the countries involved in the recent financial crises are adopting its institutional bases: transparent financial systems and deeper financial markets which allow hedging of foreign currency risk, and either a floating or rigidly fixed exchange rate regime as in a currency board or a monetary union.

Capital Control

Yet many distinguished mainstream economists[42] are arguing that developing countries should prevent or tax the free flow of short-term capital to and from their economies through various forms of capital controls. China and India, with their tight capital controls, are cited as shining examples of countries

117

which escaped the contagion from the recent Asian financial crises. The temporary controls on outflows of capital in Mahathir's Malaysia are commended. I believe these views are profoundly mistaken.

We need to distinguish between transitory and permanent capital controls. While there may be a case for maintaining capital controls in the transition of repressed economies to full-fledged market ones, allowing time for their domestic banking and financial systems to deepen, there can be none for permanent capital controls. There may also be a case for temporary capital controls on capital outflows as instituted in Malaysia, but (though this did not happen in this case) there is a danger as with emergency trade protection that they will become permanent. Maintaining permanent capital controls, besides being an important denial of the economic freedom central to the efficient working of a market economy,[43] also impedes the associated efficiency gains.[44] Moreover, in an economy with a liberal foreign trade regime, capital controls will always be leaky, as the "leads" and "lags" in payments associated with trade can be used to make the desired capital transfers. Finally, as with trade controls, there are the additional costs of corruption and rent seeking.

Advocates of capital controls, recognizing these baneful effects of administrative controls on capital flows, seek instead to merely influence their composition through a tax system like the one used by Chile in 1978–82 and 1991–98. In these two periods, foreigners moving funds into Chile had to make non–interest bearing deposits at the Central Bank. The purpose was to slow down, and change the composition of capital flows: by discouraging short-term and encouraging long-term flows. Other aims were to prevent the appreciation of the real exchange rate, and to allow Chile to conduct an independent monetary policy by maintaining a differential between domestic and international rates. My UCLA colleague Sebastian Edwards' empirical study finds that "the effectiveness of Chile's controls on capital inflows has often been exaggerated. Chile's controls did appear to increase the maturity of its foreign debt significantly. However, even in 1966 more than 40 percent of Chile's debt to banks . . . had a residual maturity of less than one year, and the total volume of aggregate capital flows moving into Chile in the 1990s did not decline. The controls on inflows had no significant effect on Chile's real exchange rate, and a very small effect on interests rates. . . . [Also] the controls were unable to isolate Chile from the very large financial shocks stemming from East Asia in 1997–1999."[45] Also there were significant costs to the controls. The most important was the rise in the cost of capital for small and medium-sized firms which could not evade the controls.

"Fear of Floating"

It has been argued, in particular by Michael Bordo,[46] that in both the nineteenth century and late twentieth century, developing countries (or emerging market economies as they are now called) have had difficulty in adopting the exchange rate regime of the "core" countries—the gold standard in the nineteenth and the floating rate regime of the late twentieth century. This it is claimed is due to their financial immaturity which leads to the "original sin" of not being able to borrow abroad in their own currencies, hence their adoption of various intermediate exchange rate regimes in both periods. Today, most emerging market economies claiming to run clean floats are in fact engaged in various forms of dirty floating through managed floats. But, as Anna Schwartz has rightly noted, of this purported cause for the current "fear of floating":[47] "financial immaturity may be a euphemism for misguided monetary and fiscal policies."[48] As noted above, the problems caused by "original sin" are greatly exaggerated, and if developing countries did adopt a clean float the necessary markets for hedging foreign currency risk would emerge.

What of the tight controls on capital movements in India and China, the stability of their exchange rates, and their avoidance of any contagion from the Asian crises? In both countries, with the substantial liberalization of their trade and payment regimes, the major reason for maintaining capital controls is to keep the nominal exchange rate undervalued. India does this through a "dirty" managed floating system, China (till recently) by a fixed exchange rate to the dollar. This policy amounts to protecting their traded goods sectors, and is hence aptly called "exchange rate protection." It engenders economic inefficiency like any other form of protection and thus could damage long-run growth. It also leads to protectionist pressures in the United States and Europe.[49] Furthermore, to maintain the undervalued exchange rate, capital flows have to be continually sterilized and put into foreign exchange reserves. As these reserves are usually kept in the form of U.S. government bonds, there is the absurd situation that these poor countries[50] are unrequitedly financing the growing trade and fiscal deficits of the world's richest country, the United States. In India, moreover, the desire to prevent the rupee's appreciation by maintaining tight capital controls and partial sterilization of the inflows allowed, has led to economic growth being lower than it would otherwise have been.[51] It would make sense for both countries, once their financial systems have been strengthened, to abandon capital controls and float their currencies.

The classical liberal conclusions on capital controls stand. They are a major infringement of economic liberty. They are based on the wholly unjustified assumption that private agents are myopic, irrational, or both, and that benevolent, omniscient governments can save them from themselves. While temporary controls on capital can be a stopgap measure, long-run concerns about vulnerability from international capital flows are best met by pursuing sound macroeconomic policies, avoiding rigid exchange rates, promoting forward markets for hedging foreign currency–denominated debt, and instituting supervision of domestic banks to reduce moral hazard and corruption. As we saw, even in poor developing African countries, private agents can be expected to deal satisfactorily with any volatility in income streams, caused by those in capital flows or the terms of trade. Similarly, given the irreducible uncertainty and the accompanying problems of information they face, governments cannot be expected to run an "optimal" discretionary exchange rate system. It is best to maintain one of the automatic adjustment mechanisms—a fixed or floating exchange rate—which allows the balance of payments effects of the innumerable "gambles" of a myriad of private agents to be mediated smoothly. As between these two alternative exchange rate regimes, if there are rigidities in nominal wage and prices in the economy, a floating rate will provide a better alternative. Also, with the growing practice of maintaining a nominal anchor for domestic fiat money through an independent central Bank targeting inflation, and by maintaining fiscal balance, governments can ensure that their own policies are not adding to the unavoidable volatility to which any dynamic capitalist economy must be subject.

Multinationals

Direct foreign investment (DFI) and equity investments do not give rise to the above discussed risks of the "currency mismatch" of portfolio lending in the borrowing country. The multinational company, which is the embodiment of DFI, has become a major catalyst and instrument in implementing the emerging international division of labor (chapter 3). From being looked upon as instruments of neocolonial exploitation for much of the postwar period, multinationals are now being welcomed and wooed, not least by Communist China. But, for many they still remain the ugly face of global capitalism.

In the nineteenth-century period of globalization, portfolio investment was much more important than direct investment. In 1999, Lipsey[52] estimated that nearly 30 percent of the total world capital outflow was accounted for by DFI.

In the early postwar period much of the DFI was from the United States. In 1960, almost half of the world's outward stock of DFI was owned by the United States. This raised nationalist hackles not only in the Third World but also in countries like France.[53] Since then, ownership has become much more diffused, with many developing countries also participating. By 1999 they owned 10 percent of the outward stock of DFI, while the United States' share had fallen to 25 percent. Mining and public utilities were the main avenues for DFI in the past. Both have declined with the nationalization of natural resource and public utility sectors in many countries. With the increasing privatization of public utilities this might change in the future.

Much of the recent DFI has been in manufacturing. The share of this internationalized production in world manufacturing output has been estimated by Lipsey to be about 16 percent in 1990. The share of world employment absorbed by internationalized production was much smaller, about 1 percent in the late 1990s. Thus, though the importance of DFI in global manufacturing has grown, it is still quite modest compared with the inflated sense one gets of its global significance from the anti-globalization rhetoric.

Much of European DFI has stayed within Europe, though both it and Japan have been net suppliers of DFI. The United States in the 1980s was a net recipient of DFI, a net supplier in the early 1990s, and again became a net recipient in the second half of the 1990s. Developing Asia and Latin America have been the steady net recipients of DFI.

The virtues and vices of DFI in manufacturing are seen to stem from the associated attributes it brings (apart from the capital) of managerial expertise, new technology, and modern marketing methods, including advertising and foreign marketing connections.[54] Much of the passion surrounding DFI concerns the welfare effects on the host country. The only rational way to evaluate these is to examine the costs and benefits of DFI to the host country. Such studies done in the 1970s found that these welfare effects were by and large negatively correlated with the degree of effective protection provided.[55]

Much of the anti-multinational rhetoric is overblown. Multinationals have been accused of exploiting developing country labor by paying coolie wages. The evidence shows that, on the contrary, they pay (on average) higher wages than domestic enterprises, and also provide training whose benefits accrue partly to the nationals receiving it.[56]

Nor is there much merit in the oft-repeated charge that many multinationals are larger in size than the economies in which they operate, the implication being that there is therefore an unequal exploitative relationship. But, first, in these comparisons like is not often being compared with like: with the size of the multinational firms being measured by sales while that of countries is rightly measured by value added. When the appropriate adjustment is made for the multinationals, it turns out that rather than General Motors' "economy" being the world's twenty-third largest it is but the fifty-fifth, after the Ukraine.[57] As regards the purported domination by multinationals of the world, those large multinationals (like the oil majors) whose assets were arbitrarily confiscated by "small" states only wish it were so. For as long as any state has the monopoly of coercion within its borders, any multinational assets can be arbitrarily taken by force.

Nor is the bogey that multinationals lead to "a race to the bottom" as regards labor and environmental standards borne out by the evidence, as we saw in the last chapter. Nor have their activities led to a decline in the tax take of governments (as we have seen in chapter 2). The anti-globalizers have created a bogeyman to frighten us. All we need to say to them is—Boo!

The Global Financial Infrastructure

There has been much talk about restructuring the global financial infrastructure. Here the continuing atavism concerning credit and capital markets needs to be noted, as it explains the jaundiced view even many economists take of the workings of the capital markets.

Economic historians consider the creation of the national public debt and the Bank of England in 1694–96 as an essential element in the rise in economic and social status of the merchant and financier from the sixteenth to the eighteenth centuries.[58] This rise, however, posed severe problems for the "Aristotelian" ethical beliefs of European societies. Those beliefs concerned the ethical problem of ascribing virtue to the acquisition of wealth by the lending of money. The ban on interest was common to all the ethical systems of the pre-modern world. It was based on Aristotle's unequivocal statement that usury is detested above all and for the best of reasons. It makes profit on money itself, not for money's natural object. Money was intended as a means of exchange, not to increase with interest. This ban on interest was gradually lifted in the West. But ethical worries about the "unreality" of credit and the socially unproductive nature of interest resurfaced vigorously in eighteenth-century England following the financial revolution of the 1690s, which had created a vastly expanded credit mechanism, leading to the rise of the rentier. The stocks that were his title to a return upon the loans he had made, themselves became a commodity, and their value was manipulated by a new class: stock jobbers.[59] This posed a severe problem for the traditional value system shared both by opponents and friends of the new goddess Credit. In the traditional ethical system, the foundation for civic virtue and moral personality was independence and real property. Property in the form of land was the most real; and although the trader's and the merchant's wealth was movable, and hence not as reliable in inducing civic virtue as the landlord's, it at least consisted of things. By contrast, the wealth of the stockholder and the stock jobber created by the new system of public credit appeared to be unreal and fantastical: when the commodities to be bought and sold were paper tokens of men's confidence in their rulers and one another, the concept of fantasy could more properly be applied. It could bear the meaning not only of illusion and imagination but also of men's opinions of others' opinions of them.[60]

This is a view of commerce and the speculation it necessarily engenders that survives to our day in the outpourings of the various critics of global financial and capital markets. Lest it be considered the untutored prejudice of economic illiterates, one has only to remember Keynes's peroration on the stock market in his *General Theory*. The same suspicion of international capital markets is shown by those who want to throw sand in its works by imposing the so-called "Tobin tax" on capital flows.[61] This would be an international tax levied on short-term capital flows to reduce them and thence stem their volatility. There can be no justification for this: consider the absurdity of imposing a similar tax on domestic stock market transactions so as to damp their volatility. Similarly, many of the current proposals to improve the so-called international financial architecture are misconceived. Clearly, with the IMF exacerbating rather than preventing debt crises it can have no role in a liberal financial economic order, except perhaps as an international country risk-rating agency such as Moodies that can make use of its existing intellectual capital and access to national statistical data. The World Bank's intermediation role is also no longer required. Its only role left, if one believes this is needed, is as an "aid agency," which in effect is what the Meltzer Commission has proposed (to be discussed in chapter 5). This would demolish the now archaic structure put in place at Bretton Woods to meet the very different requirements of a moribund international financial system inherited from the aftermath of the Great Depression.

Would any replacement be needed? No is the short answer. Without the IMF, there would be no international moral hazard exacerbating the domestic moral hazard already facing domestic banking systems worldwide because of deposit insurance. Although it would be logical to end deposit insurance and with it the moral hazard that is endemic in a system with the mismatched maturities central to banking, it is politically infeasible in this democratic age; hence the calls for greater surveillance of bank portfolios by national or international authorities. But as the governor of the Bank of England Mervyn King[62] has rightly noted, in the limit this amounts to a call for the nationalization of banks.

Nor are the calls credible for the IMF to be converted into an international lender of last resort. Such a lender is required in domestic banking systems to counter the bank runs to which a fractional reserve banking system is prone. In such a system banks keep reserves to cover only a fraction of their deposits, lending out the rest to earn profits. As the bank's assets (the loans) have longer maturity than their liabilities (deposits), if the soundness of the bank's loans comes under suspicion, all depositors will seek to remove their deposits. As the bank's reserves are limited, they will find that they do not have sufficient liquid assets to cover the run on deposits. The lender of last resort is needed to provide them with the necessary liquid currency to meet the depositors' demand and thence stop the bank run.

There are two functions that a lender of last resort has to perform, as set out in Bagehot's famous rules.[63] First, it should be able to quickly create high-powered money to on-lend to solvent banks to prevent a liquidity crisis. Second, it must be able to distinguish between good and bad "paper" and thus to judge the soundness of the banks to which it is extending liquidity, while shutting down those which are insolvent. The IMF can perform neither task.

123

It can lend only after lengthy negotiations with a country's government and the approval of its own board. Also, it has no way of sorting out the "good" from the "bad" loans made, for instance, by foreign banks to residents in a country, liquidating only those that are "bad." The lender-of-last-resort function for the money center banks involved in foreign lending must therefore continue to be provided by their parent central banks.

It has been suggested that one of the functions of domestic central banks is not only to act as a conventional lender of last resort, but also to be a financial crisis manager.[64] A recent example is the 1998 rescue of Long Term Capital Management (LTCM) by the U.S. Federal Reserve, which instead of using any of its own funds got LTCM's creditors to lend in concert to keep the firm afloat. Similarly, when through his losing bets on forward markets, a young employee Nick Lesson brought the venerable Barings Bank to its knees, the Bank of England helped to find a new owner, but did not bail out Barings' shareholders.[65] It is now being suggested first, that this role of crisis manager is a part of the central bank's traditional lender-of-last-resort functions, and second, that this role should be internationalized. The chief advocate of the proposal is the former first deputy manager of the IMF, Stanley Fischer. On the first point, clearly the central bank's role of crisis management, though performed by the same institution, is distinct from that of the classic lender of last resort—a crisis lender. One can envisage this role being performed independently of the central bank. This lends some plausibility to Fischer's proposal that, even though the IMF cannot act as a crisis lender, it could and should act as a crisis manager.

But, it is not at all obvious what this means. Countries are not like domestic financial institutions. Both LTMC and Barings were financial institutions in crisis, refloated by the crisis manager organizing their takeover by other private agents. What would be analogous in the international sphere: that the IMF in its role as crisis manager should arrange for a country in financial crisis to be taken over? This rhetorical question shows the absurdity of the analogy. It could be argued that instead of this absurd role, it would be to facilitate an orderly restructuring of the country's unsustainable foreign debt which caused its financial crisis.

This is the basis of the recent proposal by the IMF's current First Deputy Managing Director Anne Krueger[66] for the IMF to oversee the orderly restructuring of sovereign debt along the lines of the U.S. Chapter 11 domestic bankruptcy procedures. It appears to have some prima facie plausibility. As Krueger explains, when a debtor country is unable to service its sovereign debt, a minority of bondholders can hold up the restructuring of the debt, even if agreed to by the majority. The recent success of the "vulture fund"—Elliot Associates—in suing Peru for full repayment and interest on the $20 million of government-guaranteed commercial loans it had bought highlights the problem posed by the lack of an orderly mechanism for restructuring sovereign debt. Elliot Associates refused to accept the Brady bonds, which other creditors were willing to accept in Peru's debt restructuring. Instead, it obtained a judgment for $56 million and an attachment order against Peruvian assets used for commercial activity in the United States. It targeted the interest payments that Peru was due to pay to its Brady bondholders, who had agreed to the restructuring. Rather than be pushed into default on its Brady bonds, Peru settled. This contrasts with the outcome of the Latin American debt crises in the 1980s, when most of the debt was in the form of syndicated bank loans that could be restructured in an orderly way by a steering committee of fifteen people holding about 85 percent of the debt. There was little incentive for holdout creditors to pursue claims through litigation, because they would have had to share any proceeds with fellow creditors.

This explains the proposal for a formal mechanism for sovereign debt restructuring. This mechanism would allow a country to come to the IMF and "request a temporary standstill on the repayment of its debts, during which time it would negotiate a rescheduling or restructuring with its creditors, given the Fund consent to that line of attack. During this limited period, probably some months in duration, the country would provide assurances to its creditors that money was not fleeing the country, which would presumably mean the imposition of exchange controls for a temporary period of time" (Krueger 2001).

The major flaw with this proposal is that, unlike a domestic bankruptcy court where the debtor has to disclose all its assets, on which creditors can be given a fair share of their claims, no such provision is included in the IMF proposal, and for a very good reason. Unlike domestic private debtors under Chapter 11, sovereign debtors will be *unwilling* to pay their debtors well before they are unable to do so. This is precisely because only their assets in foreign jurisdictions can be legally attached by their foreign creditors when they default. Peru after all settled with Elliot Associates, showing that it was *able* to pay. Similarly, in the major 1990s debt crises in Mexico and Indonesia, both countries had large state-owned oil companies whose assets could well have covered their debt payments if they had been willing to use them. The IMF proposal would therefore reduce the limited incentives currently existing for sovereign borrowers not to overborrow, and lead future creditors to further curtail their lending to these emerging markets. It would of course provide yet another possible play for the IMF. But apart from the difficulties involved (which are recognized by the IMF) in changing the legal system in most countries, the proposal is basically flawed. It does not recognize that unlike domestic bankruptcies, it is the very invulnerability to creditors' claims on the domestic assets of a sovereign borrower which makes it impossible to have an international sovereign bankruptcy scheme.

A simpler way to deal with the problem posed by a minority of creditors holding out in the restructuring of a country's debt is to adopt the practice of the London capital markets, which insert collective action clauses into international bonds. These clauses allow a 75 percent majority in a meeting with a quorum to amend the bonds. This stops a minority of bondholders preventing the restructuring of a country's debt. It is a decentralized and market-based solution, which the IMF too is now supporting. It is also favored by the U.S. Treasury[67] and the international banks. There would be no need for the IMF as an international crisis manager if it is widely adopted.

Does this imply that the volatility of international capital flows and the periodic "bubbles" in financial markets are unavoidable? The simplest answer is to think of international capital markets as merely an extension of domestic stock markets. No one has credibly argued that domestic stock markets, despite their undoubted volatility and proneness to "bubbles," should be shut down or have sand thrown in their works, as these purported cures would be worse than the presumed disease. The same line of argument applies to competitive international capital markets.[68] Although they are volatile and subject to "bubbles"—and "bubbles" always burst—any public intervention will only make matters worse.[69] So I can only echo the sage counsel of Lord Palmerston in 1848 when faced by calls for public action in the face of spectacular defaults on foreign bonds. In a circular eschewing any public action, he wrote: "The British government has considered that the losses of imprudent men who have placed mistaken confidence in the good faith of foreign governments would provide a salutary warning to others."[70]

5

Poverty and Inequality

In his recent book Joseph Stiglitz, Nobel Prize winner, former vice president of research at the World Bank, and the academic icon of the anti-globalization movement, writes: "A growing divide between the haves and have-nots has left increasing numbers in the Third World in dire poverty, living on less than a dollar a day. Despite repeated promises of poverty reduction made over the last decade of the twentieth century, the actual number of people living in poverty has actually *increased* by almost 100 million. This occurred at the same time that total world income actually increased by an average of 2.5 percent annually."[1] He cites World Bank statistics for his conclusion. This puzzled me because, on the basis of the detailed comparative study of the post–Second World war economic histories of twenty-five developing countries, one of the firmest conclusions of the Lal and Myint study was that growth above a certain level invariably decreased poverty—that "trickle-down" did work. So, how was it possible that, at a time in which the two largest Third World economies—India and China—with the largest numbers of the world's poor in 1980 and which had grown spectacularly at average rates between 6 percent and 8 percent in the two subsequent decades, the numbers of the world's poor had grown? Similarly, if these two of the poorest countries were growing at nearly twice to thrice the rate of the rich countries, how could the statement made in the World Bank's World Development Report for 2000/2001: "The average income in the richest twenty countries is thirty-seven times the average in the poorest twenty—a gap that has doubled in the past forty years" (p. 3) be correct? If true, these "facts" would support the rhetoric of the anti-globalizers, one of whom declaimed at the Doha meeting of the WTO in November 2001: "Globalization leads to the North getting richer, and the South getting poorer. . . . This is a direct consequence of globalization, and we need to stop this from continuing,"[2] or as another has stated: "the dramatic advance of globalization and neo-liberalism . . . has been accompanied by an explosive growth in inequality and a return to mass poverty and unemployment."[3]

Poverty Head Counts

Fortunately, an old colleague of mine at the World Bank, Surjit Bhalla, who now sensibly runs an economic research and asset management firm in New Delhi, has solved the mystery in an important book.[4] The answer concerns the misuse of statistics, as well as their unreliability in many cases, to support ideological conclusions about the state of the world. This gives me a tremendous sense of déjà vu.

In the early 1970s, I spent a year working as a high-level consultant to the Indian Planning Commission. For one of my tasks I had to examine how real wages of agricultural laborers had changed in India over the recent past. This was at a time of the Green Revolution in agriculture—concentrated in the states of Haryana and Punjab. The wage data, which were based on periodic detailed surveys undertaken by the staff of the highly respected National Sample Survey (NSS), showed that real wages were stagnant and might even have declined. On a field trip to the region, the growing prosperity, even of agricultural laborers, was evident. During the peak season, employers citing a chronic shortage were importing workers from across the country in Bihar. A local district commissioner confirmed that the large increase in the demand for labor flowing from the Green Revolution had led to a very large rise in real wages. How then, I asked him, was it possible that from the NSS data real wages had declined? He took me to a teashop, and pointed out some people sitting around gossiping and having tea in the middle of the morning. These he told me were the NSS investigators who were meant to provide the data by asking informants scattered all over the countryside to fill in the official questionnaires. Instead of going out into the field, they just drank tea and filled in virtually the same numbers as they had done on previous occasions. As real wages had hardly changed before the Green Revolution, this dereliction of duty went unnoticed. But it came to the fore when the fictitious real wage evidence they provided was used by all those who feared or hoped that the Green Revolution would turn Red![5]

A similar story emerged when, in early 2000, I was working at the National Council of Applied Economic Research (NCAER) in New Delhi, trying to reconcile the figures for poverty which emerged from their annual Market Information Survey of Households (MISH), with the numbers for the poor produced by the Indian Planning Commission based on the official NSS surveys. While the NCAER survey figures showed a marked decline in poverty with the acceleration of growth after India's 1991 economic liberalization, the Planning Commission figures showed no change or even a slight increase in poverty. Having found that there were no significant differences in the design, coverage, and size of the MISH and NSS surveys, we found that all the differences were due to the differences in the poverty figures for the states which had embraced economic liberalization and grown the fastest. While the MISH survey found a marked decline in poverty in these states, the NSS found none.[6] My suspicion (which we have no way of verifying) was that something like the process I had observed with the fictitious real wage data in the 1970s must have been operating. This suspicion is strengthened by noting that, while all the NSS investigators are permanent public employees with little prospect for advancement (and hence without any incentives or sanctions against shirking), the MISH investigators were freshly recruited each year from graduating students of various universities, trained, and then monitored with surprise visits by supervisors to ensure that they were not cheating. As with real wages in the 1970s, the NSS investigators were probably filling in the same data year after year sitting in their teahouses. In states where growth was stagnant and hence little alleviation of poverty could be expected, they would not be found out, but the fictitious data would show up in the unchanged poverty numbers in states where growth had been fastest and likely to have led to a decline in the numbers of the poor.

This unreliability of the statistics from the NSS is not merely of anecdotal value. It also lies behind a major statistical puzzle: why the divergence in the per capita consumption figures derived from these surveys of expenditure, and that derived from the national accounts, has been growing in India since the 1980s. While some divergence is to be expected because of the different coverage of the two sets of statistics, it is difficult to explain why this divergence should have been growing over time. In the past, because of the well-known divergence between the survey and national account data, the per capita consumption figures from the NSS were adjusted in line with the figures from the national accounts to derive the poverty figures. But, in 1993, the Indian Planning Commission decided to drop this practice and to rely on the NSS figures alone. Why? Because the World Bank had decided this was the best way to calculate the poverty figures in its 1990 World Development Report.

This was deeply ironic. The Indian Planning Commission and Indian economists were the pioneers of this poverty numbers game. Their method was a simple and persuasive one. You first decide the minimum basket of goods consumed which would demarcate those who were on the poverty line. Value this at current prices, and see what would be the income needed to acquire it. Anyone with a lower income than this poverty line would be classified as poor, and the numbers below this poverty line would be counted as the numbers of the poor. By adjusting for yearly inflation, this would provide a national poverty line which would allow the changing number of poor below it to be counted.

In the early 1970s, when Robert MacNamara became president of the World Bank, he decided to expand its role, from an agency intermediating capital flows between rich and poor countries, to an "aid" agency whose mission was to eradicate world poverty. Under his chief economist, Hollis Chenery from Harvard, a large research program was set up. One of its earliest tasks was to measure the extent of world poverty. Montek Ahluwalia, an Indian economist (who subsequently was one of the official leaders of the Indian economic liberalization of 1991) was put at the head of this effort. The Bank adopted the Indian method of deriving poverty numbers, including the Indian poverty line.

It also began a program to obtain the income (consumption) distribution data from developing countries which was required to estimate their poverty numbers. It began a program in association with the United Nations to estimate so-called purchasing power parity (PPP) exchange rates to make the Indian poverty line consistent across countries. These PPP exchange rates were needed to convert the rupee value of nontraded goods (like housing, haircuts, etc.) into their dollar equivalents. One can assume that Indian prices of internationally traded goods when converted into dollars at the official exchange rate would be broadly similar to the prices of these goods in the United States. But this is not the case for nontraded goods like haircuts, whose prices would be much lower in the poorer countries than the richer, as these prices depend in large part on local wages. The PPP calculations were to make adjustments for converting rupee haircut prices into dollars, so that a basket of goods consumed in rupees could be converted into its true dollar value.

With an international poverty line defined in these PPP dollars, and knowing the distribution of consumption in the relevant country, the numbers that fell below it could be readily estimated. This was the practice till the early 1990s. As no one had the necessary resources to provide the worldwide data needed to provide these estimates of global poverty, the World Bank has had a virtual monopoly in providing these figures, strengthened by the fact that till very recently it did not put the underlying data on which its estimates were based in the public domain.

In the 1990s, the World Bank inexplicably changed its practices in deriving these poverty numbers. This is the central contention of Surjit Bhalla's extensive detective work, done once the World Bank published its basic data in the late 1990s and independent researchers could check the derivation of its poverty numbers. Bhalla found that, in the early 1990s, the Bank switched from using the standard PPP exchange rates to its own consumption-based purchasing power parity rates, and most momentously to using the mean consumption from surveys like the NSS rather than from the national accounts to derive its poverty numbers.

No explanation is provided for the use of the "new" consumption-based PPP exchange rates instead of the traditional "official" PPP exchange rates. Bhalla found that, while for the developing world as a whole there was not much difference between the two rates, the new Bank rate was 18 percent below the official (UN) PPP rate for India and 5 percent higher for Africa. This means that the average consumption rate of Indians is reduced by 18 percent and that of Africans increased by 5 percent. This statistical sleight of hand by itself increases the number of poor in India and reduces them in Africa. But the increase in India, given its size relative to Africa, means that just by this one adjustment world poverty goes up!

Also the choice of mean consumption is crucial. For example, to estimate the consumption and income levels of the poorest fifth (the fifth quintile) of the population, one needs to multiply the fifth quintile's share in total consumption (obtained from the survey data) to the mean consumption level. Given the growing discrepancy between mean consumption estimated from expenditure surveys and the national accounts not only in India (where the mean consumption shown by the NSS surveys in 2000 was only 55 percent of that provided by the national accounts), but in many other parts of fast-growing Asia, the Bank's recent choice of the survey-based consumption mean to get its poverty figure inflates the numbers of the poor. When changes in these poverty numbers based on lower survey consumption means are related to the changes in income derived from the national accounts, the growing divergence between the survey and national account means leads to the higher poverty figures based on consumption means being illogically related to changes in the higher national account means. This by itself will lead to the paradoxical result about globalization and poverty claimed by Stiglitz. For, suppose that in 1980 the mean per capita income was $100 from the national accounts, and mean per capita consumption as shown by surveys was $95 (a 5 percent divergence between the survey and national income means). In 1990, the national income mean is $200, but because of the growing divergence between the two means, the consumption survey mean is only $110 (that is, it diverges from the national income mean by 55 percent as in India). The change in the poverty head count ratio (HCR) is say, a fall of 10 percent. If this change is then related to the change in the national income mean, which has doubled, it will appear that the marked increase in national income has had no effect on poverty alleviation. But, if the changes in poverty are based on the survey consumption mean, we should be comparing these with the changes in the consumption means, which is only 10 percent in this example. So, apart from the upward bias given to the poverty numbers by using the lower survey consumption mean, its increasing divergence from the national income mean gives the false impression that the true fast growth in per capita income has had little effect on poverty reduction.

These statistical tricks—using "new" and unexplained PPP exchange rates rather than the "official" PPP rates used till the 1990s, switching to survey consumption means rather than national account means previously used to derive the poverty HCRs, and comparing these consumption-survey based poverty numbers with the changes in the national account means—explain how the World Bank has come to lend support to the anti-globalization case: that globalization and its associated rise in per capita income has not alleviated poverty.

So what *has* happened to poverty in the developing world in the age of globalization? Bhalla answers this by resorting to the old World Bank and Indian methodology to obtain the poverty numbers. He finds that the proportion of people in the developing world living below $1 a day in terms of 1993 purchasing power declined from 30 percent in 1987 to 13.1 percent in 2000, which is a much steeper decline than the reduction from 28.7 percent to 22.7 percent estimated by the World Bank. Xavier Sala-Martin (2000a) of Columbia University, using the same data but slightly different methods, reaches much the same conclusion as Bhalla. There has been a substantial reduction in poverty in the developing world in the 1980s and 1990s. This was the period when, with China's opening under Deng Tsiao Peng, India's economic liberalization in 1991, and the gradual movement in Latin America from the plan to the market, brought much of the Third World into the global economy. Outside the former Soviet empire, Africa—which has not integrated into the world economy, and faces serious problems of governance—is the only region where poverty has risen. So, since 1980, when the growing integration of the Third World into the global economy signaled the true beginning of the current period of globalization, contrary to Stiglitz, the World Bank and the anti-globalization brigade, there has been a historically unprecedented decline in Third World poverty.

Bhalla, using other data assembled by World Bank researchers, also computes how world poverty had changed from 1820 to 2000.[7] Figure 5.1 shows the changing head count ratio (HCR) of poverty and the number of poor in the world, using the same poverty line and methods of estimation he used for the post–Second World War poverty numbers, while table 5.1 shows the changes in income and the reductions in the world HCR of poverty for various periods. From these, three periods can be broadly identified: the nineteenth-century period of globalization; the interwar period from 1929 to 1950 when the process of globalization stalled and was reversed; and the period from 1950 when a new international liberal economic order was reconstructed. But, as the Third World did not join this LIEO till 1980, the true second period of globalization is from 1980. Bhalla then calculates what he

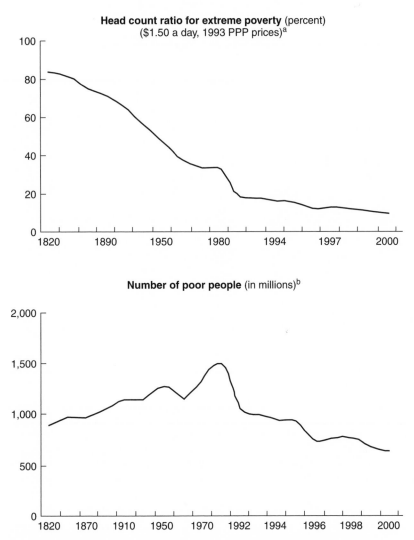

Head count ratio for extreme poverty (percent)
($1.50 a day, 1993 PPP prices)[a]

Number of poor people (in millions)[b]

Figure 5.1: World Poverty 1820–2000. a. The poverty line used is $1.50 a day, national accounts means, at 1993 prices. This is roughly equal to the popular $1-a-day, 1985-prices poverty line, when such a line is used with survey data. The $1.50-a-day poverty line incorporates within it the tendency for the rich to understate their expenditures to a greater degree than poor people, as well as the tendency for the rich to not be fully covered by surveys. b. Figures for the number of poor are computed by multiplying the estimated head count ratio by the world population. Source: Bhalla (2002), fig 9.1, p. 144. Derived from Deininger and Squire (1996); World Income Quality Database, available at http://www.wider.unu.edu/wiid; Asian Development Bank 2002; World Bank, *World Development Indicators*, CD-ROM. For years prior to 1950, data were taken from Bourguignon and Morrisson (2002).

TABLE 5.1
Poverty Reduction Yield of Growth

Time period[1]	Income		Head Count Ratio		
	Change	Equivalent 20-year change	Change	Equivalent 20-year change	Yield
1820–50	11.1	7.4	−2.4	−1.6	2.2
1850–70	19.0	19.0	−6.1	−6.1	3.2
1870–90	22.4	22.4	−3.6	−3.6	1.6
1890–1910	27.1	27.1	−6.1	−6.1	2.3
1910–29	21.9	23.0	−9.3	−9.8	4.3
1929–50	16.6	15.8	17.3	16.5	10.4
1950–70	51.3	51.3	−12.4	−12.4	2.4
1960–80	42.9	42.9	−4.6	−4.6	1.1
1970–90	28.2	28.2	−14.6	−14.6	5.2
1980–90	11.2	22.4	−13.6	−27.2	12.2
1990–2000	12.6	25.2	−9.7	−19.4	7.7
1980–2000	23.8	23.8	−23.3	−23.3	9.8
Mean		25.7		−9.4	3.5
Standard deviation			11.6	11.5	5.6

a. When a time period is either less or more than 20 years, the 20-year "equivalent" income or head count ratio change is presented, i.e., the actual change is multiplied by a fraction equal to (20 divided by the number of years); e.g., figures for 1910–29 will be multiplied by (20 divided by 19).

Note: The yield of growth is defined as the decline in poverty (head count ratio) brought about by each 10 percent growth in per capita incomes (data up through 1950) or per capita consumption (data for 1950 to 2000). Both income and consumption figures are national accounts based. The poverty line used is $1.50 a day, national accounts means, 1993 prices, for data for 1950–2000.

Sources: Bhalla (2002) p. 145. Derived from Deininger and Squire (1996); World Income Inequality Database, available at http://www.wider.unu.edu/wiid; Asian Development Bank (2002); World Bank, *World Development* Indicators, CD-ROM; for years prior to 1950, data taken from Bourguignon and Morrisson (2001).

calls the "poverty reduction yield of growth": the decline in the poverty head count ratio brought about by each 10 percent growth in per capita incomes— the "bang for the buck" in poverty reduction. From table 5.1 it is apparent that the head count poverty ratio was falling during both the nineteenth century and current periods of globalization, but rose during the period of anti-globalization in the interwar period. The highest yield in terms of poverty reduction has been since 1980, when the Third World started to integrate with the world economy. Africa is the only region where poverty has not declined and it is also the region that is least integrated into the world economy. The largest decline in poverty has been in Asia, but Latin America and the Middle East have also seen declines in poverty. So poverty today is by and large an African problem, and it is the behavior of its predatory elites, as well as their failure to join the globalization bandwagon, which explains most of to-day's poverty in the Third World. Thus, whereas in 1980—when the numbers of the world's poor peaked—the majority of the world's poor were in Asia, to-day they are in Africa.

It has also been claimed by the World Bank and others—particularly in the anti-globalization movement—that the growth which occurred was not "pro-poor," so that, despite the rapid growth promoted by global integration, not much poverty reduction took place. Bhalla shows that this is not true. He asks a simple question: did the consumption of those considered to be poor in 1980 (the bottom 44 percent) grow faster than that of the rest of the popula-tion (the remaining 56 percent) between 1980 and 2000—the period of glob-alization? For the developing world as a whole, its poor increased their income twice as fast as those who were not poor. Thus, the growth generated by glob-alization has not been anti-poor as the Jeremiads claim. Instead, globalization and the rapid growth it has promoted has reduced world poverty by histori-cally unprecedented amounts. Growth has not merely "trickled down" to the poor, it has been a flood!

Income Gaps

One of the major complaints of the anti-globalizers is that globalization in-stead of reducing has increased the disparity of average incomes between rich and poor countries. Similar claims were made in the 1950s by various dirigistes that integration with the world economy had led to a widening income gap between rich and poor countries because they were "unequal partners," as one of these authors titled his book. Global integration benefited the rich coun-tries at the expense of the poor. Various theories were developed to explain and deal with this "income gap." They created the Dirigiste Dogma which, I argued in my *The Poverty of "Development Economics,"* led to the disastrous policies which held the poor in developing countries in thrall. It was not till the new Age of Reform in the 1980s that parts of the Third World began to integrate with the world economy. But now new voices, whom we may label the New Dirigistes, are propounding another version of the Dirigiste Dogma, based on this purported growing gap between rich and poor.

So what is the evidence? Again, in the 1990s, the World Bank and its researchers have been at the forefront of the statistical conjuring yielding this result. They look at the per capita income of the twenty richest countries and compare them with those of the twenty poorest, at different points in time. This shows that, while in 1960 per capita incomes of the richer countries were twenty-three times that of the poorest twenty countries, by 2000 this gap had increased to thirty-six.[8] The trick lies in using the *shifting* composi-tion of the poorest countries over time to make the comparison. This is like

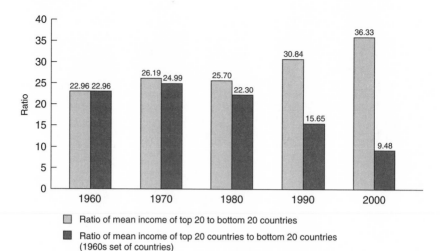

Figure 5.2: Convergence or Divergence? It Depends. For each year, the unshaded bar represents the income ratio of the mean-to-20 poorest countries in that year; the shaded bar represents the constant set of 20 richest and poorest countries in 1960. Source: Bhalla (2002), fig. 2.4, p. 26. Derived from World Bank, *World Development Indicators*, CD-ROMS, 1998, 2001; Maddison (2001); Penn World Tables, various years.

using an elastic ruler. For the comparison to have any meaning, one must keep the base constant, that is, one should see what has happened to the gap between the *same* set of countries—rich and poor—over time. Bhalla does this. The results from the World Bank method (using the shifting composition of countries) and Bhalla's method (of using the same set of countries) is shown in figure 5.2. The gap, on the correct method, instead of rising, declines substantially from 23 in 1960 to 9.5 in 2000. Moreover, the largest decline in the gap between rich and poor countries has occurred in the two decades of globalization since the 1980s. The World Bank has again perpetuated a myth based on statistical chicanery which has aroused anti-globalization passions.

But, whereas some might find it of interest to see how the gap between rich and poor *countries* has changed with globalization, from the viewpoint of judging the changes in welfare of *people*, we need to see how the incomes of the world's citizens have changed over the years. For this we need estimates of the distribution of income between all the people of the world, ignoring their place of residence—their countries. Bhalla has estimated these distributions for the post–Second World War period, as has Sala-Martin (for 1970–1998) based on the same data but using somewhat different methods. Their results are very similar.

A summary statistic to measure inequality is the Gini coefficient.[9] If

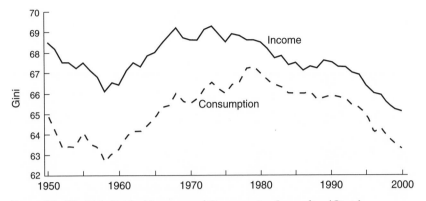

Figure 5.3: World Individual Income and Consumption Inequality (Ginis), 1950–2000. The simple accounting procedure method is used to derive world income distribution from individual country distributions. Source: Bhalla (2002), fig. 11.1, p. 174. Derived from Deininger and Squire (1996); World Income Inequality Database, available at http://www.wider.unu.edu/wiid; Asian Development Bank 2002; World Bank, *World Development Indicators*, CD-ROM.

there is complete equality the Gini will be zero, if complete inequality it will be 1. Figure 5.3 shows Bhalla's estimates of the Ginis for both the income and consumption of all the world's individuals from 1950 to 2000. These show a U-shaped pattern till 1980, as world individual inequality peaks, and then a steep decline from the 1980s, the period of globalization. So that, by 2000, world individual inequality was at its lowest since the previous trough in 1958. No better picture shows the equalizing forces of globalization.

Finally, figure 5.4, charting Bhalla's estimated income distributions for all the individuals in the world for 1960, 1980, and 2000, also shows the same equalizing effect of globalization since the 1980s. But more important, it graphically shows the growth of a world middle class, with the mean of the distribution shifting to the right. If the middle class is defined as the population above the U.S. poverty line of $10 per capita per day (= $365 annual per capita income) and below that of $40 per capita per day (= $ 14,600 annual per capita income), implying an annual income of $70,000 for a household of four, figure 5.4 shows a massive growth of a world middle class since 1980— the era of globalization. Most of this growth in the middle class has occurred in Asia. In 1960, only 6 percent of the world's middle-class population was Asian, with 63 percent in the industrialized world. Today, 52 percent of the world's middle class is Asian.[10] This is the miracle that globalization has wrought in the most populous part of the world.

Since the Great Divergence began with the rise of the West in the eleventh century (see chapter 1), the gap in per capita incomes between the West and the East (charted in figure I.1) inexorably widened, leading to rising

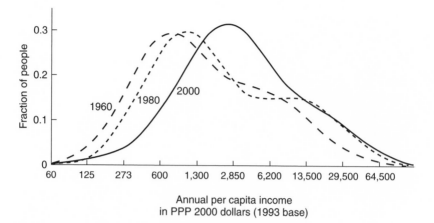

Annual per capita income
in PPP 2000 dollars (1993 base)

Figure 5.4a: World Income Distribution, 1960, 1980, and 2000. Note: Per capita income is calculated at 2000 prices. An 18 percent increase in prices between 1993 and 2000 (equal to U.S. inflation for the period) is used to convert 1993 prices to 2000 prices. The simple accounting procedure method is used to derive world income distribution from individual country distributions. Source: Bhalla (2002), fig. 11.3, p. 176. Derived from Deininger and Squire (1996); World Income Inequality Database, available at http://www.wider.unu.edu/wiid; Asian Development Bank 2002; World Bank, *World Development Indicators*, CD-ROM.

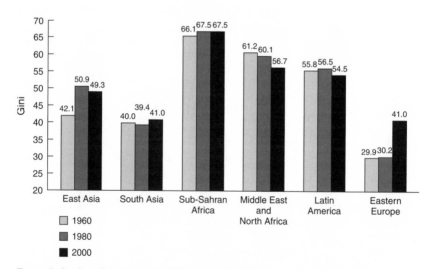

Figure 5.4b: Simple Accounting Procedure (SAP) Regional Measures of Income Inequality (Ginis), 1960–2000. Note: To obtain regional distributions of income, country data are pooled using the SAP method. Source: Bhalla (2002), Fig. 11.4, p. 177. Derived from Deininger and Squire (1996); World Income Inequality Database, available at http://www.wider.unu.edu/wiid; Asian Development Bank 2002; World Bank, *World Development Indicators*, CD-ROM.

world inequality. It is only in the current era of globalization that this gap has begun to decline. It was the rise of the West and the stagnation of the great Asian civilizations which was responsible for this growing gap. It was only with their most recent attempt to modernize and catch up with the West, by belatedly and still half-heartedly following the classical liberal policies (discussed in chapter 2), that these ancient civilizations have begun to close the gap. Growing global integration has been the motor for this transformation. Thus, contrary to the chants of the protestors marching through the streets of Seattle or Genoa, and despite the many financial crises which have plagued the developing world, globalization has been good for the world's poor and has reduced global inequalities.

Finally, what of inequality within countries during this globalized period of growth? In the historical case studies on which the Lal-Myint comparative study was based, we found no systematic relationship between growth and inequality. This had been confirmed in more recent studies.[11] There seems to be no systematic trend in Gini coefficients in developing countries.[12] Bhalla, however, finds that if one averages across the Ginis for all countries in the world, then compared with the pre-globalization period 1960–1980, in the post-globalization period this average world Gini has risen. But, this does not tell us much in itself. For, as Bhalla himself notes, "for long periods of time, inequality at the country level, does not display any significant change either way."[13] Since the 1980s some countries—notably the United States, China, the United Kingdom, Nigeria, and most spectacularly Russia and the East European countries—have seen an increase in their national inequality indices. Others, like Sweden, Brazil, and Mexico, show declining inequality, while in four of the largest Asian economies—India, Indonesia, South Korea, and Vietnam—there is no trend in inequality. As some of these countries have grown in the era of globalization while others (like the East European countries and many in Africa) have not, it is not possible to claim that globalization and the growth it engenders leads to growing inequality within countries. In any case, from the classical liberal viewpoint, this concern for inequality as opposed to poverty reduction is dubious at best. Even for those of a cosmopolitan egalitarian bent—as most anti-globalizers claim to be—it is surely the changes in the distribution of individual incomes in a world without borders which should be of relevance, and this as we have seen has unequivocally improved.

Foreign Aid

Why should the Indian Planning Commission, the World Bank, sundry UN agencies, and NGOs seek to show that the growth associated with globalization has not reduced world poverty and has increased inequality? Ideological reasons could be cited, but a much more powerful and persuasive reason is in terms of interest. The poverty numbers matter in India, because the allocation of central government grants to the states by its Planning Commission depends in part on the extent of poverty in each state. Each state, therefore, has an interest in seeing an inflation of its poverty numbers. Similarly, the varied NGOs who raise money for alleviating Third World poverty by appealing to the charitable instincts of Western citizens need to claim that the problem of world poverty is grave and not improving, so that more money is needed. The same is true of the various official foreign aid agencies. In fact, poverty alleviation has become a large international business, from which a large number of middle-class professionals derive a good living. It is not in the interest of these "Lords of Poverty," as a former East African correspondent of *The Economist* has labeled them,[14] to see poverty decline—as that would put them out of business.[15]

But, why should the World Bank, which was set up at Bretton Woods to mediate capital flows from rich to poor countries at a time when Western capital markets were closed to the Third World, want to play this game? The answer lies in the gradual transformation of the Bank into an aid agency. This was done through expanding the size and role of the International Development Association (IDA) set up in 1960 to provide loans at concessional interest rates to the poorest developing countries. By contrast, the original International Bank for Reconstruction and Development (IBRD) provided loans at nonconcessional rates to poor countries from the capital it raised by issuing its own bonds in Western capital markets. This intermediating role clearly helped in the more efficient allocation of global capital. As the World Bank's bonds carried the multilateral guarantee of the large number of states who were its owners, they carried the best rating for risk. This allowed the IBRD to borrow at somewhat lower interest rates than the "market" rate, a saving it passed on to its borrowers. By contrast, the money for the IDA—partly generated by the profits from the IBRD's intermediation role as a banker—came from periodic subscriptions made to IDA by rich country governments. These "soft" loans at highly concessional rates were meant to go to the poorest countries not able to afford the near market rates charged by the IBRD.

IDA, and the World Bank's overall lending, were expanded by member governments in the 1970s. The Bank's new mission was to alleviate poverty. This was reflected in the new research program noted above. The then World Bank President Robert MacNamara's obsession with numbers, however flimsy, led to a strong emphasis on the measurement of poverty.

As figure 5.5 shows, since the OPEC price coup in the early 1970s, and the recycling of the OPEC financial surpluses to developing countries by the offshore money center banks, private capital accounted for a growing and larger share of total capital flows to poor countries. This trend was reversed for some years in the mid-1980s because of the debt crisis, but has re-emerged

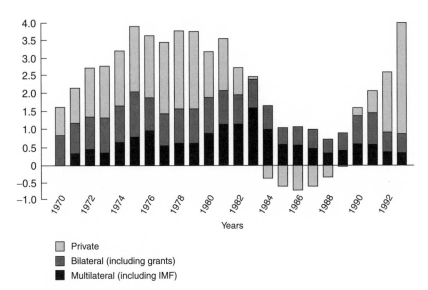

Figure 5.5a: Net Capital Flows to Developing Countries, 1970–1993. Source: World Bank 1995. Annual Bank Conference on Development Economics 1995, ed. M. Bruno and B. Pleskovic, p. 70.

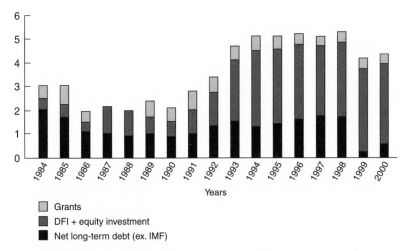

Figure 5.5b: Capital Flows to Developing Countries, 1984–2000. Source: World Bank: World Debt Tables and Global Financial Indicators.

more strongly in the 1990s. The intermediation role of the World Bank is thus no longer needed by well-managed economies, and some major foreign aid recipients like India have recently announced their decision to abjure official aid in the future. For the "lords of poverty" this is a disaster, and particularly for the World Bank as the largest "aid" agency in the world. If the millennium target for reducing world poverty to an HCR rate of 15 percent by 2015 has already been met, as the Bhalla estimates show, how can they continue to pull on our heartstrings to fund their hitherto profitable business? It is in this context that the debates about global poverty and inequality are of vital importance to all those well-meaning people who live well by claiming they are helping the world's poor.

But, is even this last claim true? The first thing to note is that foreign aid as a form of capital flow is novel both in its magnitude and global coverage.[16] Though there are numerous historical examples of countries paying "bribes" or "reparations" to others, the continuing large-scale transfer of capital from official sources to developing countries is a post–Second World War phenomenon. Its origins lie in the breakdown of the international capital market in the interwar period, as well as in the rivalry for political clients during the Cold War.

The first of these factors provided the impetus, as we have seen, for the creation of the World Bank by the Bretton Woods conference to provide nonconcessional loans to developing countries. With developed country capital markets, especially its largest—the United States, being shut to the Third World, official flows to LDCs at *commercial* interest rates, as laid down in the charter of the World Bank's parent—the IBRD, were justified on the grounds of efficiency in intermediating the transfer of capital from where it was abundant to where it was scarce.

This purely economic case was buttressed by political and later humanitarian justifications for *concessional* official flows. On the political reasons for giving aid, little can be added to Lord Bauer's devastating critique[17] that, by and large, Western political interests have not been well served by foreign aid, which instead fostered the formation of anti-Western coalitions of Third World states seeking "bribes" not to go Communist.[18] Moreover, as a statistical study by Mosley concluded: "as an instrument of *political leverage*, economic aid has been unsuccessful."[19] The end of the cold war has made this political motive redundant, as witness the growing "aid fatigue" bemoaned by the aid lobbies in the West. It is the humanitarian and economic case for foreign aid which is currently emphasized, though each has seen a metamorphosis over the years.

The humanitarian case for concessional flows was based on an analogy with the Western welfare state. But as many commentators not necessarily hostile to foreign aid[20] emphasized, the humanitarian motives for giving aid may have justified transferring Western taxpayers' money to poor *people* but not poor *countries*, and that giving money to the latter may have no effect on the former. Nor can the poor of the world claim a moral *right* for welfare transfers from the rich, on the line of argument used to justify *domestic* welfare payments. For the latter depends upon the existence of *national* societies with some commonly accepted moral standard. No similar *international* society exists within which a *right* to aid can be established.[21]

Nor has the foreign aid given to alleviate poverty been markedly successful in achieving its aims. Thus, the statistical study by Mosley concludes that foreign aid "appears to redistribute from the reasonably well off in the West to most income groups in the Third World *except* the very poorest" (1987, p. 23). This is in consonance with the evidence from both developing and developed countries that public transfers tend to be captured by the middle classes. By contrast, private transfers either through traditional interfamily channels or through private charities (currently called nongovernmental organizations—NGOs) are more efficient in targeting these transfers to the poor, as well as in delivering the so-called "merit goods" of health and education.[22] The centralized bureaucracies of the Western aid agencies are particularly inept in targeting these transfers to the truly needy as they lack the local knowledge on which it depends. Moreover, there is evidence that these inefficient public transfers tend to crowd out more efficient private transfer.[23] Not surprisingly, therefore, despite the continuing rhetoric (for instance of the World Bank's President John Wolfensohn) that the mission of official aid agencies is to alleviate Third World poverty, they are increasingly subcontracting this role to the NGOs. An increasing quantity of ODA is channeled through NGOs. In 1970, official sources accounted for 1.5 percent of NGO budgets. By "1998 they channeled $10 billion to developing countries of which half came from official sources" (World Bank 2001, p. 200).

Whether this official embrace of the NGOs is in the latter's long-term interest is arguable.[24] But in order to prevent this public embrace from crowding out the charitable private impulse which has fueled NGOs and set their performance above those of their public counterparts, I have argued that, if public transfers are to be made (for whatever reasons), they are best made through NGOs but with the proviso that the NGOs raise equivalent private funds on a matching basis.[25]

What of the purely economic arguments for foreign aid? The argument that official capital flows (albeit nonconcessional) were required to overcome the closure of private capital markets to developing countries in the first two postwar decades was supplemented by justifications for such flows based on the "two gap theory."[26] This claimed that foreign aid was required to fill one or the other of two shortfalls—in foreign exchange or savings—which depressed the growth rates of developing countries below some acceptable limit. Little need be said about the unrealism of the "foreign exchange" gap as it was, amongst other dubious assumptions, based on the extreme export pessimism that characterized the postwar climate of opinion in developing countries.[27] As both experience and theory have shown the irrelevance of this assumption, the "foreign exchange gap"–based justification for foreign aid has lost all force.

Nor has the "savings gap" justification proved to be any more cogent. Contrary to the theory that foreign capital is necessarily required to supplement fixed and inadequate domestic savings, the savings performance of developing countries in the post–Second World War period shows that nearly all of them (including those in Africa until the early 1970s) have steadily raised domestic savings rates since the 1950s.[28] Moreover, a comparative study of the experience of twenty-one developing countries between 1950 and 1985 confirms the commonsense expectation that differences in economic performance (in terms of growth rates) seem to be related more to the differences in the productivity of investment than its level.[29] Finally, statistical studies of the effects of foreign aid on growth and poverty alleviation have not been favorable. An earlier study found that, even after correcting for the link between aid and income levels and growth, the effect of aid on growth is often negative,[30] while a recent survey of subsequent studies finds that "there is now widespread skepticism that concessional assistance does have positive effects on growth, poverty reduction or environmental quality."[31] More recently two IMF economists (Rajan and Subramanian 2005) have surveyed the past literature and provide the most comprehensive statistical cross-section study of the effects of aid on growth. They conclude: "We find little robust evidence of a positive (or negative) relationship between aid inflows into a country and its economic growth. We also find no evidence that aid works better in better policy or geographical environments or that certain forms of aid work better than others" (p. 1).

This is hardly surprising, for, except for sub-Saharan Africa, under 2 percent of investment in developing countries is financed by the World Bank.[32] Most of the Bank's lending continues to finance projects. Though these projects have earned rates of return of more than 10 percent, this cannot be taken as a measure of the true effects of the "aid" provided. For money is fungible. So a country which finances a high-yielding project it would have undertaken in any case through "aid" can use its own resources freed by this "aid" to finance a project with a low rate of return (say, more armaments). This problem led to the growth of "program" lending in the 1980s in the form of "structural adjustment" loans. But they never accounted for more than one-fifth of World Bank lending.[33] It was hoped that, through applying conditions to the program loans, the general policy environment and thence the effectiveness of aid would improve.

But, numerous studies have found this policy "conditionality" to be ineffective. Not only is aid not necessarily used for what it had been intended, but on average it has no effect on growth, either directly, or indirectly through improved government policies. What matters is the policy environment, but this is not directly affected by official lending.[34] This is hardly surprising, for, as the adage has it: "You can lead a horse to water, but you can't make him drink." Governments make all sorts of promises to get the loan, which they renege once they have taken the money and run. Moreover, the Bank cannot call their bluff, for, since McNamara's expansion of its role and lending, it has been an institution geared to lending as much as possible. The individual Bank bureaucrat's prospects depend upon how much he lends, not on the outcome of the lending. There is thus a mutual interest of both the principal (the Bank) and the agents (recalcitrant governments) to turn a blind eye to the nonfulfillment of the conditions on economic policy.

Not surprisingly, the effectiveness of "aid" and policy advice will depend on the nature of the governments. Most of the technocratic advice offered is based on the assumption that all governments are made up of Platonic Guardians. But, there are good reasons to believe that many Third World governments are likely to fit the predatory mold rather than the Platonic. Moreover as the Lal-Myint study documents, it is the relative resource endowments of their economies which determine their behavior. Governments in countries with relatively rich natural resource endowments behave in a more predatory fashion than those without.[35] The East Asian NIC's fall into the latter category, most in Africa and Latin America in the former. It is not surprising therefore that both Nyereres Tanzania and Castros Cuba, client states of the West and the East respectively in the Cold War, should have suffered foreign aid–mediated development disasters. It would also explain another finding that "aid has had a significant effect on development in Asia and very little in Africa."

Nor is it credible that it was the "conditionality" of the structural adjustment and stabilization programs, and the accompanying money, which turned the debt crisis countries—and others—from the plan to the market. As the Lal-Myint study documents, the economic liberalization that has occurred was due to the "crisis" in governability which past dirigisme had engendered. The chronic fiscal deficits, hyperinflation and balance of payments problems, and growing black economies—as private agents sought to escape the government's explicit and implicit tax net—were symptoms of the collapsing fiscal base of these dirigiste governments. As happened in the last great Age of Reform in the nineteenth century, economic liberalization was undertaken to restore the tax base (see Hecksher 1955). No multilateral conditionality was required for these self-interested predatory states to undertake the liberalization which was motivated by their own interest rather than that of their prey—the general populace. On the other hand, the money which flowed into the public coffers as part of these multilateral aid programs, to the extent it eased the predator's fiscal problem, would have reduced rather than increased their incentive to reform.

145

The latest play in the "aid" game is to suggest that as the current "ex ante" conditionality has failed, "ex post" conditionality should be used instead. This implies that, rather than seeking promises for better future actions, Third World governments should be judged by their past actions, and "aid" be given only to those whose policy environment has been known to be better than their comparators. This will, besides providing an incentive to the laggards to improve their policies, also mean that whatever aid is given will be effective. But, there are two objections. The whole purpose of aid was supposed to improve the economic performance of countries that could not help themselves. If the basket cases are to be left behind because of their predatory governments, what happens to the humanitarian arguments which have supported aid? Second, and most important, with the opening up of the world's capital markets to well-run developing countries, what incentive is there for them to turn to the Bank, and its onerous procedures and conditions for loans, when they can get these as easily and with much less effort from a syndicate put together by Goldman Sachs? The argument that well-run countries might still be shunned by the private credit market because of bad neighborhood effects—investors assume that even a well-run country is like the average badly run country in Africa—can be countered by the Bank providing credit ratings for countries like Moody's. No loans would be required.

It is, however, being suggested[36] that even in this latest phase of the revival of private capital flows to the developing world, multilateral conditionality can provide a collective stick to keep Third World governments honest, which in turn could stimulate larger private capital flows. But, this must imply that the multilateral agencies were given positions on the boards of private lending agents, for otherwise what sanctions could they apply if they were not lending their own money.

Nor is it persuasive that there is still a role for official flows to those countries—mainly in sub-Saharan Africa—shunned by the private market. Private investors—both domestic and foreign—are unwilling to invest in these countries because of the predatory nature of their governments. Without dealing with these problems of governance—which short of imposing some new form of imperialism cannot be imposed externally—there is little chance of these loans leading to any development. Worse, from the viewpoint of the multilateral agencies, with all the sound borrowers avoiding them because of their access to an apolitical private capital market without any onerous "conditionality," the only remaining borrowers are the "lemons." This would have serious repercussions in their credit rating in Western capital markets, and thence in their ability both to raise money and provide loans at subsidized interest rates to their clients.

Various intangible benefits are also adduced from the operation of the World Bank and the IMF. These have more merit. My colleague Al Harberger[37] has always maintained that the most important benefit of these institutions has been their "tutelage" role, through both the in-house train-ing offered to its international staff—many of whom have become policy makers in developing countries—in the lineaments of sound economic meth-ods and policies, and in conveying ideas about development policy to the whole developing world. For this task, these institutions not only collect a vast amount of data on developing countries, but also conduct research which has broadened our understanding of development. On this view, the World Bank should become a "Knowledge Bank."

Although these arguments may have carried weight in the past—and I myself have justified the Bank's operations in these terms[38]—they increas-ingly carry less weight. Unlike the 1950s and 1960s when many countries did not have the necessary domestic technical personnel to conduct sound eco-nomic policy, there has been a sea change in their availability over the last two decades—except perhaps for Africa. Moreover, the "tutelage" and educa-tional role crucially depends upon the soundness of the curriculum. Till the coming of James Wolfensohn as president of the World Bank, despite passing fads, the World Bank's intellectual stance was in consonance with main-stream economics. But this has changed.

As Anne Krueger—a former Vice President for Research at the Bank—noted, the World Bank faced three choices in the mid-1990s with the opening up of world capital markets to most developing countries outside Africa. These were: "(1) continue to be a development institution, focusing only on those countries that are truly poor and gradually phasing out activities in the middle-income countries; (2) continue to operate in all client countries, focusing on the "soft issues" of development such as women's rights, preservation of the environment, labor standards, and the encouragement of nongovernmental organizations (NGOs); (3) to close down."[39] For the reasons given above, the first alternative is becoming more and more difficult, and would involve a considerable downsizing of the Bank. No bureaucrat wants that, and least of all the adoption of the third alternative, as it implies loss of power, prestige, and money.[40] So, Wolfensohn has understandably chosen the second alterna-tive.[41] The political support for "aid" had in the past come from the "right" concerned with security, and from the "left" on humanitarian grounds. With the end of the Cold War, support from the Right eroded, and Wolfensohn has probably sought to broaden the Bank's political support base by embracing so-called civil society issues.[42]

The battle between the "old" and "new" curriculum centered around the World Bank's *World Development Report 2000/1: Attacking Poverty*. This cre-ated a fierce storm between Joseph Stiglitz, Wolfhenson's chief economist—representing the "new"—and the IMF with its First Deputy Managing Direc-tor Stanley Fischer, and the U.S. Treasury with its Deputy Secretary Lawrence Summers—representing the "old." This is not the place to go into the ensuing denouement.[43] However, the report's chief author Ravi Kanbur[44] has perceptively outlined the issues separating the two sides, which he has labeled the "finance ministry" and "civil society" views. The former group includes finance ministries around the world, economic analysts, the economic policy managers in the IFIs, the international financial press, and most mainstream economists. The second group consists of officials of the NGOs and "people who worked in some of the UN specialized agencies, in aid ministries in the North, and social sector ministries in the South. Among academics, noneconomists would tend to fall into this group."[45] So, clearly the former groups consist of the professionals in the economic development business, the second of the self-serving and the uninformed, with their own special—often ideological—agendas (see chapter 8).

What are the issues separating them? They all concern the so-called "Washington Consensus," the classical liberal package of economic policies which has the capacity to eliminate world poverty through the globalization it promotes. The finance ministry types are in favor, the civil society ones are against. Their differences arise, says Kanbur, because of disagreements about aggregation, time horizons, and market structure and power.

On aggregation, while the finance ministry views are based on the type of aggregate statistics we have discussed in this chapter to see the changing incidence of poverty, the civil society view is concerned much more with the changes in poverty levels of much smaller groups, regions, villages. As Kanbur says, for a ground-level NGO, even though the incidence of poverty has declined: "If the number of people turning up at soup kitchens, the number of indigents who have to be provided shelter, the number of street children increases, then those who work in these organizations, quite rightly from their perspective argue that poverty has gone up." But, surely the whole purpose of economic analysis and measurements is to go beyond these local impressions, and see what is happening to the whole.

On the time horizon, Kanbur states, whereas civil society is concerned with the short-run effects of policies, the economists of the finance ministry views are concerned with the medium term. The economists are surely right, as the effects of any policy take time to work themselves out. All economic policy change must lead to gainers and losers in the short term, but if in the medium term when the necessary adjustments have been made, the change in policy leads to everyone gaining, should one concentrate merely on the short-term pain and forget the long-term gains? For the short-term losers every economist has advocated social safety nets to alleviate this conjunctural poverty.[46] But, if the policy is sound, we would expect everyone to be better off once the adjustments to the new economic circumstances have been made. However, these social safety nets do not need to be public ones. For, human beings have known for millennia that change is ubiquitous and have found numerous ways of insuring against its vagaries—the most important being through the family. The major social safety nets that have existed over time are in the form of private intra-household transfers. These are still wide-spread and robust in many developing countries. Where these private social safety nets do not exist or are weak, there is clearly a case for public safety nets. But these require an efficient and functioning government.

The third area of disagreement concerning market structure and power reflects an old complaint about capitalism which I discuss more fully in chapters 6 and 7. Many dirigiste economists have chimed in, not least Joseph Stiglitz, by recommending smart government interventions on the basis of their *theoretical* deductions. But, as we saw in chapter 2, these are of little use in designing policy in the real world.

Thus, though Kanbur makes a plea for understanding and mediation between the finance ministry and civil society types, this is like asking a scientist who has through measurement and analysis found the earth is round to take account of the views of the man in the street who sees and knows it is flat. In this purported dialogue between the deaf, what the proponents of civil society and their acolytes at the World Bank need is a hearing aid.

Clearly, the second of the three paths chosen by Wolfensohn is unviable. In championing civil society, it is supporting highly contentious issues on which there is limited agreement about either ends or means. In part this is because some of these issues raise important differences in cosmological beliefs (see chapter 6), and in part because, like labor standards—which Wolfensohn's Bank has made a requirement for its multilateral investment guarantee branch (MIGA)—they are not only rejected by developing countries, but rightly so for going against the development objective of alleviating poverty which the World Bank has rightly espoused.[47] This leaves only the third of Krueger's options for the future of the World Bank. It should be shut down.

Our conclusion can be brief. The foreign aid programs of the last half-century are a historical anomaly. They are best seen as part and parcel of the disastrous breakdown of the nineteenth-century liberal economic order spanned by the two world wars. But, just as a new liberal economic order is gradually being reconstructed, with a milestone being the collapse of the Second World and its growing integration in the world economic order, the various palliatives devised to deal with the dreadful woes bred by the past century's economic breakdown are becoming more and more redundant. It is time to pension off the Lords of Poverty. Foreign aid is an idea whose time has passed!

6

Morality and Capitalism

Introduction

The arguments I have advanced and the evidence presented in previous chapters will not convince the Western anti-globalizers. For their real case against globalization is that it promotes global capitalism, of which they disapprove. Their disapproval is not merely based on the erroneous belief that global capitalism promotes poverty and inequality, but on an underlying belief in the immorality of capitalism. These are old objections, but not for that reason to be dismissed. Capitalism, it is believed, is based on the power of the economically strong to coerce the weak. It is fueled by that ancient Christian sin of greed. It is necessarily corrupt, as the rich steal from the poor, as witness the recent Wall Street scandals surrounding Enron and WorldCom. It leads to a growing concentration of economic and thereby political power in the hands of unelected and thence undemocratic captains of business who run the multinational companies which are the hallmarks and whipping boys of global capitalism. These bosses are only interested in feathering their own nests and keeping the rest of humanity as wage-earning helots in a consumerist society, whose advertising and the media feed various forms of mind-numbing sedation, leading to that *mauais foi* which keeps the oppressed from recognizing their miserable state. The prosperity globalization fosters is only at the expense of destroying the natural world of Spaceship Earth. These complaints are as old as the Romantic revolt against the Enlightenment and its "disenchantment of the world." These moral concerns of many in the West about global capitalism are juxtaposed with the desire of others in the

West, to use the current American imperium to legislate their "habits of the heart" around the globe.

For the cultural nationalists of the Third World, the economic arguments advanced in the previous chapters in support of globalization will also seem beside the point. For them, too, like the Romantics, globalization and the modernization it brings is "a desert in which everything has been leveled, and all beauty been stamped out to create a mundane serviceable world of use objects."[1] Globalization is seen as a Faustian pact where prosperity is bought at the cost of losing one's soul.

What is the relationship between morality and capitalism? Are the cultural nationalists right that the modernization that globalization entails will lead to Westernization and the losing of their souls? Are there some universal moral norms which will allow us to appraise particular economic arrangements? Is the "rights talk" used to justify various dirigiste regulations cogent? Is there a Third Way between capitalism and the failure of the countries of "really existing socialism"—for "capitalism with a human face"? These are the questions I will address in this and the next chapter, as they are central in countering both the fear of globalization of the cultural nationalists in the Third World and the New Dirigisme of the traditional enemies of global capitalism in the West.

Analytical Framework

From an economist's perspective, morality is best looked upon as part of the institutional infrastructure of a society. This institutional infrastructure, broadly defined, consists of informal constraints like cultural norms (which encompass morality) and the more formal ones which are embodied in particular and more purposeful organizational structures. Inter alia such formal rules embrace the Common Law which forms a spontaneous order in Hayek's sense[2] as having evolved without any conscious design—which constrain human behavior.

But as soon as we talk about constraining human behavior, we are implicitly acknowledging that there is some basic "human nature" to be constrained. While we take up this question in greater detail below, as a first cut we can accept the economists' model of "Homo Economicus" which assumes that human beings are self-interested and rational: maximizing utility as consumers and profits as producers. So as a start, the function of the rules constraining human nature which comprise institutions must be to limit self-seeking behavior.

This immediately points to another significant feature and reason for the existence of institutions. If Robinson Crusoe was alone on his island, he would have no reason to constrain his basic human nature. It is only with the appearance of Man Friday that some constraints on both him and Crusoe

151

might be necessary for them to cooperate in order to increase their mutual gains: and to do so by specializing in tasks in which each has a comparative advantage. This, then, immediately leads us to the notion of "transactions costs"—a concept that is even more slippery than that of institutions.

The reason there is a close relation between institutions and transactions costs is that, as Robin Matthews pointed out several years ago, "to a large extent transactions costs are costs of relations between people,"[3] and institutions are par excellence ways of controlling or influencing the form, content, and outcome of these interactions.

Culture is the informal aspect of institutions which constrain human behavior. But if "institutions" are a murky concept, "culture" is even more so. I have found an interpretation adopted by ecologists particularly useful. They emphasize that, unlike other animals, the human one is unique because of its intelligence and its ability to change its environment through learning. It does not have to mutate into a new species to adapt to the changed environment. It learns new ways of surviving in the new environment and then fixes them by social custom.[4] These social customs form the culture of the relevant group, which are then transmitted to new members of the group (mainly children) who do not then have to invent these "new" ways de novo for themselves.

This definition of culture fits in well with the economists' notion of equilibrium. Frank Hahn has described an equilibrium state as one where self-seeking agents learn nothing new so that their behavior is routinized. It represents an adaptation by agents to the economic environment in which the economy "generates messages which do not cause agents to change the theories which they hold or the policies which they pursue."[5] This routinized behavior is clearly close to the ecologist's notion of social custom which fixes a particular human niche. On this view, the equilibrium will be disturbed if the environment changes, and so, in the subsequent process of adjustment, the human agents will have to abandon their past theories, which would have been falsified. To survive, they must learn to adapt to their new environment through a process of trial and error. There will then be a new social equilibrium, which relates to a state of society and economy in which "agents have adapted themselves to their economic environment and where their expectations in the widest sense are in the proper meaning not falsified."[6]

This equilibrium need not be unique or optimal. But once a particular socioeconomic order is established, and is proved to be an adequate adaptation to the new environment, it is likely to be stable. For, unless the environmental parameters change, there is no reason for the human agents to alter it in any fundamental way. Nor is this social order likely to be the result of a deliberate rationalist plan. We have known since Adam Smith that it is possible for an unplanned but coherent and seemingly planned social system to emerge from the independent actions of many individuals pursuing their different ends, with final outcomes very different from those intended. Thus, the self-interested actions of individuals, coordinated through an unplanned market, can lead to unintended mutual gains.

It is also useful to distinguish between two major types of beliefs relating to different aspects of the environment. These are the *material* and *cosmological* beliefs of a particular culture. The former relate to ways of making a living, involving beliefs about the material world, in particular about the economy. The latter relate to our understanding of the world around us and mankind's place in it, which, in turn, determine how people view the purpose and meaning of their lives and interpersonal relationships. There is considerable cross-cultural evidence that material beliefs are more malleable than cosmological ones. Material beliefs can respond rapidly to changes in the material environment. There is greater hysterisis in cosmological beliefs, on how, in Plato's words, "one should live."[7] Moreover, the cross-cultural evidence shows that, rather than the environment, it is the language group to which people belong that influences these worldviews.[8]

This distinction between material and cosmological beliefs is important for economic performance as it translates into two distinct types of transactions costs. These are of importance for explaining not only "market" but also "government" or "bureaucratic failure." Broadly speaking, transactions costs can usefully be distinguished as those associated with the efficiency of exchange, and those associated with policing opportunistic behavior by economic agents. The former relate to the costs of finding potential trading partners and determining their supply-demand offers, and the latter to enforcing the execution of promises and agreements.

These two types of transactions costs are distinct. The economic historian Douglass North (1990) and the industrial organization theorist Oliver Williamson (1985) have both evoked the notion of transactions costs and used them to explain various institutional arrangements relevant for economic performance. While both are primarily concerned with the costs of opportunistic behavior, for North these arise as a result of the more idiosyncratic and nonrepeated transactions accompanying the widening of the market, whilst for Williamson they stem from the asymmetries in information facing principals and agents, in cases where crucial characteristics of the agent (employees) relevant for measuring performance can be concealed from the principal (employer). In both of these cases, it is the policing aspects of transactions costs which are at issue, not those concerning exchange.

To see the relevance of the distinctions concerning beliefs and those concerning transactions costs for economic performance, it is useful to briefly delineate how material and cosmological beliefs have changed since the Stone Age in Eurasia.

Changing Material and Cosmological Beliefs

On Human Nature

Evolutionary anthropologists and psychologists maintain that human nature was set during the period of evolution ending with the Stone Age. Since then, there has not been sufficient time for any further evolution. This concept of human nature appears darker than Rousseau's and brighter than Hobbes' characterizations of it. It is closer to Hume's view that "there is some benevolence, however small . . . some particle of the dove kneaded into our frame, along with the elements of the wolf and serpent."[9] For even the hunter-gatherer of the Stone Age would have found some form of (what evolutionary biologists term) "reciprocal altruism" to his own benefit. He would have discovered that in his various tasks, cooperation with one's fellows yielded him gains, but which might be further increased if he could cheat and be a free rider. In the repeated interactions between the selfish humans comprising the tribe, such cheating could be mitigated by playing the game of "tit for tat." Evolutionary biologists claim that the resulting reciprocal altruism was part of our basic human nature in the Stone Age.

Archaeologists have also established that the instinct to "truck and barter," the trading instinct based on what Sir John Hicks used to call the "economic principle"—"people would act economically; when an opportunity of an advantage was presented to them they would take it"[10]—is also of Stone Age vintage. It is also part of our basic human nature.

Agrarian Civilizations

With the rise of settled agriculture and the civilizations that evolved around them, social stratification arose between three classes of men—those wielding respectively the sword, the pen, and the plow. In these agrarian civilizations most of the Stone Age basic instincts would be inadequate or dysfunctional. Thus, with the multiplication of interactions between human beings in agrarian civilizations, many of the transactions would have been with anonymous strangers who might never be seen again. The reciprocal altruism of the Stone Age which depended upon a repetition of transactions would not be sufficient to curtail opportunistic behavior.

Putting it differently, the "tit for tat" strategy for the repeated Prisoners Dilemma (PD) game among a band of hunter-gatherers in the Stone Age would not suffice with the increased number of one-shot games consequential upon the arrival of settled agriculture, and the widening of the market for its output. To prevent the resulting dissipation of the mutual gains from cooperation, agrarian civilizations internalized restraints on such "antisocial" action through moral codes which were part of their "religion." But these "religions" were more ways of life as they did not necessarily depend upon a belief in God. The universal moral emotions of shame and guilt are the means by which these "moral codes" embodied in cultural traditions are internalized in the socialization process during infancy. Shame was the major instrument of this internalization in the great agrarian civilizations. Their resulting cosmological beliefs can be described as being "communalist."

The basic human instinct to trade would also be disruptive for settled agriculture. Traders are motivated by instrumental rationality which maximizes economic advantage. This would threaten the communal bonds that all agrarian civilizations have tried to foster. Not surprisingly, most of them have looked upon merchants and markets as a necessary evil and sought to suppress them and the market which is their institutional embodiment. The material beliefs of the agrarian civilizations were thus not conducive to modern economic growth whose major institutions can be summed up as capitalism.

The Rise of the West

The great divergence of Western Europe from the other Eurasian civilizations occurred, I have argued in *Unintended Consequences,* because of a change in the cosmological and material beliefs mediated by the Catholic Church in the sixth through eleventh centuries, through its promotion of individualism, first in family affairs and later in material relationships. The first were a series of pronouncements by Pope Gregory I in the sixth century on family matters,[11] and the second those by Gregory VII in the eleventh century on property and institutionally related issues.[12] These can be called the twin papal revolutions of which Gregory VII's in the eleventh century included the introduction of all the legal and institutional requirements of a market economy, which eventually put the West on a different economic trajectory from its Eurasian peers.

These twin papal revolutions arose because of the unintended consequences of the Church's search for bequests—a trait that goes back to its earliest days. From its inception it had grown as a temporal power through gifts and donations—particularly from rich widows. So much so that, in July 370, the Emperor Valentinian had addressed a ruling to the Pope that male clerics and unmarried ascetics should not hang around the houses of women and widows, and try to worm themselves and their churches into their bequests at the expense of the women's families and blood relations. Thus, from its very beginnings the Church was in the race for inheritances. In this respect, the early Church's extolling of virginity and preventing second marriages helped it to create more single women who would leave bequests to the Church.

This process, of inhibiting a family from retaining its property and promoting its alienation, accelerated with the answers that Pope Gregory I gave to some questions that the first Archbishop of Canterbury, Augustine, had sent in 597 concerning his new charges. Four of these nine questions concerned issues related to sex and marriage. Gregory's answers overturned the traditional Mediterranean and Middle Eastern patterns of legal and customary practices in the domestic domain. The traditional system was concerned with the provision of an heir to inherit family property, and allowed marriage to close kin, marriages to close affines or widows of close kin, the transfer of children by adoption, and finally concubinage, which is a form of secondary union. Gregory banned all four practices. There was, for instance, no adoption of children allowed in England until the nineteenth century. There was no basis for these injunctions in Scripture, Roman law, or the existing customs in the areas that were Christianized.

This papal family revolution made the Church unbelievably rich. Demographers have estimated that the net effect of the prohibitions on traditional methods to deal with childlessness was to leave 40 percent of families with no immediate male heirs. The Church became the chief beneficiary of the resulting bequests. Its accumulation was phenomenal. In France, for instance, it is estimated that one-third of productive land was in ecclesiastical hands by the end of the seventh century![13]

But this accumulation also drew predators from within and without the Church to deprive it of its acquired property. It was to deal with this denudation that Pope Gregory VII instigated his papal revolution in 1075, by putting the power of God—through the spiritual weapon of excommunication—above that of Caesar's. With the Church then entering into the realm of the world, the new church-state also created the whole administrative and legal paraphernalia which we associate with a modern economy.[14] This provided the essential institutional infrastructure for the Western dynamic (as outlined in the Introduction) that was to lead to Promethean growth. Thus, Pope Gregory VII's papal revolution lifted the lid on the basic human instinct to "truck and barter," and in time to a change in the traditional Eurasian pattern of material beliefs with their suspicion of markets and merchants. This in time led to modern economic growth.

But the first Papal Revolution of Gregory the Great also led to a change in the traditional Eurasian family patterns which were based on various forms of "joint families" and family values. This essentially removed the lid placed on the other opportunistic basic instincts by the shame-based moral codes of Eurasia. To counter the potential threat this posed to its means of making a living by way of settled agriculture, the Church created a fierce guilt culture in which the concept of Original Sin was paramount, and morality was underwritten by the belief in the Christian God.[15]

Communalism versus Individualism

Of the major Eurasian civilizations, the ethic of the Sinic (and its derivatives in Japan and Korea) and the Hindu has remained distinctly "communalist" rather than individualist for millennia. But there were important differences in the cosmological beliefs of these two ancient civilizations.

Hindu Civilization

The ancient Hindu, unlike the Sinic civilization, did have a role for a form of individualism, which was reminiscent of that found among the Greek Stoics. The anthropologist Louis Dumont has labeled this as "out-worldly" individualism as contrasted with the "in-worldly" individualism, which is the hallmark of the "modern" individual. Hinduism allows the person who renounces the world and becomes an ascetic to pursue his own personal salvation without any concern for the social world. Like the Greek Stoic, this Hindu "renouncer is self-sufficient, concerned only with himself. His thought is similar to that of the modern individual, but for one basic difference: we live in the social world, he lives outside it."[16]

For a Hindu, who had not renounced the social world, Western individualism is impossible, as Ernest Gellner tellingly shows by imagining a Hindu Robinson Crusoe, a polyglot called Robinson Chatterjee. "A Hindu Crusoe," he notes, "would be a contradiction. He would be destined for perpetual pollution: if a priest, then his isolation and forced self-sufficiency would oblige him to perform demeaning and polluting acts. If not a priest, he would be doomed through his inability to perform the obligatory rituals."[17]

Sinic Civilization

The ancient Sinic civilization did not even have this "out-worldly" individualism of the Hindus and the Greeks. Its central cosmological beliefs have been summarized as its optimism, its familialism, and its bureaucratic authoritarianism.[18] Interacting and influencing these characteristics were the embedded customs of "ancestor worship and its social and political correlates involving hierarchy, ritual deference, obedience and reciprocity."[19] There is little room for even the "out-worldly" individualism of the Hindus or Greeks in these cosmological views which have been labeled "Confucianism"; this in spite of the continuing controversy over whether the ancient sage should be lumbered with whatever have been seen to be the distinctive features of Chinese civilization.

In our own day and age, partly provoked by the events surrounding

Tianenmen Square, there has been an attempt to reconcile Confucianism with Western notions of "human rights."[20] But, apart from the murkiness surrounding the notion of "rights" even within the Western philosophical tradition, as Henry Rosemont rightly notes: within the Confucian framework

> rights—talk was not spoken, and within which I am not a free, autonomous individual. I am a son, husband, father, grandfather, neighbor, colleague, student, teacher, citizen, friend. I have a very large number of relational obligations and responsibilities, which severely constrain what I do. These responsibilities occasionally frustrate or annoy, they more often are satisfying and they are always binding . . . And my individuality, if anyone wishes to keep the concept, will come from the specific actions I take in meeting my relational responsibilities.[21]

As he rightly notes, the attempt to reconcile a different "way to live" with the universal claims of Christianity has been a constant factor in the West's encounter with China. Views differed between those seeking converts, who thought the Chinese way was incompatible with universal Christian beliefs, and others of a less imperialist bent, who sought a syncretism which made Chinese beliefs fit the universal Christian ethic.[22]

Christianity

In this context it is worth noting the important difference between the cosmological beliefs of what became the Christian West and the other ancient agrarian civilizations of Eurasia. Christianity has a number of distinctive features which it shares with its Semitic cousin Islam, and in part with its parent Judaism, but which are not to be found in any of the other great Eurasian religions. *First* and most important is its universality. Neither the Jews nor the Hindu or Sinic civilizations had religions claiming to be universal. You could not choose to be a Hindu, Chinese, or Jew, you were born as one. *Second*, this also meant that, unlike Christianity and Islam, these religions did not proselytize. *Third*, only the Semitic monotheistic religions have also been egalitarian. Nearly all the other Eurasian religions believed in some form of hierarchical social order. By contrast, alone among the Eurasian civilizations, the Semitic ones emphasized the equality of men's souls. Dumont (1970) has rightly characterized the resulting and profound divide between the societies of *Homo Aequalis* which believe all men are born equal (as the *philosophes*, and the American constitution proclaim) and those of *Homo Hierarchicus* which believe no such thing.

Christianity, as we shall see, is and remains at the nub of the West's beliefs, and at the heart of that "clash of civilizations" posited by Huntington. There can be little doubt that neither the Hindu nor the Sinic civilizations have adhered to the Western notions of liberty and equality based on individualism.

But, for a long time, neither did the West. For, although Christianity came inadvertently to promote the "in-worldly" individualism which is a hallmark of Western civilization, in its basic teachings it did not differ greatly from the communalism found in the other great ethical beliefs systems of antiquity. Like the Greeks and the Hindus it provided a place for "out-worldly" individualism. As Dumont notes: "There is no doubt about the fundamental conception of man that flowed from the teaching of Christ . . . man is an individual in—relation to God; . . . this means that man is in essence an out-worldly individual."[23]

It was St. Augustine in his *City of God*, who by substituting the absolute submission of the State to the Church for the previous endorsement of sacral kingship, analogous to the Hindus, brought the Church "into the world" with Gregory VII's proclamation: "Let the terrestrial kingdom serve—or be the slave—of the celestial."

The Course of Western Individualism

But the course of Western individualism has not been simple. It would take me too far afield to go into this in detail, but the importance of St. Augustine's "City of God" must be noted. Throughout the last millennium, the West has been haunted by its cosmology. From the Enlightenment to Marxism to Freudianism to Eco-Fundamentalism, Augustine's vision of the Heavenly City has had a tenacious hold on the Western mind. The same narrative, with a Garden of Eden, a Fall leading to Original Sin and a Day of Judgment, keeps recurring. Thus, in their refurbishment of Augustine, the eighteenth-century philosophers of the Enlightenment displaced the Garden of Eden by classical Greece and Rome, and God became an abstract cause—the Divine Watchmaker. The Christian centuries were now taken to be the Fall, with the Christian revelations considered a fraud. As for the enlightened, God expressed his purpose through his laws recorded in the Great Book of Nature. The Enlightened were the elect and the Christian paradise was replaced by Posterity. By this reconfiguration of the Christian narrative, the eighteenth-century philosophers of the Enlightenment thought they had been able to salvage a basis for morality and social order in the world of the Divine Watchmaker. But once, as a result of Darwin, he was seen to be blind, as Nietzsche proclaimed from the housetops at the end of the nineteenth century,[24] the Christian God was dead, and the moral foundations of the West were thereafter in ruins.

The subsequent attempts to found a morality based on reason are open to Freidriech Nietzsche's fatal objection in his aphorism about utilitarianism. He wrote: "moral sensibilities are nowadays at such cross purposes that to one man a morality is proved by its utility, while to another its utility refutes it."[25] Nietzsche's greatness lies in his clear recognition of the moral abyss that the death of its God had created for the West. Kant's attempt to ground a rational morality on the principle of universalizability—harking back to the biblical injunction "therefore all things whatsoever ye do would that men should do to you, do even so to them"—founders on Hegel's two objections: first, it is merely a principle of logical consistency without any specific moral content, and second, as a result it is powerless to prevent any immoral conduct that takes our fancy. The subsequent ink spilled by moral philosophers has merely clothed their particular prejudices in rational form.[26]

The death of the Christian God did not, however, end variations on the theme of Augustine's "City." It was to go through further mutations in the form of Marxism and Freudianism, and a more recent and bizarre mutation in the form of Ecofundamentalism.[27]

Marxism, like the Christian faith, looks to the past and the future. There is a counterpart to the Garden of Eden, that is, the time before "property" relations corrupted "natural man." The Fall is represented by the "commodification" which leads to a class society and a continuing but impersonal conflict of material forces. This in turn leads to the Day of Judgment with the Revolution and the millennial Paradise of Communism. Marx also claimed that this movement toward earthly salvation was mediated, not as the Enlightenment sages had claimed through enlightenment and the preaching of good will, but by the inexorable forces of historical materialism. Another secular "City of God" has been created.

Ecofundamentalism is the latest of these secular mutations of Augustine's "City of God."[28] It carries the Christian notion of *contemptus mundi* to its logical conclusion. Humankind is evil, and only by living in harmony with a deified Nature can it be saved.

From Victorian Virtues to Modern Values

But even with the death of the Christian God there was a way to ground the morality needed to reduce the "policing" type of transactions costs for economic efficiency. The path was clearly charted by the other sage of the Scottish Enlightenment, Adam Smith's close friend, the philosopher David Hume. In his *Treatise of Human Nature*, Hume begins by recognizing that morality is essential to control man's self-aggrandizing instincts to garner the gains from cooperation. However, he does not try to ground morality either in a belief in God or reason but rather in tradition. As he notes: "the sense of justice and injustice is not derived from nature, but arises artificially, though' necessarily from education and human conventions."[29] Once they are in place, "a sympathy with public interest is the source of moral approbation, which attends that virtue [justice]" (p. 551). This leads parents "to inculcate in their children from the earliest infancy, the principles of probity, and teach them to regard the observance of those rules by which society is maintained as worthy and honorable, and their violation as base and infamous."[30] Hume, while clearly accepting the role of morality in maintaining the social cement of society, believes that this morality is primarily dependent on a society's traditions and forms of socialization, based on utilizing the moral emotions of shame and guilt. Neither God nor Reason needs to be evoked to justify these conditioned and necessary habits. This is very much the view of ethics taken by the older Eurasian civilizations with their moral ecology based on shame, and also by those contemporary philosophers who see morality and manners as arising by conventions which allow us to live together peacefully in a viable society.[31]

This was also the basis of the morality of that bourgeois capitalist society par excellence—Victorian England. For as Adam Smith, that votary of commercial society, had argued in his Theory of Moral Sentiments: "the man of the most perfect virtue, the man whom we naturally love and revere the most, is he who joins, to the most perfect command of his own original and selfish feelings, the most exquisite sensibility both to the original and sympathetic feelings of others."[32] Healthy ambition and individual desire were to be combined with an empathetic conscience to promote social stability and order.

But, Smith was at pains to distinguish this "sympathy" from that preached by "those whining and melancholy moralists, who are perpetually reproaching us with our happiness, while so many of our brethren are in misery, who regard as impious the natural joy of prosperity, which does not think of the many wretches that at every instant laboring under all sorts of calamities, in the languor of poverty, in the agony of disease, in the horrors of death, under the insults and oppression of their enemies."[33] But he says: "this extreme sympathy with misfortunes which we know nothing about, seems altogether absurd and unreasonable . . . and those who affect this character have commonly nothing but a certain affected and sentimental sadness."[34] Sentimentality, it is worth noting, has become a hallmark of "the Third Way" proponents like Bill Clinton, Tony Blair, and James Wolfensohn.[35]

The Victorians from Charles Darwin, Samuel Smiles, to John Stuart Mill recognized that "character," which embodied these traditional virtues of self-control and empathy, was required to tame our baser instincts. These culturally acquired higher moral sentiments needed to be cultivated against those darker dispositions genetically endowed to us by natural selection. "The truth" Mill wrote, "is that there is hardly a single part of excellence belonging to human character, which is not decidedly repugnant to the untutored feelings of human nature."[36]

Peter Gay, in his magisterial reconstruction of "The Bourgeois Experience" encompassing the rise of a middle-class culture across Europe and North America in the Victorian age, and summarized in his Schnitzler's Century, shows how the Victorian virtues embedded in their morality provided the bulwark against the basic instincts unleashed by the two papal revolutions, and which put a lid on the socially disruptive self-seeking that the rise of capitalism would otherwise have entailed. He writes:

> [T]he standard by which Victorians hoped to live was that of free individuals who set their own course, though within a given, gladly accepted framework of family, society, and state. Institutions, especially religious commitments, were authoritative markers, so many monitory uplifted fingers, which demanded a good measure of conformity. Yet this social and spiritual discipline implied a realm of individual autonomy. . . . Their new hero was a man in a frock coat, perhaps wearing galoshes, carrying a briefcase and certainly an umbrella, thinking on his business and his family. He was or claimed to be a loving husband, a doting father, an honest business partner, a moderate in politics and the consumption of wine, and addicted, if at all to inexpensive pleasures. He read the newspaper at breakfast, and, religious or not, probably went to church . . . the family was the icon that the nineteenth-century middle class worshiped, domestic felicity the motto that, as it were, hung over the marital bed.[37]

These Victorian virtues, of work, discipline, thrift, self-help, self-discipline, Gertrude Himmelfarb notes, "were neither the classical nor Christian virtues; they were more domesticated than the former and more secular than the latter[38] . . . they were the standards against which behavior could and should be measured. And when conduct fell short of those standards, it was judged in moral terms, as bad, wrong, or evil—not, as . . . today, as misguided, undesirable, or inappropriate."[39] These Victorian virtues are today to be found more often among the burghers of Bombay and Shanghai than those of Wall Street or Hollywood.

The embodiment of these Victorian virtues was the English gentleman. The term was used to denote a distinction of character, rather than class. "As James I is reputed to have said 'I can make a lord' . . . when [his old nurse] begged him to make her son a gentleman, 'but only God Almighty can make a gentleman'."[40] The gentleman was defined by his virtues of "integrity, honesty, generosity, courage, graciousness, politeness, consideration for others."[41] Anyone, even a working-class man who embodied these virtues, could aspire to be a gentleman.

It was Nietzsche who transmuted "virtues" as the basis for morality to "values." "His 'transvaluation of values' was to be the final, ultimate revolution, a revolution against both the classical virtues and the Judaeo-Christian ones. The 'death of God' would mean the death of morality and the death of truth—above all the truth of any morality. There would be no good and evil, no virtue and vice. There would be only 'values'."[42] Thus began the demoralization of much of Western society.

Keynes in his *Economic Consequences of the Peace* recognized that the nineteenth-century LIEO which had brought prosperity around the world "depended on a shared morality, which emphasized above all the virtues of abstinence, prudence, calculation and foresight—the basis for the accumulation of capital. . . . The world's economic organization ultimately rested on the Victorian virtues."[43] But, it was his generation of Cambridge Apostles who did more than most to undermine these Victorian virtues. Lytton Strachey's satirizing of the repression and hypocrisy of the Victorians in his *Eminent Victorians* began that process whereby subsequent generations came to associate the Victorians with all that was fuddy duddy, arcane, and reactionary.

But, Keynes's generation, as adduced to by Keynes's paper on "My Early Beliefs," still had a need for "true beliefs," albeit in a godless universe. His generation found a justification for their own beliefs in the incoherent intuitionism of G. E. Moore, whose *Principa Ethica*, according to Keynes, had a "religion" and "morals." His generation "accepted Moore's religion . . . and discarded his morals. Indeed, . . . one of the greatest advantages of his religion was that it made morals unnecessary—meaning by 'religion' one's attitude to oneself and the ultimate and by 'morals' one's attitude towards the outside world and the intermediate."[44] They, Keynes continued, "repudiated entirely customary morals, conventions and traditional wisdom. We were, that is to say, in the strict sense of the term, immoralists. The consequences of being found out had, of course, to be considered for what they were worth. But we recognized no moral obligations on us, no inner sanction, to conform or obey."[45]

But, as Keynes's biographer Robert Skidelsky rightly notes, the striking difference between his generation and ours is "not so much that we have lost our beliefs as that we have lost the belief in the possibility of having true beliefs."[46] This is, of course, the modern progression from Nietzsche's "transvaluation of values" to Derrida's philosophy of "deconstruction." The shift from "virtues" to "values" as the basis of morality meant that instead of being an authoritative yardstick to judge behavior in society, it became a flexible ruler. For, as Himmelfarb notes: "values . . . do not have to be virtues; they can be beliefs, opinions, attitudes, feelings, habits, conventions, preferences, prejudices, even idiosyncrasies—whatever any individual, group, or society happens to value, at any time, for any reason."[47] They can be relativistic, peculiar to specific individuals, societies, races, classes or even sexes. Nonjudgmental amorality becomes the characteristic of a society ruled by a set of subjective and relative values. While the empathy adduced descends into the sentimentality castigated by Adam Smith: not least when contemplating the plight of the unfortunate millions in the Third World.[48]

The 1960s Cultural Revolution provided the final "coup de grace" to the traditional morality of the West. It changed traditional family relationships, created new standards of sexual behavior. "All the statistical evidence," writes the historian Arthur Marwick, "suggests that permissive behavior continued to spread at accelerating rates, with only the utterly unforeseen occurrence of AIDS to bring any kind of caution; single parent families proliferated, the term 'husband' and 'wife' became almost quaint, giving place to 'lover' and 'partner'."[49] This subversion of traditional morality was aided and abetted by the growing entertainment and leisure industries. In America "some pollsters, such as Daniel Yankelovich, believe that the values of the so-called counter culture—"creativity, leisure, autonomy, pleasure, participation, adventure, vitality, stimulation, tender loving care"—have triumphed among a majority of the educated and affluent."[50] The traditional constraints on self-seeking which classical liberals such as Hume and Smith saw as a necessary means to create a good society have been removed. But, "the hope that unbridled passion was capable of not merely transforming society but of changing those within it, that it would give lasting meaning to otherwise empty lives, was as dangerous as it was naive."[51] The resulting ills of contemporary Western society, with it "Slouching Towards Gomorrah" as one observer has it,[52] are less to do with capitalism, as some have claimed,[53] but to the West's demoralization.

The West's cosmological beliefs today are incoherent. As the philosopher Alasdair Macintyre has powerfully argued, the current Western notion of self has three contradictory elements. The first derives from the Enlightenment. It views individuals as being able to stand apart from external social influences and constraints, and allows them to mold themselves in accordance with their own true preferences. The second component of the Western self concerns the evaluation of oneself by others. Here the standards are increasingly those of acquisitive and competitive success, as nurtured (so some would believe) by a bureaucratized and individualist market economy. The third element of the Western self derives from its remaining religious and moral norms, and is open to various "invocations of values as various as those which inform the public rhetoric of politics on the one hand and the success of Habits of the Heart on the other."[54] This aspect of the self harks back to the Christian conception of the soul and its transcendental salvation.

These three elements comprising the Western conception of self are not only mutually incompatible, they are incommensurable. They also lead to incoherence as there are no shared standards by which the inevitable conflicts between them can be resolved. So, as Macintyre puts it, "rights-based claims, utility-based claims, contractarian claims, and claims based upon this or that ideal conception of the good will be advanced in different contexts, with relatively little discomfort at the incoherence involved. For unacknowledged incoherence is the hallmark of this contemporary developing American self, a self whose public voice oscillates between phases not merely of toleration, but admiration for ruthlessly self-serving behavior and phases of high moral dudgeon and indignation at exactly the same behavior."[55]

Many in the West can be seen as going back to the worship of the multiplicity of "gods" and personal moral codes (particularly in the realm of sexuality) which are reminiscent of the pre-Christian Graeco-Roman world. The growing popularity of New Age religions which is occurring at a time when the traditional churches continue to lose followers is a testament to the growing "neo-paganism" in the West.

But there is a growing reaction in the West to the last century's demoralization of its society. Western philosophers are now discovering the importance of "virtue" as the basis for morality.[56] While in the ongoing culture wars in the United States, the so-called moral majority seeking to restore traditional values in this bastion of contemporary bourgeois civilization seems, at least judging from the 2004 elections, to indeed be becoming a majority.[57] But, meanwhile, the seeming moral disintegration of the West, and in particular the effects of the first papal revolution in the domestic domain with the disappearance of sin in the West, continues to provide reasons for the cultural nationalists in the Rest to oppose the modernization promoted by globalization. They see this globalizing capitalism as the Trojan horse which will lead to Westernization and the adoption of Western mores, especially concerning sex, marriage, and the family.

Modernization and Westernization

The Response of Wounded Civilizations

With the rise and global expansion of the West, the other Eurasian civilizations faced a dilemma. With their ancient equilibrium disturbed, most often by force of superior arms, how could their wounded civilizations come to terms with the West without losing their souls? There were essentially three responses. The first was to modernize by imitating the West: by adopting its material beliefs including the accompanying artifacts which provide military and economic strength, but without adopting Western cosmological beliefs. The second was to adopt the attitude of the clam for fear of a modernization that would undermine ancient traditions. The third was to find a middle ground between tradition and modernity.

During the Meiji Revolution, Japan, following its opening by Commodore Perry's "black ships," took the first route. It was the first to recognize that modernization (involving a change in material beliefs) did not entail Westernization (a change in its cosmological beliefs). The second route was advocated by sundry cultural nationalists, particularly in India by Gandhi and his followers—including till recently the Bhartiya Janata Party— the Hindu nationalist party. The third route was taken by all those countries which found a middle way in various variants of socialism to reconcile modernity with tradition. India and China have epitomized this route. The countries of Islam have tried all three routes, from Attaturk's Turkey to Nasser's Egypt (which took the first and third routes), to the current Islamists of the Muslim world (who want to follow the second route).

The third route of finding a middle ground between tradition and modernity was the most commonly taken. This usually took some socialist form. For socialism has its roots in both the Enlightenment, which sees all social and economic structures as open to rationalist manipulation to subserve universal human goals, and the romantic critique of modernization based on these rationalist ideas. The young Marx and the indigenous English socialist tradition represented by William Morris and R. H. Tawney took up the romantic critique. Fabian socialism, which has had the most appeal in the Third World, combined these two faces of socialism—the manipulative, utilitarian socialism of the Webbs (the Enlightenment strand) with the passionate critique of a dehumanizing capitalist society of Morris and Tawney (adherents of the romantic expressivist tradition). This form of socialism provided a formula for reconciling the two ambivalent rejections of the traditional and the modern which is the unique feature of this route.[58]

The Emerging Giants—India and China

Jawaharlal Nehru was the most eloquent exponent of this form of reconciliation of tradition with modernity.[59] In his autobiography he wrote:

> [R]ight through human history the old Indian ideal did not glorify political and military triumph, and it looked down upon money and the professional money making class. Honor and wealth did not go together, and honor was meant to go, at least in theory, to the men who served the community with little in the shape of financial reward. Today (the old culture) is fighting silently and desperately against a new all-powerful opponent—the Bania (Vaishya) civilization of the capitalist West. It will succumb to the newcomer. . . . But the West also brings an antidote to the evils of the cut-throat civilization—the principle of socialism, of cooperation, and service to the community for the common good. This is not so unlike the old Brahmin ideal of service, but the Brahminization— not in the religious sense, of course—of all classes and groups and the abolition of class distinctions.[60]

By contrast, Gandhi, the cultural nationalist, was an unwavering adherent of maintaining the traditional Hindu socioeconomic system—albeit cleansed of some aberrations. He never deviated from the views he expressed in 1909 in a booklet called *Hind Swaraj*. This work is an uncompromising attack on Western civilization. He was implacably opposed to Western education, industrialization, and all the other modern forces, like lawyers, railways, and doctors, which could undermine the ancient Hindu equilibrium. Above all, even though he was against untouchability, he nevertheless upheld the caste system and its central feature of endogamy. He wished to see a revival of the ancient and largely self-sufficient village communities which were an essential part of the ancient Hindu equilibrium. He did not succeed in his aims, for soon after Independence in 1947 he was dead at the hands of an assassin, and it was his anointed successor Nehru's Fabian socialist views which determined Indian economic policy. But Gandhi's ideas were picked up and refurbished by the Hindu nationalist party, the Jan Sangh, which later transmogrified into the Bhartiya Janta Party (BJP).

The dirigiste system of planning and controls set up in the Nehruvian era was much influenced by the success of Stalin's Russia, which within a generation had created a massive military machine through forced industrialization. India too adopted a similar inward-looking, import-substituting, heavy industry–biased development strategy. But this soon ran into the sands, and since the late 1960s India was in a quiet crisis of low growth and undiminished poverty. Beginning in the mid-1980s partial economic liberalization began. But it took a balance of payments cum fiscal and inflationary crisis in 1991 for India to finally turn its back on planning with its Permit Raj, and to begin reintegration into the global economy. This process is still ongoing, but seems irreversible. It has raised the economy's growth rate of about 3–4 percent p.a. in the era of planning to 6–7 percent p.a. since economic liberalization was undertaken (see table 6.1).

China, by contrast, after nearly a century of turmoil following the Opium Wars when British gunboats shattered its self-imposed isolation, with the victory of the Communists in 1949 turned to the purely Enlightenment strand of socialism. This Communism pioneered in Soviet Russia which in Lenin's apt phrase equals "Soviet power + electrification" also led to an even more extreme version of the inward-looking heavy industrialization strategy adopted in India. Its denouement came sooner. The collectivization of agriculture (which never occurred in India) during the Great Leap Forward led to one of the worst famines in human history, with an estimated 30 million excess deaths,[61] as the "peasants simply downed tools and turned their bottoms to the sun."[62] The chaos of the ten-year Cultural Revolution which followed further retarded Chinese progress.

With the fall of the Gang of Four and the ascendancy of Deng Tsiao Ping, China began the process of economic liberalization. Its movement from the plan to the market began when Deng reversed the collectivization of agriculture in 1978 with the introduction of the household responsibility system. This in effect restored, in all but name, privately run and owned family farms. This reversal of policy was the pragmatic response to the deep economic and social crisis caused by Mao's collectivization, Great Leap Forward, and Cultural Revolution. The peasant's response was stupendous. Agricultural output, which had grown at 2.9 percent p.a. between 1952 and 1978, grew at 7.6 percent p.a. from 1978 to 1984.[63] The large increase in farm incomes led to a rapid rise in savings to 42 percent in 1999. The rise in savings was also fostered

TABLE 6.1
China–India Comparison

I. Growth Rates (%p.a.)

	China			India		
	GDP	Population	Per Capita GDP (Level PPP $1990)	GDP	Population	Per Capita GDP (Level $1990)
(1950)			(439)			(619)
1950–78	5.0	2.1	2.9	3.8	2.2	1.6
1978–91	7.0	1.6	5.4	4.5	2.2	2.3
1991–2001	7.5	1.1	6.4	6.1	1.9	4.2
(2001)			(3583)			(1957)

Source: Maddisson, A. (2003), pp. 174, 184.

II. Gross Domestic Savings(S) and Investment (I) (% GDP)

	China		India	
	S	I	S	I
1965	24.8	24	11.6	14.4
1973	29.8	29	14.6	15.4
1980	30	30	18.9	20.3
1990	38	35	23.1	26.3
1999	42	40	22.3	23.3

Source: China: World Bank: *World Tables* and *World Development Report 2001, and 2002.* India: Lal, D. (1988/2004), p. 294.

by China's forced demographic transition, with its one-child policy which reduced the dependency ratio (the number of the old and young to workers) and thus—on the lines of the life cycle theory of savings—to a rise in the savings rate.[64]

The crucial difference between China and Russia in their transitions from the plan to the market lay in their initial conditions. Russia and Eastern Europe had about 90 percent of their labor force in state-owned industrial enterprises, while most of the labor force in China (80 percent) was in agriculture. For Russia and Eastern Europe the only route to a more efficient private market economy was a "big bang" to dismantle the state-owned industrial enterprises. China could, through its own rural big bang, immediately convert the majority of state employees into private owner operators, and see a rise in output rather than the losses experienced by Russia, leaving time for gradual reform of its inefficient state-owned industrial enterprises.

A momentous unintended consequence of the privatization of agriculture was the initiation of a boom in small-scale nonfarm rural enterprises.[65] This began with Deng's injunction that it was virtuous to be rich. The local party officials took this to heart, becoming directors and managers of township and village enterprises (TVEs). With the rise in farm incomes, the pent up demand for manufactured goods and housing was met by these TVEs. Collectively owned but run as profit-making capitalist enterprises, they provided the local authorities with extra budgetary resources, and legal opportunities for their officials to become rich. Unlike the state enterprises, they did not carry any welfare responsibilities and were free to hire and fire the abundant local labor in a completely free market. With Deng's creation of the Special Economic Zones in China's southern rim in the early 1980s, these TVEs and later individually owned private firms became the spearhead of a Dickensian capitalism. Using the cheap labor in the Chinese countryside with foreign technology, self-financing from household savings and enterprise profits, and (some) foreign capital from the Chinese diaspora[66] and a myriad of multinationals, and engaging in fierce locational competition, these nonstate enterprises have made China into the processing center for manufactured goods in the world. This labor-intensive industrialization is now spreading inland along the Yangtze.[67]

Total employment in TVEs rose from 28 million in 1978 to 60 million in 1996. There was dramatic growth in individually owned enterprises. Their numbers rose from nothing in 1978, to 4 million in 1984 and 23 million in 1996, employing 76 million people. They have been the motor of China's spectacular labor-intensive industrialization. Angus Maddison[68] estimates that real value added in this new small-scale sector rose by about 22 percent a year from 1978 to 1994. It has made China the workshop of the world.

These spin-offs from the privatization of agriculture were aided by the massive buildup of infrastructure by the state. Labor-intensive export industries were further helped by domestic price reforms and one of the largest unilateral liberalizations of foreign trade in history. Today, most relative prices in China (unlike India) are closely aligned to world prices. Chinese exports have exploded, growing eightfold between 1978 and 1995. By 2003, China was the world's third largest trading country, when its trade *increased* by over $200 billion—twice the *level* of India's total trade in 2002. Its share of global trade is six times that of India's.[69]

The rapid export-led industrialization in the private sector is based on processing imported components with domestic cum foreign capital and technology and cheap domestic labor. This private sector has grown so rapidly that its share of manufacturing output is now over 70 percent compared with that of the moribund and unviable state enterprises, whose share has fallen from about 80 percent in 1978 to about 28 percent in 1998.[70] This has led to spectacular growth rates of the Chinese economy of 9–10 percent p.a. (based on official estimates) and 7–8 percent p.a. on independent estimates, for nearly two decades[71] (table 6.1). But, the state sector still controls more than 70 percent of all fixed assets and 80 percent of all working capital in manufacturing.

As its nonstate sector grew, China undertook a gradual reform of its state-owned industrial enterprises. Most were set up, as in India, under the unviable heavy industry–biased industrialization strategy. In the reform period they have been kept alive to avoid losses in output and employment, till the dynamic nonstate sector is large enough to absorb the labor their closure would release. Most state firms are making losses, worsened by the "social" welfare burden they continue to carry. Worried about the social disorder entailed in their wholesale closure, the Chinese government has tread warily. Closing the worst loss-making units has reduced state employment from 109 million in 1995 to 70 million in 2002, of which 10 million is in manufacturing. The rest have been kept alive by subsidies through the banking system. The consequent debauching of the financial system and inefficient use of massive domestic savings pose serious problems for China's economic future.

The drag that the state enterprises still exert on Chinese economic performance can be best illustrated by the contrasting savings rates in India and China and the economic growth these have yielded (see table 6.1). The Chinese savings rate of about 40 percent is about twice that of India, yet its growth rate is only higher than India's by about 2–3 percentage points. The reason is that nearly 90 percent of Chinese household savings are placed in the state-owned banks, which channel them at subsidized rates to the low-return and often loss-making state enterprises. The efficient private sector is crowded out of access to the bulk of Chinese savings, and the overall growth rate is then brought down by the low-return state sector.

The heart of the problem lies in the financial repression, which is a necessary feature of a capital-intensive heavy industry–biased development strategy. It requires government monopolization of the mobilization and deployment of savings in the economy. In China this was done through the complete control of the economy by the planners. The savings were provided by the profits of the state enterprises. With the reforms these profits collapsed. In the rural sector they now accrued to private agents. But in the industrial SOEs the price reforms and growing competition from the efficient non-SOE sector led to the previous profits being replaced by losses, particularly as the SOEs still had to carry the welfare commitments for health, housing, education, pensions, and jobs for life of the planned era. As a result, the central government's revenues fell from 32 percent of GDP in 1978 to 11 percent in 1995. The decline was made worse by the various tax concessions the local authorities offered in their locational competition for joint ventures with foreign investors. This acute fiscal crisis was met by two fortuitous circumstances. The large increase in private savings with rising incomes in the rural and small-scale nonstate sector was held as deposits in the state banks, whose deployment was determined by the central authorities. Moreover, the privatization of the rural sector and its growing incomes led to a rapid monetization of the economy with the ratio of money supply to GDP rising from a third to equality from 1978 to 1995. This gave large seignorage gains to the Central Bank. Nevertheless, the government has run large fiscal deficits funded by bonds held by the state banks during the reform period. Apart from public investment in infrastructure, much of government expenditure is on implicit or explicit subsidies to the loss-making SOEs. With savings having reached a plateau and future seignorage gains likely to be limited, the continuing incipient fiscal crisis of the state requires a reform of the SOEs.

Currently, nearly 90 percent of household savings are still held in deposits with the state-owned banks, in part because of the lack of alternative savings instruments. Most of the deposits in the banks are loaned to the SOEs, while most of the investment in the viable private non-SOE sector is either self-financed or else dependent on foreign capital.[72] With few of these nonstate growth enterprises being willing or allowed to issue stocks in their companies, the stocks traded on the domestic stock exchanges are mainly those in the SOEs whose nontransparent accounting practices and perceived unviability deter households from holding much of their savings in their stocks. Hence, the domestic stock markets are thin and volatile.

This lack of adequate savings vehicles, and the low return households currently get from their savings in the state-owned banks, pose a threat to the maintenance of China's high savings rate. The state-owned banks cannot promote higher savings by raising their deposit rates without a rise in their lending rates to the unviable SOEs whose losses would increase, leading the banks to further increase their loans to cover these losses and thus to a further increase in the nonperforming loans in the banking system.

These microeconomic difficulties in using the interest rate to stimulate savings and for the efficient sifting and deployment of investments through a well-functioning stock market are further compounded by the macroeconomic consequences of financial repression. As the interest rate cannot be used as an instrument for managing aggregate demand, heavy-handed administrative measures with all their inherent inefficiencies and limited effectiveness (given the self-financed nature of most private (non SOE) investment) are needed to cool the economy.

Furthermore, given the fragility of the banking system, fully opening up the capital account of the balance of payments followed by a move to a fully flexible exchange rate system is ruled out as it could lead to a serious financial crisis. I do not think that China's export-led growth has depended as many other observers believe on maintaining an undervalued exchange rate. For, as most of Chinese manufactured exports are processed goods with little domestic value added (estimated to be about 20 percent of the value of output), changes in the exchange rate would not markedly affect their profitability.

171

A flexible exchange rate would not therefore hurt China's phenomenal export-led growth. This move to a flexible exchange rate is needed not only for a more efficient use of China's national savings but also to fend off the growing pressures for a revaluation of the Yuan from both private speculators and China's major trading partners.

Behind all these prospective dangers currently facing the Chinese economy lie the "policy" and "social" burdens carried by the SOEs because of China's past planned development strategy. The answer must be to eliminate these burdens so that the viable SOEs can be privatized and prosper in a globally integrated market economy, while the unviable ones are allowed to be taken over or are shut down without causing domestic disorder. Fortunately, China's large buildup of foreign exchange reserves (which in October 2004 were about 60 percent of GDP) provides the means to do so. I have suggested that they could be utilized to create a Social Reconstruction Fund (SRF) at the Central Bank, whose income, based (like any large pension fund) on investing a large part of foreign reserves in an international portfolio of securities, could be used to finance the remaining "social burden" of the SOEs.[73] They could then be privatized. They could then be treated as normal commercial enterprises which could be privatized if viable, and closed down if not. This would end the subsidies from the banking system which have led to its fragility, allow transparent accounting of SOE stocks traded on the stock market, allow the banks to perform their primary intermediating function of efficiently mobilizing domestic savings and transferring them to high-yielding investment projects, and with the restoration of health to the financial system allow China to float the Yuan. With the end of the SOE burden, the SRF could be used to finance a social security system for China's rapidly aging population.[74]

The current draft on the massive private savings by the inefficient state sector also poses a further challenge for China's future prospect. Demographers seem to agree that countries undergoing a demographic transition, when the dependency ratio starts declining as the birth rate and population growth rate begin to fall, see a temporary bonanza in terms of higher savings rates. Thereafter, as the population ages this bonanza ends, as the dependency ratio begins to rise.[75] China, with its one-child policy, has already experienced the demographic transition and its currently high savings rates are partly its reflection (table 6.1). But by 2010, China's population will begin aging.[76] The ratio of working-age people to retirees will fall from 6 today to 2 in 2040, and this savings bonanza can be expected to end in the following decade. This makes it imperative that, during the remaining period of its demographic bonus, China's high savings are productively employed. If they are wasted in subsidizing inefficient state enterprises, the economic prospects of future generations will be damaged, as less productive capital will be left to them than would otherwise have been the case. By contrast, India has just entered its demographic transition (table 6.1) and can expect a rise in its savings rate. If by then it has completed the second generation of economic reforms and fully integrated itself into the global economy, we might yet find that the tortoise overtakes the hare in the race for economic growth between these two Asian giants.

India, too, has a continuing problem with privatizing its public sector, particularly with the political constraints imposed by the current (2004) Congress government's alliance with the Communist parties, which seem to have learned little from the collapse of Communist economies in the rest of the world. It also has been unable, for political reasons, to curb a host of uneconomic subsidies which have led to a burgeoning fiscal deficit. Its Communist allies have also prevented the repeal of the colonial labor laws (discussed in chapter 3) which have hampered the development of labor-intensive industry in India for nearly a century. These, along with the "reservations" for small-scale industries introduced to pacify the Gandhian cultural nationalists, have meant that much of light industry cannot grow to achieve economies of scale. Thus, India, which was the pioneer of industrialization in the Third World in the nineteenth century,[77] has not been able to employ its most abundant resource—unskilled and semiskilled labor—to become the workshop of the world. The rapid labor-intensive industrial growth of the Chinese oceanic rim (and increasingly its hinterland) still remains a pipe dream in India. Instead, it has been able to utilize the unintended consequence of its state-sponsored production of a surplus of engineering graduates, and its partial liberalization of foreign trade, to become the major world center for the outsourcing of hitherto nontraded services from developed countries. It is becoming a major exporter of IT and back office services for many multinational firms.

In both China and India the dynamics of their recent growth have been provided by areas which the state had overlooked as being of little importance: the small-scale rural industries in China, and the IT-based service sector in India. These were the areas where capitalism was allowed to take its natural course, and once foreign markets were opened with the liberalization of foreign trade, the native entrepreneurial wit of economic agents not subject to the dead hand of the state generated a dynamism which no planner could have created. Unlike the Indians, the Chinese policy elite seem to have fully embraced capitalism. The new (often Western trained) mandarins who run the Chinese state recognize, as many in India still do not, that this is the only route to both prosperity and power for their nation—and like mandarins of yore it is the Chinese State and not any ideology that they serve. They are desperately seeking for ways to remove the remaining vestiges of their dirigiste past: the loss-making state enterprises. India by contrast seems stuck with its "Left" still unwilling to abandon its past dirigisme, who continue to block the necessary privatization of its public enterprises.

Thus, the most striking development in the last decades of the past century is the abandonment of the socialist route, and acceptance of the route first pioneered by Japan, by the two major Eurasian civilizations of India and China. They are now catching up rapidly after their years of relative decline with the rise of the West (see figure I.1). They are set to become the two largest economies after the United States in this century. After a near century detour, they have realized, as Japan did in the late nineteenth century, that they can modernize by joining the bandwagon of globalizing capitalism without westernizing and losing their souls. The most important sign that these two emerging giants are now willing and able to join the bandwagon of globalization is its acceptance, nay celebration, by the cultural nationalists represented by the BJP in India. In the late 1980s I remember witnessing numerous demonstrations organized by the BJP where they burned effigies of the then director general of GATT, Arthur Dunkel. But, in their last government (1999–2004), they embraced globalization and economic liberalization, and fought the 2004 election on a platform of further economic reforms. They have accepted that embracing globalization does not damage their cultural program of Hindutva.

Similarly, on a recent (October 2004) visit to Shanghai, after a gap of over six years, I saw an astonishing symbol of China's acceptance of globalizing capitalism. On my previous visit in the mid-1990s I visited the house where the Chinese Communist party was born. It was a small but elegant old-fashioned house surrounded by old traditional and new Communist housing—which have now all gone. Today it stands rather forlorn in an alley off a large pedestrian mall which is covered with the icons of global capitalism—Starbucks, Pizza Hut, McDonalds, Kentucky Fried Chicken, elegant French restaurants, luxury shops selling every Western brand, and the ubiquitous karaoke bars. It is filled with the burgeoning and prosperous Chinese middle class. Could those revolutionaries meeting in the small house off the lane have ever imagined that their sought-for revolution would lead to this: a capitalist paradise in an ostensibly Communist country?

If further proof were needed that capitalism is here to stay in China, the Communist party's attitude to the private sector has evolved over the years. In 1988, the constitution was revised to provide for the first time in China a legal basis for private enterprise, "and providing it with a status as a supplement to economic activity based on public ownership. By 1997, at its Fifteenth National Congress, the party went further, elevating the role of the non-state sector . . . to 'an important, integral part of China's socialist market economy.' By 2000, policy had evolved again, not only acknowledging the contribution that the private sector was making to the economy but also promising that private firms would be put on an equal footing with state-owned firms."[78] China also accepted much more onerous terms relating to domestic liberalization on its entry into the WTO than many other countries.

Long Yongtu, vice minister of foreign trade and China's chief global trade negotiator, confirmed in 2000 that China is fully converted to being part of global capitalism when he said: "Countries with planned economies have never been a part of economic globalization. China's economy must become a market economy in order to become part of the global economic system, as well as the economic globalization process."[79] The Chinese Communists seem well on the way to achieving this goal, not least because they see this as the route to popular opulence on which the legitimacy of this latest Chinese dynasty depends. The race for growth between the two emerging Asian giants is set to be the most dramatic event of this century.

The Polity

Will the rising prosperity of China lead to the democratization of its polity, as many in the West hope and the Communist party dreads? Can Indian democracy deliver the second generation of reforms that are required to complete India's integration into global capitalism? And what of Africa and the Middle East, which still lag behind in embracing global capitalism? I have argued elsewhere[80] that political habits are also part of a civilization's cosmological beliefs. They were formed in large part by the exigencies of geography in the region where these civilizations were born. But, as the Japanese first showed, it is possible to modernize and wrap one's traditional polity in Western trappings.[81]

Thus, for example, Chinese civilization originated in the relatively compact Yellow river valley, constantly threatened by the nomadic barbarians from the steppes to its north. It developed a tightly controlled bureaucratic authoritarianism as its distinctive polity which has continued for millennia to our day. The 1949 Communist victory is best seen as the establishment of another Chinese "dynasty," which since Deng's reforms has also recreated a modern mandarinate of technocrats, initially schooled abroad but increasingly at home in all the material beliefs and technologies of modernity. The Chinese Communist party is now co-opting capitalists. Some believe that this embourgeoisment of the party with the entry of Red capitalists will in time lead to the spread of democracy. But in a study based on survey research of the attitudes of these Red capitalists Bruce Dickson finds that, as with other studies of their attitudes, "private entrepreneurs in China have been reluctant to promote democratization . . . China's entrepreneurs are focused primarily on business interests, rather than overtly political ones. They believe local officials are as much part of the solution as they are part of the problem. This fits nicely with the idea that a market dynamic is leading to the formation of a noncritical sphere of civil society that is not necessarily a threat to the state, but is largely beneficial to it."[82] Thus, those who believe that its increasing prosperity will lead China to become democratic are, in my view, likely to be disappointed.

175

By contrast, Hindu civilization developed in the vast Indo-Gangetic plain, protected to a greater extent by the Himalayas from the predation of barbarians to the north. This geographical feature (together with the need to tie the then-scarce labor to the land) accounts for the traditional Indian polity, which was notable for its endemic political instability caused by numerous feuding monarchies, and for its distinctive social system embodied in the institution of caste.[83] This social system, by making war the work of professionals, saved the mass of the population from induction into the deadly disputes of its changing rulers. The tradition, whereby a certain customary share of the village output was remitted to the current overlord, discouraged any victor from disturbing the daily business of his newly acquired subjects. The democratic practices gradually introduced by the British have fit these ancient habits like a glove. The ballot box has replaced the battlefield for the hurly-burly of continuing "aristocratic" conflict, and the populace accepts with weary resignation that its rulers will through various forms of rent seeking take a certain share of output to feather their own nests.

But can India's democratic system with its equilibrium of rent-seeking interests complete the required economic liberalization? Many since the 1960s have predicted a dismal outcome for India's polity.[84] But it has shown a remarkable resilience. It has survived a direct assault on democracy during Indira Gandhi's Emergency in the mid-1970s; the breakdown of the Congress party's dominance in the 1980s; various bloody separatist movements; the emergence since the late 1980s of a succession of coalition governments with a large number of regional parties; and the emergence of the Hindu nationalist party (BJP) as the major contender to replace the Congress as the dominant party at the national level. Despite this political turbulence, the polity did succeed in reversing the dysfunctional Nehruvian settlement. While even with the shifting coalitions at the center, economic reform has continued over a decade—slowly but surely. Rob Jenkins (1999) explains and documents how the political players, particularly at the Center, used both a rearrangement of the previous spoils system, and the various conflicts of interest among the numerous rent seekers, to both institute and consolidate reforms in the 1990s. The improved productivity of the economy resulting from economic liberalization provided larger rents—through the new means documented by Jenkins—to the predators. They got an unchanged share of a larger pie. Jenkins rightly notes that an understanding of the dynamics of India's successful democracy and its ability to institute and continue economic reform requires abandoning many of the preconceptions of Western democratic theory. I believe that it will continue to surprise us by continuing, however slowly, to integrate India with global capitalism.

The continent of Africa has suffered most from the "precious bane" of natural resources. It is also the part of the Third World where its traditional polities, based on the legitimacy of tribal chiefs, were shattered by the Western scramble for Africa in the nineteenth century. The artificial states they established and bequeathed to their nationalist successors cut through ancient configurations or amalgamated historically opposing tribes within their borders. So, apart from intertribal conflict within these states, they have also been threatened by claimants from "across the border." The ensuing problems of governance have led the Four Horsemen of the Apocalypse to gallop with fury through the subcontinent. But, there is one shining exception— Botswana. It was a state which the British allowed to preserve its pre-colonial internal autonomy and tribal chiefs. Though its major source of wealth lies in the diamonds found after its independence, these have not as in so many other parts of Africa turned into a precious bane.[85] The tribal elites have been able to utilize the revenues for the general weal and Botswana's economic performance has matched that of the fastest growing economies of the Far East. Thus, unlike Asia where globalization has been thwarted by the fears of Westernization, there is no such dissonance between the cosmological beliefs of Africans and the material beliefs engendered by modernization. Its problems, and with them its failure to fully join the globalization bandwagon, are mainly due to the depredations of the nationalist predatory elites who inherited the artificial states created by colonialism.

Latin America too is a continent plagued with the curse of natural resources. Given its Christian heritage, its egalitarian cosmological beliefs are in dissonance with its ecology which generates large inequalities of income and wealth. Its neo-Thomist beliefs, which it inherited from the conquistadores of Spain and Portugal, involve a form of fundamentalist universalism not found in its Protestant neighbor to the north.[86] As Gary Wynia has noted: "politically, North Americans confine their feuds primarily to selecting officials and debating policies, but in Latin America feuds are more fundamental . . . democrats, authoritarians, and communists . . . all insist they know what is best for themselves and their neighbors."[87] This fundamentalist universalism also accounts, in my view, for the continent-wide swings and fashions in economic policy over the last two hundred years. These swings in intellectual fashion are rather like religious conversions—Carlos Menem in Argentina and Henrique Cardoso being major examples, while the dissonance between an unequal social reality and egalitarian cosmological beliefs has led to political cycles of democratic populism followed by authoritarian repression as the distributional consequences of the populist phase are found unacceptable by the upper classes. Chile is the one country which seems (at least to date) to have broken this cycle. Moreover, in the emerging tripartite international division of labor, with the emerging Asian giants now like the industrial North in the nineteenth century providing burgeoning markets for Latin American natural resource exports, the region can once again be expected to prosper through integration in the world economy.

The cosmological beliefs of Islam are not incompatible with democracy

177

or the market. After all, the Prophet Mohammed was a merchant. But despotism and a disjunction between state and society have characterized Muslim society from its origins.[88] Neither need prevent the countries of Islam from embracing global capitalism. It is the fear that the resulting modernization will also bring Westernization, and all that implies for their habits in the domestic domain, which is holding them back.

The Family

Most Eurasian civilizations had similar family patterns, based on extended families and arranged marriages. They had settled families to maintain their way of making a living through settled agriculture. The first papal revolution (in the sixth century) concerning the family changed these "family values" in the West, with the rise of nuclear families and marriages based on that primordial passion—love. But, traditional values concerning the sanctity of marriage were preserved through the fierce guilt culture based on sin promoted by the medieval Church. Even with Darwin's undermining of the Christian God, as we have seen, the Victorians still maintained these family values as part of their virtues. But in the last century, particularly since the 1960s, with the demoralization of its society, the West has gone back to the primordial practices of its hunter-gatherer ancestors in the domestic domain. It is this undermining of traditional family values and in particular the sexual license of the West which the cultural nationalists, particularly in the Muslim world, most fear.[89]

But, these fears are misplaced. Japan, and increasingly India and China, have shown that modernization need not entail the erosion of these traditional family values.[90] The examples of India and China are particularly instructive.

In India, with growing urbanization and industrialization, there is a growing disjunction between caste and occupation. But this change in material beliefs is not matched by any marked change in cosmological beliefs.[91] Their cornerstone remains the value of hierarchy and the importance of the endogamous caste/subcaste unit in personal affairs like marriage, though the notion of the "suitable boy" is no longer confined to the subcaste but encompasses a wider definition of the caste group. Equally important, a belief in hierarchy still forms a major part of the Hindu psyche, but with "hierarchical notions based on purity and pollution on the decline, and giving way to secular criteria such as education, income, kind of work performed, place of residence and life style."[92] Nor has the nuclear family replaced the joint family. A recent survey, of the attitudes of 18–35-year-old urban Indians, further supports the view that India's increasing modernization is not leading to the acceptance of Western mores in the domestic domain. This group is in the vanguard of globalization in India. Seventy percent said they would rather live in a joint rather than a nuclear family; 71 percent would not consider an old age home for an elderly person in their family; 75 percent would not want to have a live-in relationship with someone prior to marriage; and 88 percent find kissing in public unacceptable.[93] Cultural nationalists need not worry. Traditional values still predominate amongst the young. Modernization in India is not leading to the loss of its soul.

The Chinese family has been both excoriated and hailed. As Whyte notes in an excellent survey of the Chinese family, there has been a virtual 180-degree shift in views. The traditional view associated with Max Weber and various modernization theorists was that the Chinese family was a major brake on economic progress because its nepotism, initiative-sapping patriarchy, and personal rather than universalistic value system would make enterprises based on it inefficient. This is of course the view that both Stalin and Mao adopted in their assault on the family to establish their Communist nirvana. But Stalin proved more successful than Mao. Most scholars agree that, despite the state's constant threats and attacks, family obligations and loyalties have survived.[94] For, today, the Chinese family is being hailed as the engine of growth in the Sinic world, based on the undoubted success of the family-based businesses of Hong Kong and Taiwan and the growth of family-based industry in the nonstate sector in China.

Without going into the debates about the economic efficiency of the Chinese family, one unintended consequence of the Communists' assault on the family needs to be noted. The Maoist attack on the family, in particular the "one-child policy," has had some unintended consequences. The first is the highly biased sex ratio. There is a ratio of 118 boys to 100 girls at birth according to official statistics. The normal ratio is about 105 to 100. This reflects parents' desire to have a son to look after them in their old age. This need has become more acute with the smashing of the Maoist "iron rice bowl" with Deng's reforms. Health, education, and housing, which were free in the past, have in effect been privatized. This is putting an inordinate burden on the young. In urban China what is called the "4-2-1 phenomenon" is growing: four grandparents and two only-child parents being supported by one child. This poses a severe social problem for the future. But there are signs that the government might be moving to a two-child policy. The Chinese family today remains an essential institution for dealing with life's risks as it has for millennia.

But, as in India, many aspects of the traditional family have altered. Whyte summarizes these as a greatly improved status of women; fewer joint families; decline in parentally arranged marriages; increased female participation in the labor force outside the home; and a sharp decline in fertility. Nevertheless, other features have not changed: universal marriage is still the norm, extended families are overwhelmingly patrilocal, and "even though there is some increase in older Chinese living by themselves, still the great majority of Chinese spend their final years living with a grown child and his or her (usually his) family." The most important aspect of the Chinese family that has not changed is "the overwhelming loyalty that Chinese in all settings continue to feel towards their families. Obligations to the larger family are heavily stressed in child socialization . . . and young people seem to accept the message and fulfill its obligation."[95]

The survival of the Chinese family on the mainland, despite Mao's spirited attack, is due to its central role in Chinese cosmological beliefs. "To the extent that it is possible to speak of one strategic custom or institution in the mix of early China's cultural variables—strategic because of its pervasive ability to sanctify all other aspects of life and to legitimate and reinforce the lineage—it would seem to be ancestor worship and its social and political corollaries involving hierarchy, ritual deference, obedience and reciprocity."[96] The family has been the only dependable institution for the Chinese for millennia—a lesson reinforced by the turbulence of the last century. "For better for worse, for richer for poorer, in sickness and in health, in the last resort the family is all there is."[97]

Conclusions

My conclusions can be brief. Capitalism has always needed a moral underpinning to reduce the policing type of transactions costs resulting from unconstrained self-seeking. The cosmological beliefs of the various Eurasian civilizations provided these internalized moral codes, which were transmitted to the young through the processes of socialization using the moral emotions of shame and guilt. The West diverged from the Rest because of two papal revolutions, the first concerning the family, which changed its cosmological beliefs from the communalist ones it shared with other Eurasian civilizations to individualism. The contingent consequences of this on the accumulation and subsequent depredation of Church property led to the second papal revolution in the eleventh century, concerning the law and its enforcement through the church-state. This changed the material beliefs of the West by removing the lid most Eurasian civilizations had placed on the novelty and profit-seeking capitalist entrepreneur. It also created the legal and institutional infrastructure needed for the functioning of a market economy. This led to the Rise of the West.

The Rest had to come to terms with this rise after the West's global expansion led to direct or indirect imperialism and the wounding of their civilizations. Much of the history of the Rest over the last two hundred years has been to find a way to achieve the modernization they all seek—not least to overcome their military weakness—while maintaining their ancient traditions (their own cosmological beliefs). One of the major impediments to the

Rest joining the bandwagon of globalizing capitalism has been their fear that modernization (by changing their material beliefs) would lead to Westernization (a change in their cosmological beliefs). But, as I have argued elsewhere,[98] although in the rise of the West the change in cosmological and material beliefs were conjoined, this is not necessary, once the transferable legal and other infrastructure for a market and commercial society were created by Gregory VII's eleventh-century papal revolution. The Rest of the world has the option—as dramatically illustrated by the Japanese example—of adopting the West's material beliefs which are necessary for prosperity, without adopting the West's cosmological belief's and surrendering their own morality. In short, it is possible to modernize without Westernizing.

Japan was the first non-Western country to realize this, and the two Asian giants, India and China, after a century of fruitlessly trying to find a middle way to marry tradition with modernity, are now following the Japanese example. The only ancient civilization which has still not recognized this fully is Islam. Its cultural nationalists continue to pose a threat to the spread of globalizing capitalism in their lands. In Africa, it is not a dissonance between cosmological and material beliefs that has prevented the subcontinent from partaking in the globalization of capitalism. Rather, it is the failure, due in large part to the predation of nationalist elites in natural resource rich countries, to govern in the common interest.

While the fears of most of the cultural nationalists in the ancient Eurasian civilizations about globalization may have been allayed, the same cannot be said of the other group of anti-globalizers: those in the West who claim capitalism itself is immoral. We turn to their discontents in the next chapter.

7

"Capitalism with a Human Face"

Introduction

The "new dirigistes" form the second group of anti-globalizers. Unlike the cultural nationalists of the Third World, they are not necessarily against globalization but rather against capitalism and its globalization. Their moral objections against capitalism are based in part on the Romantic critique of its dehumanizing effects but also in a growing "social paternalism." This in turn has fed what Ken Minogue has called "constitutional mania," which emphasizes substantive social and economic rights in addition to the well-known liberties—freedom of speech, contract and association—emphasized by classical liberals. The "new dirigisme" seeks to use the law to enforce these "rights" based partly on "needs" and partly on the "equality of respect" desired by a heterogeneity of self-selected minorities differentiated by ethnicity, gender, and/or sexual preference. This attempt to define and legislate a newly discovered and dense structure of rights (including, for some activists, those of non-human plants and animals) requires a vast expansion of the government's power over people's lives.

In addition, the new dirigistes are also "moral paternalists" who want to coerce individuals to follow a new code of manners and morals which Himmelfarb has labeled the "New Victorianism." This morality, while condoning various forms of permissiveness, seeks to regulate its expression. Thus, writes Himmelfarb, "the New Victorians do not condemn promiscuity; they only condemn those men who fail to obtain the requisite consent for every phase of sexual intercourse. They do not denounce drunkenness; they only denounce those who take 'advantage' of their partner's drunkenness . . . They are not concerned with the kinds of crime that agitate most citizens [blaming these on economic and social conditions]; they only propose to pass new legislation to punish speech or conduct normally deemed uncivil rather than illegal."[1] This New Victorianism is different from the Victorian code of manners and morals which was an internalized moral code based on convention and tradition. The New Victorian code by contrast "is novel and contrived, officially legislated and coercively enforced."[2] Thus, the New Victorians "require employees, students and professors to attend 'sensitivity' and 'consciousness-raising' sessions to combat their supposed racism, sexism, and homophobia."[3] All this is reminiscent of Mao's Cultural Revolution. Like it, this "moral paternalism" seeks to use the state to legislate a particular morality.

This is of course a voice of Oakeshott's "enterprise" view of the state (discussed in chapter 1) which inevitably involves dirigisme. In my view, the Oakeshottian taxonomy distinguishing between the "civil association" and "enterprise" view of the state allows us to think clearly about the links between ethics, economics, and politics. The fog created by distinctions like negative and positive liberty and continuing attempts to reconcile these irreconcilables[4] can be readily dispelled by keeping Oakeshott's distinction between these two interpretations of the state in mind. The state seen as a civil association does not seek to legislate morality. The state seen as an enterprise association does.

With the death of "really existing socialism" in 1989, it was no longer feasible to argue against capitalism per se as it was the only remaining viable system to organize economic life. So, the "new dirigistes" have changed their tack. They want to reform capitalism in the name of freedom and justice: to create "capitalism with a human face."

Justice and Freedom

Contemporary classical liberals have found it difficult to counter this "new dirigisme" because it claims to be based on notions of justice and freedom; notions which remain central to their own traditions. In a penetrating analysis, the philosopher-economist Anthony de Jasay has provided a cogent reworking of the principles underlying classical liberalism, which enables us to counter many of the moral claims on which current critiques of global capitalism by the new dirigisme are based.

Jasay begins with an audacious move. He states: "The notion whether freedom is valuable or a free society is good, ought not to enter at all into a properly thought out political doctrine, liberal or other."[5] For, of the two arguments on which individual freedom can be considered to be of value, the *first*, that freedom is itself a final value, is one which opens the way to relativism. For while individual freedom may be valuable to me, there is no reason it should be valuable to someone in a different culture, and as our earlier discussion of the Sinic ethic showed, there are many cultures which have not valued it as the only or even an end. The *second* possible justification is that it allows us to choose what we prefer. But this ability to lead one's life as one chooses, or autonomy as others have called it, makes individual freedom merely of instrumental value. But then, what final value is this instrument serving? If we reply "freedom," we are in a circular argument. For if we posit some other final value, someone from another culture could once again deny it as being valuable.

But, the most basic reason for not relying on the concept of freedom to justify a classical liberal society and polity is because freedom in ordinary speech involves not having deliberate obstacles being placed in the way of individuals' actions. This immediately leads to the slide whereby "being *free* to do something and being *able* to do it"[6] are confounded. "One depressing end result is that we now call without the least semantic embarrassment, both the freedom to choose and the set of things available to be chosen by the same name freedom, distinguishing between them only by the misplaced adjective 'negative' and 'positive'."[7] The discourse of freedom then degenerates into one about all good things, and their availability is also called "freedom." An example is the recent book by the Nobel Prize–winning economic theorist Amartya Sen entitled *Development as Freedom*. This allows various policies forming part of the "social paternalist" enterprise view of the world to be smuggled in as being part of freedom.[8]

Instead Jasay, relying on the English Common Law tradition, defines the basic rules which should govern a civil association, and which the State seen as a civil association should uphold. "The basic rule is that a person is free to do what is *feasible* for him to do. This presumption is subject to two compatibility conditions. One relates a person's proposed actions to his own obligations, the other to harm to others."[9] This is, of course, J. S. Mill's famous principle of liberty. The burden of proof lies with someone who wants to prohibit individuals' actions, because he has an obligation—as in a contract, or promises made—not to do it, or if it would harm others. This process is equivalent to presuming the accused is innocent unless found guilty by due process.

In contrast to this Common Law tradition of justice, there is an alternative which may be called the Continental system of justice[10] or of "public law," as Jasay calls it. Unlike the Common Law tradition where people are free to do what is feasible and not expressly forbidden by the two compatibility conditions, individuals in this alternative tradition are presumed to be forbidden to undertake feasible actions unless they are expressly *permitted* by various "rights" granted under constitutional provisions. In fact, these "bills of rights" are only coherent if they provide a suspension of a tacit presumption that everything not covered by them is forbidden by "legislative discretion if not by legislative fiat." These "rights" ignore the central norm underlying classical liberalism that "whoever proposes to stop another from doing what is feasible must show a right to prohibit or obstruct the particular feasible action."[11]

But, just as with freedom as a final value, this norm of liberty too could be questioned by someone from a different culture. Jasay uses an epistemological argument, not a moral intuition, to justify this "liberty" norm. The epistemological argument concerns what can be verified. Of the two alternative legal traditions, the Common Law based on a list of *prohibited* actions is more readily verifiable than the Public Law tradition based on a list of *permitted* actions. As feasible actions are limitless, listing what we must not do is less onerous than listing what we are permitted to do. Even if the Public Law tradition accepted the liberal norm that individuals were at liberty to undertake feasible actions unless they harmed others or violated an obligation, it would have a problem. For it presumes that "*unless* it can be shown that the proposed action *is* harmless and breaches no obligation, it must *not* take its course."[12] If, as is usually the case, there is no clear boundary to the possible harms a particular action could cause, it will be impossible to prove (verify) that a feasible action is harmless. Similarly with obligations (which confer corresponding rights), it will be impossible to prove that some right has not been violated. In the common law tradition, the *prosecutor* has to prove that the defendant has in pursuing a particular action violated obligations or caused harm to others. In the Continental law tradition it is for the *defendant* to prove that he has not violated *any* right or caused *any* possible harm.

The Public Law tradition based on "bills of rights" also leaves the judicial process open to all kinds of opportunistic behavior, where innumerable third parties can make claims (even spurious) of limitless harms and obligations being violated. These "render ordinary processes of social cooperation excessively legalistic, litigious, costly and precariously dependent on judicial, administrative and regulatory review,"[13] a judgment which is corroborated by the experience of the leading "rights"-based polity, the United States.

Rights

If we accept the liberty norm of the Common Law based on prohibitions of feasible actions as being epistemologically more sound (being verifiable) than that of the Continental tradition based on permissions, what of property rights and human rights—which so many votaries of freedom have sought to defend?[14]

Property Rights

So-called property rights are mistakenly called rights. If an individual is free to do something which is not wrong, that is, it does not violate obligations

185

and causes no harm to others, this liberty must include the freedom to do what he likes with his property which includes his body as well as various material possessions like his car or his clothes. *Liberties are different from rights.* I own a house which I am at liberty to do with what I will. Suppose I lease it out to a tenant through a contract. This contract obliges me to relinquish my liberty to use my property in certain ways by giving up the liberty to live in it, and gives the tenant a right to use it in the way and on terms stipulated in the lease. While the property owner has the *liberty* to use his property, the nonowner has to get the *right* to use it which is provided by the lease. Thus, whereas liberties are not conferred by anyone, rights require someone else to have agreed to fulfill some obligation.

But how do I come to own property which I am at liberty to use as I may? Much is acquired through the proceeds of work, others through exchange like that of assets, and still others from gifts and inheritance. As in each of these ways of acquiring property, besides those based on exercising my own liberties, I am also the beneficiary of others who have exercised their liberty of using what they themselves own as they wish. These means of acquiring property meet the requirements of justice, as they are exercising a liberty without transgressing any obligation or causing harm to others.

But, as regards land there is the question: as we go back in history how did land that was free, a gift of nature, come to be owned? Over time, as land became scarce it was appropriated and enclosed, largely for economic reasons: when the marginal benefits for an individual from enclosing land were equal to or greater than the marginal costs of excluding others.[15] As it was not owned by anyone else, no one else's liberties were thereby infringed and hence this appropriation cannot be called morally unjust. But, conquest and seizure have been equally important in acquiring land. These would be morally unjust and calls for restitution would be justified. This is, of course, at the heart of the controversy about the "right to return" of the Palestinians in the Arab-Israeli dispute. But, though the claim maybe morally just, it is not expedient. For most societies throughout history have recognized the chaos that would be caused by seeking to redress any fault in the historical descent of every current title to property, no matter how far back the chain of transfers stretches. They have, therefore, correctly applied some form of statute of limitations—if for no other reason than recognizing that the sins of their fathers should not be visited upon their grandchildren and great-grandchildren.

Human Rights

What of "human rights"? We have seen that rights arise from contracts—actual or implicit—which give rise to obligations that have been accepted by someone else. Thus, "every right of one person has the *agreement* of another as its source, cause and evidence."[16] Agreement is crucial in generating rights and the corresponding obligations. Thus, what are often called social rights are not rights but *entitlements*. For instance, the right of the unemployed to unemployment insurance, or of the poor to welfare, are not rights but entitlements created by the state, which as they are not based on contract can be changed or repudiated. By contrast, a genuine right arising from a contract cannot be limited or withdrawn without the right holder giving his consent. These rights are sometimes called *specific* rights.

In addition, it has been claimed that there are human rights—a *general* right arising from the assumption that being *human* in some sense provides a justification for some rights which go beyond specific rights. They are the modern descendants of natural rights.[17] Hart claims that they arise from the general right, namely "the equal right of all men to be free."[18] They include the right to free speech, free worship, to walk about, to breathe. But, this right is redundant in the Common Law tradition. One is simply free to undertake any feasible action which does not infringe one's obligations (the specific rights of others) and does not cause harm to others.[19] It is only in the Public Law tradition that these rights would need to be specified, because all feasible actions require *permission*—including these human rights to breathe, to be able to speak freely, to perambulate, and so on. But as there are an infinite number of such rights, it will be impossible to delineate them all, leading to endless legalistic disputes. Individual freedom of action is much better protected by the Common Law tradition where one is free to take any feasible action subject to the constraints of harm and specific obligations (rights).

Social Paternalism and Dirigisme

We can now briefly outline the various ways in which enemies of capitalism have used the notion's of freedom and rights to insinuate various "enterprise" views of the state while seeming to subscribe to the classical liberal view of the state as a "civil" association. Most of these seek to provide justifications for redistributive measures. They all deny that there can be a just distribution of property based on contract, just transfers, and first possession—constrained by the necessary expedient of a statute of limitations to rectify past unjust acquisitions. For them property arises from the mutual gains provided by social cooperation.

It is argued that much of the existing stock of wealth is the result of social cooperation going back to Adam and Eve. It is in that sense a social inheritance, and belongs to the whole of society. But, largely for efficiency reasons, as the failure of "really existing socialism" has shown, it is inexpedient to rule out some private appropriation of this social wealth. Hence, some of this social wealth can be allowed to be converted into private property, on the terms and conditions specified by the co-owner—society. One of these conditions is that there should be no *social exclusion* from this social wealth of those who have been disadvantaged because of lack of talent or luck from partaking of the benefits produced by social cooperation. Hence, the state as the co-owner of this social wealth should use its coercive powers to force the fortunate to give up part of their property or income to the disadvantaged.

This edifice is, however, based on the myth that it is impossible to trace the individual contributions to past and present social cooperation which has generated this social wealth. Hence, all wealth must be taken to be the wealth generated by society as a whole. But, while there is no doubt that social cooperation has generated the wealth in the world, it is false to claim that no tracing of the individual contributions is available. Everyone who contributed by work was paid for their contributions in voluntary exchanges. Some of these payments were consumed and some saved and invested, with the resulting assets having the contributor's title to them. To coerce them to give away what is theirs, and which they are at liberty to use as they see fit, would be unjust. Though, undoubtedly, everyone has contributed to the generation and accumulation of a society's wealth over the millennia, this does not mean that everything is owed to society. "*Nothing is owed*," Jasay rightly notes, "everything has been paid for, one way or another, in a manner and to an extent sufficient to call forth the contribution. There is no further common pool claim overhanging the lot, for no payment must be made twice. He who sees and overhanging claim in favor of 'society' is seeing a mirage, or the wishful image of one."[20]

Equally tendentious is the claim that, because of the social cooperation required to obtain the mutual gains in a business or corporation, everyone is a *stakeholder*, who must be consulted and if necessary assuaged. But a corporation consists of a series of voluntary exchanges based on a contract where the worker has an obligation to perform certain specified tasks in payment for the agreed remuneration. The obligation to consult may be given by the employer to workers as part of the contract, thereby granting them a specific right matching the voluntarily agreed obligation.[21] But there can be no general right to consult "stakeholders," unless one believes that the sharing of the fruits of cooperation cannot be assigned by voluntary contract, and hence this social product has to be shared by continual negotiation or mediation by the co-owner of society's capital—the state. The dirigistes claim that the capital the employer deploys has only been implicitly leased to him, for reasons of efficiency, from society's capital owned by the state on its behalf. But this claim is false. The employer has justly acquired his capital from his past savings, and he can do with them what he pleases. There is nothing which belongs to society which has been leased out to the employer.

Another illegitimate claim is that employers wield coercive *economic power*, as they can force the weak to give in to the demands of the strong because of necessity. But this is to mistake the *actual options* open to the weaker party with their *hopes* for a better deal. The first is part of the set of feasible actions they can take, based on the offer made by the strong, which does not infringe the rules of justice that the owner is free to dispose of his endowment as long as he does not violate the constraints of harm and obligation. The hope depends upon what turns out to be a false expectation. To use the coercive power of the state to enforce this hope of the weak would be to violate the strong party's liberty to use their endowments as they wish. It would be unjust.

Similarly, any other coercion by the state to take a person's justly acquired property and to give it to someone else would also be ruled out in a state seen as a classical liberal civil association. This would rule out *redistributive taxes* as being unjust. Would it also rule out public transfers to the destitute? Most societies have made provision for the destitute: those incapable of making any living. This social safety net usually has been provided through private transfers from other family members or public charity. With the fraying of families in the West, these private social safety nets have also become frayed. Public charity remains the only alternative. Whether this should be voluntary or coercive will depend upon particular circumstances. But unless the coercive power is voluntarily and unanimously given by free agents to the State, its exercise would be unjust. However, where private charity can no longer be relied on to alleviate destitution, such near-unanimity of agreement for some form of public transfers may be forthcoming.[22]

Moral Paternalism and the New Victorians

In the early 1960s, while I was reading Philosophy-Politics and Economics at Oxford, there was a famous debate which we undergraduates followed avidly. It was between Lord Devlin, a law lord, and Professor H.L.A. Hart, the professor of jurisprudence at Oxford. The debate arose from the Wolfenden Report into sexual mores, particularly concerning homosexuality and prostitution. The Commission took a classical liberal line based on the arguments of J. S. Mill's *On Liberty*, and argued that as both homosexuality and prostitution were consensual acts between adults they should be permitted in private but not in public—as that would offend public decency. So prostitution should be legal but prostitutes should not be allowed to solicit on the streets. This recommendation was enacted into law but that consensual homosexuality in private should be legalized was rejected. Hart, in his *Law, Liberty and Morality*, basing himself on Mill argued that legal coercion of homosexuals was unjustified as consensual homosexuality did not harm others. Devlin in his *The Enforcement of Morals* demurred and argued that "the suppression of vice is as much the law's business as the suppression of subversive activities" because he stated "a recognized morality is as necessary to society's existence as a recognized government."[23] A shared morality is the cement of society and

189

the law is justified in enforcing it. Hart, in a subtle analysis which need not concern us here, argued against Devlin by basically supporting Mill's principle of liberty, namely: "The only purpose for which power can rightfully be exercised over any member of a civilized community against his will is to prevent harm to others . . . His own good either physical or moral is not a sufficient warrant . . . He cannot rightfully be compelled to do or forbear because it will be better for him to do so, because it will make him happier, because in the opinions of others, to do so would be wise or even right."[24]

But, on one point Hart demurred from Mill's position on moral paternalism, which Mill rules out with specific examples like restrictions on the sale of drugs (Mill, chapter 5) as being an infringement of the liberty of the would-be purchaser. Hart by contrast states: "paternalism—the protection of people against themselves—is a perfectly coherent policy. Indeed, it seems very strange in mid-twentieth century to insist upon this, for the wane of laissez faire since Mill's day is one of the commonplaces of social history, and the instances of paternalism now abound in our law, criminal and civil." This, he goes on to say, "is due, in part to a general decline in the belief that individuals know their own interests best, and to an increased awareness of a great range of factors which diminish the significance to be attached to an apparently free choice or to consent. Choices may be made or consent given without adequate reflection or appreciation of the consequences; or in pursuit of merely transitory desires; or in various predicaments when the judgment is likely to be clouded; or under inner psychological compulsion; or under pressure by others of a kind too subtle to be susceptible of proof in a court of law."[25]

Here is the modern "liberal" voice in its making. It takes part of the classical liberal principle of the individual's liberty to undertake feasible actions if they do not harm others, to permit every consensual private sexual activity. But, it abjures the classical liberal case against moral paternalism, on the specious grounds that individuals are not really free to choose. So, while permissiveness is legitimate, all forms of paternalistic supervision or coercion are needed to ensure that individual choices are in fact freely made. As these choices are supposed to be psychologically determined, it also becomes imperative to exercise thought control: to make "windows into men's souls." This is not classical liberalism but the route to 1984 and Big Brother, and classical liberals would eschew this moral paternalism, however politically correct it is currently.

This moral paternalism is also being fed by the so-called "communitarians" whose leader is the sociologist Amitai Etzioni. His themes have been taken up by politicians of the "Third Way" like Tony Blair and Bill Clinton. The notion of "social capital" has also been developed in support of these views, most famously by the political scientist Robert Putnam. The third-way politicians were searching for floating voters "who liked lower taxes and limited government but were put off by the celebration of egoism in the

Thatcher-Reagan years. Community and its attendant watchwords—voluntarism, civic virtue and neighborly responsibility—arrived like a gift to politicians trying to 'redefine' government."[26] Social ills from poverty, street crime, vandalized urban housing, and urban anomie—epitomized by the title of Putnam's article and book "Bowling Alone"—were seen as the results of an erosion of community and the running down of social capital.

Communitarianism is a broad church, which in part recognizes the demoralization of Western society.[27] But unlike classical liberals, instead of emphasizing the role of tradition in socializing the young in a morality which provides the cement of society, communitarians want the state to enforce a form of moral paternalism. "A skeptic about the movement once joked that communitarians want us to live in a Puritan Salem but not believe in witches."[28] Having eschewed a morality based on religion or tradition, and also—with the rise of Freudianism—the use of the moral emotions of shame and guilt in the socialization of children, the only instruments left to communitarians to reverse the demoralization of Western society are exhortations or the enforcement of morality by the state.

Not surprisingly, therefore, it is the proponents of the Oakeshottian "enterprise" view of the state—Fascism and Catholic corporatism—which have upheld the claims of the "community" against the individual. For communitarianism is a philosophy which believes that there is a common good that resides in the national community. The state can override individual liberties to subserve this common good. Moral paternalism by the state is therefore justified. For, on this view, the community is indivisible, needs to speak with a single voice, and adopt a uniform line of conduct. Dissenters must be silenced or "reeducated" to conform to the views and behavior of the community. It is Mao's Cultural Revolution. It is a profoundly illiberal philosophy which seeks to extend state power into numerous private spheres where on classical liberal principles the state has no right to tread. This does not mean that communitarians are not right to diagnose the disease as the demoralization of society. It is the proposed means—a further extension of the state into what were hitherto private spheres—which are in question.

Nor is the notion of "social capital," which provides a technocratic gloss to this illiberal creed, any more cogent. As both the economist Nobel Laureates Kenneth Arrow and Robert Solow have argued, an essential element in the notion of capital is that it implies the deliberate sacrifice in the present (usually designated as "consumption foregone" by economists) for future benefits (consumption). The type of "social networks" emphasized by theorists of "social capital" as its main component are often built up for noneconomic reasons and may not involve any foregone consumption. "People may get jobs through networks of friendship or acquaintance, but they do not, in many cases, join the networks for that purpose."[29] What the proponents of social capital seem to be after are good behavior patterns which lead

191

to trust and thence the lowering of the policing type of transactions costs which affect economic performance. But this was precisely the role of cosmological beliefs or "morality." To put this into a meaningless concept of social capital shows at the least a certain maladroitness, but even more importantly the reluctance to face up to the factors which have led to the demoralization of the West.

Capitalism and Happiness

The romantic critique of capitalism has also had one other refrain. Capitalism breeds unhappiness. Many, from Marx to Etzioni, have seen this leading to imminent trends for capitalism's self-destruction.[30] But, as Robert Lane has rightly noted, "Given the thriving economic success of the U.S. version of individualist capitalism at the end of the twentieth century, there is an anachronistic quality to these accounts of capitalism's tendency to destroy itself. It is the theories of immanence and not capitalism that seem to destroy themselves."[31]

Recently many economists have examined this presumed blemish of capitalism. Basing themselves on the cross-country and cross-cultural data provided by the *World Values Survey*, they find that on its measures of subjective happiness there is a moderate positive correlation with per capita income (in PPP $), which is strongest with countries with a per capita GNP up to $10,000 (in 1995). "There are no rich countries where people's happiness, on average is low. But, for the rich countries, it does not seem that higher per capita income has any marked effect on happiness."[32] This is hardly surprising, because real income is likely to be only one element in a person's happiness, and as economic theory postulates diminishing marginal utility from increased income (consumption) we would expect rich countries to have reached what the Cambridge economist Frank Ramsey and John Maynard Keynes postulated as the "Bliss" level of utility. Nevertheless, happiness economics—as we may call it—has both tried to econometrically estimate the determinants of "happiness" and to argue that the standard microeconomics of utility theory need to be revised. These byways need not detain us.[33]

More serious are the implications various dirigistes have drawn from this line of research. Some[34] have argued that the estimated "happiness functions" provide an approximation to the social welfare function, which hitherto had been a merely theoretical construct of modern welfare economics. The constrained maximization of the estimated "happiness function" is supposed to yield the optimal values of its determinants which public policy is then expected to implement. But, as Frey and Stutzer rightly note, even if one accepts the validity of the empirical estimates of this happiness function as a reasonable approximation to the theoretical social welfare function (which is dubious) there are still problems in using it for public policy.[35] The first arises from

Arrow's famous Impossibility Theorem, which showed that under a set of "reasonable assumptions" it was not possible to aggregate individual preferences into a social welfare function which consistently ranked outcomes; something which a dictator would obviously be able to do. Despite a lot of useless ink spilled by "social choice theory" on trying to determine the robustness of the theorem with the weakening of its assumptions,[36] the economic theorist Peter Hammond rightly concluded that "there is no way we can use empirical observations on their own to produce an ethically satisfactory cardinalization,[37] let alone an ethically satisfactory social welfare ordering."[38] The second problem is that, like all forms of dirigisme advocated by public economics, this happiness economics assumes that the agents of the state charged with its implementation are benevolent Platonic Guardians—an assumption we have questioned.

The other implications some others have drawn from this way of thinking are more disturbing. In the late 1970s, Fred Hirsch in his *Social Limits to Growth*[39] argued that the fight for social status, and so-called "positional goods," would only lead to subjective unhappiness. For, by definition, unlike other consumer goods the supply of "positional goods" was limited. Hirsch and other economists, therefore, wish to deter this socially wasteful competition for status through heavy taxation of the winners in the status race.[40] More recently Richard Layard[41] has argued that as working too hard is one source of unhappiness in capitalist economies, work should be taxed more heavily, so that people substitute leisure for work at the margin—something the French government has imposed by fiat with its statutory reduction of the working week with no apparent improvement in happiness to offset the obvious losses in economic output.

These are all, of course, voices of Oakeshott's "enterprise association" view of the state. The most extreme form of this voice was the book by the Marxist economist John Roemer,[42] who argued that as in modern economies most inequalities were due to the differing intellectual endowments of individuals, higher IQ individuals should be taxed more heavily. Without having read Roemer, the Khmer Rouge leader Pol Pot followed this advice to its logical conclusion when he had anyone with any education clubbed to death in the killing fields of Cambodia. A gentler dirigiste form is being followed by New Labour in Britain which, in the name of ending "social exclusion," wants university entrance to be based not on merit but on social circumstances, and further, wants universities to stop classifying their graduates to prevent employers from using these grades to "discriminate" against those with poorer degrees. Perhaps the best course to level the educational playing field would be for the government to give every child at birth along with their birth certificate another one for a first class honors degree from a university of their parents' choice!

The trouble with all these critiques of the psychologically dysfunctional effects of capitalism is that they confuse two aspects of any society: questions of how best to make a living (its material beliefs) with those concerning in Plato's words "how one should live" (its cosmological beliefs). Capitalism provides a new and highly productive way of making a living. That is why, despite century-old predictions of its imminent collapse, it has not only survived but despite many false starts is spreading globally. But how the ensuing prosperity can best be used to lead a good life will depend upon a society's cosmological beliefs. Many of the social ills adduced to capitalism, by Lane for example, like the decline in family values and companionship,[43] have less to do with capitalism (the change in the West's material beliefs flowing from the second eleventh-century papal revolution) than individualism (the change in its cosmological beliefs promoted by the first sixth-century papal revolution in family affairs). It is the subsequent demoralization of its society rather than the instrument of its prosperity—capitalism—which is to be blamed for the social ills cited by the "happiness researchers."

This would not have come as a surprise to the sages of the Scottish Enlightenment. Discussing happiness in his *Theory of Moral Sentiments*, Adam Smith wrote:

> Happiness consists in tranquility and enjoyment. Without tranquility, there can be no enjoyment; and where there is perfect tranquility there is scarce any thing that is not capable of amusing. But in every permanent situation, where there is no expectation of change, the mind of every man, in a longer or shorter time, returns to its natural and usual state of tranquility. In prosperity, after a certain time it falls back to that state; in adversity after a certain time it rises up to it. . . . The great source of both the misery and disorders of human life, seems to arise from overrating the difference between one permanent situation and another. Avarice over-rates the difference between poverty and riches; ambition, that between a private and a public station; vain-glory, that between obscurity and extensive reputation . . . Except the frivolous pleasures of vanity and superiority, we may find, in the most humble station, where there is only personal liberty, every other which the most exalted can afford; and the pleasures of vanity and superiority are seldom consistent with perfect tranquility, the principle and foundation of all real and satisfactory enjoyment. . . . Consider the . . . conduct of almost all the greatly unfortunate, either in private or public life, . . . and you will find that the misfortunes of by far the greater part of them have arisen from their not knowing when they were well, when it was proper for them to sit still and be contented. The inscription upon the tombstone of the man who had endeavored to mend a tolerable constitution by taking physic; "*I was well, I wished to be better; here I am*"; may generally be applied with great justness to the distress of disappointed avarice and ambition.[44]

Thus, it is the pursuit of the classical virtues that led to happiness. The Scottish sages never believed, nor should their classical liberal followers, that material prosperity is necessarily the route to happiness. This is of course the truth recognized by the various Eurasian religions, for whom their respective codes of conduct and the virtues they propagated were the very cements of their society that were assumed to promote happiness. Thus my conclusion that the complaints about the unhappiness that capitalism has caused are better addressed to the causes of the West's demoralization (the course of its individualism) than the instruments of its prosperity (capitalism).

The Corporation under Attack

Most of these attacks on global capitalism have coalesced into an attack on the modern corporation—particularly in its Anglo-American and multinational form. It is argued that the corporation must assume various social responsibilities if it is to be acceptable. Various activist spokesmen of an imagined "international civil society" will otherwise take action, ranging from protests, consumer bans to public interest litigation and pressure on governments to regulate socially irresponsible corporations. Most of their claims about the damage inflicted by multinationals on poor countries are false (see chapter 4). Nevertheless, the recent scandals following the dot-com speculative bubble have bred moral outrage at the behavior of corporations and led to demands that governments should find ways to improve their governance. Many are advocating the adoption of stakeholder capitalism to replace the shareholder capitalism enshrined in the Anglo-American classical liberal tradition, and many corporations have succumbed to the demands for corporate social responsibility. But, these are again old and atavistic beliefs and demands.

In an important book, *Saving Capitalism from Capitalists*, Raghuram Rajan and Luigi Zingales have argued that financial repression has been a powerful means of maintaining the wealth and power of the few. As financial capitalism has evolved it has meant greater access for those without inherited wealth or powerful connections to obtain the financial means "to escape the tyranny of collateral and connections.[45] The contemporary American search fund which funds an idea is the ultimate symbol of the most highly developed financial market "where a person's ability to create wealth and attain economic freedom is determined by the quality of her ideas [and skills] rather than the size of her bank balance."[46] By contrast, in financially underdeveloped or artificially repressed economies the monopolization of access to finance by financiers, through implicit or explicit collusion with the state, prevents such outsiders from challenging the incumbent insiders. It has been a powerful means for the rich and well connected to maintain their wealth and power. Stakeholder, or as Rajan and Zingales term it, "relationship capitalism," has been the modern version of this exclusion, as have the various nationalized banking systems in both communist and socialist countries like China and India. These are attempts to prevent the creative destruction of capitalism to do its work. By contrast, the Anglo-Saxon corporation as it has evolved has allowed the economic opportunities of those without resources to expand, and enabled outsiders to challenge the insiders to impart the dynamism of death and rebirth which is involved in the most efficient deployment of an economy's resources. But the insiders even within this Anglo-Saxon form of capitalism, as Adam Smith well knew, will still collude or use the political process to keep out outsiders.

But, how did this modern corporation evolve? Though it has various antecedents, particularly in the guilds found in most of the ancient agrarian civilizations, the notion of a "corporate person" whereby loose associations of persons were given a legal persona goes back to the Middle Ages. It was the result of the legal revolution of Pope Gregory VII in the eleventh century. These corporations included universities, towns, religious communities, and the guilds. These "corporate persons" "honeycombed medieval society, providing security and fellowship in a forbidding world. They also provided a means of transmitting traditions—not to mention considerable wealth—to future generations."[47]

It was the transmission of and preservation of wealth which was of particular concern to the Pope, and led to the canon law which provided the legal basis for the corporation. It was to become the most important part of the legal infrastructure required for a market economy which was to lead to the rise of the West.

But, the corporation has always had an uneasy relation with the state. Feudal monarchs worried about its immortal status. "They circumvented feudal fees by never dying, never coming of age, and never getting married."[48] The state has always sought to regulate them. Till the sixteenth century most of the economic corporations were guilds which were little more than trade unions. It was the growth of the great chartered companies during the age of exploration, of which the East India Company was the longest lasting and the most famous, which gave these corporations their modern form. They were joint stock companies issuing shares that could be traded. They also limited the liabilities of the shareholders. They thus provided for the sharing of risk among a group of shareholders. Most of the companies were chartered monopolies, and as such they roused the ire of Adam Smith.

With their stocks being traded, these corporations were liable to speculative bubbles. The most famous was the South Sea Bubble of 1720, when a chartered company the South Sea Company originally set up with a monopoly of trade with South America, switched its operations in 1719 to the market in the new public debt created by the Glorious Revolution. It obtained parliamentary approval for taking over the entire national debt. There was a speculative frenzy to acquire South Sea shares. This was aided and abetted by the company's securing a Bubble Act in 1720 which made it extremely difficult to set up a new joint-stock company and deprived investors of alternative avenues for deploying their capital. When the speculative mania faded, and the company's share price fell with it, the government had to nationalize the company. Many—including the well-born and well-connected—lost their shirts. This led to a reaction against all joint-stock companies for at least a generation. But gradually the dead hand of the state in regulating joint-stock companies was lifted.

It was not till Gladstone's 1862 Companies Act that the modern corporation was born. This made incorporation a "liberty" and not a privilege. The most powerful instrument for sharing risk, dispersing ownership, and maximizing profits was thereby created. In the United States, chartered companies had existed from its inception, but the state began to step back earlier, in the early part of the nineteenth century. Germany and Japan, as they began to industrialize, also saw the corporation as an essential instrument for economic progress. But it was a different animal from the Anglo-American variety.

After Germany's unification in 1871, it soon came to rival Britain and the United States in its industrial advance based on its corporations. But there were four main differences between Germany and its Anglo-American cousins. First, Germany did not prohibit cartels. Nor was there any anti-monopoly legislation like the U.S. Sherman Antitrust Act. This tolerance of combination was based on the belief propagated by Frederic List that the basic economic unit was not the individual but the nation and that industry should serve the national weal. Second, unlike the Anglo-American version, there were incestuous connections between the industrial corporations and the commercial banks. Third, German corporations had a two-level system of corporate control. It was enshrined in an 1870 law allowing free incorporation but requiring companies to not only have a management board responsible for day-to-day decisions, but also a supervisory board consisting of various stakeholders. Besides shareholders, these stakeholders included various interest groups: banks, cartel members, local politicians, and trade unions. In this stakeholder corporatism, companies were required by Bismarck in the late 1880s to be socially responsible: by providing social insurance to their employees and "co-determination" by giving a formal voice to workers on company boards.

In Japan, after its opening with the Meiji Revolution, the reformers scouted around for Western models for all aspects of their march to modernization. They also chose a form of stakeholder capitalism through the *zaibatsu*. These were conglomerates at whose center was a family-owned holding company, with other associated firms linked by cross-shareholding and interlocking directorships. The conglomerates included banks and insurance companies which channeled private savings to the various other enterprises in the group. They recruited high flyers from universities to be professional managers and offered lifetime employment with attendant perks to their employees.

After the Second World War, the Allies tried to introduce more Anglo-American types of capitalism in the two countries, most notably in General MacArthur's busting of the *zaibatsu*. But old habits die hard. The German "social market" recreated Bismarckian corporatism, while in Japan the *zaibatsu* was reborn as the *keiretsu*. This corporatist model was then exported to other Asian countries, most notably South Korea, whose *chaebol* represented another example of this corporatist capitalism. Since, until recently, these corporatist countries were undoubtedly economically successful, they were held up as examples of countries where stakeholder capitalism had proved to be both as efficient and more socially cohesive than Anglo-American shareholder capitalism. But the recent travails of the Asian model of capitalism (discussed in chapter 4) show that at the turn of the millennium all is not well with this corporatist form of capitalism.

Micklethwait and Wooldridge suggest that German industrial success depended less on its stakeholder capitalism than the German cult for scientific and vocational education and the respect accorded to managers, many of whom were technicians. The Japanese success depended much more on catching up with the West, for which its particular form of corporatism proved highly useful. For late developers with abundant labor, it is easy to discern the initial industrial structure in line with their comparative advantage. It consists of small-scale enterprises producing labor-intensive goods like shoes and clothes. In these small-scale enterprises the capital required can usually be mobilized from within the extended family or small partnerships. Most of these will be run by owner-managers. But, as with growth, the country's comparative advantage shifts toward more capital-intensive lines, individuals will not have the requisite capital available unless there is a concentration of wealth, with some individuals or households having the large amounts of capital required to establish the business and retain control. In Japan and Korea the state used the banks, which were indirectly under their control, to create these concentrations of wealth in the zaibatsu and chaebol. Thus, the characteristic form of corporatism of the Asian model developed, with its close cooperation between the state, the banks, and industrial enterprises.

In England and America, the growth of shareholder capitalism allowed this agglomeration of large amounts of capital to occur naturally. But, as the firms became larger, ownership tended to get more diffused among a larger number of shareholders. This trend was accompanied by the increasing use of professional management to run the business. In time this led to the rise of managerial capitalism with a growing potential divergence between the objectives of the shareholders (the owners) and the managers (their agents). The former were interested in maximizing the returns to their investments which came from the profits the firm earned. The larger the profits, and the more they were as paid out in dividends, the higher the return to the shareholders. Managers, though not indifferent to profits, would be more interested in using these to serve their own ends: paying themselves higher salaries and reinvesting profits into the expansion of the firm to acquire greater power and status. These managerial objectives would not necessarily maximize the returns to shareholders. This "agency" problem, as it has been called, arises whenever there are many principals who find it difficult to act collectively because of the problems of free riding to which large group decision making is subject.[49] They will be unable to collectively monitor the actions of their agents—the managers—to see that they are maximizing shareholder value.

This problem can be avoided by creating large concentrations of wealth or finding ways for some concentrated wealth holders—like rich families—to indirectly control enterprises run by managers.[50] This in effect was the path chosen by the countries which adopted various forms of corporatism. The financial institutions which were part of the ultimately family-owned conglomerates channeled the savings of the general public to the enterprises. As the businesses grew larger, this bank finance became the major source of capital for the firms. This process was directed by the state as a major stakeholder in the enterprises. But, this could and did lead to immense moral hazard in this form of capitalism. Neither the controlling family owners, whose own financial stake was progressively diluted over time, or the managers, or the bankers found it necessary to undertake prudent investments, as they knew that with the involvement of the state as the ultimate stakeholder, they would always be bailed out by the government. Once the easy "catch-up" stages of industrialization were completed, this led to many bad investment decisions, and thence financial crises.

After painstaking detective work, Albert Ando has quantified the effects of stakeholder capitalism in Japan. He finds that the cumulative net savings of the Japanese household sector (at 1990 prices) between 1970 and 1998 was 1,250 trillion yen. The change in the net worth for this sector during the same period was 860.7 trillion yen. Thus, the Japanese "household sector suffered a real capital loss of 389 trillion"! Roughly three-fourths of this huge capital loss is attributable to the loss of market value by Japanese corporations. Over this period they "managed to incur capital losses of 405.5 trillion in their market value." How did this happen? Working out the rates of return of nonfinancial corporations and both for them and financial corporations for 1996, he finds that the returns were just above 2 percent for the former and 1.6 percent for the latter. These low returns are due to Japanese corporations having "over-invested in plant and equipment using funds retained through a very high rate of depreciation and the large savings channeled through financial institutions."[51] This led to very high capital-output ratios—which continued to rise during the depressed 1990s—and very low rates of return. Thus, an aging population finds that its stakeholder capitalism lost 31 percent of its lifetime savings over thirty years. It is hardly surprising that they continue to save rather than spend to see them through their uncertain old age. The Japanese example is a salutary warning to all those enamored of stakeholder capitalism. For a generation of ordinary Japanese, who through their thrift and productivity saw Japan rise like a phoenix from its wartime destruction, it has meant that as they aged, their hopes along with their savings have turned to ashes.

But what then accounts for the postwar Japanese and German economic miracles, which many have ascribed to their stakeholder corporatism. A detailed study of the comparative growth experience of OECD countries by Maurice Scott shows that there was no such miracle. The Japanese growth rate of 9 percent between 1960 and 1973, and the German rate of 6 percent between 1955 and 1962, can be explained entirely by the investment rate, the growth of the quality adjusted labor force and a catch-up variable. The stakeholder model of capitalism had little to do with it. But the subsequent decline in their growth rates and the continuing stagnation of their economies can be blamed on the rigidities and inefficiencies in their markets for labor and capital caused by the stakeholder model. They are reluctantly and slowly moving away from this to the shareholder model of the Anglo-Americans.

If the stakeholder model with its collusion between industry, banks, governments, and trade unions has led to these inefficient outcomes, can the Anglo-American shareholder model with its "agency" problem caused by the separation between ownership and management do any better? Are the latest scandals following the bursting of the dot-com bubble, and those associated with the greedy 1980s, a sign that this model too bilks the multitudinous private investors for the benefit of fat cat managers of the system?

With the separation of ownership from management, managers were prevented from milking shareholders in the Anglo-American model through the threat of hostile takeovers—hostile to the company's management but friendly to its shareholders. If a management was not maximizing shareholder value, and using the company's profits for its own ends, its share price would decline compared to other companies in the industry. A corporate raider could offer the shareholders a deal whereby he offered to buy their shares at a premium, and took over the corporation to serve shareholder rather than managerial interests. The existing management would of course be sacked. It is this market for corporate control which would control bad managers.[52] Gordon Gekko is good for the market.

In the late 1950s to mid-1960s there was a fairly unregulated market for corporate control in the United States. In the takeovers that ensued, shareholders received on average 40 percent over the pre-bid price for their shares. But, following the howls of protests by threatened managers, the U.S. Congress passed the Williams Act in 1968. This removed the highly profitable el-

ement of surprise in hostile takeovers and made it more expensive for outsiders to mount a successful bid. But, it did not kill hostile takeovers—a wave
of them in the 1980s restructured U.S. business. Over half of U.S. corporations became targets, while many others restructured to avoid becoming targets. This led the managements of the largest U.S. corporations to petition
state governments for protection from corporate "raiders." The legislatures
and courts obliged, by allowing managers to protect themselves from
takeovers with so-called "poison pill" defenses. The number of hostile bids
declined precipitously. The takeovers which took place were through friendly
mergers. In these, the incumbent managers agree to cede control in return for
lucrative consulting arrangements, stock or stock options in the acquiring
company, generous severance packages, and other bonuses. In these mergers,
the managers, not the shareholders, get the largest share of the premium being
paid for control of the company. As hostile takeovers declined from 14 percent
of all mergers in the 1980s to 4 percent in the 1990s, not surprisingly executive
compensation soared. "Every statute, adjudication, or regulation that in any
way inhibited the free functioning of the market for corporate control simply
raised the real cost of ousting inappropriate managers. Dollar for dollar, every
increase in those costs could be claimed by incumbent managers, either in
greater rewards for themselves or in inefficient management policies. Until
the real cost of wastefulness equals the cost of a successful takeover fight, they
remain secure behind a legal barrier to their ouster, at least until the whole
house of cards collapses."[53]

This is, of course (as we argued in chapter 2), the predictable outcome
of regulations which seek to tamper with the free functioning of the market—
in this case the market for corporate control. This attenuation of the market
by making hostile takeovers more difficult was worsened by another feature of
the postwar fiscal system—the double taxation of dividends. In both America
and Britain the profits of corporations which belong to shareholders were first
taxed through corporation tax. When part of these post-tax profits were paid
as dividends to shareholders, they were again taxed as part of their income.
This greatly reduced the post-tax return to investors from shares in corporations. Most of their returns then depended upon rises in the share price,
which in turn depended upon the reinvestment of the company's profits into
new, and hopefully profitable investments. One means of motivating managers to take account of shareholder value was to link their remuneration to
stock options. Both managers and shareholders now had a common interest
in seeing an increase in the company's shares price. This gave managers an incentive to manipulate their share price through the fraudulent practices
shown up by the Enron and other scandals during the 1990s stock market
bubble. But, though there is a lot of wringing of hands at these clearly illegal
accounting practices, as Demsetz notes, "indeed I wonder just how many
shareholders might have objected to these misrepresentations if they had be-

lieved they would remain undiscovered."[54] The proposed removal of the tax on dividends in the United States will help corporate governance, for with the tax on corporate profits still in place, it will provide incentives to managers to retain less of post-tax profits and pay more out in dividends, shifting resources from management to shareholder control.

The perceived ills of Anglo-American shareholder capitalism shown up in the bursting of the 1990s stock market bubble are not therefore a sign of some decrease in corporate morality—though there have been some clearly illegal practices which are rightly being dealt with by the courts—but due to the perverse incentives created for managerial "rent seeking" by the regulations limiting hostile takeovers, and the unintended effects of fiscal policy through the double taxation of dividends. With the double taxation of dividends due to end, if all the regulations preventing hostile takeovers can also be repealed, the unregulated market for corporate governance would again provide checks on predatory managements. Executive compensation will begin to fall, accountants will have less pressure to cook the books, and the Anglo-American corporation would pursue the innovation, efficiency, and profitability that has till now been its hallmark.

But there is one final cloud on the horizon. Various activists have been successful in persuading many people and corporations in the previous citadels of Anglo-American capitalism that corporations have a social responsibility to pursue "sustainable development." We will discuss this issue in greater detail in chapter 8. Though this corporate social responsibility is not as yet being legislated in the bastions of Anglo-American capitalism, there are clearly pressures to do so. This would create a moral version of stakeholder capitalism with dire results. For, as David Henderson has shown in his devastating critique of this program of what he labels the "global salvationists,"[55] the objectives to be subserved are unclear, the means to do so and judge their success even more so. As long as the pursuit of this moral agenda is not made compulsory in the Anglo-American shareholding countries—as the stakeholder form of capitalism was in Germany and Japan—then, as this form of capitalism is compatible with a thousand flowers blooming, companies which favor the corporate social responsibility agenda will have to compete with those interested in the traditional objective of maximizing shareholder value. If shareholders prefer "ethical" companies irrespective of their relatively poorer earnings (as they serve many other gods besides profits), they will bid up their share price relative to their earnings. If not, their share price will decline compared to their more politically incorrect peers, with the consequent threat to their future survival. This has already happened to some of the firms and funds which have adopted this moral stance. Thus, in the recent bear market, the ethical mutual funds which eschewed holdings of tobacco stocks on ethical grounds have found that their performance has been worse than their more economically hard-headed peers, as tobacco shares proved more resilient to the downturn than other stocks. Similarly, Levi Strauss, which created denim jeans, embarked under its CEO Robert Haas on what has been described as "a failed utopian management experiment"[56] in which it "was intent on showing that a company driven by social values could outperform a company hostage to profits alone." The outcome was declining sales, profits, and share value. As Nina Munk entitled her article, this was "How Levi's Trashed a Great American Brand."

Conclusions

Our conclusions can be brief. The major difference between the first liberal international economic order (LIEO) established under British leadership in the nineteenth century and the contemporary LIEO fostered under the U.S. Imperium is that while the former embodied the classical liberal view of the state—it did not seek to legislate morality—the latter is infected by the enterprise view in both the domestic concerns for social welfare and the desire to export Western values like "human rights" and "democracy" to the Rest of the world.[57] But, the notion of human rights is (as Bentham rightly observed) "nonsense on stilts." A state seen as a civil association will seek to uphold its citizens' liberty to undertake feasible actions which are only constrained by avoiding harm to others, and keeping one's obligations. Rights arise as the other side of a voluntary agreement between two parties whereby one party willingly takes on obligations to the other party, who thus acquires rights. This classical liberal notion of justice is embodied in the Common Law tradition. We have seen that "rights talk" is based on the alternative Continental Public Law tradition where justice requires agents to get permission to undertake feasible actions. As the set of possible feasible actions is infinite, this leads in these "rights"-based systems to endless legal disputes about what is or is not permitted. By contrast on the Common Law tradition, as the list of prohibited actions is limited to those causing harm and keeping one's obligations voluntarily determined, there is less room for dispute about the actions individuals are allowed. They are at liberty to do anything which is not prohibited by the two constraints on their liberties.

We have also shown that, with the end of "really existing socialism," those still infected with the collectivist virus underlying the enterprise view of the state have shifted their focus from destroying capitalism to providing it with a "human face." The arguments for stakeholder capitalism and corporate social responsibility have been shown to be wanting. This desire by many current critics of globalization to use the state to legislate their preferred ethics is antithetical to the Western classical liberal tradition. As the above discussion should make clear, these socialist impulses are atavistic. The state should restrict itself to providing the public goods which are an essential part of the infrastructure for efficient globalization, upholding its citizens' liberty to undertake any feasible action which does not do anyone else any harm and which does not renege on obligations. All other aspects of morality are best left to the family and other institutions of civil society.

8

The Greens and Global Disorder

Introduction

A myriad of nongovernmental organizations (NGOs) are the storm troopers of the anti-globalization movement. A large number support various environmental causes. They are enemies of global capitalism, which they see as undermining "sustainable development" and endangering Spaceship Earth. They are major purveyors of the "new dirigisme."

Who are these "global salvationists"—as David Henderson[1] has aptly labeled them? How have their views come to have such resonance in the West? What are their true aims? Is there any international civil society of which they can be taken to be the spokesmen—or spokespersons in politically correct discourse—as they claim? These are the questions I consider in this chapter. For this global salvationist movement poses a major threat to the processes of globalizing capitalism and the redressal of poverty it offers to the Third World.

The Rise of the NGOs

NGOs are pressure groups. For 200 years they have been a feature of the political system in both the United Kingdom and the United States. In nineteenth-century Britain many pressure groups were created to deal with the seeming evils of the emerging industrial capitalism. Most, like the trade unions, were concerned with promoting sectional interests. But many sought to promote causes based on Christian morality. Some of these causes, like the

205

abolition of slavery, involved international commerce. But most concerned domestic secular issues, like the rights of women and the extension of the franchise, as well as strictly moral ones like gaming, and temperance.[2]

For the United States, De Tocqueville provides the best account and justification for these pressure groups. In his great book, *Democracy in America*, De Tocqueville maintained that "all the causes which contribute to the maintenance of a democratic republic in the United States are reducible to three heads: 1. The peculiar and accidental situation in which Providence has placed the Americans. 2. The laws. 3. The manners and customs of the people" (vol. 1, chap. 17). Of these he assigned the greatest weight to customs. He wrote: "These three great causes serve, no doubt to regulate and direct American democracy; but if they were to be classed in their proper order, I should say that physical circumstances are less efficient than the laws, and the laws infinitely less so than the customs of the people. I am convinced that the most advantageous situation and the best possible laws cannot maintain a constitution in spite of the customs of a country; while the latter may turn to some advantage the most unfavorable positions and the worst laws."

Among the customs that De Tocqueville identified as being most important for maintaining democracy in America were the myriad civil voluntary associations he found in the country.

> The political associations that exist in the United States are only a single feature in the midst of the immense assemblage of associations in that country. Americans of all ages, all conditions, and all dispositions constantly form associations. They have not only commercial and manufacturing companies, in which all take part, but associations of a thousand other kinds, religious, moral, serious, futile, general or restricted, enormous or diminutive. The Americans make associations to give entertainments, to found seminaries, to build inns, to construct churches, to diffuse books, to send missionaries to the antipodes; in this manner they found hospitals, prisons, and schools. If it is proposed to inculcate some truth or to foster some feeling by the encouragement of a great example, they form a society. Wherever at the head of some new undertaking you see the government in France, or a man of rank in England, in the United States you will be sure to find an association. (vol. 2, chap. 5)

De Tocqueville argued that, once the traditional aristocracy—with its sense of "noblesse oblige"—standing between the rulers and the ruled in the Ancient Regimes in Europe had been extinguished with the rise of democracy, these voluntary associations were necessary as an intermediating layer between the ruling elites and the masses to prevent abuses of power, and to allow ordinary citizens to participate in the political process.[3]

This benign view of pressure groups was adopted by the influential American "pluralist" school of political sociology.[4] They argued that free competition among pressure groups leads to a process similar to Adam Smith's "invisible hand" to subserving the general welfare, even though each group is only promoting its own particular interest. Perfect competition among interest groups, with the state acting as an umpire, is thus the political analogue of the perfect competition paradigm of the economist. With free entry and exit (as in the economy), the size of the associations would not necessarily pose a problem. Any untoward pressure by one group would call forth pressure by a countervailing group—if necessary being newly created for this purpose.

Mancur Olson has questioned this benign view of pressure groups.[5] Unlike the rather vague objectives assigned to participants in pressure groups by political sociologists, Olson rightly looks upon these groups—at least in the economic sphere—as engaging in attempts to use the political process to obtain special economic benefits for their members. Olson argued that small concentrated interest groups are more likely to form and succeed in their aim of influencing the democratic political process to their ends than larger, more diffused groups (see chapter 3). Olson's theory provides an explanation for the stylized fact that in developing countries—with a preponderance of farmers—agriculture is taxed for the benefit of urban consumers, while in developed countries it is subsidized at the cost of a much larger number of urban consumers. Those larger pressure groups which are formed and are effective— such as trade unions—attract members, argues Olson, by offering "selective" not collective benefits. Thus, workers may have to join trade unions if union membership is a condition for obtaining a particular job. But this is likely to leave the common interests of many large groups unorganized. As Olson concludes: "Only when groups are small, or when they are fortunate enough to have an independent source of selective incentives, will they organize or act to achieve their objectives. . . . But the large unorganized groups [with common interests] not only provide evidence for the basic argument of this study: they also suffer if it is true" (p. 167). Thus, far from being the benign social equilibrium of the political sociologists, for the economist, a pressure group equilibrium may not serve the common weal.[6] Olson's arguments about the predatory nature of pressure groups are supplemented by those of the political scientist Schattschneider, who notes their class bias: "The flaw in the pluralist heaven is that the heavenly chorus sings with such an upper class accent. Probably about 90 percent of the people cannot get into the pressure group system."[7]

While Olson and other critics of domestic pressure groups criticized them for the promotion of sectional interests, the currently active internationally oriented pressure groups—which can be collectively included in the acronym NGOs—are mainly dealing with specific causes whose resonance comes from some form of moral claim. But, like the domestic pressure groups in the United States castigated by Schattschneider, they too reflect the ideals of the global "rich" even while claiming to speak for the global "poor."

Of the several thousand NGOs which currently have a formal status in the UN system, only several hundred are from developing countries, and of the developed-country NGOs an overwhelming majority are from the United States.[8] Most of these are environmental groups. They have large bases around the world. Thus, Greenpeace based in Amsterdam has members and national organizations in twenty-eight countries. They are also very rich and bring large resources for lobbying and litigation. Thus, of the U.S. environmental NGOs, Conservation International has assets of nearly $10 million and income of $18 million; the Environmental Defense Fund has assets of $18 million and income of $27 million; Greenpeace (U.S.) has assets of nearly $15 million and income of $9 million, while Greenpeace's global income is $101 million; the National Audubon Society has assets of $109 million and income of $106 million; the National Wildlife Federation has assets of $69 million and income of $102 million; the National Resources Defense Council's assets are $39 million and income of $26 million; the World Resources Institute has assets of $47 million and income of $18 million; the Sierra Club's assets are $52 million and income $73 million; the World Wildlife Fund has assets of $89 million and income of $320 million.[9] These resources dwarf those available to many poor countries to counter the lobbying and litigation in which these environmental NGOs engage. Furthermore, these NGOs are increasingly becoming massive bureaucratic organizations whose interests lie in creating scares to maximize their income and thereby the salaries, perks, and size of their bureaucracies.

Colonizing the UN

How have they come to have the influence they do? The crucial element has been their colonization of the UN and increasingly its specialized agencies, including the World Bank under the presidency of James Wolfensohn (see chapter 5). Article 17 of the UN charter required its Economic and Social Council (ECOSOC) to consult nongovernmental organizations but in an arm's-length fashion, with an "insistence that their status is peripheral to the state."[10] This provided the route for the entry of the NGOs into the international system. Since the fall of the Berlin Wall, the UN has shifted its focus from its traditional role of maintaining the peace, to economic and social issues with a greatly expanded role for ECOSOC, which moved to center stage with the mandating of nine conferences in the 1990s by the UN General Assembly. These were to produce a "global consensus on the priorities for a new development agenda for the 1990s and beyond."[11] Conferences were held on education, children, environment and development, human rights, population and development, social development, women, human settlement, and food. Many of these touched upon subjects where the cosmological beliefs of many poor countries conflicted with those of the rich countries, most notably in the women's conference in Beijing in 1995, and on population and development in Cairo in 1994—where the Islamic and Catholic countries opposed the pro-abortion agenda of the West.

In each of these conferences the NGOs provided a parallel forum in which they networked with conference organizers. "As they became an integral part of the 1990s conference process, NGOs were transformed from arm's-length consultants to full participants in the development and implementation of UN policies and programs."[12] The UN Secretary General Kofi Annan enthusiastically endorsed this embrace of the NGOs. In 1997 he stated, "I see a United Nations keenly aware that if the global agenda is to be properly addressed, a partnership with civil society is not an option it is a necessity."[13] The UN Development program (UNDP)—though not as yet the UN secretariat—has endorsed the NGOs' demands for the UN constitution to be changed so that they have equal status with governments! The puzzle remains why member governments, particularly those of developing countries, have supported and acquiesced in this takeover of the UN by the NGOs.

International Civil Society and Participatory Democracy

NGOs and their apologists claim that, analogously to their role in domestic politics, they represent the world's citizens and thence an international civil society. But this claim is patently false. There are no world citizens as there is no world polity. There are only citizens of nation-states to whom—at least in democracies—their governments are accountable.[14] The chief characteristic of a state is its monopoly of coercive power. In democracies this power is granted to governments responsible to the electorate. As Martin Wolf of the *Financial Times* has cogently argued: "to grant *any* private interests a direct voice in how coercion is to be applied is fundamentally subversive of constitutional democracy . . . Only elected government can be properly responsible for the making of law, domestically and internationally."[15]

Along with other pressure groups, the NGOs do seek to influence national politics. But, if their claim that they represent "civil society" were true, the proponents of their ideas would be in power in national polities. They are not, except in some countries of Northern Europe. So, far from representing a fictitious world citizenry, they are not even representative of their own polities. Hence they have sought to hijack the bureaucratic international institutions through the tactic of "entryism." They then use the "conventions" and "soft agreements" of these international institutions to subserve their partisan and wholly unrepresentative ends.

The NGOs' moral claim that they represent the views and interests of a fictitious world citizenry is false. Thus, Shaffer has noted: "While northern environmental NGOs may be 'internationalist' in orientation . . . they do not represent a 'global civil society.' They have a specifically northern perspective,

209

and often, even more specifically, an Anglo-Saxon one. Their representatives were raised and educated in the North. Almost all of their funding comes from contributors from the North. They obtain their financing by focusing on single issues that strike the northern public's imagination."[16]

The underlying theory behind the NGOs' claims, and source of their popular appeal, is the wholly illiberal theory of *participatory* democracy. The Western notion of a liberal democracy is based on *representative* democracy. From the Founding Fathers of the American Republic to liberal thinkers like Immanuel Kant, direct or participatory democracy on the model of the Greek city-states has been held to be deeply illiberal. Subject to populist pressures and the changing passions of the majority, it can oppress minorities. Greater popular participation does not necessarily subserve liberty. The great liberal thinkers have therefore advocated indirect representative democracy hedged by various checks and balances to prevent the majority from oppressing the minority. Both James Madison and Immanuel Kant liked to call their preferred political system based on representative government a republic, rather than a democracy—which they saw as being of the direct sort and subject to illiberal rule by the mob. In a representative democracy, citizens choose their representatives for a legislature which legislates, instead of directly writing and passing legislation. The ideal of representative democracy was best expressed by Edmund Burke in a speech to his constituents in Bristol: "Your representative owes you, not his industry only, but his judgment: and he betrays it instead of serving you if he sacrifices it to your opinion . . . You choose a member indeed; but when you choose him, he is not a member of Bristol, but he is a Member of Parliament."[17]

But in both the bastions of representative democracy, the United States and United Kingdom, there has been a gradual move toward direct participatory democracy. With the rise of the pollsters, and the weakening of party loyalties, politicians, particularly of the Third Way, have come to rely increasingly upon "focus groups" to discover and pander to public opinion—a practice which Burke decried. Nowhere is this more evident than in the politics of California, where legislative tasks concerning taxation and public spending are increasingly decided not by elected representatives but by plebiscites. The ostensible opening up of the legislative process to greater scrutiny and accountability has paradoxically left it more open to influence by pressure groups. This has led to what has been called *Demosclerosis*,[18] with well-funded interest groups increasingly hijacking domestic politics. As Zakaria sums up, these attempts to democratize the system, to "listen to the people," where "the people" do not have the time or inclination to monitor the legislators and various laws on a daily basis, have meant that "well-organized interest groups—no matter how small their constituencies—can ensure that governments bend to their will. Reforms designed to produce majority rule have produced minority rule."[19] The transference of such a system to the international arena would have even more dire consequences, and national governments, particularly those in developing countries, need to fiercely resist this NGO takeover of the international system.

Sustainable Development

But what is the agenda of the NGOs? It is a left-wing agenda to extend the regulatory system of the U.S. New Deal to the international arena.[20] Peeters has argued that the new left has hijacked the economic and social programs of the UN. "The new model defies traditional values, national sovereignty, the market economy, and representative democracy. It demands radical changes in individual and social behavior and perceives culture as the last frontier of global change. The standard denounces as unethical the principles of modern industrial civilization, individualism, profit and competition."[21]

The origins of this international "new left" movement lie in the various reports produced by the world's great and the good. One of the earliest was the Brandt Report in the early 1970s, which provided ammunition for the dirigiste demands of the NIEO. The most influential has been the 1987 Brundtland Report of the United Nations World Commission on Environment and Development (WCED) with its recommendation for "sustainable development" to be a global objective. It asserted, "sustainable development seeks to meet the needs and aspirations of the present without compromising the ability to meet those of the future" (WCED, the Brundtland report, 1987, p. 40). This vague and general principle is like "motherhood and apple pie," something to which no one could possibly object. And therein lies its emotive appeal. Being broad enough, it is open to different interpretations. A voluminous literature on sustainable development has developed. The most widely adopted interpretation, widely adopted in the business world, in the words of the World Business Council, is that sustainable development "requires the integration of social, environmental and economic considerations to make balanced judgments for the long term" (WBC 2000, p. 2).

But, this seemingly bland objective is not without fundamental disagreements about what is to be sustained. "On the one hand, there are those who think of this in relation to human beings: their sole or main concern is with the sustainable welfare of people, now and for the future. By contrast, others think in terms of ecosystems rather than humanity, so that sustainability is identified with ecosystem resilience. In the 2000 BBC Reith Lectures, the leader of the Southern California Sierra Club argued that sustainable development has become a buzz-word for human-centered destruction of the wild planet. Such a view is common among environmentalists and their NGOs" (Henderson 2001, pp. 47–8). If it is human welfare which is to be sustained, there is nothing new in the notion of sustainable development.[22]

In estimating the costs and benefits of investment projects, economists have devoted much thought to quantifying the distributional (social) effects and externalities (environmental effects) associated with the project. This allows estimates of more inclusive measures of aggregate social welfare. In fact, I spent a large part of my misspent youth on such a task.[23] Part of this task requires making current and future costs and benefits commensurate. In our personal accounting, we convert the likely future income we are likely to get from our current investments into their present value by discounting the income stream at the market interest rate, and comparing it with the cost of the investments. Why should this future income stream be discounted at the market interest rate to get its present value (in terms of current dollars)? Because, if the investment had not been made, the money could have been put in the bank and earned the market interest rate. For the investment to be worthwhile it must at least yield as much as money left in the bank.

A similar argument carries over when we consider investments in the aggregate economy from the viewpoint of society's welfare. But, here, the reason for discounting future income streams made possible by current investment is based on slightly different considerations. Any act of investment means giving up current consumption which has intrinsic value. Any productive investment made from this current consumption foregone must yield future consumption which is at least as large. But does it have to be larger? Would not the consumption foregone (in dollar notes, say) put under the mattress which (without inflation) provides equivalent consumption in the future be enough? For individuals there is still a cost in this postponement of consumption: being mortal, they may die before they can indulge in the future consumption for which they have saved. They are, therefore, likely to put a premium on current over future consumption. This private "impatience," as it has been called, requires them to be given something extra (in the form of interest) to forego current consumption.

But what about society? As it is immortal, why should it be impatient? Why should it put a premium on current consumption over future consumption through discounting the future? The answer is provided by thinking of the very long run, where the "present" and "future" relate not to the consumption levels of a single individual's life at different dates (as in the private decision) but of two generations: the present and future ones. Investment becomes a means of transferring consumption from present to future generations. When we value the future consumption made possible by current investment, we are valuing the extra consumption made possible for future generations by cutting the consumption of the current generation. This value necessarily depends upon an intergenerational distributional judgment. If we discount future consumption to make it commensurate with the present consumption foregone, we are assuming that one dollar accruing to the future generation is socially less valuable than the dollar given up by the current

generation. Some economists have argued that there should be no such discounting of the future. One should be distributionally neutral about income
transfers to one generation from another. One dollar for the current generation is of the same social value as one dollar to a future generation. My late
mentor and colleague at Christ Church, Oxford, Sir Roy Harrod, used to say
that any social discounting of benefits accruing to future generations was a
"polite word for rapacity."

Against this is an argument, particularly relevant for poor countries,
that it is regressive to raise the consumption of a rich future generation by a
dollar through cutting the consumption of the current poor generation. For,
with economic growth future generations will be richer than the current generation. So taking a dollar from the current generation and transferring it to a
future generation would be to take a dollar from a poor person and give it to a
rich person. For this reason we should value the dollar accruing to future generations at a lower (discounted) value than the dollar that the current generation is sacrificing. This social discount rate, therefore, summarizes society's
value judgments about intergenerational equity. As with all value judgments,
the appropriate discount rate can be a matter of controversy. But for the
Greens this very logic is dismissed as "economism."

Similarly, economists are perfectly happy to include natural resources as
part of the capital stock of an economy. Some of these resources are finite
(like oil and other minerals) and their current use leads to their future ex-
haustion. Does this mean that for development to be sustainable they should
not be used by the current generation? The answer is no. For the current use
of these exhaustible resources allows both the consumption of the current
generation and its investments to be higher. This investment adds to the material capital supplementing the natural resource stock which is passed on to
future generations. The economic rate at which the exhaustible resource is
exploited will depend upon the discount rate. The higher the discount rate,
the faster the rate of depletion. It is often argued that, currently, natural resources are being exhausted too quickly. This must be a claim that the market
rate of interest at which private producers are discounting their future rents
from mines and wells is above the social discount rate. But this is not an argument for leaving the ore in the ground for future generations. In fact, a fairly
precise rule can be given for the current generation's optimal rate of exploitation of exhaustible resources which leaves the next generation no worse off.[24]
Assuming that various forms of reproducible capital (including methods of
reprocessing, and investment in R & D) are substitutes for the natural resource, then the current generation should replace the currently depleting finite resource stocks with new reproducible capital such as roads, buildings,
and machines, or financial assets of equivalent value for future generations.

The island of Nauru provides an example of how these economic principles work. It is a small island in the Pacific which consists of coral reefs

213

made from bird droppings. These yield guano, a valuable fertilizer. The citizens of Nauru have been mining this natural resource, so the "country" is literally disappearing. The proceeds from the sales of guano have been used to invest in real estate and other assets in Australia, to provide its citizens future income and consumption when their only resource is exhausted. Should the citizens of Nauru have continued to eke out a miserable living so that they could have handed over their stock of natural "coral reefs" untouched to their future generations? This would be absurd. But it is in effect what many of the Green panaceas desire.

Nor is there any sound economic reason to maintain the level of any current stock of renewable resources like fisheries. It all depends upon the regeneration rate of the natural resource, population change, our value judgments about intergenerational equity (summarized by the social discount rate), and technological progress. Many renewable resources, however, face the "problem of the commons." If the renewable resource is not owned by anyone, there is an incentive for everyone to use it excessively. Thus, a commonly owned lake will be overfished. The answer lies in creating ownership rights which provide the owner the incentives to conserve his resource to the optimal extent. The African elephant provides an example of how creating private ownership of commonly owned renewable resources can prevent their uneconomic use. The elephant population in sub-Saharan Africa was declining because of poaching for ivory. The Convention on International Trade in Endangered Species sought to stem the decline by banning trade in ivory. This merely sent the ivory trade underground. As the legal trade was suppressed but demand remained undiminished, ivory prices soared. The profits of the poachers involved in the illegal trade also soared, along with their incentives to kill even more African elephants. South Africa bucked the trend. It allowed herds to be privately owned for eco-tourism and safari hunting. Its elephant population was stabilized and even increased,[25] so much so that when I and my wife visited the Krueger National Park in the late 1990s there were worries about the danger to crops from the burgeoning elephant herds, and a program of official culling was in progress.

But, this will seem like pettifogging economism to environmentalists. For it is not human welfare they are concerned with but with preserving the ecosystem—Spaceship Earth.

The Greens and Ecological Imperialism

Global Warming

I fortuitously got involved in debates on the environment when I was preparing the 1990 Wincott lecture. I had aimed to show that various arguments based on "pecuniary" externalities for international macroeconomic and exchange rate coordination were invalid, as pecuniary externalities were mediated through the market mechanism and hence were Pareto-irrelevant.[26] For balance, I hoped to argue that the "global warming" then making the headlines was a "technological" externality which was Pareto-relevant and would require international action. Wishing to inform myself on the issue of global warming, I got in touch with the late Julian Simon. He sent me a reading list and put me in touch with a scientist—Fred Singer. He was a respected atmospheric physicist who was skeptical of any evidence of man-made global warming, and hence of any need to counter it by public action. After reading the scientific literature, I was appalled at how scientists—like Stephen Schneider—openly admitted they were creating alarm for what they themselves recognized was a highly speculative phenomenon.[27] My lecture not surprisingly also ended up as an attack on this scientific attempt to bamboozle the public.[28]

My late friend, John Flemming, then chief economist at the Bank of England, was also chairing a subcommittee of one of the United Kingdom's research councils on the environment. On reading the lecture he told me that I would get nowhere by taking on the scientists. For, at a meeting he attended to distribute funds for climate research, the scientists had explicitly said that they would maintain a united front and not behave like economists by disagreeing with each other! Of course, the cornucopia of research funds that the climate change scare has generated provides a baser rent-seeking motive—well known to economists—for this closing of ranks. It would take me too far afield to describe the shenanigans of the International Panel of Climate Change (IPCC),[29] but just judging from its flip-flopping around even about the likely extent of global warming, I think it is fair to say that the scientific basis of any great global catastrophe following from the undisputed increase in greenhouse gases is highly insecure.[30] But the Greens had found a cause which resonates with the public, with any hurricane or flood or unseasonable warmth being easily sold as a sign of global warming.

A number of points can be made about the ongoing controversies surrounding global warming. First, emissions of CO_2—one of the greenhouse gases—will increase with growing global economic activity. But there is general scientific agreement that this poses no danger of runaway global warming. As Patrick Michaels, a research professor of environmental sciences at the University of Virginia, shows in an excellent book, *Meltdown*, we now know precisely how much

> the climate will warm in the policy-foreseeable future of 50 years, a modest three quarters of a degree (C)(1.4 degrees F). NASA's James Hanson, whom many credit with lighting the fire over the greenhouse issue with his incendiary 1988 congressional testimony, wrote this in the *Proceedings of the National Academy of Sciences* in 2001: "Future global warming can be predicted much more

accurately than is generally realized. . . . we predict additional warming in the next 50 years of 3/4 C +/– 1/4 C, a warming rate of 0.15 C +/–0.05 C per decade." That warming rate is about four times less than the lurid top figure widely trumpeted by the UN in its 2001 compendium on climate change and repeated ad infinitum in the press. (2004, p. 19)

Second, the global warming that has occurred to date is well within the climatic variations that have occurred over millennia. The highest estimate of the likely future rise in temperature falls within this historical range. Even the most rabid environmentalist does not expect a runaway greenhouse effect making the earth inhabitable. As Schneider notes: "from the perspective of the overall existence of life on earth, even a 15 degree Centigrade (27 degree Fahrenheit) temperature change is not threatening. For example 100 million year ago dinosaurs roamed a planet some 15 degrees C warmer than today, and tropical plant and animal forests have been found in high latitude locations such as Alaska."[31] The IPCC's expected rise in global temperature of 2.5 degrees Centigrade by the end of this century is well within this range. Figure 8.1, from the book (*Global Warming: The Complete Briefing*) by Sir James Houghton, who has been the cochairman of the science assessment working group of the IPCC, shows the derived record from direct and indirect sources of the average temperatures for Central England for the past thousand years. A recent warming trend is discernible which will continue, but will not lead to even the temperatures seen in the medieval warm period between A.D. 1100 and 1300. This warming trend is merely reversing the "Little Ice Age" between A.D. 1450 and 1850. The current warming attributable to human

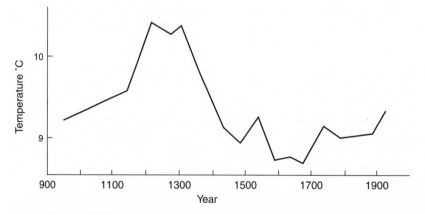

Figure 8.1: Global Warming? Average temperature in Central England during the last thousand years. Source: Figure taken from *Global Warming: The Complete Briefing* by *John Houghton*, published by Lion Hudson plc, 1994. Figure copyright © 1994 Hardlines, Charlbury. Used with permission.

carbon emissions of 3/4 degree Centigrade over the next fifty years is a mere blip in the large natural variations in climate that mankind has lived with over the last thousand years. As Houghton admits, "there is as yet no certain explanation for these warm and cold periods during the past thousand years" (p. 49).

Third, the major economic effects of increasing CO_2—the major greenhouse gas—will be regional, with some regions being better off and others worse off, particularly from the effects on their agriculture. Moreover, industrialization and urbanization—the last century's two great forces of economic progress—have made making a living in developed countries virtually climate-proof. This will also happen in most developing countries through the same process of economic growth.[32] Nor are rising temperatures necessarily something to be deplored. In the United States, millions have voluntarily moved from colder northern to warmer southern climates. Even a sudden rise of temperature from global warming will not lead to a more drastic change in their local climates than is involved in this voluntary migration. The benefits from global warming and in particular of CO_2 emissions are rarely cited. Increased CO_2 emissions are already increasing global vegetation, including the tropical forests that are so dear to the hearts of many Greens. Moreover, through human history warm periods like that in the Middle Ages was marked by prosperity, while the subsequent Little Ice Age was characterized by famines, pestilence, and social disorder. What then of the 11,000 who died in France during the 2003 heat wave? A study of weather-related deaths (W. R. Keatings et al., 2000) found that an on annual basis in all regions cold-related mortality greatly exceeds heat-related mortality.

Fourth, the fear of rising sea levels with global warming concerns distributional effects. Even if the projected rise in sea levels—which along with so many of the scientific predictions is now estimated to be much less than originally predicted—leads to the erosion of many coastal areas, it will be no worse than what is already happening through sea erosion.[33] If some Pacific islands are threatened with extinction, they should follow the Naurians in ensuring their future with a trust fund. The Green NGOs and the various international institutions currently trying to convince developing countries to reduce their carbon emissions to prevent climate change should instead organize a trust fund to be paid out to the citizens of countries threatened by sea level rises if the worst happens.

This last point raises the important question of whether, even if the most dire (but non-Apocalyptic) predictions of global warming turn out to be true, it is better to adapt to this global warming—as humans clearly have been doing for millennia in the long swings in climate shown in figure 8.1—or to try to prevent it, as proposed in the Kyoto Protocol.

Fortunately, there is a sophisticated cost-benefit study which quantifies the various alternative scenarios and uncertainties surrounding both the extent of the likely climatic effects of the increase in greenhouse gases and its effects on the economies of different regions of the world.[34] Nordhaus considers seven alternative policies for dealing with climate change:

> The first is . . . "laissez-faire" . . . in which there are no controls on greenhouse gasses . . . The second is the "optimal" policy, a scenario in which GHG controls are set so as to maximize the discounted value of the utility of consumption. The third is a scenario in which we wait 10 years to implement policies so that our knowledge might be more secure. The fourth and fifth policies are ones that stabilize emissions—one at the 1990 rate of emissions and the other at 80 percent of the 1990 emissions rate. The sixth proposal is to undertake geo-engineering, while the final approach is to curb emissions sufficiently to slow climate change and eventually stabilize climate. (p. 79)

Nordhaus's results for the best-guess case are: "Among these seven [policy options] the rank order from a purely economic viewpoint is geo-engineering, economic optimum, 10-year delay, no controls, stabilizing emissions, cutting emissions by 20 percent, and stabilizing climate. The advantage of geo-engineering over other policies is enormous" (p. 96). These results are fairly robust and are not changed markedly by the introduction of "uncertainty and realistic constraints on the resolution of uncertainty" (p. 186).

There are two points worth noting about these results. First, the geo-engineering option, which according to a U.S. National Academy of Sciences survey could be implemented "at relatively low costs," involves various options including "shooting smart mirrors into space with 16-inch naval rifles or seeding the oceans with iron to accelerate carbon sequestration." But, as Nordhaus notes, these technological fixes are opposed by environmentalists "because of the grave reservations about the environmental impacts of the geo-engineering options."[35] Whether these reservations are rational is not discussed. For reasons set out in the next section, my suspicion would be they are not!

Second, the ten-year delay and laissez faire alternatives dominate the various alternatives about stabilizing emissions—the policies endorsed by the Rio conference, and adopted enthusiastically by the United Kingdom and the European Union with the Kyoto Protocol. Moreover, the optimal policy implies a reduction in GHG emissions from their laissez faire level of 21.96 billion tons of carbon equivalent in 2075 to 19.01 billion tons (a mere 13 percent reduction from laissez faire)! And the gain from this policy over laissez faire is only a 0.06 percent annual increase in world annual consumption! By contrast, all the alternatives to stabilize emissions involve losses of from 1.5 percent to 8 percent of world annual consumption.[36] Given the political difficulties in implementing the optimum solution, and the trivial gains to be thereby secured, the only rational conclusion is that the only sensible policy on climate change is to let well enough alone—that is laissez faire!

But, the Greens will not be convinced by this and will invoke the precautionary principle: "It is better to be safe than sorry." This has some resonance with the Western public, as it has echoes of Pascal's famous wager about the existence of God, that is, if God did not exist, one would only have eschewed the finite pleasures from forsaking a sinful life, but if he did exist, a sinful life would lead to damnation and the infinite pain of Hell. In expected utility terms (as economists would call it), it was better to give up the finite pleasures of a sinful life for even an infinitesimally small probability of burning forever in Hell.

Julian Simon had a riposte to Paul Ehrlich's well-known restatement of this wager: "If I'm right we'll save the world by curbing population growth. If I'm wrong, people will still be better fed, better housed and happier, thanks to our effort [all the evidence suggests he is wrong. JLS] Will anything be lost if it turns out later that we can support a much larger population than seems possible today." But, says Simon, note that " 'Pascal's' wager applies entirely to one person. No one else loses if she or he is wrong. But Ehrlich bets what he thinks will be the economic gains that we and our descendants might enjoy against the unborns' very lives. Would he make the same wager if his own life rather than others' lives were at stake?"[37] So it does come down to a question of values after all—not facts or logic.

Green Misanthropy

What of the other Green scares? Even though they have been countered by rational and scientific arguments, it has had no effect on them. For those who need the evidence (till 1993), Julian Simon's *The Ultimate Resource* provides a comprehensive compilation. More recently, Bjorn Lomberg, an environmentalist who sought to disprove Simon, found to his astonishment that Simon was right. His comprehensive examination of all the available evidence on green scares, in his book *The Skeptical Environmentalist*, is a tour de force which has predictably raised the hackles of the Greens. The ensuing debate has shown up the ideological motives of so many of the scientists in bed with the Greens. Lomberg, like Simon, has found that trying to engage the Greens in rational debate is futile. Their position is not based on reason but is a new secular religion (see chapter 6).

Most of the Green scares are without any foundation. The world is not running out of resources. The commercial reserves of nonrenewable resources have risen markedly since 1970 (with those for oil rising by 63 percent and natural gas by 163 percent), and declines in their price trends as well as in their current consumption as a proportion of reserves, all point to a growing abundance rather than scarcity of many nonrenewable natural resources. The world is not going to starve because of the growth in its population. Even with low technology the world could support one and a half times the 2000 world population, and over nine times that using the United Nation's recommended calorie intake per head.[38] Lomberg, summarizing the evidence at the end of the millennium, writes of the other scares:

> We will not lose our forests; we will not run out of energy, raw materials or water. We have reduced atmospheric pollution in the cities of the developed world, and have good reason to believe that this will also be achieved in the developing world. Our oceans have not been defiled, our rivers have become cleaner and support more life.... Acid rain did not kill off our forests, our species are not dying as many have claimed, with half of them disappearing over the next 50 years—the figure is likely to be about 0.7 percent. The problem of the ozone layer has been more or less solved. The current outlook on global warming does not indicate a catastrophe—rather there is good reason to believe that our energy consumption will change towards renewable energy sources before the end of the century ... And, finally, our chemical worries and fears of pesticides are misplaced and counterproductive."[39]

So why do the Greens persist with their crusade? The reason is that, like any religion, their beliefs are not based on reason but on faith. For those who do not profess the same faith the time has surely come to take on these new cultural imperialists. The first point of resistance is to recognize what they are seeking to do. Bluntly, they would like to perpetuate the ancient poverty of the great Eurasian civilizations—India and China—with, as they see it, their burgeoning unwashed masses increasingly emitting noxious pollutants as they seek to make their people prosperous, and achieve economic parity with the West.

For, as economic historians have emphasized, it was not until the Industrial Revolution that mankind found the key to intensive growth—a sustained rise in per capita income—which, as the example of the West and many newly industrializing countries have shown, has the potential to eradicate mass structural poverty—the scourge which in the past was considered to be irremediable (pace the biblical saying that the poor will always be with us). For in the past most growth was extensive—with output growing in line with (modest) population growth.[40] As pre-industrial economies relied on organic raw materials for food, clothing, housing, and fuel (energy), whose supply in the long run was inevitably constrained by the fixed factor of land, their growth was ultimately bounded by the productivity of land. Even transport and traditional industry—depending upon animal muscle for mechanical energy, and upon charcoal (a vegetable substance) for smelting and working crude ores and providing heat—would ultimately be constrained by the diminishing returns to land, which would inexorably set in once agriculture had expanded to the land frontier. In these organic economies[41] with diminishing returns to land conjoined with the Malthusian principle of population, it seemed inevitable that the economy would converge to a long-run stationary state where the mass of the people languished at a subsistence standard of living. No wonder the classical economists were so gloomy!

But even in organic economies there could be some respite, through the adoption of market "capitalism" and free trade as propounded by Adam Smith. This could generate some intensive growth as it would increase the productivity of the economy as compared with mercantilism, and by lowering the cost of the consumption bundle (through cheaper imports) would lead to a rise in per capita income. But, if this growth in popular opulence led to excessive breeding, the land constraint would inexorably lead back to subsistence wages. Technical progress could hold the stationary state at bay, but the land constraint would ultimately prove binding.

The Industrial Revolution led to the substitution of this organic economy by a mineral-based energy economy. It escaped from the land constraint by using mineral raw materials instead of the organic products of land. Coal was the most notable, providing most of the heat energy of industry and with the development of the steam engine virtually unlimited supplies of mechanical energy. Intensive growth now became possible, as the land constraint on the raw materials required for raising aggregate output was removed.

Thus, the Industrial Revolution in England was based on two forms of "capitalism," one institutional, namely that defended by Adam Smith—because of its productivity-enhancing effects, even in an organic economy—and the other physical, the capital stock of stored energy represented by the fossil fuels which allowed mankind to create, in the words of E. A. Wrigley: "a world that no longer follows the rhythm of the sun and the seasons; a world in which the fortunes of men depend largely upon how he himself regulates the economy and not upon the vagaries of weather and harvest; a world in which poverty has become an optional state rather than a reflection of the necessary limitations of human productive powers" (1988, p. 6). The Greens are of course against both forms of "capitalism"—the free trade promoted by Smith, as well as the continued burning of fossil fuels—leaving little hope for the world's poor.

The U.S. disengagement from the Kyoto Protocol is therefore to be commended. India, along with China, rightly stood firm at Kyoto against any restriction of their CO_2 emissions. It is unfortunate that the Russians' arm was twisted by the EU, whereby its support for Russian entry to the WTO was made conditional on its signing the Kyoto treaty. But, as President Putin's economic advisor rightly maintained till the end, given the junk science on which the treaty is based, it is likely to inflict long-term damage to the economic prospects of its signatories.[42] Perhaps the lesson will then be learned that, instead of chasing the chimera of controlling climate change, the world needs to adapt to it (if it happens) as it has done so notably in its past.

There are a number of other treaties and conventions the Greens have

221

been able to promote which are inimical to the interests of developing countries. The following are worthy of note.

(i) Basle Convention: This defines various metals as "hazardous," and controls trade in waste, scrap, and recyclable materials. Greenpeace is using the treaty to organize a total embargo on such trade with developing countries, excluding them from global scrap metal markets. This is already having deleterious effects. There are press reports that a recently highly profitable industry—ship-breaking—at Alang in Gujarat is likely to fall afoul of this convention.

Ship-breaking was till the 1970s performed with cranes and heavy equipment at salvage docks in big shipyards. When rising labor costs and environmental regulations made this uncompetitive, the industry shifted to Korea and Taiwan. But in the 1980s, enterprising businessmen in India, Pakistan, and Bangladesh realized that wrecking a ship did not require expensive docks and tools. They could just drive the ship up onto a beach, as they might a fishing boat, and tear it apart by hand. The scrap metal obtained can be profitably sold in South Asia with its insatiable demand for low-grade steel, mainly for ribbed reinforcing bars used in constructing concrete walls. These rods are produced locally from the ships' hull plating by small-scale re-rolling mills, of which there are close to one hundred near Alang alone. Today nearly 90 percent of the world's seven hundred condemned ships annually broken up are wrecked on South Asian beaches—nearly half of them at Alang. The economic benefits are substantial. "Alang and the industries that have sprung from it provide a livelihood however meager for perhaps as many as a million Indians."[43] This industry is sought to be destroyed by Greenpeace under the auspices of the Basle Convention. India should walk away from this convention, just as is being urged by some influential people for Australia.

(ii) POPs and DDT: The Persistent Organic Pollutants (POPs) framework convention is being negotiated under pressure from environmental groups, who want a binding treaty to ban "persistent organic pollutants"—defined as pesticides, industrial chemicals, and their by-products. DDT is sought to be banned under the treaty. Signing this convention will seriously damage the health of developing countries.

DDT is the most cost-effective controller of diseases spread by bugs—like flies and mosquitoes—which has ever been produced. The U.S. National Academy of Sciences estimated it had saved 500 million lives from malaria by 1970. In India, effective spraying had virtually eliminated the disease by the 1960s, so much so that the mosquito nets which were ubiquitous in my childhood had disappeared from urban houses by the time I was at University in the late 1950s. DDT spraying had reduced the number of malaria cases from 75 million in 1951 to around 50,000 in 1961, and the number of malaria deaths from nearly a million in the 1940s to a few thousand in the 1960s.

Then in the 1970s, largely as a result of an environmental scare promoted by Rachel Carson's book *Silent Spring*, foreign aid agencies and various UN organizations began to take a jaundiced view of DDT. The use of DDT declined. Not surprisingly, the mosquitoes hit back and endemic malaria returned to India. By 1997, the UNDP's Human Development Report 2000 estimates there were about 2.6 million malaria cases.

The same story of a decline and rise in disease with the increase and decrease in DDT spraying can be told about kala-azar, which is spread by the sand fly. DDT largely rid India of kala-azar in the 1950s and 1960s. But, with the subsequent decline in DDT use, it has come back. The state minister of health in Bihar recently informed the Assembly that 408 people had died, and 12,000 were afflicted with the disease in 30 districts of Northern Bihar.

So, why did DDT fall out of favor despite its demonstrated merits? Rachel Carson in 1962 started the DDT scare with her claim that its use had devastating effects on bird life, particularly those higher up the food chain. It was also claimed DDT caused hepatitis in humans. Numerous scientific studies showed these fears to be baseless. It was shown to be safe to humans, causing death only if eaten in the size of pancakes! In 1971, the distinguished biologist Philip Handler, then president of the U.S. National Academy of Science, said, "DDT is the greatest chemical that has ever been discovered." Commission after commission, expert after Nobel Prize–winning expert has given DDT a clean bill of health.[44]

Yet in 1972, President Nixon's head of the U.S. Environmental Protection Agency, William Ruckelshaus, banned DDT against all the expert scientific advice he had been given. He argued that the pesticide was "a warning that man may be exposing himself to a substance that may ultimately have serious effects on his health." Most developed countries followed the U.S. and banned the chemical for all uses. Many developing countries followed suit by banning the pesticide in agriculture, and some for all uses. USAID and the WHO, who had been at the forefront of the mosquito eradication programs based on house spraying with DDT, turned their backs on DDT. USAID has maintained that as DDT is not registered by the EPA for use in the United States, foreign assistance is not available for programs that use DDT. Thus, despite the WHO's Malaria Expert Committee's ruling that DDT is safe and effective for malaria control, since 1979 the WHO itself has championed a strategy which ignores the causal link between decreasing numbers of houses sprayed and increasing malaria, by emphasizing curative and de-emphasizing preventive measures. Instead of fighting malaria by the only effective method known, the WHO is instead spending its limited resources on the politically correct but highly dubious campaign against smoking.[45]

The decline in house spraying created DDT-resistant mosquitoes. Nevertheless, whenever DDT was vigorously used—as in Mexico—malaria rates declined despite the increased DDT resistance of mosquitoes. Today, DDT is needed more than ever as the Anopheles mosquito has become resistant to the pesticides currently used—synthetic pyrethroids.

The favored WHO strategy of distributing pesticide-impregnated mosquito bed nets and using chloroquine to treat the disease is vitiated by two factors. First, distributing and monitoring the use of bed nets is even more complicated than house spraying, and likely to be much less effective. Second, the chloroquine resistance built up by mosquitoes in the 1960s in South East Asia and South America has subsequently spread to most malarial countries around the world. There are some promising new drugs on the horizon, but the hope of a malaria vaccine is at least seven years away. While curative measures must continue to form part of a malaria control program, preventive measures are just as important, and for this, killing the mosquitoes with DDT remains the most efficient and cost-effective measure.[46]

If both the science and economics favor DDT, why has this growing ban on DDT spread? Ruckelshaus's reason for his unscientific decision to ban DDT in the early 1970s provides the clue: the environmental movement's supposedly key concept of "sustainable development." This was endorsed by the World Commission on Environment and Development's report, "Our Common Future," whose chair was the then Norwegian prime minister, Gro Harlem Bruntland, and who subsequently was the head of the WHO. The notion of sustainability—at least in its strong form—asserts that natural capital, such as forests, wildlife, and other natural resources, cannot be substituted by man-made capital. As pesticides are assumed to have adverse effects on natural capital, they are inconsistent with sustainable development. Hence, instead of using pesticides to control bugs, bed nets and drugs to fight the disease they cause should be used. The argument that there is no scientific evidence that DDT spraying to kill mosquitoes damages natural capital is once again countered by the so-called precautionary principle. Once again, the environmentalists are willing to ban DDT because they are willing to sacrifice human lives for those of birds and bugs.

This underlying misanthropy of the environmentalists is explicitly brought out by the following statement by Paul Ehrlich about India: "I came to understand the population explosion emotionally one stinking hot night in Delhi . . . The streets seemed alive with people. People eating, people washing, people sleeping, people visiting, arguing, and screaming. People thrusting their hands through the taxi window, begging. People defecating and urinating. People clinging to buses. People herding animals. People, people, people."

Not surprisingly, many environmentalists have argued since the 1950s that, in the words of one: "It maybe unkind to keep people dying from malaria so that they could die more slowly of starvation. [So that, malaria may even be] a blessing in disguise, since a large proportion of the malaria belt is not suited to agriculture, and the disease has helped to keep man from destroying it—and from wasting his substance on it." Or more recently: "Some day antimalarial vaccines will probably be developed, which may even wipe out the various forms of the disease entirely, but then another difficulty will arise: important wild areas that had been protected by the dangers of malaria will be exposed to unwise development."[47]

(iii) Biodiversity and GM Foods: Another convention promoted by the Greens is the Biodiversity Convention, which seeks to control the genetically modified (GM) food seen to threaten biodiversity. This scare about GM food needs to be resisted. The Green Revolution having disproved the doomster's predictions that the world would not be able to feed a burgeoning population, they are now attempting to stop the next stage of the agricultural revolution offered by biotechnology. As the father of the Green Revolution Norman Borlaug has recently noted: though "the Green Revolution is [not] over, [as] increases in crop management productivity can be made all along the line: in tillage, water use, fertilization, weed and pest control and harvesting, however, for the genetic improvement of food crops to continue at a pace sufficient to meet the needs of the 8.3 billion people projected to be on this planet at the end of the quarter century both conventional technology and biotechnology are needed."[48]

In 1995, there were 4 million acres of biotech crops planted, which had risen to 100 million in 1999. In the United States, 50 percent of the soybean crop and more than one-third of the corn crop were transgenic in 1999. These GM crops provide major economic benefits as they have reduced pesticide applications, and brought higher yields and lower consumer prices.[49] They have been readily adopted where they have been introduced. Yet, particularly in Europe, the Greens—again led by Greenpeace—have created mass hysteria about these crops, calling them Frankenstein foods.

But if GM crops are the creation of a Frankenstein, so is virtually everything we eat. Any method that uses life-forms to make or modify a product is biotechnology: brewing beer or making leavened bread is a "traditional" biotechnology application. As Borlaug states:

> The fact is that genetic modification started long before humankind started altering crops by artificial selection. Mother Nature did it, often in a big way. For example, the wheat groups we rely on for much of our food supply are the result of unusual (but natural) crosses between different species of grasses. Today's bread wheat is the result of the hybridization of three different plant genomes, each containing a set of seven chromosomes, and thus could easily be classified as transgenic. Maize is another crop that is the product of transgenic hybridization. Neolithic humans domesticated virtually all of our food and livestock species over a relatively short period 10,000 to 15,000 years ago. Several hundred generations of farmer descendants were subsequently responsible for making enormous genetic modifications in all of our major crop and animal species. To see how far the evolutionary changes have come, one only needs to look at

the 5,000-year-old fossilized corn cobs found in the caves of Tehuacan in Mexico, which are one-tenth the size of modern maize varieties. Thanks to the development of science over the past 150 years, we now have the insights into plant genetics and plant breeding to do what Mother Nature did herself in the past by chance. Genetic modification of crops is not some kind of witchcraft; rather it is the progressive harnessing of the forces of nature to the benefit of feeding the human race. (Borlang 2000)

For what biotechnology merely does is to isolate individual genes from organisms and transfer them into others without the usual sexual crosses necessary to combine the genes of two parents.

Nor is there any danger to health or the environment from GM food, as has been repeatedly noted: by a 2,100-signatory declaration in support of biotechnology by scientists worldwide, by the U.S. National Academy of Science, by the U.S. House of Representatives Committee on Science, and by a Nuffield Foundation study in the United Kingdom. Since 1994, more than 300 million North Americans have been eating several dozen GM foods grown on more than 100 million acres, but not one problem with health or the environment has been noted.[50] Yet the hysteria continues. To see the misanthropy at its heart, there is no better example than that of the miracle "golden rice."

Scientists from the Swiss Federal Institute of Technology (Zurich) and the International Rice Research Institute (Philippines) have successfully transferred genes producing beta-carotene—a precursor of vitamin A—into rice to increase the quantities of vitamin A, iron, and other micronutrients. As the GM rice produces beta-carotene it has a bronze-orange appearance, hence its name "golden rice." It promises to have a profound effect on the lives of millions suffering from vitamin A and iron deficiencies which lead respectively to blindness and anemia. It has been estimated that more than 180 million children, mostly in developing countries, suffer from vitamin A deficiency, of whom 2 million die from it each year. About a billion people suffer anemia from iron deficiency. The new golden rice is being distributed free of charge to public rice breeding institutions around the world. Millions will be able to reduce their risks of these disabling diseases at little or no cost.

Yet, as the inventor of "golden rice" Professor Portykus has noted, though it satisfies all the demands of the Greens, they still oppose it. The new rice has not been developed by or for industry; benefits the poor and disadvantaged; provides a sustainable, cost-free solution, not requiring other resources; is given free of charge and restrictions to subsistence farmers; can be re-sown each year from the saved harvest; does not reduce agricultural biodiversity; does not affect natural biodiversity; has no negative effect on the environment; has no conceivable risk to consumer health; and could not have been developed with traditional methods.

But, notes Portykus, "the GMO opposition is doing everything to prevent 'golden rice' reaching the subsistence farmer. We have learned that the GMO opposition has a hidden, political agenda. It is not so much the concern about the environment, or the health of the consumer, or the help for the disadvantaged. It is a radical fight against technology and for political success."[51]

Conclusions

There we have it. The Green movement is a modern secular religious movement engaged in a worldwide crusade to impose its "habits of the heart" on the world. Its primary target is to prevent the economic development which alone offers the world's poor any chance of escaping their age-old poverty. This modern-day secular Christian crusade has exchanged the saving of souls for saving Spaceship Earth. It needs to be fiercely resisted.

First, by standing up to the local converts—the modern-day descendants of what the Chinese called "rice Christians" and "secondary barbarians"—the Arundhati Roys, Vandana Shivas, and Medhka Patkars in India. Their argument that their views are in consonance with Hindu cosmology are reminiscent of those used by the proselytizing Christians promoting a syncretized Christianity in the nineteenth century, and are equally derisory.

Second, by refusing to accept the transnational treaties and conventions which the Greens are promoting to legislate their ends. As many of the environmental ministries have become outposts of their local converts, the economic ministries must play a central role in resisting this Green imperialism, by insisting on having the last say on any transnational treaty signed by their country. Through its continuing production and use of DDT and continuing development of GM technology, China has shown that there is no need to give in to this latest manifestation of Western cultural imperialism. In this fight there are still many in the West itself (like Julian Simon—or his legacy, at least—and Bjorn Lomberg) who, not having been infected with this secular Christian religion, will join in showing up the Greens and their agenda as paper tigers, much as the Christian missionaries found in the last phase of Western imperialism.

Toward World Disorder

There are ominous parallels between the last decades of the nineteenth and the present century. In both periods it seemed that a world increasingly closely knit through foreign trade and capital flows would bring universal peace and prosperity. This dream came to an end on the fields of Flanders. The First World War (which has been aptly described as a wholly unnecessary war) put an end to the first Liberal International Economic Order (LIEO) created under British leadership. It took nearly a century to resurrect a new LIEO under the United States.

One of the causes of the First War was the imperial competition for colonies. This late imperialism was fueled by the territorial imperative as well as the "white man's burden"—to save the heathen souls. In nineteenth-century India, as Stokes demonstrated, there was an unholy alliance of Evangelicals—with their belief in the Gospels, and Utilitarians and Radicals—with their faith in reason, who believed in the superiority of Western ways, both religious and secular. Today we see a similar alliance between some scientists and the eco-fundamentalists with a similar imperialist form though differing content. But history never repeats itself. Whereas the nineteenth-century battles for "hearts and minds" were fought within and between "nation-states," the arena for today's cultural imperialists is provided by various transnational organizations. It is instructive to see how this has happened and its likely consequences.[52]

Stephen Toulmin's (1990) brilliant reconstruction of the origins of "modernity" provides the necessary clues. Toulmin argues that there were two strands in modernity: the skeptical humanism of the late Renaissance epitomized by Montaigne, Erasmus, and Shakespeare, and the rationalism of the late sixteenth century epitomized by Descartes' search for certainty. The latter underpinned the triumphs of the scientific revolution, and the methods of mechanistic Newtonian physics as the exemplary form of rationality. Toulmin's most original insight is that the rationalist project was prompted by the Thirty Years War that followed the assassination of Henry IV of France in 1610. Henry's attempt to create a religiously tolerant secular state with equal rights for Catholics and Protestants mirrored the skeptical humanism of Montaigne. Henry's assassination was taken as a sign of the failure of this tolerant Renaissance skepticism. With the carnage that followed the religious wars in support of different dogmas, Descartes set himself the project of overcoming Montaigne's skepticism—which seemed to have led to such disastrous consequences—by defining a decontextualized certainty.

This rationalist project, which created the scientific revolution, found resonance—argues Toulmin—in the coterminous development of the system of sovereign nation-states following the peace of Westphalia. The ascendancy of these two "systems" continued in tandem till the First World War. But chinks were appearing in the armor of the rationalist Cartesian project—with its separation of human from physical nature—with the developments in the late nineteenth century associated with Darwin and Freud. Despite the replacement of Newtonian physics by the less "mechanistic" physics of Einstein and his successors, the political disorder of the 1930s led as in the 1630s to a search for certainty and the logical positivist movement was born.

The final dismantling of the scaffolding of the rationalist project begun with the peace of Westphalia, according to Toulmin, occurred in the 1960s—

with Kennedy's assassination being as emblematic as Henry IV's. Many hoped that Kennedy was about to launch a period ending the Age of Nations and beginning one of transnational cooperation through transnational institutions. Thus, since the 1960s, the world has been trying to reinvent the humanism of the Renaissance which was sidelined by the rationalist Cartesian project of the sixteenth century. As he writes: "By the 1950s there were already the best of reasons, intellectual and practical for restoring the unities dichotomized in the seventeenth century: humanity vs. nature, mental activity vs. its material correlates, human rationality vs. emotional springs of action and so on." He then goes on to argue that the postwar generation was the first to respond: "because they had strong personal stakes in the then current political situation." The Vietnam War

> shocked them into rethinking the claims of the nation, and above all its claim to unqualified sovereignty. Rachel Carson had shown them that nature and humanity are ecologically interdependent, Freud's successors had shown them a better grasp of their emotional lives, and now disquieting images on the television news called the moral wisdom of their rulers in doubt. In this situation, one must be incorrigibly obtuse or morally insensible to fail to see the point. This point did not relate particularly to Vietnam: rather, what was apparent was the super-annuation of the modern world view that was accepted as the intellectual warrant for "nationhood" in or around 1700. (Toulmin 1990, p. 161)

This is the place to introduce the insights of Douglas and Wildavsky concerning the cultural and political characteristics of the environmental movement. They define a hierarchical center which has been characteristic of the nation-state—much as Toulmin does. Opposing it have been what they call "border" organizations. They comprise "secular and religious protest movements and sects and communes of all kinds" (p. 102). They argue that: "the border is self-defined by its opposition to encompassing larger social systems. It is composed of small units and it sees no disaster in reduction of the scale of organization. It warns the center that its cherished social systems will wither because the center does not listen to warnings of cataclysm. The border is worried about God or nature, two arbiters external to the large-scale social systems of the center. Either God will punish or nature will punish; the jeremiad is the same and the sins are the same: worldly ambition, lust after material things, large organization" (p. 123).

Like Toulmin they see the Vietnam War, and Watergate, undermining support for the center in the United States, and giving greater legitimacy to the "border"—particularly to the segment which emphasizes Nature. There are various more complex reasons why the moral authority of the center in many Western states has been undermined (chapter 5). This has given rise to sources of moral authority outside the hierarchical structure of the nation-state, which echoes a return to pre-modern Western medieval forms. As Toulmin notes: "One notable feature of the system of European Powers established by the Peace of Westphalia . . . was the untrammeled sovereignty it conferred on the European Powers. Before the Reformation, the established rulers . . . exercised their political power under the moral supervision of the Church. As Henry II of England found after the murder of Thomas a Becket, the Church might even oblige a King to accept a humiliating penance as the price of its continued support" (ibid., p. 196).

With the undermining of the moral authority of Western nation-states, this moral authority is increasingly being taken over by nongovernmental organizations (NGOs) like Amnesty International, and in many cases the environmental NGOs. This unraveling of the Westphalian system and a partial reversion to the world of the Middle Ages pose, in my view, the real threat of eco-imperialism, modeled less on the nineteenth-century scramble for Africa than the Crusades. The new imperial power, the United States, remains infected with this moralism. Its eco-moralists might try to promote their "habits of the heart" around the world.

For, whilst the West may be turning its back on modernity, the Rest are seeking its technological fruits, without giving up their souls. Hence, even religious fundamentalists in the Rest recognize the need for economic progress, if for no other reason than to acquire the ability to produce or purchase those arms which they feel are essential to prevent any repetition of the past humiliation they have suffered at the hands of superior Western might. The attempts by the eco-moralists to curb their development of the industrial bases of this power to save Spaceship Earth will be fiercely resisted. It is the major future source for global disorder.

9

Conclusions

At the end of the second millennium, the world presents a number of paradoxes. One of these is best illustrated by the recent elections in two of the
largest democracies in the world—the United States and India. In both election campaigns questions concerning globalization were to the fore. But, paradoxically, in one country—India—globalization was accepted by all the con-
testing parties, with the party of the cultural nationalists, the BJP, pointedly
pinning globalization and economic liberalization to their electoral mast. In
the United States, the Democrats made a major election issue of the irrational fears aroused by "outsourcing" of jobs to China and India, whilst the
purportedly free-trading Republicans had earlier placed tariffs on steel and increased domestic agricultural subsidies to buy votes in battleground states.
This represents a sea change in the respective positions of the two countries
concerning globalizing capitalism, particularly relating to the merits of free
trade. In previous chapters we have seen how this has come about. I have argued that the major problem lies in the United States failure to accept and
adopt the correct classical liberal principle of unilateral free trade upheld by
its nineteenth-century imperial predecessor. It still foolishly clings to reciprocity in its trade policy. By contrast, an erstwhile Communist country,
China, has carried out a massive unilateral trade liberalization over the last
twenty years. Many Third World countries, like India and Chile, are fearful of
completely removing their trade barriers, as they would have nothing to bargain with the United States and European Union in the reciprocity game the
largest trading entities still insist on playing. Thus, the promoters of the new
LIEO have paradoxically become its weakest adherents.

Just as paradoxically, as the former repressed economies of the Third and Second Worlds are gradually adopting the other dyad of the twin classical liberal policy of laissez faire, there has been hardly any change in the bloated size and role of government in the United States and EU—the erstwhile rhetorical champions of free markets and limited government intervention. Again by contrast, China, a supposedly socialist state, has in its burgeoning southern rim the freest labor market in the world.

Underlying both these paradoxes is the interaction of the income distribution effects of globalization with Demos. The short-term losers from globalization can use the political process to prevent or mitigate these changes at the expense of their own, and their compatriots', future standards of living. But, as the Northern losers in the new LIEO are the unskilled, there is a simple means for them to maintain and raise their incomes: go to school. This would allow them to participate in the emerging new international division of labor: with the highly skilled jobs of the "head" in the North and the low- and semi-skilled jobs of the "body" in the South—mainly in Asia, whilst the natural resource–rich countries of Africa and Latin America specialize in primary commodities. The skills needed in the North include not only those which are increasingly in demand in the production of traded goods, but also the interpersonal skills which are important in the production of nontraded services in the North. The Northern failure to adjust smoothly to this new international division of labor is partly due to its departure from classical liberal principles of providing targeted benefits to the deserving poor and of publicly *financing* but not *producing* the merit good of education. With the growing awareness of the unintended consequences of the welfare state on personal behavior, belated attempts have begun to reverse the policies begun by Bismarck in Germany, Lloyd George in Britain, and Roosevelt in the United States.

The necessary reforms are made more difficult by pressure group politics and the gradual though subtle shift in many countries of the North from representative to participatory democracy. The growing influence of virtually continuous opinion polling on public policy leads to populist pressures reflecting changing, ephemeral passions. The rational considerations of alternative policy choices by the people's representatives in a democracy is replaced by implicit or explicit referenda where emotion and "spin," not reason, determine the outcomes.

It is therefore ironical that the current panacea for development is the introduction of democracy in the Third World.[1] It is claimed that a number of statistical studies have found a relationship between democracy and development.[2] But, the statistical proxies used for the political variables in these studies do not inspire much confidence, which are further plagued by the econometric problem of identification. In our recent comparative study of the thirty-year economic histories of twenty-five developing countries, Myint and I found no relationship between the form of government and economic performance.[3] Rather than the polity, the initial resource endowment—in particular the availability or lack of natural resources—was a major determinant of policies which impinged on the efficiency of investment and the rate of growth. This was basically due to the inevitable politicization of the rents from natural resources, with concomitant damage to growth performance. By contrast, resource-poor countries, irrespective of the nature of their government, were forced to develop their only resource—their human subjects. Thus, the economic performance of resource-poor countries—like the Far Eastern Gang of Four—tended to be much better on average than that of those with abundant natural resources—like the countries in Africa and Latin America. Countries whose factor endowments fell in between these extremes—like India and China—swerved between following the policies of their resource-abundant and resource-poor cousins, with a resultant indifferent intermediate economic performance.

There is an important distinction between political and economic cum civil liberties, which explains the link between the polity and the economy. While political liberty is an end in itself, it need not necessarily promote prosperity as De Tocqueville knew well, when he wrote in *The Ancien Regime* "It is true that in the long run liberty always leads those who know how to keep it to comfort, well being, often to riches: but there are times when it impedes the attainment of such goods, and other times when despotism alone can momentarily guarantee their enjoyment. Men who take up liberty for its material rewards, then, have never kept it for long . . . what in all times has attracted some men so strongly to liberty has been itself alone . . . Who seeks in liberty something other than itself is born to be a slave."[4] It is economic cum civil liberties and not necessarily political which are required for prosperity. Thus, whilst democracy may be preferred as a form of government as it promotes the valuable end of political liberty, its instrumental use to promote prosperity may well backfire. What matters for development is not political but economic liberty, and for that a state which views itself as a "civil association" in Oakeshott's terms is more likely to promote development. These truths about the links between good governance and prosperity were well known to the classical liberal fathers—Hume and Smith. They recognized that the characteristics of good government are more important than its particular form. There is no better example of these classical liberal insights than the shining example of Hong Kong, which had the most stellar growth performance amongst the Gang of Four. It maintained civil and economic liberties but, as a British colony, it was clearly not a democracy.

The current Western obsession with promoting democracy is linked to the West's desire to promote its "habits of the heart" around the world. This process has been exacerbated by the propaganda of the NGOs, most of whom espouse various environmental causes. Their bread and butter is obtained by arousing the fear of "Apocalypse Now," which has been an enduring superstition of mankind. But they also play on the moral emotions and on the muddled cosmological beliefs of the West. Many of their moral claims, I have argued, can be shown to be the culture-specific beliefs of Western Christendom. Their "rights talk" is illogical even within their Western ethic. Their attempts to infiltrate and use the transnational institutions created after the Second World War to legislate their Western morality around the world are a potential source of serious disorder. Based on my distinction between material and cosmological beliefs, there is also a distinction between modernization which requires accepting Western material beliefs concerning the operations of the economy, and cosmological beliefs, which means accepting Western beliefs about "how one should live" (Plato).

In the West, two papal revolutions changed its cosmological and material beliefs. The sixth-century Papal Revolution of Gregory the Great changed its cosmological beliefs, particularly in the domestic domain, and made individualism their dominant component. The eleventh century Papal Revolution of Gregory VII changed its material beliefs by creating the commercial and legal infrastructure for the functioning of a market economy. It was this second papal revolution which led to the economic rise of the West.

In the subsequent clash between the dominant West and the Rest, the defeated civilizations of Eurasia were faced by a choice—either to modernize and adopt the West's material beliefs, which meant adopting the commercial and legal infrastructure of a market economy created by the Papal Revolution of Gregory VII, allowing them to catch up with the West. Or imitating the clam and closing their shells. Japan speedily chose the former route and modernized without Westernizing. Others, like China and India (and arguably Russia), chose to temporize. They feared that modernizing would also involve Westernizing and losing their souls. So they adopted the dirigiste alternatives provided by Fabian socialism and Communism, whereby they hoped to reconcile tradition with modernity. It is the demonstrable failure of this alternative that has led these two ancient Eurasian civilizations to realize that they can modernize without Westernizing. Like the Japanese before them, they too have joined the bandwagon of globalizing capitalism without sacrificing their cosmological beliefs. The attempt by the Western global salvationists and their converts in these civilizations (the rice Christians as the Chinese called them) to legislate their cosmological beliefs will be fiercely resisted. It could even lead to a backlash by their cultural nationalists against globalization, as the modernization it breeds is once again erroneously identified with Westernization. The global salvationists need to be fiercely resisted.

Another paradox is the widespread impression created by the New Dirigisme that instead of engendering unprecedented prosperity in most parts of the Third World, globalizing capitalism has led to rising inequality and perpetuated poverty. This has been shown to be false. Just as in the first LIEO, the countries of the Third World which have accepted global capitalism have seen historically unprecedented prosperity and a massive reduction in poverty. It has led to the growth of a large non-Western middle class. It is the parts of the world not integrated into the global economy (mainly in Africa, Central Asia, and the Middle East) which have failed to share in the prosperity engendered by globalizing capitalism. Despite its critics, global capitalism (of the Anglo-Saxon shareholder variety) has shown its power to bring prosperity and banish poverty wherever it has been given its head.

The final paradox is that the transnational institutions the United States created to promote its LIEO after the Second World War are now either dysfunctional, or are supporting the New Dirigisme. It is the very success of the World Bank and IMF in bringing much of the Third and Second Worlds into the globalization process which has made them redundant. The IMF, created to manage the Breton Woods quasi–fixed exchange rate system, lost its rationale after the world moved to various forms of flexible exchange rates. It then found a role in managing various financial crises, but the moral hazard this has fostered has brought this role too into question. The World Bank lost its financial intermediation role when the well-managed economies of the Third and Second Worlds gained access to private capital markets. Its foreign aid role has been undermined by the manifest failure of "conditionality" to change the behavior of predatory states. Instead it has become a purveyor of the New Dirigisme, espousing all the soft causes promoted by the NGOs. Ideally it and its sister institution should be shut down, having accomplished their original purposes. But international institutions, like old soldiers, never die. I have suggested elsewhere that they should be amalgamated and given a new role.[5]

This would be to deal with the natural resource rents which are the cause of the failure of so many failed or failing states. As the Lal and Myint comparative study showed, there is a strong temptation for anyone controlling the state to appropriate the rents from natural resources for their own personal purpose. In failed or failing states the political struggle surrounds the capture of these rents. Lacking any assurance about their tenure, the time horizon of incumbent predators is understandably very short: he may be killed or overthrown in the next battle for the control of the rents. Hence, it is rational to get as much, as soon as possible, out of the country. Once we have such a failing state, an obvious solution is to follow the Alaskan example. It distributes its oil revenues to citizens by writing checks through the tax system. But such a policy is not available in countries without a functioning state.

A conjoining of the staff of the World Bank and the IMF to form an International Natural Resources Fund (INRF) could be the answer. The INRF would obtain the rents from the natural resources of failed or failing states and put them in escrow for use *only in the country in which they were generated*. These funds would only be released on the authority of the INRF for purposes

235

determined by the fund's managers in consultation with the local government—mainly for social and economic infrastructure projects. To prevent predators from attacking the mines and wells generating the rents, the military prowess of an imperial power or coalition of great powers would be required. This could provide a solution to the problem of natural resources which have become a precious bane in so many Third World countries.

There is no such useful purpose that any of the other specialized UN agencies can fulfill. They along with the UN's ECOSOC are now enemies of a LIEO. Along with the NGOs to whom they offer succor, though speaking in their name they are the enemies of the world's poor. They are the most important channels through which the New Dirigisme is being promoted. They should be shut down.

This leaves the WTO. Till recently it has been spectacularly successful in promoting multilateral free trade. But with the United States's move to unilateralism and bilateralism in its trade policy, the WTO's role and usefulness are seriously threatened. The only hope is that the United States, by giving up its illogical belief in reciprocity, will unilaterally adopt free trade.

In the early 1980s I wrote a small book preaching the virtues of classical liberalism in redressing the ancient poverty of the Third World. For a variety of reasons, these developing countries have begun to heed that message. I did not imagine that it would now be necessary to preach a similar message to the countries of the North. But this is now required with the rise of the New Dirigisme. It is time for the North to put into practice the classical liberal principles it rhetorically espouses. Though the globalization glass can be looked upon as either half empty or half full, there is a growing danger that the New Dirigisme will undermine the current LIEO as the Dirigiste Dogma did its predecessor. But, Cassandra is hoarse and is due for a vocational change.

Notes

Preface

1. Lal (1983/1997/2002).

2. Thus *The Economist* (March 24, 1992) noted: "During the past ten years a great change has swept through the developing world: governments everywhere are turning against economic interventionism and putting their trust in market forces. . . . This bloodless revolution is a triumph for the relatively small group of economic thinkers who for years withstood the contempt of the development-economics establishment. . . . In the 1990s Lord Bauer and economists such as Anne Krueger, Bela Balassa, Deepak Lal, and Ian Little are regarded—above all in the third world itself as largely vindicated" (p.103).

3. Polonius would have said: "That's an ill phrase, a vile phrase" (*Hamlet*, Act 2 scene 2, line 11). It is a meaningless term. As the Peruvian novelist and politician Mario Vargas Llosa (2000) has argued: "A 'neo' is someone who pretends to be something, someone who is at the same time inside and outside of something; it is an elusive hybrid, a straw man set up without ever identifying a specific value, idea, regime, or doctrine. . . . To say 'neoliberal' is the same as saying 'semi-liberal' or 'pseudo-liberal.' It is pure nonsense. Either one is in favor of liberty or against it, but one cannot be semi-in-favor or pseudo-in-favor of liberty, just as one cannot be 'semi pregnant,' 'semi-living,' or 'semi-dead.' The term has not been invented to express a conceptual reality, but rather as a corrosive weapon of derision, it has been designed to semantically devalue the doctrine of liberalism" (p. 16).

Moreover, by liberal I mean "classical liberal" throughout this book, and not "liberal" as it is currently used in the political discourse in the United States, where it means socialist. As Schumpeter (1954) noted: "The term [classical or economic liberal] has acquired a different—in fact almost the opposite meaning—since about 1900 and especially since 1930; as a supreme if unintended compliment, the enemies of the system of private enterprise have thought it wise to appropriate its label" (p. 394).

Introduction

1. Baechler (1975), p. 33.
2. Whybrow (2004), p. 97.
3. See Cavalli-Sforza (2000).
4. See Chen et al. (1999) and Chang et al. (1996).
5. Whybrow (2004), p. 99.
6. Ibid., p. 98.
7. This is the "7 allele of the D4 dopamine receptor." See Whybrow (2004), p. 93.
8. Ibid., p. 53.
9. See Greif (1994).
10. Hicks (1969), p. 33.
11. Schumpeter (1954), p. 78.
12. Dumont (1986), p. 40.
13. Berman (1983), p. 338.
14. Ibid., pp. 349–50.
15. Ibid., p. 521.
16. Tawney (1926/1990), p. 26.
17. See Lal (1998). Intensive growth which leads to a sustained rise in per capita income is to be distinguished from extensive growth where output grows pari passu with population leaving per capita income virtually unchanged. The world has seen extensive growth for millennia with the expansion of population leading to rises in agricultural output with more land being brought into cultivation or being used more intensively. In these agrarian organic economies, as Wrigley (1988) has labeled them, the fixed land constraint implied that at some stage diminishing returns would set in, and along with the expansion of population following any rise in per capita on Malthusian lines, there would be no sustained rise in per capita income. The intensive growth due to the extension or creation of empires would lead to a temporary rise in per capita income (Smithian intensive growth), but it was not till the Industrial Revolution and the substitution of mineral energy resources—fossil fuels—for the products of land as the source of the economy's energy that unlimited intensive growth which I label Promethean became a possibility first in the West and subsequently in the Rest.
18. See Lal (1988/2004).
19. Chinese per capita income rose to c $600 (in 1990 international $) and the population to 100 million. But, following the depredations of the Mongol invasions, there was a decline in the population to 65 million by the fourteenth century. When the Ming dynasty (1368–1644) replaced the Mongols, and restored peace and stability, the population began rising again from 65 million to 400 million by 1800 (Maddison 2001, table B -21).
20. See Lal (1998), chap. 3.
21. "In the first and second century of the empire neither population nor product per head nor aggregate product increased noticeably, i.e., by say more than 0.1 % and 0.2% per year" (Goldsmith 1984, p. 287).
22. Ibid., p. 263.

23. See Bernardi (1970).

24. Ibid., p. 81.

25. Ibid., p.73.

26. See Lal (1987); Lal and Myint (1996).

27. Goldsmith (1984), p. 283.

28. It should, however, be noted that Jones (1981)—following in the footsteps of Kant (1784), Gibbon (1787), and Weber (1920/1958)—has maintained that the Rise of the West was due to the political and institutional competition which existed in the European "states system" after the fall of the Roman Empire. But, as I have argued (in Lal 1998, 2004b), this explanation is inadequate as India too had a "state's system" for much of its history and it did not lead India into the Industrial Revolution. Instead, the rare periods of political stability under dynastic Imperial rule extending over the subcontinent were the most prosperous and glorious periods of Indian history, when innovation and growth occurred. The Rise of the West, as I argue in *Unintended Consequences*, cannot be explained in purely materialist terms. It cannot be understood without the distinctive change in the cosmological and material beliefs of Western Europe from those of other Eurasian civilizations, associated with the twin Papal Revolutions of Gregory I (concerning the family in the sixth century) and Gregory VII (concerning the law in the eleventh century).

29. S. E. Finer (1997), vol. 1, p. 34.

30. See Berman (1983).

Chapter One: Liberal International Economic Orders

1. Keynes (1919/1971), pp. 6–7.

2. See A. M. Taylor (2002).

3. Hecksher (1955).

4. See Aftalion (1990).

5. See Cain and Hopkins (2002).

6. O'Brien (1998), p. 71.

7. Ibid. One measure of the prosperity this order created is given by the large increase in the productivity of shipping due to the suppression of piracy. Douglass North (1968) has estimated that from the mid-seventeenth to the end of the eighteenth century, as a result freight rates on the Atlantic trade fell by half, and from 1814 to 1850, before the technological revolution associated with steamships, productivity in shipping increased by 3.5 percent p.a. The decline in piracy with the extension of the British international order also reduced insurance costs by about two-thirds between 1635 and 1770.

8. See my *In Praise of Empires* for details.

9. O'Brien (1998), p. 64.

10. Ibid., p. 67.

11. Hecksher (1955), p. 325.

12. But see Temin (2003), who shows that even in the early Iron Age there is evidence from underwater archaeology that there was trade in bulk commodities across the Mediterranean where transport costs were low. This trade was of the

Hecksher-Ohlin variety and thus should have had similar effects as predicted by the model.

13. Given the continuing confusion in popular discussion about comparative and absolute advantage, it maybe useful to set out a variant of Ricardo's numerical example (Ricardo (1821/1951, p. 135). Assume that both Mexico and the United States produce vegetables and cars. Mexico needs five labor days to produce one ton of vegetables, the United States, only four labor days. Mexico needs thirty labor days to produce one car, the United States, only twenty labor days. So the United States can produce both vegetables and cars more cheaply in labor days than Mexico. The United States has an *absolute* advantage in producing both cars and vegetables. But the United States has a *comparative* advantage in producing cars, Mexico has a *comparative* advantage in producing vegetables. Without trade (that is under *autarky*), and as there is only one factor of production, labor, the relative price of cars to vegetables will be given by the ratio of the relative costs of producing each good in terms of labor days in each country. Thus in Mexico, one car will exchange for 6 (= 30/5) vegetables, while in the United States, one car will exchange for 5 (= 20/4) vegetables. As long as with the opening up of trade the relative "world" price, the *terms of trade*, settle between these two ratios, both countries will gain from trade. Thus, suppose the "world" prices settle at the autarkic domestic price ratio in Mexico (viz.1 car for 6 vegetables). It will be profitable for the United States to specialize in producing cars, exporting them to Mexico and obtaining imports of 6 vegetables in exchange through trade, whereas under autarky it would only be able to get 5 vegetables by giving up one car. Foreign trade therefore provides it a new and superior indirect way ("technology") of transforming cars into vegetables. Similarly, suppose the terms of trade after the opening up of trade settle at the U.S. autarkic price ratio (1 car for 5 vegetables); then it would be profitable for Mexico to export 5 vegetables and get one U.S. car in exchange, which is better than the rate at which it could transform vegetables into cars domestically without trade, viz., 6 vegetables for 1 car. Thus, as long as the terms of trade facing a country after opening up to trade differ from its autarkic domestic price ratio it will gain by specializing in the good it has a *comparative* advantage, even though it has an *absolute disadvantage* in producing both goods. . . . Apart from lowering the price of the imported good in each county with trade (the consumption gain), the fall in the price of the imported good will lead labor to be shifted to the production of the good in which the country has a comparative advantage, with the total supply of both cloth and wine being higher in the trading world than under autarky (the production gain). This Ricardian example also shows that talk which is current in business and many lay circles about the *competitiveness* of any economy is meaningless in a trading world. As the numerical example shows, the United States is more competitive than Mexico in producing both goods but Mexico still has a comparative advantage in producing vegetables. That a country *must* have a comparative advantage in producing some goods even if it produces all goods more expensively (so is uncompetitive, i.e., has an absolute disadvantage) than its trading partners is a *logical* truth. It is one of the irrefutable though counterintuitive propositions of economics.

14. For an empirical validation of this process of "real cost" adjustment, see Harberger (1998).

15. Mill (1969), p. 581.

16. See Irwin (2002), chap. 21. Huber (1971) and Bernhofen and Brown (2000) find that the opening up of Japan in 1858 after a long period of autarky led to substantial gains from trade. For the postwar period, the most important empirical evidence is provided by a series of comparative studies based on detailed historical case studies of many developing countries. The pioneers of these studies are Little-Scitovsky-Scott (1970) for the OECD, Balassa (1971, 1982) for the World Bank, Bhagwati (1979) and Krueger (1978) for the NBER. Later comparative studies which are relevant are Michaely, Papageorgiou, and Choksi (1991) and Lal and Myint (1996) for the World Bank. While these are the studies which provide the most detailed and carefully evaluated evidence for the effects of "openness" on growth, there has also been an attempt to test this proposition econometrically through cross-country regressions. A survey of these till the late 1980s is provided in Lal and Rajapatirana (1987), which is updated in Lal (1993a). Recently there has been an explosion in these studies. See Srinivasan and Bhagwati (2001) for an evaluation of these studies and for reasons why not much faith can be placed in this flawed enterprise. They note the "mutual assured destruction (MAD)" that has been wrought by two sets of these regression warriors, Rodriguez and Rodrik (1999) and Sachs and Warner (1995).

Mention should also be made of the spread of this "mad(ness)" to econometric studies of the nineteenth century. It begins with Bairoch's crude correlations between average tariff levels (given by tariff revenue divided by imports) and growth rates in the North as summarized in Bairoch (1993). The most sophisticated subsequent study is by O'Rourke (2000), which by and large confirms Bairoch's findings that between 1875 and 1914 in the ten Northern countries he examined, tariffs were positively correlated with growth. But see Irwin (2002a), who also uses regression analysis to reach the contrary conclusion, namely, "these findings suggest that tariffs were not a critical factor behind the late nineteenth century growth experience." But as in the regression studies for the twentieth century, the measure of protection used in these historical studies is deeply flawed, as it does not provide any idea of the "effective protection" provided by a tariff structure. As O'Rourke notes: "Cross-country regressions need to be supplemented with more individual country and industry studies" (p. 478). To which we can say Amen! Also, Lal and Myint (1996, chap. 2.4), after surveying the new theories and cross-country regressions trying to establish a link between "openness" and growth, show that a more sophisticated three-factor model based on Krueger (1977), as well as the incorporation of various "costs of agency" involved in industrial development, are required to explain the divergent growth outcomes in their 25-country sample.

17. In Lal (1980) I argued against the common presumption that, because of the terms of trade argument for protection, free trade will have to be enforced. The conventional position is clearly expressed by Kindleberger (1976), for example, who states: "In the international economy it has all along been recognized that the world of the benign invisible hand does not obtain. Unlike the households and firms of the national economy, countries in the international economy and especially in the international polity have power . . . so that it is useful to simulate the world of the invisible hand by commitments to the rule of free trade and the gold standard" (p. 16). The implicit model underlying this view is the two-person noncooperative game like the Prisoner's Dilemma. I argued that while this model may be appropriate if the

world consisted of two mutually opposed trading blocs, in a multicountry trading world in which all traders are to some extent "price makers," the relevant model is of N person cooperative game theory. Within this framework, it can be demonstrated that, following from a famous theorem of Edgeworth's which has been revived in the mathematical theory of the "core" of an economy, when there are many trading partners with some "monopoly" power and those nations have the preferences of *homo econimicus*, the only stable equilibrium point in the process of higgling and haggling among these "rational" nations will be where they act as if they were price takers, namely the free trade, competitive equilibrium (see Malinvaud 1972; Arrow and Hahn 1971, pp. 186–7). The only international trade theorist as I noted to the best of my knowledge who was aware of this deficiency (based on game-theoretic considerations) in the classical terms of trade argument was Frank Graham (1948), pp. 10–12.

18. See H. G. Johnson (1953–54/1958); Lal (1980/1993), pp. 134–36; and note 14 above.

19. Thus Irwin (2003) has recently quantified the possible gain to the antebellum United States from an "optimum tariff" on cotton in which it had close to a monopoly position in world markets. The optimal export tax would have been "in the range of 45–55%." With this "optimal tariff" the welfare gain to the United States would have been about "0.24–0.32 percent of U.S. GNP in 1859," and even just looking at the South, it would have been "between 0.9% and 1.2% of the South's GNP." As Irwin concludes, "the antebellum U.S. may have been the quintessential example of a 'large' country in world trade, but that does not necessarily imply that the optimal tariff was high and the welfare gains from it would be large"(p. 290).

20. Bhagwati in his introduction to Bhagwati (2002) shows how, while for the "small" country which cannot influence its terms of trade, unilateral free trade remains the ideal policy, for "large" countries which can influence their terms of trade there could be an argument for reciprocity. But, if for most countries the "terms of trade" argument is a theoretical curiosity, the policy implications of this theoretical possibility would be minimal. Bhagwati summarizes the three basic propositions arising from the economics of unilateralism and reciprocity as follows: "Proposition 1: Go alone if others do not go with you. . . . Proposition 2: If others go with you, so that there is (simultaneous) reciprocity, that is better still. . . . Proposition 3: If you go alone, others may liberalize later: Unilateralism then begets sequential reciprocity" (pp. 4–7). These propositions are sufficient to make the case I make later in this book that it would be best for the United States today as the world's hegemon to eschew its policy of reciprocity and adopt unilateral free trade.

21. See Crafts (1985).

22. See Irwin (1996).

23. In my *Unintended Consequences* (1998) I have distinguished between material and cosmological beliefs. The former involve beliefs about how the world works, the latter, those concerning in Plato's words "how we should live."

24. Cameron (1993), p. 277.

25. Also, see Conybeare (2002) for a fuller discussion.

26. Irwin has persuasively documented that even "Hamilton preferred modest duties, because in his view, the tariff was more important as a tool of fiscal policy than as instrument for promoting manufactures" (2002, p. 16). Similarly, the German customs union (the Zollverin) was motivated by the economies of scale in fiscal adminis-

tration which raised total government revenue, and not the need to protect Germany from English competition (Dumke 1994).

27. See Williamson (1996); O'Rourke and Williamson (1999).

28. See Rogowski (1989).

29. "The Populists' fusion with the Democrats in 1896 under the presidential candidacy of William Jennings Bryan severed the older party's ties not only to Eastern financiers and industrialists but to the urban working class and the less land-intensive farmers of the East and Middle West. In a realignment of American politics that endured until the late 1920s, workers joined owners in support of a triumphant, highly protectionist, and increasingly imperialist Republican party" (Rogowski 1989, p. 44).

30. Ibid., p. 40.

31. Williamson (1985), p. 48.

32. This was caused both by the convergence of commodity prices as a result of free trade and falling transport costs, as well by the massive migration of labor from the Old to the New world. See O'Rourke and Williamson (1999).

33. See Phelps-Brown (1983).

34. See Lal (1983, 1994).

35. Eichengreen (1996).

36. There is a controversy about the origins of the price deflation of the 1870s (Saul 1976; Lewis 1978). But it is indubitable that there was a fall in the rate of growth of the world's monetary stock from the 8 percent of the 1950s to only 1 percent between 1875 to 1887 (Saul 1976, p. 17). This was partly because many countries adopted the Gold Standard after 1870 and sought to build up gold reserves to maintain a fixed exchange rate. This sterilization of gold supplies occurred without any new gold discoveries until the gold mines in Australia and South Africa opened up at the end of the 1880s. Cagan argues that as he found that "price movements in the United States reflect primarily changes in the monetary stock, the same explanation must hold for countries, including England, that were on the Gold Standard and had close commercial ties with the United States" (Cagan 1965, p. 250).

37. Lipson notes that these principles were: "foreigners were deemed subject to local laws, as they had been since the Middle Ages, but national jurisdiction over aliens and their property had to comply with a variety of international standards" (1985, p. 8).

38. See Berman (1983); Lal (1998).

39. Lipson (1985), p. 14.

40. See Hopkins (1973).

41. Lipson (1985), p. 15.

42. In an important article Gallagher and Robinson (1953) had described this indirect imperialism as the "imperialism of free trade."

43. Cain and Hopkins (2002), p. 650, emphasis added.

44. Bairoch (1981).

45. Bairoch (1967).

46. Maddison (2001), p. 47.

47. This is in *EHNet*, October 2002. Also see Maddison (2004).

48. Gunder Frank (1998), p. 284.

49. See Lal (1988) for the following.

50. See Hopkins (1973); Bauer (2000).

51. Rogowski (1989), p. 57.

52. Copans (1980), p. 91.

53. See Collier and Lal (1986).

54. On the origins of Western individualism and its exceptionalism in the context both of its own "communalist" past and that of other Eurasian civilizations to our day, see Lal (1998).

55. Hicks (1969), p. 99.

56. The causes of the Great Depression are still being hotly debated by scholars. Most, however, agree that it was caused by domestic and international monetary factors. But some, like Temin (1976), have emphasized the importance of real factors like demography, technology shocks, and structural change in the United States. The monetary factors are the decline in money supply (M2) by 33 percent between August 1929 and March 1933 in the United States, caused by banking panics which closed nearly 30 percent of U.S. banks in less than four years (Bordo et al. 1998, p. 8). Friedman and Schwartz (1963) blame this on the Federal Reserve's ineptitude in using well-known monetary tools to prevent the panic. Moreover, Bernanke and Gertler (1995), Eichengreen (1992) emphasize the role of the Gold Standard as both causing and propagating the Great Depression. The rules of the Gold Standard led the United States and other countries to follow deflationary policies in the face of external shocks, with the fixed exchange rates transmitting this deflation to other countries which could not (given convertibility of their currencies) use domestic monetary policy to reflate. But Meltzer (1995) demurs, arguing that at least the United States was not in "golden fetters" as it had sufficient gold reserves to follow an expansionary policy.

57. See Kindleberger (1973). This view has now had a long life as part of the theory of "hegemonic stability" in academic international relations, but has rightly been abandoned as it is incoherent (see Lake 1993; and Eichengreen 1989). There is one sense in which Kindleberger's view about the effects of the U.S. actions in the interwar period can be rescued. This is the example set by the leading economic power adopting inimical economic policies which went against classical liberal policies and which others then adopted. But no imperial hegemon is required (except to maintain international property rights) for the correct classical liberal policies of free trade and free capital mobility to be adopted in their own self-interest by all participants in the LIEO. This in fact was the correct classical liberal case against empire. The United States in the interwar period not only failed to provide the public good of protecting international property rights and peace, but foolishly went against free trade and capital mobility which were clearly in its own self-interest to maintain, for the reasons spelled out in this chapter and the two following.

58. Lipson (1985), p. 66.

59. See Knock (1992).

60. See Lal (2003a) for why even in the modern theory of trade and welfare the two should again be linked. Also see chapter 5 below.

61. P. Bairoch (1993), p. 34.

62. See Baldwin (1969) for the flaws.

63. Bairoch (1993), p. 36.

64. Corden (1977).

65. W.A. Lewis (1978a), p. 49.

66. As shown by the detailed study by Collier et al. (1997).

67. See Lal (1983/1997/2002).

68. The distinction between "inward" and "outward" looking policies was first made by Hla Myint in his inaugural lecture at the London School of Economics. See Myint (1967).

69. The one contemporary cartel which has bucked this trend is the diamond cartel run by DeBeers which was originally created by Cecil Rhodes. See "The Diamond Business," *The Economist*, Dec. 20, 1997, pp. 113–15, for an account of how this has been done, and why it might come unstuck in the future.

70. Having risen from $4 in 1972 to $30 in 1983, it collapsed in 1986 and in 2004 was about $50, which is still lower in real terms than the price in 1983.

71. See Rajan and Zingales (2004), pp. 260–2b.

72. The costs and benefits of direct foreign investment are outlined and case studies for India and East Africa are presented in Lal et al. (1975).

73. See Lal (1996).

74. It is still unclear to what extent the collapse is due to the internal factors resulting from the economic consequences of past dirigisme which impels reform (see Lal 1987), or external factors such as the threat of Star Wars, which upped the ante in terms of unsustainable defense expenditures for the Soviet Union. Certainly Deng's reforms in China were motivated by a threatened internal economic collapse rather than any external factors.

Chapter Two: From *Laissez Faire* to the *Dirigiste Dogma*

1. See Wyatt-Walter (1996).

2. See the excellent book by Razeen Sally (1998) for a clarification of what classical liberalism stands for, and how it has subsequently evolved in discussions of international economic order.

3. D. Hume (1740/1978), part 2.

4. Ibid.

5. Smith (1759/1982), part 2, p. 82.

6. Lal (1988, chap. 13.2); Lal and Myint (1996).

7. Robbins (1952), p. 37.

8. Smith (1759/1982), vol. 2, pp. 184–5.

9. Keynes (1926), pp. 46–7.

10. The "Washington Consensus" was the term coined by Williamson (1990) to describe the policy package which had emerged as best able to promote efficient poverty alleviating growth as a result of the experience of developing countries in the 1970s and 1980s. It is close to that advocated in Harberger (1984) as constituting the best technocratic advice based on experience. It is also the one emerging from the Lal and Myint (1996) study of twenty-five developing countries. Recently Williamson (2000) has sought to partly disown it, as the anti-globalization backlash has used it, particularly in Latin America, as the whipping horse in its denouncement of what it calls the "neo-liberal" policies adopted in Latin America. But, as Vargas Llosa (2000)

has argued, there are hardly any countries in Latin America, apart from Chile, who have in fact adopted the full package, and hence to announce its failure on the half-baked liberalization attempts in many countries is rather premature. Srinivasan (2000) rightly takes Williamson to task for his partial recantation.

11. Nozick (1974), p. 163. Thus, suppose you start off from what is considered a just, say equal, distribution of income. People then voluntarily go to a basketball game and give Wilt Chamberlain, the famous basketball player, a large part of their income to watch him play. The distribution of income will then become unequal. The adherents of a patterned distribution would then have to say this is unjust and force a return to the original distribution of income!

12. See the discussion in Lal and Myint (1996).

13. Conservatism as defined by its major proponent Edmund Burke can, according to John Micklethwaite and Adrian Wooldridge (in their important book *The Right Nation*), be "reduced to six principles: a deep suspicion of the power of the State; a preference for liberty above equality; patriotism; a belief in established institutions and hierarchies; skepticism about the idea of progress; and elitism" Micklethwait and Wooldridge (2004), p. 11. Classical liberals share the first three of these principles but not the last three.

It may also be instructive to see the similarities and differences in the thinking of the leading contemporary conservative thinker Michael Oakeshott and classical liberal Fredrich Hayek. They both agree on the dangerous illusion of constructing social institutions on the basis of a rationalist plan. They also agree on the distinction between the "civil association" and "enterprise view" of the state. Thus, Hayek states in vol. 2 of his *Law, Legislation and Liberty*, "I understand Professor Michael Oakeshott, in his oral teaching, has long used the terms *teleocratic* (and *teleocracy*) and *nomoccratic* (and *nomocracy*) to bring out the same distinction [between an organization and a spontaneous order]. . . . We shall occasionally make use of these terms when we want to stress the end governed character of the organization or the rule-governed character of the spontaneous order" (Hayek 1976, p. 15).

But they differed on the role of ideologies in promoting liberty as well as on the role of liberty in promoting economic efficiency and prosperity. Hayek wished to formulate a classical liberal ideology to combat collectivist ideologies; Oakeshott, however, argued against all doctrines (ideologies). Thus, while agreeing with Hayek's devastating critique of planning in *The Road to Serfdom*, he wrote that the main significance of the book "is not the cogency of the doctrine, but the fact that it is a doctrine. A plan to resist all planning may be better than its opposite but it belongs to the same style of politics" (Oakeshott 1990, p. 26). This is precisely the conservative attitude that Hayek deplored in "Why I am not a Conservative." By its "fear of ideas" and "distrust of theory" conservatism "deprives itself of the weapons needed in the struggle of ideas" (Hayek 1960, p. 404).

Furthermore, though both Hayek and Oakeshott defend free markets, Oakeshott "harbored deep reservations about Hayek's instrumental defense of liberty in terms of its propensity to promote economic efficiency and prosperity" (Franco 2004, p. 12). He looks upon classical liberalism's "plausible ethics of productivity" as a questionable moral ideal, and argues that "the political economy of freedom rests upon the clear acknowledgment that what is being considered is not 'economics' (not the maximization of wealth, not productivity or the standard of life) but *politics* that is, the custody of a manner of living" (Oakeshott 1990, p. 406).

They also disagree about the role of tradition in politics. Hayek notes this adherence to tradition is objectionable as "by its very nature it cannot offer an alternative to the direction in which they are moving" (Hayek 1960, p. 398). Or, as Himmelfarb (1975) observed, if Oakeshott's traditionalism is accepted, how can conservatives criticize the 1960s counterculture when it becomes the dominant culture (the tradition)?

Finally, unlike the classical liberal Hayek who embraces and welcomes change, the conservative Oakeshott seems to be against change. He derides innovation as "almost always an equivocal enterprise, in which gain and loss are so closely interwoven that it is extremely difficult to forecast the final upshot: there is no such thing as an unqualified improvement" (Oakeshott 1990, p. 411). "To be conservative," he writes, "is to prefer the familiar to the unknown, to prefer the tried to the untried, fact to mystery, the actual to the possible, the limited to the unbounded, the near to the distant ... the convenient to the perfect, present laughter to utopian bliss" (p. 409). This attitude is diametrically opposed to the classical liberal's optimistic view of change, as the quotation in the text from Hayek exemplified.

Franco (2004) provides a judicious account of Oakeshott's philosophy and its relationship to many other philosophers.

14. Hayek (1960), p. 400.

15. Ibid.

16. Hayek (1960), p. 402. He goes on to say, "this may also explain why it seems to be so much easier for the repentant socialist to find a new spiritual home in the conservative fold than in the [classical] liberal."

17. Ibid., p. 404.

18. Ibid., p. 405.

19. Ibid., p. 409.

20. Micklethwait and Wooldridge (2004), p. 348.

21. Who is rightly described as more an American conservative than a traditional British Tory by Micklethwait and Wooldridge (2004), p. 345.

22. Keohane (1984); Ruggie (1983).

23. Hayek (1954), p. 6.

24. Remember William Blake's rhetorical lines in his poem "Jerusalem":

> And was Jerusalem builded here,
> Among these dark Satanic Mills?

(*The New Oxford Book of English Verse*, Oxford University Press, 1972, p. 486)

Moreover, as Hayek (1954) has noted, the pessimistic view about industrialism began not in the manufacturing heartland in Northern England, but in the "belief about the 'horrible' conditions prevailing among the manufacturing populations of the Midlands and the North of England was in the 1830s and 1840s widely held among the upper classes of London and the south" (p. 19). It was not based on first-hand experience but on writings of various radical writers, novelists, and poets.

25. Crafts (1985), p. 112.

26. Ibid.

27. Hicks (1969).

28. Mill (1848/1970), bk. 2, chap. 1, pp. 349–50.

29. Though with the contemporary failure of alternatives to what is derisively called "Anglo-Saxon capitalism" by some, this is dubious.

30. Gray (1983), p. 102.

31. Bardhan (1989), p. 1389.

32. See Buchanan and Tullock (1962); Olson (1965); and Stigler (1988).

33. See Barry (1978).

34. Newberry and Stern (1987), p. 653.

35. To see this irrelevance, consider one example. Public economics argues that, to minimize the deadweight social welfare losses associated with distortionary taxation, governments should levy the Ramsey optimal taxes to raise given revenue. Ramsey taxes are named after their inventor, Frank Ramsey, who as a young Cambridge don was set a task by Keynes: to devise the least cost of raising a *given* revenue through distortionary taxation. Any non-lump-sum tax has deadweight losses associated with the consumer surplus lost net of the tax revenue. This loss will be greater for any given tax rate the more elastic the demand curve (the more sensitive consumers are to price in the quantity of the good they buy), for the rise in the price facing a consumer from the tax will lead to a larger reduction in quantity purchased than if demand was more inelastic. Hence Ramsey's solution that to minimize the cost of taxation, the taxes should be placed on goods for which demand is inelastic. But, suppose the government is predatory, and is not interested in merely raising a given revenue but in *maximizing it*. What pattern of commodity taxation will it choose? Ramsey taxes! See Lal (1990a); Brennan and Buchanan (1980). Thus, the tax recommendations of public economics are exactly those that would best serve the interests of a revenue-maximizing predatory government. If the normative analysis is in the interests of the prey, then what should be recommended is a system of taxation that prevents predatoriness while providing enough revenue for public good provision. This, as Brennan and Buchanan argue, would assign only goods with elastic demand to the government for taxation, not those in inelastic demand à la Ramsey.

Recently there has been a spurt of interest in flat taxes to limit the fiscal predatoriness of governments. In its pure version, a flat tax replaces multiple marginal tax rates with a single marginal rate, and abolishes all of the complex systems of allowances and reliefs which governments use for social engineering or for buying votes. A high personal tax–free allowance allows the poor to be taken out of the tax net and imparts progressivity to the system. All taxes, corporate, personal income, and commodity taxes (e.g., VAT) are set at the same rate, amounting to in effect a consumption tax which abolishes any double taxation such as taxation on dividends. The advantages of a flat tax are its simplicity and transparency leading to greater tax compliance and increased tax revenues, faster economic growth due to greater incentives to work, and the removal of various disincentives and distortions caused by existing tax systems. The main costs to the fisc in the short run could be a loss of revenue with the reduction in rates and the increased income tax threshold to help low earners.

Apart from the Channel Islands (in 1940 and 1960) and Hong Kong (since 1947), flat taxes have been recently introduced mainly in the East European countries moving from the plan to the market (Estonia and Lithuania in 1994, Latvia in 1995, Russia in 2001, Serbia and Ukraine in 2003, Slovakia in 2004, and Georgia and Romania in 2005. Poland, the Czech Republic, and Slovenia are considering a move to flat taxes; see Rabushka 2004, 2005).

One of the major advantages of a flat tax from a classical liberal point of view is that its transparency prevents governments from playing the zero sum political redistributive game by robbing Peter to pay Paul. In this game it is usually the middle classes who benefit, as political parties seek to placate the median voter. Unlike the new East European tax systems which were replacing a defunct *ancien regime*, in most developed economies with mature tax systems which are the result of this political redistributive game over many generations, the most likely losers from a flat tax are likely to be the past beneficiaries—the middle classes—who will use the democratic process to resist it. So, even though a number of developed countries which include the United States, the United Kingdom, Germany, Spain, Italy, and Greece, are considering the introduction of a flat tax, it is not likely to be of the pure form with the abolition of all middle-class entitlements, as a British advocate, the Shadow Chancellor of the Exchequer, George Osborne, has conceded. If, however, a flat tax could be implemented, because of its transparency and simplicity it would make it more difficult for governments to increase predatory public expenditure, as *all* taxpayers would know it would imply a rise in the flat tax they would have to pay. This should aid the tax resistance of all the prey who can no longer be played off one against another by the predatory state.

The progenitors of the flat tax were Robert Hall and Alvin Rabushka in 1985 (see their updated Hall and Rabushka 1995). The major political proponent has been Steve Forbes in the United States (see Forbes 2005). The major UK proponents have been the Adam Smith Institute (see Grecu 2004). The UK treasury in its uncensored examination of the flat tax also found much to commend (UK Treasury 2005). A useful UK website which provides concise details of flat tax systems and references is reform.co.uk.

36. See, e.g., Dasgupta (1980); Hahn (1984); Sen (1983). The theorems are proved for a perfectly competitive economy, which has universal markets for all commodities distinguishable not only by their spatial and temporal characteristics but also by the various conceivable future "states of nature" under which they could be traded. (That is, there is a "complete" set of future markets for so-called "contingent commodities.") But the lack of markets for all current and future "contingent" commodities in the real world is patently obvious and hence makes the theorem little more than a theoretical curiosity. Equally unrealistic are the assumptions for perfect competition, where there are large numbers of consumers and producers for every commodity, so that neither producers nor consumers can effect price—they all are "pricetakers." For this happy state to exist, first, there must not be interdependencies in either production or consumption not mediated through markets—that is, no externalities. Second, there must not be too many industries with decreasing costs of production, as these are likely to lead to monopoly.

37. See Lal (1983, 1987a).

38. This is Demsetz's (1969) splendid phrase.

39. Stiglitz (1994).

40. Greenwald and Stiglitz (1986), note 7, p. 234.

41. Blaug (1987), p. 445.

42. Demsetz (1989), p. 94.

43. Baumol, Panzar, and Willig (1982).

44. See Stigler (1988).

45. Schumpeter (1954), pp. 84–5.

46. Demsetz (1995), p. 146.

47. Ibid.

48. I have found this theory particularly useful in thinking of the natural monopoly which is the state. In Lal (1988/2004) I develop a model of the predatory state in which "contestability" plays a central role. The model is used to explain the rise and fall of empires in India over the millennia (see ibid., chap. 13.2).

49. Also, there is no reason why there should not be contractual conditions attached to the possibility of renegotiation of the terms of the franchise before its expiration. In fact, given uncertainty on this account, the rivals bidding for the franchise will take account of these renegotiation costs in their bids. Similarly, if there are likely to be future cost reductions because of technical progress, which would lead to future rents for the incumbent, these too would be taken into account in the rivals' bids for incumbency if they can be forecast, and the best bid again will involve the whittling away of these potential future rents.

Positive or negative windfalls, which are the result of unavoidable uncertainty, need not be inefficient. For instance, even in the near perfect markets for commodities, economic agents suffer positive and negative windfalls all the time, but this does not provide a case for regulation. However, in the case of natural monopolies, as these windfalls could continue for some considerable period of time, there could be political pressure for their curtailment if they are positive, and the danger of bankruptcy for the incumbent and hence of a disruption of supply if they are negative. This would provide a case for some renegotiation clause in the contract granting a franchise to a natural monopoly.

50. In contrast with this UCLA view on regulation, we have the emerging technocratic view on the regulation of natural monopolies. This is based on the frail framework of noncooperative game theory. (See Gilbert and Newberry 1994, which also provides references to this literature.) As the leading lights of game theory recognize, it is of very limited practical relevance because of the plethora of Nash equilibrium which can be generated (Binmore 1990, and Kreps 1990). Though of use in training the intellectual muscles of the young, it has not as yet yielded any robust policy-relevant results in my view. (But see Laffont and Tirole 1993 for an attempt to provide a textbook for the dirigiste technocratic regulator.) Its use in designing the auction for mobile phone licenses in the United Kingdom is better seen as a predatory scheme to transfer potential shareholder wealth to the state than any necessary subserving of efficiency.

51. Schumpeter (1954), p. 100.

52. Hacker (1954), pp. 82–3.

53. Ibid., p. 86.

54. Ibid., p. 79.

55. Ibid., p. 87.

56. Ibid., p. 80.

57. Two excellent accounts of the rise and content of business regulation in the United States are provided in Freyer (2000) and Vietor (2000) in the *Cambridge Economic history of the United States*, vols. 2 and 3. Vietor highlights five chronological stages in the evolution of regulatory policy in the United States. These are "(1) the period between World War I and the Great Depression, in which the growth of

nationwide markets and national firms outstripped the power of state and local authorities to fulfill public objectives; (2) the Great Depression through the 1960s, in which New Deal–inspired regulatory regimes shaped most of the industries that comprised the national infrastructure and fostered development and integration in a relatively non-competitive environment; (3) the years from the mid-1960s through the late 1970s, in which a rights revolution extended government controls to a variety of social problems; (4) an overlapping era (1968–1983) of deregulation, in which New Deal controls on competition were removed or redirected; and (5) the period after 1983, in which government-managed competition and market-oriented controls emerged as the basis for a new regulatory regime" (p. 971). His concluding net historical judgment on regulation is that "it has worked well at times and failed at others. . . . At the very least, regulation during the twentieth century has provided the Untied States with a politically acceptable means for preserving enterprise, while controlling it" (p. 1012). Once again it is the politics not the economics of regulation which has been important in regulating U.S. business.

Chapter Three: The Changing Fortunes of Free Trade

1. Lal (1983/1997/2002) provides a summing up of the arguments that turned the tide against the Dirigiste Dogma.

2. The major ones are Little, Scitovsky, and Scott (1970); Balassa (1971, 1982); Bhagwati (1979); Krueger (1978). For a comparative study which takes the story up to the early 1990s, see Lal and Myint (1996).

3. Corden (1997), p. 2.

4. The optimum tariff was the only first best argument dealing with a divergence between private and social values in foreign trade, and hence required interventions in foreign trade to remove this divergence.

5. Rimmer (1992), p. 136.

6. This is the title of an excellent collection of essays on the Great Depression and the American economy in the twentieth century edited by Bordo, Goldin, and White (1998).

7. Rockoff (1998) p. 125.

8. Stigler (1965/1986).

9. Myint (1987), p. 108.

10. Tanzi and Schuknecht (2000) also argue that the rise in public spending in all developed countries since the First World War cannot be explained by various theories (see Holsey and Borcherding 1997 for a survey) which have been advanced, but "resulted from changing views on the role of the government in the economy" (p. 15).

11. Friedman and Friedman (1980).

12. Tanzi and Schuknecht (2000), p. 15.

13. In their authoritative survey of global public spending in the twentieth century, Tanzi and Schuknecht (2000) conclude that whereas in the pre-1960 period "the growth in public spending from a very low level generated significant gains in social and economic welfare. For the period after 1960, however, when the rapid increase in public spending became largely of a redistributive kind, the earlier link between

growth in government spending and improvements in social and economic objectives seems to have been broken. In our analysis we have found that the industrial countries with small governments and, to some extent, the newly industrialized countries with low public spending, were able to achieve levels of socioeconomic indicators similar to those achieved by countries with much higher levels of public spending. This has led us to the conclusion that there must be considerable scope for redefining the role of the state in industrialized countries so as to decrease public spending without sacrificing much in terms of social and economic objectives" (p. 131).

14. I first realized this when working on the World Bank's *World Development Report* for 1984. The dangers were spelled out in Lal and Wolf (eds.) (1986), and a model developed in Lal and Wijnbergen (1985) showed how, through global interactions, the fiscal deficits in industrialized countries would crowd out investment in the Third World. With China and India now increasingly financing the U.S. trade deficit, this has come to pass.

15. G. N. Mankiw, "Deficits and Economic Priorities," *The Washington Post*, July 16, 2003.

16. By Jagadeesh Gokhale of the Federal Reserve Bank of Cleveland, and Kent Smitters, former deputy assistant secretary of economic policy at the U.S. Treasury, as reported in N. Ferguson and L. Kotlikoff, "The Fiscal Overstretch That Will Undermine an Empire," *Financial Times*, July 15, 2003.

17. Olson (1965).

18. Irwin (2002), p. 152.

19. Thus, in figure A.1, the VER of Q3Q4 would generate rents of gdeb which would be transferred to foreign producers.

20. Francois and Baughman (2001).

21. See Keesing and Wolf (1980); Wolf (1984); Goto (1989).

22. U.S. ITC (1999); Harrison, Rutherford, and Tarr (1996); De Melo and Tarr (1992); Hufbauer and Elliot (1990).

23. Irwin (2002), p. 127.

24. The most succinct and balanced treatment of these arrangements with references is Krueger (1999). Also see the spirited defense of multilateralism and the case against preferential trade arrangements by Bhagwati (2002a).

25. See Krueger (1992).

26. See Bhagwati (2002a) which along with Irwin (2002) provides the best and most succinct account of the current threats to the multilateral trading system.

27. See Krueger (1999a).

28. Snape (1996).

29. Bhagwati (2002a), p. 112.

30. See Malcolm (1995).

31. For a critical discussion of regulation and how it has replaced planning as the chief method of current dirigisme, as well as ways to escape it, see Lal (1998a).

32. Wolf (1994).

33. Irwin (2002) p. 174.

34. See Lal (1988).

35. Bhattacharya (1979), p. 171.

36. Ibid.

37. Ray (1979), p. 67.

38. Lal (1981).

39. See Goldsmith (1994), and the refutation by Hindley (1994).

40. Corden (1997).

41. Levinson (1996).

42. Wilson (1996).

43. Claire (1977).

44. Basu and Tzannatos (2003) provide a summary of the arguments and evidence on this issue.

45. Krueger (1996), p. 295.

46. Irwin (2002), p. 217.

47. See Basu (1999); Cigno, Rosati, and Guarcello (2002).

48. Edmonds and Pavcnik (2001).

49. *The Economist*, June 3, 1995, p. 59.

50. Wood (1995); Leamer (1996, 1999).

51. Bhagwati (1999); Lawrence and Slaughter (1993).

52. Berman et al. (1994) and Baldwin and Cain (1997).

53. It has also been argued by Borjas et al. (1997) that immigration, particularly of the unskilled (mainly but not entirely) from Latin America, has adversely affected U.S. unskilled wages. Between 1960 and 1996, the share of the U.S. population which is foreign born increased from 5.4 percent to 9.3 percent. They estimate that, in 1995, whereas less than 12 percent of native-born Americans lacked a high school diploma, 40 percent of legal immigrants had not completed high school. This led to a 15 to 20 percent increase in the relative supply of unskilled labor without a high school diploma, which led to a 5 percent fall in the relative wages of high school dropouts between 1980 and 1995, and accounts for nearly half the 11 percent decline in their wages over this period. By contrast, trade with developing countries accounted for only 8 percent of the decline. But these inferences are unwarranted. It is a common error among labor economists to assume that if the supply of labor goes up, then wages must fall (see Lal 1988; Bhagwati 1999; Bhagwati and Rodriguez 1975). But this will not happen in an open economy, as a famous theorem named for its discoverer Tad Rybczynski shows. In an economy which, say, just produces two traded goods, an importable that uses the scarce factor labor and an exportable which uses the abundant factor of production capital, an increase in the domestic supply of labor—whether from population expansion or immigration—will not alter the wage relative to the return to capital, because the ratio of factor prices is uniquely determined by the given and ex-hypothesi unchanged prices of the two goods in international trade. All that will happen is that, with the expansion of the labor supply, the output of the labor-intensive good (importables) will expand in absolute and relative terms to that of the capital-intensive good (exportables). Hence, once again the inferences drawn about the effects of immigration causing the decline in real wages are invalid.

54. See Feenstra (1998) for evidence on the size and importance of this "virtual" production.

55. Ibid., p. 41.

56. A fuller discussion of this is in Lal (1998). Also see Murray (1984); Magnet (1993); Himmelfarb (1995).

57. A succinct and up-to-date account of this modern welfare theory and compensation tests is given in Little (2002).

58. This is Ian Little's (1957) famous dual welfare criterion, including a separate distributional judgment expounded in his *A Critique of Welfare Economics*. He has defended it against various misconceptions in Little (1979), arguing that it is valid and useful and forms the basis of most cost-benefit analyses.

59. One example from my time at the Indian Planning Commission may be relevant. One of the major projects we were asked to evaluate was a gigantic iron ore project. This involved mining virtually a whole mountain and converting the iron ore extracted into pellets to be exported. The analysis showed that the project could not be justified at the current and prospective export price of iron ore pellets. The price at which the pellets could be exported would have to be above twice the world price. The prime minister of the day when the project analysis went up to her, only wanted to know what the effect would be on some local election if she accepted or rejected the project! Meanwhile, the Steel Ministry had contacted with the shah of Iran to organize a sale of pellets to Iran for about twice the world price. This deal was signed. We at the Planning Commission warned that this uneconomic deal for Iran would only stick if the shah of Iran remained in power. Our advice was ignored and the project went ahead for political reasons. Of course, the shah of Iran fell before the project could be completed and India was left with a massive white elephant. This convinced me that supposedly technocratic cost-benefit analysis in the real world would end up as little more than cosmetic social cost-benefit analysis because of the inevitable politicization of the process.

60. There may be cases of public projects, like airports and dams, where actual compensation may be required. There is a large and older cost-benefit literature on this which can be consulted. See for instance Little and Mirrlees (1974); Harberger (1972); Lal (1980a).

61. Epstein (2004), p. 34.

62. My UCLA colleague Jack Hirshleifer (2001) has been a pioneer in developing economic models which incorporate two ways of obtaining income: (a) by making—through the productive processes, and (b) by taking—through conflict (war). The role of the state in protecting "property" is to prevent this "taking." The losses arising from the changing values of the specific labor and capital owned by individuals in a dynamic productive process by contrast reflect what under changing economic circumstances this "property" can command in voluntary exchanges. These "losses" cannot be looked upon as theft.

63. Epstein (2004), p. 36. He also writes: "The willingness to protect individuals against physical loss to person or property, or against defamation and other forms of molestation that involve misrepresentation or threats of force, has the great virtue of allowing individual lawsuits to go forward when private and social welfare are perfectly aligned. But any offer of compensation or other protection to the disappointed trader has the exact opposite effect: it places a giant wedge between individual and social welfare. The point here does not depend on the particulars of the product or service that is offered. It is not undermined by the most painful stories that novelists can write about the havoc that demonic competition imposes on those who have found themselves displaced by market forces. It is a general proposition that is capable of general affirmation"(ibid.). Also see Epstein (2003).

64. Boldrin and Levine (2002) have argued in favor of patents for the first sale of intellectual property but not for further copies.

65. Maskus (2000).

66. Barfield (2001), p. 5.

67. As Colambato and Macey (1996) have argued.

68. Lardy (2003), p. 3. Also see Lardy (2002).

69. One contemporary thinker, the late Jan Tumlir (1984, 1985) who was for many years the director of research at the GATT, saw clearly the link between domestic disorder bred by dirigisme and international order. He recommended that the leading Western powers incorporate the unconditional MFN clause into their separate national laws as a *private right*. This would give both nationals and foreigners the freedom to trade across borders in national jurisdictions, enforced by domestic courts. This would move foreign economic policy out of discretionary diplomacy into the rule-based sphere of law. Sally (1988), chap. 4, provides a lucid account of his views.

70. In the 1970s many development economists of my ilk played this game by trying to persuade governments to apply the "second best"shadow pricing rules based on "world prices" devised by Little and Mirrlees (1974) for public investment in economies where existing protection cannot be removed because of interest groups. My stint at the Indian Planning Commission to estimate and implement these "shadow prices"convinced me of the delusion involved in promoting "second best" policies. Lal (1990b) provides an account of the reasons for this disillusion.

71. Keynes (1936), chap. 24, p. 383.

72. The Appendix is based on Lal (2003a).

73. A poll tax is an example of a lump-sum tax, and the checks each citizen of Alaska receives as a share of the state's oil revenues is one of a lump-sum subsidy.

74. The economists' notion of "consumer surplus" can be explained simply as follows. The demand curve (DD) summarizes what consumers are willing to pay for different quantities of the good, say cloth. If the price is say $150 for a unit of cloth (pd in figure 3.1), consumers, say, will wish to purchase 1,000 units (OQ4). If the price were lower, say $100 per unit, they will wish to purchase more, say 1,500 units (OQ2). But at this lower price they are getting all the units of cloth from 0 to 1,499, for a price which is lower than what they were willing to pay. Hence, on these intramarginal units they buy they will be earning consumer surplus given by the price they would be willing to pay for each unit and the lower $100 per unit they are in fact paying. Hence, the area above the demand curve at the price they are purchasing any given quantity will represent the consumer surplus they have obtained. Thus, when the price falls from $150 (pd) to $100 (pf), they will be consuming an extra 500 units of cloth (Q4Q2) for which they would have been willing to pay more than $100. They will thus have obtained a consumer surplus given by the triangle def in figure 3.1.

75. Little (1970–71), p. 132.

76. This is the tax system devised by Frank Ramsey to solve a problem posed by Keynes to him: how to minimize the deadweight loss associated with raising a given revenue. He came up with the inverse elasticity rule, that is, the taxes should be placed on goods with the most inelastic demand/supply. Thus, in figure 3.1, if demand was completely inelastic (the demand curve were vertical), the net consumer surplus triangle def would vanish.

77. Krueger (1974); Tullock (1967); Bhagwati and Srinivasan (1980).

78. For a recent consolidated survey of where the theory of domestic distortions stands, taking account of DUP activities including subsidy seeking, see Srinivasan

(1996). He also incorporates the numerous paradoxes, which are inevitable in comparing various second-best situations, when in theory, almost anything can happen.

Chapter Four: Money and Finance

1. Thus, the Bardi and Peruzzi banks were ruined by Edward III of England's default in the fourteenth century, while the British Council of Foreign Bondholders formed in 1868 continued till 1988 to seek compensation for the losses suffered in the repudiation of a number of American state governments of their bonds to British investors. When it was disbanded in 1988, one U.S. state was still in default on its nineteenth-century bonds (see Makin 1984).

2. The excess of the face value over the cost of production of currency is called seignorage, because it accrued to the *seigneur* or ruler who issued the currency.

3. Salter (1959); Swan (1963); Corden (1977) provide a lucid account of the model and its applications to a host of international monetary issues.

4. If the nominal exchange rate; p_n—the price of nontraded goods, p_f—the foreign currency price of traded goods; p_t—the domestic price of traded goods; e—the nominal exchange rate and e_r—the real exchange rate, then by definition:

$$e_r = (p_n/p_t) = (p_n/e \cdot p_f).$$

5. Latin Americans being upside down define it as the inverse of this definition, that is, the ratio of traded to nontraded prices.

6. Thus, as $e_r = p_n/e \cdot p_f$, the required rise in e_r can come about with a fall in e, with p_n and p_f unchanged.

7. Named after the Dutch who when they discovered large natural gas reserves in the 1960s found that their utilization led to a shrinkage of the industrial traded goods sector.

8. Corden (2002) provides a lucid account of the choice of exchange-rate regimes, and references to the voluminous literature on the subject. My own position was set out in Lal (1980) and, as the introduction to Lal (1993) notes, I have not had any reason to change these views.

9. The efficient market hypothesis which was based on similar theoretical arguments maintained that stock prices could not deviate from fundamentals, as smart operators could profit by arbitraging the difference. The fundamental value of a stock should reflect the present value of the profits (dividends) the firm will pay into the future. More recent research has found, however, that this theoretical prediction is not borne out by the empirical evidence. The problem seems to be that the "riskless" arbitrage assumed by the theory cannot be conducted in practice. Together with a supply of "naive" investors whose speculative appetite is fed by smart money, asset prices can deviate from fundamentals for some time, leading to bubbles, but the asset prices cannot deviate forever from the fundamentals. This leads to the cycles of booms and busts in financial markets, as was amply demonstrated in the recent Internet bubble. See Rajan and Zingales (2004), pp. 85–105 for a lucid account of the theory and evidence. Also see Shleifer and Vishny (1997); Shiller (2001).

10. See Edwards (1989).

11. Many countries, particularly those in the southern cone of Latin America, tried to use the nominal exchange rate as an anchor to lower inflationary expectations as part of the stabilization programs they instituted to deal with chronic or hyperinflation. The most common form was the "tablita," or a preannounced downward crawl of the nominal exchange rate equal to the difference between the officially desired inflation rate and the expected world rate of inflation. But most of these exchange rate–based stabilization programs broke down because the underlying fiscal deficits causing inflationary pressures were not dealt with. The actual inflation rate did not fall as desired, and the net effect was a substantial appreciation of the real exchange rate, which further worsened the balance of payments. See Little et al. (1993) for evidence.

12. Bergsten (1996) notes, "The EU accounts for about 31 percent of world output and 20 percent of world trade. The U.S. provides about 27 percent of global production and 18 percent of word trade. The dollar's 40–60 percent of world finance far exceeds the economic weight of the U.S. The total also exceeds the share of 10–40 percent for the European national currencies combined" (p. 83).

Portes and Rey (1998) state that: "the dollar is used in 83 percent of two-way transactions in foreign exchange markets. . . . In 1992 . . . 48 percent of world exports were invoiced in dollars, 15 percent in DM, 18 percent in other European currencies, and only 5 percent in yen" (pp. 311–12).

Rogoff (1998) concludes that based on various estimates about "40–50 percent of U.S. currency is held abroad" in the underground economy, a large part of which is related to drugs (p. 270).

13. Portes and Rey (1998) estimate that the seignorage derived by the United States from the use of the dollar as an international currency is about 0.2 percent of its GDP.

By contrast, the purported savings in transactions costs of converting one European money into another are likely to be trivially small. The oft-repeated experiment of a traveler taking a fixed sum in one currency and then converting into other European currencies in local foreign exchange bureaus ignores the fact that only a moron would now do this. As any well-traveled teenager will tell you, they should carry a piece of plastic which gives them local currency and bills them in their home currency at the market rate without incurring any of these costs of "dealing."

14. See Wyplosz (1997) (esp. pp. 8–10) for a summary of the studies which have tried to see if empirically the EU meets the optimum currency criteria. Of the three criteria, openness to mutual trade, the diversification of individual economies, and mobility of inputs particularly labor over the area, the evidence on the first two is ambiguous, but it clearly shows that on the third criterion of labor mobility, Europe is not an optimal currency area compared with the United States.

15. Bhagwati (1998); Krugman (1998); Stiglitz (2002).

16. Romer (1999), p. 33.

17. Ibid., p. 41.

18. Basu and Taylor (1999), p. 49.

19. This is argued in a persuasive article by Bradford Long (2000).

20. Meltzer (1995), p. 69.

21. In Lal (2003b), I provide a Hayekian perspective on the ongoing Japanese slump. For those who believe in long swings in growth based on mechanical analogies,

Solomou (1990) provides a necessary corrective based on analysis of national and international growth trends from 1850 to 1973. He finds there is no support for the Kondratieff waves, and some for the Kuznets waves at the national level.

22. See Zarnovitz (1999). Also see Prescott (2002) for a "real business" cycle explanation of the major business cycles in developed countries.

23. Ranciere, Tornell, and Westerman (2003). They explain the link between higher growth and a propensity for crises in a two-sector long-run growth model with a traded and nontraded good sector in which financial crises can occur, but are low probability events. The nontraded sector is financially constrained, while the traded good sector is unconstrained as it has access to world capital markets. As unlike the traded good sector when the nontraded good sector borrows abroad, it borrows in foreign currency but its output being nontraded is sold for domestic currency. This currency mismatch of the foreign currency debt of the nontraded good sector leads to financial fragility. As nontraded goods are required as inputs into traded goods production, traded goods producers are willing to pay an implicit tax to provide bailout guarantees that insure lenders only against systemic risk (like a devaluation of the domestic currency). In their model this leads to higher growth as it allows the nontraded sector to break its financial constraint, even though this implies risky borrowing.

24. See Rimmer (1992) for details.

25. See Bevan, Collier, and Gunning (1999) for details.

26. Findlay and Wellisz (1993).

27. This is the so-called intertemporal approach to the balance of payments of modern macroeconomics and is lucidly discussed in Obstfeld and Rogoff (1996), while Edwards (2004) provides references, qualifications, and empirical evidence on the anatomy of current account imbalances around the world during the last three decades.

28. Reserve Bank of India (2004).

29. A quantitative survey of the Asian financial crisis and its similarity to those in the nineteenth century is provided in Delargy and Goodhart (1999). In both cases the cause of the crises was overexpansion by the private sector (unlike the 1980's Third World debt crises, which were caused by overexpansion of the public sector). They note that "prior to 1914 the regime encouraged large-scale gold inflows in the aftermath of the crisis, a reliquification of the economy and interest rates returning rapidly to low levels. Stabilizing expectations are harder to encourage in current circumstances; in their absence the essential alternative is to reduce the burden of the foreign debt" (p. 1).

30. See Cline (1984).

31. See Eaton et al. (1986).

32. See Granville (2003) on this so-called HIPC (Highly Indebted Poor countries) initiative.

33. On the Asian crises see Corden (2002); on the Russian crisis see Desai (2003); on the Brazilian and Argentinian crises see Edwards (2002). Also see Eichengreen (2002).

34. I have long maintained this (see Lal 1980, 1987) as in a liberal international economic order with irreducible uncertainty, the authorities do not have the requisite information to run a managed exchange rate. The current "fear of floating" in developing countries whereby they are running various forms of dirty floats (see Calvo and Reinhart 2002) can at best be taken as a transitory device till they have established the

necessary institutional prerequisites for a clean float. For a contrary view which sees this "fear of floating" as "optimal" floating, see Edwards (2002).

35. See Schwartz (1996) for a judicious review of the case for currency boards.

36. See Bogetic (2000) and Edwards (2002) for a judicious review of the evidence.

37. See Lal and Myint (1996), pp. 92–9 for an economic rationale for this Asian model.

38. Rajan and Zingales (2004) provide a detailed and important critique of this "crony capitalism" or as they call it "relationship capitalism," which favors incumbent insiders against upstart outsiders. Not only does this damage the prospects of the poor who are thereby denied access to finance, but it also leads to well-known inefficiencies in the allocation of resources, by preventing that creative destruction which is the hallmark of a dynamic capitalist economy.

39. See Eichengreen and Hausman (1999); Eichengreen, Hausman, and Panizza (2003).

40. As deposit insurance means that depositors will be bailed out even if their banks fail, they have no incentive to monitor their banks' risky deployment of their deposits. This means that banks can make riskier loans than they would if they feared that their depositors would flee if they undertook this risky lending.

41. See Feldstein (2002) to see that this is not an entirely eccentric view. Also see Blustein (2003) for a riveting account of the IMF's handling of these crises.

42. See Bhagwati (1998); Krugman (1998); Stiglitz (2002).

43. Milton Friedman (1962) puts it: "there is much experience to suggest that the most effective way to convert a market economy into an authoritarian economic society is to start by imposing direct controls on foreign exchange. This one step leads inevitably to the rationing of imports, to control over domestic production that uses imported products or that produces substitutes for imports, and so on in a never-ending spiral" (p. 57).

I should also mention one other prescription that Hayek and other classical liberals have made in the postwar years to maintain stable money. Hayek (1976a) rightly argued that the intemperate monetary policies in the twentieth century were largely due to the government's monopoly in providing money. He argued for the denationalization of money and the introduction of free banking. This idea was taken up by a number of classical liberals (Vaubel 1977, 1984; Selgin 1988), who, basing themselves on the experience of free banking episodes in Scotland and the United States in the nineteenth century, question the self-serving arguments advanced by governments that national control of the money supply is required for monetary stability. White (1984) has shown that, contrary to popular presuppositions, the Scottish free banking system was not unstable, and was only taken over because of the government's monopoly of money. Issuers of competing currencies would (unlike governments) have to limit the amount of paper they issue in order to maintain its value. This would end the political management of national monies, which as we saw in the text can be held responsible for much of the macroeconomic instability of the last century. In Lal (1995d) I suggested a scheme based on free banking for Brazil. It would be a free banking system based on a common monetary standard as in nineteenth-century Scotland. The monetary standard would initially be provided by the notes of a currency board which would constitute the common outside money of the free banking system. Over time it could evolve into a full-fledged free banking system which, by depoliticizing and decentralizing the issuance of money, could succeed in abolishing the unstable monetary policy which has been the bane of the Brazilian economy.

Without going into the technicalities of the arguments (pro and con) for the removal of the government's monopoly of money in any particular country (see Dowd 1989; Dorn and Schwartz 1987; Friedman and Schwartz 1986; Goodhart 1988; Hall 1983), it is worth noting (see Lal 1990c, 1992) that in a world of floating exchange rates and with no exchange controls, in effect the world's citizens (at least in developed countries) would have competing currencies to denominate their assets. This is already happening at a rapid rate with the so-called securitization in world capital markets. All that is required to move to the "free banking" analogue at the world level is the removal of the provision that each country's money is the only legal tender within its own jurisdiction. Then, while residents would still have to pay their taxes in the national currency, they could demand payment for their own services in any currency of their choice. When conjoined with the freedom to hold their assets in any currency denomination, this would lead to a reversal of Gresham's law—with good currencies driving out the bad. For with private agents moving out of holding assets in unstable monies, and with inflationary governments being paid taxes in their depreciating currency while their expenditures on payments to private agents are in stable currencies would be faced with a worsening fiscal crisis. This would provide built-in incentives for all countries to follow stable monetary policies.

44. It is true that convincing empirical estimates of these benefits have not been made. But this was also true of the gains from trade liberalization. As liberalized capital markets are a recent phenomenon in developing countries, hopefully empirical comparative historical studies of the sort which established the incontrovertible case for liberalizing foreign trade will be undertaken for the opening up of the capital account. Meanwhile, for those who find the highly suspect cross-country econometric regressions as providing empirical evidence for their views, Prasad et al. (2003) and Eichengreen and Leblang (2002) provide some empirical evidence. The IMF study (Prasad et al. 2003) finds: "the empirical evidence has not established a definitive proof that financial integration has enhanced growth for developing countries. Furthermore, it may be associated with higher consumption volatility. Therefore, there may be value for developing countries to experiment with different paces and strategies in pursuing financial integration. Empirical evidence does suggest that improving governance, in addition to sound macroeconomic frameworks and the development of domestic financial markets, should be an important element of such strategies" (p. 58).

Eichengreen and Leblang (2002) examine data spanning 1880–1997, and examine the twin effects of capital controls: the negative effect on growth through their negative effects on economic efficiency, and their positive short-run effects in limiting the disruptive effects of the crises at home and abroad. They find that "the effects of capital account liberalization are contingent and context specific." But, taking the data as a whole, since 1914 they find that for international crises which infect the domestic economy through an open capital account, the controls have a negative effect on growth, but when combined with a crises, they find that controls did neutralize the effects of crises, particularly in the unstable interwar years.

Finally, Rajan and Zingales (2004) summarizing the evidence from a number of recent econometric studies claim that "when countries open up to foreign capital inflows . . . the country's growth rates increase significantly. Countries that open up their equity markets to foreign inflows experience an average increase in GDP growth rate of about 1.1 percent per year" (p. 113).

45. Edwards (1999), p. 82.

46. See Bordo (2003) and Bordo and Flandreau (2003).

47. This term was coined by Calvo and Reinhart (2002) to show that the de jure classification of exchange rates by the IMF did not in fact match the de facto reality, with many countries supposedly floating cleanly in fact adopting various intermediate regimes between the fixed and floating end points. Unfortunately, this purely descriptive term seems now to have become almost an apologetic for developing countries not to float cleanly, and all sorts of reasons as we see in the text are being advanced to justify this fear.

48. Schwartz (2003a), p. 469.

49. See M. Goldstein and N. Lardy (2003).

50. In a series of papers clearly motivated by the strange policies and outcomes in China, Dooley, Folkerts-Landau, and Garber (2004)(DFG) (which also lists their other papers on this theme) provide a theoretical framework for what they call the revived Bretton Woods system in Asia. Using the Bordo and Flandreau (2003) findings about the fear of floating in emerging markets in both the nineteenth- and late twentieth-century periods of globalization, they consider the problems of capital importing countries with large pools of underemployed labor. They argue that an export-led growth strategy underwritten by an undervalued exchange rate and capital inflows is the best way of employing and raising the incomes of this vast labor reserve. This is of course a variant on the famous model of industrialization with surplus labor devised by Sir Arthur Lewis, the gloss being that, whereas Sir Arthur advocated import-substituting industrialization to mop up the surplus labor, DFG advocate export-led growth instead. As an alternative, this is clearly more efficient than the import-substitution route to development and in fact was part of the Asian model which came to grief in the 1980s. But DFG add an ingenious twist to explain Chinese policies. They claim that given the very high savings rates in China, though domestic capital formation to absorb the surplus labor would be possible, it would be inefficient as compared with getting multinationals to come in and build a capital stock which is competitive in world markets. But, as the capital inflow accompanying this direct foreign investment is not needed, and if absorbed would lead to a real exchange rate appreciation that would undermine exchange rate protection, the Chinese authorities sterilize these inflows and return them to the country of origin of the multinationals by buying their government bonds and holding them in their reserves. The additional benefit from following this strategy is that the multinationals become lobbyists for allowing Chinese imports into the developed countries against the understandable howls of their import competing industries.

Goldstein and Lardy (2005), however, question this interpretation of Chinese policies. They argue that more than half of China's exports go to non-U.S. countries with currencies not pegged to the dollar; the Chinese real trade weighted real exchange rate appreciated by 30 percent between 1994 and early 2002 and then depreciated by 10 percent by end of 2004, so keeping an undervalued real exchange rate is not Chinese policy: foreign investment has only financed 5 percent of fixed investment whose effects are swamped by the misallocation of investment flowing through China's weak financial system; U.S. companies investing in China export little back to the United States, mainly servicing the domestic market, while the foreign investors from the Chinese diaspora who are the main exporters to the United States have little clout in keeping the U.S. market open to Chinese goods.

Whatever may be a plausible interpretation of recent Chinese exchange rate policies, it cannot explain why the Indians are maintaining an undervalued exchange rate by sterilizing capital inflows and building up huge foreign exchange reserves which are put into U.S. government bonds (though recently in 2004–05 there has been some diversification of these reserves). The Indians do not have a shortage of domestic entrepreneurs capable of building up a capital stock which is competitive in world markets. That depends on the incentives they are offered. Nor are they as welcoming as the Chinese to foreign investment. Nor do they have the high savings rate of the Chinese. Both the Chinese and Indians suffer from having inefficient and politicized banking and financial sectors dating from their nationalization of the banking industry. As a sound banking system is considered by many to be a prerequisite for opening the capital account and freely floating, current government actions in both countries are probably best looked upon as being transitional. In addition, India has a fiscal deficit of over 10 percent of GDP and a rising internal public debt which could lead to a 1980s type Latin American crisis. In both cases, a crisis induced by opening the capital account may well be the spur for a full-fledged move to a market economy, as is argued in Lal (1987) and documented for many developing countries in Lal and Myint (1996).

51. See Lal, Bery, and Pant (2003).

52. R. E. Lipsey (2001).

53. See J.-J. Servan-Schreiber (1968), and Lal and associates (1975).

54. See Caves (1996) for a judicious review of the theory and empirical evidence.

55. See D. Lal and associates (1975) and Lall and Streeten (1977).

56. See Caves (1996) who surveys the evidence on this and many other issues that seem to have exercised critics of multinationals.

57. Wolf (2001). His review of one of these anti-globalizers, the Cambridge Business School academic Noreena Hertz's book, *The Silent Takeover*, which has achieved iconic status in the anti-globalization movement, is devastating and correct.

58. See Lal (1993), chap. 2.

59. See Pocock (1975).

60. Ibid.

61. This was floated by the Nobel Prize–winning economist, James Tobin, for an international tax to be levied on international financial flows. The tax revenue was to be given to the United Nations. Not surprisingly it has been a continued supporter of the proposal.

62. M. King (1999).

63. W. Bagehot (1873).

64. See Fischer (1999).

65. See G. E. Wood (2003) for a lucid account of these two functions.

66. Krueger (2001).

67. J. Taylor (2002).

68. Eichengreen and Bordo (2002) examine both the two periods of globalization—pre-1914 and post-1971. Contrary to common perceptions, they find that currency crises were of longer duration pre-1914, but in banking and banking cum currency crises, recovery was faster than now. They attribute this to the fact that

nineteenth-century banking crises were less likely to undermine the currency, as most countries were expected in the long run to adhere to the Gold Standard rules.

Delargy and Goodhart (1999) provide a detailed comparison of pre-1914 crises and the Asian crisis and find great similarities.

69. See Lal (1993, chap. 8) for a fuller discussion. Minsky (1977) and Kindleberger (1978) view boom-bust cycles as being endemic in capitalist economies due to the supposedly "irrational" behavior of private speculators, so that speculative bubbles in which there is overlending are followed by collapse and crisis. A lender of last resort is then advocated to mitigate the deflationary impact of financial crises. John Flemming (1982) has commented on these views, that the mechanism they envisage for the boom-bust cycles is as follows: "Suppose an economy is subject to random shocks generated in a stationary way. A chance period of stability will be misinterpreted as implying that fewer precautions need to be taken, thus increasing the economy's vulnerability to the next "normal" shock. As applied to financial structures, enterprises adopt excessively exposed geared, levered positions in a period of stability that does not in fact reflect a favorable shift in the economy's stochastic environment. . . . The argument depends on agents failing to distinguish a run of good luck from a favorable structural shift in their environment. Such errors are not only identifiable but also optimal if agents attach the correct non-zero probability to structural changes. If Minsky believes that people are too willing to believe that such changes have occurred, he should consider suggesting to the authorities that they intervene randomly in financial markets by increasing their variance. Such intervention would hinder the recognition of genuine shifts and should also inhibit false inferences" (p. 40).

Rather than rely on "irrational" speculation to explain the boom-bust cycle, I find the classical and Austrian perspective set out in the text above more persuasive.

70. Cited in Lipson (1985).

Chapter Five: Poverty and Inequality

1. Stiglitz (2002), emphasis added, p. 5.

2. Cited in Bhalla (2002), p. 27.

3. The activist Ignacio Ramonet cited in Sala-a-Martin (2002).

4. Bhalla (2002).

5. My own contribution to this debate was Lal (1976). Also see Lal (1988), vol. 2.

6. See Lal, Mohan, and Natarajan (2001).

7. Bourguignon and Morrisson (2002). Also see Lindert and Williamson (2003), but their conclusions diverge somewhat from Bhalla's, though they both use the same database. This is because they use the same inappropriate methodology criticized by Bhalla in deriving their global inequality measure. Hence their conclusion that "the world economy has become more unequal over the last two centuries . . . all of the observed rise in world inequality has been driven by widening gaps between nations, while almost none of it has been driven by widening gaps within nations." As Bhalla shows, using the correct method, and deriving the correct distribution of income of the worlds individuals, neither statement is true.

8. World Bank (2001).

9. This is derived as follows. Suppose we could line up every human being in ascending order of their income. We then derive a curve called the Lorenz curve which relates (on the X axis) the percentage of the total population to (on theY axis) the percentage of total income in the world. If everyone's income was equal, then the Lorenz curve would just be the diagonal of the box in the accompanying figure. If all the income went to only one person so there was complete inequality, the Lorenz curve would just be the sides of the box. More usually when there is neither complete equality or inequality the Lorenz curve will be concave from the origin, as shown. The Gini coefficient is then defined as the area between the Lorenz curve and the diagonal (A) divided by the total area under the diagonal (A + B). When there is complete equality and the Lorenz curve coincides with the diagonal, the area A shrinks to zero, hence the Gini is O. If there is complete inequality so that the area A is the whole of the area below the diagonal A + B, the Gini is 1.

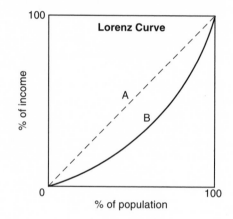

10. Bhalla (2002), p. 187.

11. Dollar and Kraay (2001). But see Lindberg and Squire (2003), who find that when they look jointly at the determinants of growth and inequality, various policy and institutional variables, they find that education, lower inflation, and improved land distribution effect growth and inequality positively, while greater "civil liberties" improve income distribution they worsen growth, and "openness"—measured by the imperfect Sachs-Warner (1995) index— while having a substantial positive impact on growth has a small negative effect on inequality. But as they themselves note, this last conclusion is based on the short-term nature of the data and estimation methods. As they note, "if adjustment costs decline over time, while the dynamic gains from better and more stable policies continue ad infinitum, then the short-run adverse effects on equality may eventually be offset by faster growth among the poor" (p. 339).

12. Li, Squire, and Zou (1998).

13. Bhalla (2002), pp. 45–6.

14. Hancock (1989).

15. The power of this motive was again on display at the 2005 Davos meeting of the world's "great and the good" who indulged in competitive altruism (mostly with other people's money) to solve the problems of Africa. The recent Millennium Development Report, produced under Jeffrey Sachs of Columbia University's direction by the UNDP, is another recycled plea for foreign aid to solve the problems of Africa. There is no recognition of the fact that without a change in governance (probably involving direct or indirect imperialism), there is no reason to believe that, as in the past, Africa's predatory elites will not once again "take the money and run."

16. A large part of this section is based on Lal (1996).

17. Bauer (1971/1976).

18. Ibid.

19. Mosley (1987), p. 232.

20. E.g., Little and Clifford (1965).

21. See Lal (1978, 1983).

22. See Lal and Myint (1996), chap. 9, for details.

23. See Lal and Myint (1996).

24. See Lal (1996a).

25. Lal (1995a).

26. See Lal (1972) for an explication of the assumptions underlying this theory.

27. See Lal (1983).

28. See Lluch (1986). Since then the rise in savings rates in China and India, two of the poorest countries and the major clients for "aid," has been spectacular. For a study of the Indian savings performance, see Lal and Natarajan (2001).

29. Lal and Myint (1996), chap. 2. Also see Easterly (2001) for a survey of the evidence based on the currently fashionable cross-country regressions.

30. Boone (1994).

31. Gilbert, Powell, and Vines (1999), p. F607.

32. Krueger (1998), p. 1990.

33. Ibid., p.1991.

34. Gilbert et al. (1999), p. F619. Also see Collier et al. (1997); and Gilbert and Vines (1999).

35. See Lal and Myint (1996), chap. 6.

36. See Rodrik (1995).

37. Harberger (1984a).

38. See Lal (1983), pp. 56–7. Also, this was the thrust of the annual reports on the Bank's research budget that, as its Research Administrator between 1984 and 1987, I had to submit to the Board to justify the expenditure on research.

39. Krueger (1998), p. 2006.

40. Vaubel (1996) argues that the IFIs engage in bureaucratic maximization, and much of their lending is to promote the bureaucracy's interests rather than to assist poor countries. Frey (1997) provides a survey of international organizations from the public choice perspective.

41. A highly readable and balanced account of Wolfensohn's presidency of the World Bank is provided by Sebastian Mallaby (2004). He outlines how Wolfensohn's embrace of the NGOs has backfired on the Bank. Its middle-income borrowers find its "social" conditionality too onerous and are unwilling to borrow from the Bank, with dire consequences for its lending portfolio in the future. Thus, China and India sought

to use Bank funds for infrastructure projects like the Narmada and Qinghai dams, but have been thwarted by the Bank's embrace of a whole host of environmental and social conditions in its lending for infrastructure projects. In its latest incarnation it is trying to relax the NGO embrace by trying to loosen these conditions. But, even this latest ploy makes little sense. For, as in the nineteenth century, much of this infrastructure in middle-income countries is being financed by a combination of local and foreign capital. The real losers from the Bank's political correctness under Wolfensohn are the poorest countries, like Nepal and Laos, which have found the costs of complying with the Bank's "social" conditionality for dam projects too onerous.

42. Ibid., fn 85, p. 2010. Also see Wade (2001) on the making of the Bank's 2000 "World Development Report." He writes: "Over the 1990s extensive consultation exercises have been held with nongovernmental organizations (NGOs) as they have demonstrated their power to affect the Bank's survival" (p. 1436).

43. Wade (2001) provides an outsider-insiders' account. The end result was that, "Stiglitz stepped down as chief economist (as part of a deal between Wolfensohn and the Treasury that Wolfensohn would get a second term if Stiglitz did not" (p. 1438). Mallaby (2004, p. 266) states that Wolfensohn denied this, saying, "I'd have told him to himself." The rather foolish book by Stiglitz (2002) is his way of settling scores with his Treasury and IMF enemies. For a robust response, see Rogoff (2002), while Fidler (2001) provides an account of the turmoil Wolfensohn has caused. For letters attacking and supporting (mainly from his subordinates) Wolfensohn's watch at the Bank, see the Nov./Dec. 2001 issue of Foreign Policy. Also see Mallaby (2004), particularly chapter 6 entitled "Narcissus and the Octopus." Mallaby is also astute about the unworldly foolishness displayed by Stiglitz. He writes about Stiglitz's scrap with the IMF: "Stiglitz had helped to create a branch of economics that explained the failure of standard market assumptions; he was like a boy who discovers a hole in the floor of an exquisite house and keeps shouting and pointing at it. Never mind that the rest of the house is beautiful—that in nine out of ten cases, the usual laws of supply and demand *do* work; Stiglitz had found a hole, a real hole, and he had built his career on it. Naturally, this had consequences for the way he viewed the world. There is nothing more satisfying for the discoverers of holes than to watch ordinary fools tumble down them" (p. 193).

44. Kanbur (2001).

45. Ibid., p. 1084.

46. For a detailed discussion of conjunctural poverty and social safety nets, see Lal and Myint (1996), chap. 9.

47. Equally deplorable is the World Bank's embrace of the WHO's politically correct crusade against tobacco. This damages rather than advances the welfare of the poor. See Lal (2000) and Lal, Kim, Lu, and Prat (2003).

Chapter Six: Morality and Capitalism

1. Taylor (1974), p. 51.

2. A spontaneous order, Hayek contends, is not planned, nor based on some design, but emerges spontaneously as the unintended consequence from the interactions of a myriad of individuals.

3. Matthews (1986), p. 906.

4. See Colinvaux (1983).

5. Hahn (1973), p. 28.

6. Ibid.

7. Bernard Williams (1985, p. 1) notes that this Socratic question is the start of any thinking about morality.

8. See Hallpike (1986).

9. Hume (1740/1985).

10. Hicks (1979), p. 43.

11. See Goody (1983).

12. See Berman (1983).

13. See Goody (1983).

14. See Berman (1983).

15. See Delumeau (1990).

16. Dumont (1986), p. 26.

17. Gellner (1988), p. 121.

18. See Hallpike (1986); Jenner (1992).

19. Keightley (1990), p. 45.

20. See De Bary (1998); De Bary and Tu Weiming (1998).

21. Rosemont (1998), p. 63.

22. See Lal (2003d).

23. Dumont (1986), p. 27.

24. The great philosopher of the Scottish enlightenment, David Hume, had reached this conclusion earlier at the end of the eighteenth century, but realizing the subversive nature of his conclusions, his "Dialogues Concerning Natural Religion," were only published posthumously (see Hume 1779/1948).

25. Nietzsche (1881/1982), p. 220.

26. A concise and lucid account of the links between contemporary philosophy, politics and economics is provided in Little (2002).

27. That Freudianism follows the same Augustinian narrative is snown in Gellner (1993); Webster (1995).

28. See Lal (1995b).

29. Hume (1740/1985), p. 535.

30. Ibid., p. 551.

31. See Lewis (1965); Sugden (1986, 1988); Little (2002), chap. 7 provides a succinct account of this "morality by convention" and the similar but less persuasive account of "morality by agreement" in some form of contract provided by various game theorists like Gauthier (1986) and Binmore (1994, 1998).

32. Smith (1759/1982), p. 152.

33. Ibid., p. 139.

34. Ibid., p. 140.

35. See Mallaby (2004), pp. 255–7.

36. Mill (1874), p. 393.

37. Gay (2001), pp. 32–3.

38. The classical virtues celebrated by Aristotle were wisdom, justice, temperance, and courage. Associated with these cardinal virtues were prudence, magnanimity, munificence, liberality, and gentleness. The Christian virtues were faith, hope, and charity. Aquinas saw these religious virtues complementing the classical ones, whereas Augustine

saw them as irreconcilable as for him virtues without any reference to God were "rather vices than virtues" (*The City of God*, bk. 19, chap. 25, p. 265). Himmelfarb (1994) notes, "Later secular philosophers, in the seventeenth and eighteenth centuries, subverted the classical virtues more subtly, and the Christian ones more radically. But all of them insisted upon the importance of virtues not only for the good life of individuals but for the well-being of society and the state. And all of them believed in the intimate relation between the character of the people and the health of the polity. Even those philosophers like Montesquieu who assigned different virtues to different regimes, and different *moeurs* to different societies, did not denigrate or deny the idea of virtue itself" (p. 9).

39. Himmelfarb (1994), pp. 12–13.

40. Ibid., p. 45.

41. Ibid., p. 46.

42. Ibid., p. 10.

43. Skidelsky (1983), p. 385.

44. Keynes (1933/1972), p. 436.

45. Ibid., p. 446.

46. Skidelsky (1985), p. 131.

47. Himmelfarb (1994), p. 12.

48. The preface to the Liberty Fund edition of Minogue (1963) provides a succinct account of this modern sensibility of the liberal mind.

49. Marwick (1998), p. 802.

50. Wasserman (1998), p. 5.

51. Ibid., p. 6. The destruction this caused to the American social fabric, and in particular to its weakest members, is powerfully argued in Magnet (1993).

52. Bork (1996).

53. For instance see Whybrow (2003).

54. MacIntyre (1990), p. 492.

55. Ibid.

56. See Nussbaum (1992).

57. See Micklethwait and Wooldridge (2004).

58. See Lal (1985).

59. This is based on Lal (1988/2004); Lal (1995c); Lin et al. (2003); Lardy (2002), which also contain detailed references.

60. Nehru (1962), pp. 431–2.

61. Lin (1990), p. 1234.

62. As a Chinese politburo member, Li Xiannian is reported to have told a visitor. Cited in Evans (1993), p. 280.

63. Justin Lin, *American Economic Review*, March 1992.

64. See F. Modigliani and S.L. Cao, *Journal of Economic Literature*, March 2004.

65. Huang (2003, p. 308) reports Deng Tsiao Ping as giving the following assessment of Chinese economic reforms to a visiting Yugoslav delegation: "In the rural reform our greatest success—and it is one we had by no means anticipated—has been the emergence of a large number of enterprises run by villages and townships. They were like a new force that just came into being spontaneously. . . . The Central Committee [of the Chinese Communist party] takes no credit for this."

66. A major portion of the foreign investment in China consists of Chinese private capital which has been recycled through Hong Kong. The importance of Hong

Kong for the growth of nonstate enterprises in China lies in its efficient financial markets and legal system. Thus, Yasheng Huang notes that Lenovo, China's largest computer maker which has bid for the personal computer business of IBM, though seemingly Chinese, is a foreign company. The father of Lenovo's founder ran a Hong Kong business and his company arranged critical financing for Lenovo in the 1980s. Lenovo organized its Chinese operations as subsidiaries of its Hong Kong branch, so it would be subject to Chinese laws on foreign investment rather than domestic business. Seven of Lenovo's Hong Kong subsidiaries were among the top 500 foreign operations in China. The startup capital from Lenovo's Chinese parent was only U.S. $40,000. The rest of the millions of dollars needed were obtained in Hong Kong. Similarly, the major Chinese home appliance makers (TCL, Galanz, and Kelon), and the four Chinese companies listed as the most dynamic by Forbes, have all found legal and financial sanctuaries in Hong Kong (Yasheng Huang, "China's Big Hope Is Not Hong Kong," *Financial Times*, Jan. 14, 2005, p.13).

 67. See "China's Growth Spreads Inwards," *The Economist*, Nov. 25, 2004, p. 13.

 68. In his *Chinese Economic Performance in the Long Run*.

 69. N. Lardy, IMF-NCAER "Tale of Two Giants" conference, Nov. 2003.

 70. Lardy (2002), p. 15.

 71. There is a continuing dispute about measurement of Chinese growth rates (see Lardy 2002). The data shown in table 6.1 are based on Angus Maddisson's estimates, which in my view provide the best attempt to reconcile the different estimates.

 72. In an important book, Huang (2003) finds that most of the foreign investment in China is by the Chinese diaspora, and this goes to the nonstate enterprises. As they are denied access to capital from the banking system, this overseas Chinese capital has been an important means for the nonstate enterprises to overcome this distortion in China's capital markets. The investment by foreign multinationals has by contrast gone mainly to the state enterprises. Much of this has been misappropriated, though some has helped some state enterprises to modernize. See the enthralling account by Clissold (2004) of his adventures in using Western hedge fund money to reform and manage inefficient Chinese state enterprises.

 73. See D. Lal, "How Foreign Reserves Could Make China Still Stronger," *Financial Times*, Dec. 29, 2004.

 74. Ibid., p. 11.

 75. See Williamson (2001).

 76. See the United Nations (2002).

 77. See Lal (1988/2004), chap. 8.

 78. Lardy (2002), p. 19.

 79. Cited in Lardy (2002), p. 21.

 80. See Lal (1998, 2000c).

 81. See Lal (1998).

 82. Dickson (2003), p. 169.

 83. See Lal (1988/2004).

 84. It began with Selig Harrison (1960), *India, The Most Dangerous Decades*, and continued through the 1980s with political scientists producing tomes entitled *Democracy and Discontent—India's Growing Crisis of Governability* (Kohli 1990). They are now editing books called *The Success of India's Democracy* (Kohli, 2001).

 85. See Samatar (1999), Acemoglu et al. (2001).

86. See Lal (2000c) and Morse (1964) for a fuller treatment.

87. Wynia (1990), p. 3.

88. See Lal (1998), chap. 4, which also provides references.

89. See my *In Praise of Empires* (Lal 2004a), pp. 92–3, for a fuller elaboration and references.

90. See Lal (1998) for evidence and explication.

91. See Lal (1988/2004); Mayer (1996); Srinivas (1996); Beteille (1996) and the references to the earlier literature on the Indian family in Lal (1998), chap. 3.

92. Srinivas (1996), p. xv.

93. "Sex, Society and the Family," *India Today International*, Jan. 31, 2005, pp. 34–7. These results are based on a poll conducted by AC Nielsen-Org-Marg of a cross-section of the population aged between 18 and 35 years across ten major representative urban centers.

94. See the contributions in Davis and Harrell (1993). Yunxiang Yan (2003) provides a unique ethnographic account of family change in a Chinese village between 1949 and 1999. There have been changes, but to this reader of the book there seems to be much more continuity in Chinese family life Yan documents than the sharp divergence he claims in his conclusions.

95. Whyte (1996), pp. 16–17.

96. Keightley (1990) pp. 44–5.

97. Jenner (1992), p. 124.

98. Lal (1998).

Chapter Seven: "Capitalism with a Human Face"

1. Himmelfarb (1994), p. 261.

2. Ibid., p. 260.

3. Ibid., p. 259.

4. For instance by Sen (1992). Sugden (1993) cogently argues that these two divergent views of the state cannot be reconciled by arguing as Sen does that classical liberals too are egalitarians, as they are concerned with the equality of liberty.

5. de Jasay (1996), p. 21.

6. Plant (1992), p. 124.

7. de Jasay (1996), p. 22.

8. See Sugden (1993, 1986).

9. de Jasay (1996), p. 23.

10. See Berman (1983), pp. 477–81. He argues that both the English "common law" and French "public law" systems were built on Roman, Canon, and Germanic law, but in the late thirteenth and fourteenth centuries the royal law of the two began to diverge. "Eventually, after another century or so, the two systems acquired many of the contrasting features that have continued to characterize them in the twentieth century. The French system came to rely heavily on written procedure, the English on oral procedures; the French relied on hundreds of highly trained professional judges, the English on lay jurors and lay justices of the peace and only a very few professional judges; the French on judicial interrogation of parties and witnesses under oath, the

English on accusation and denial by the opposing parties with resolution by the jury. With regard to substantive law, French law was more systematic, more learned, more Roman, more codified, while English royal law was more particularistic, more practical, more Germanic, more oriented to case law" (p. 478).

11. de Jasay (1996), p. 23.

12. Ibid., p. 24.

13. Ibid., p. 25.

14. de Jasay's position on rights is different from Nozick's (1974). Of one of the senses in which Nozick uses rights, "rights that is permissions to do something and obligations on others not to interfere" (p. 92), Jasay rightly notes, "rights are not permissions but claims for performance by another. Yet liberties are not permissions either; if they were they would be most confusingly misnamed. Who would be competent to grant permissions and on what authority?" (1996, pp. 5–31). He also contests Nozick's position on property rights; see his n. 2, p. 51.

15. See Demsetz (1967).

16. de Jasay (1996), p. 30.

17. See Minogue (1979).

18. Hart (1955/1967), p. 53.

19. Isaiah Berlin (1969) refers to human rights as "a frontier of freedom" which no one is allowed to cross (p. 165). But as Little (2002) rightly notes: "an infinite list of rights is not convincing as a frontier. The frontier is properly constituted by the quite limited list of things that one may not do to human beings" (p. 31).

20. de Jasay (1996), p. 51.

21. The existence of corporations depends upon there being various contracts which cannot be specified at arms length (see Coase 1937/1988). Because workers acquire various skills which are specific to the firm through on-the-job training, this form of firm-specific capital is of value to the firm but not the worker who cannot cash them by moving to another firm. These firm-specific skills are to be distinguished from the general skills acquired from on-the-job training which can be marketed outside the firm. Because of the importance of firm-level skills there will have to be a more permanent relationship between employer and employee than the arm's-length transactions of a spot market for labor. This means that the employer will now have to incur the policing type of transactions costs in monitoring the worker to see that they are not shirking. This would require the hierarchical organization of firms. As part of this task the employer may choose various forms of contracts with the workers which could include "co-determination" by having workers on boards of companies. But given the diversity of conditions faced by different firms, in a free market, the types of contracts will be varied, including the types advocated by promoters of "stakeholder capitalism." What would go against the functioning of the free market was if a particular type of contract, that is, the stakeholder type, was forced on all employers by legislative fiat.

22. See Lal and Myint (1996) for a fuller discussion.

23. Devlin (1959), p. 48.

24. Mill (1859/1910), chap. 1.

25. Hart (1963), pp. 32–3.

26. Fawcett (2004), p. 23.

27. See Himmelfarb (1996) for a concise and insightful account of the various streams which have fed the communitarian movement. Among philosophers, Sandel

(1996) represents those who are committed to both American style liberalism as well as the welfare state. This leads them into the anomalous position that they "tend to be more solicitous of community in the abstract than of particular communities which might challenge the state as the guardian of the common good." These liberal communitarians seek "to disassociate themselves from conservatism, puritanism, religion and even 'traditional values'" (Himmelfarb 1996, p. 12). They are statist. For instance, as de Jasay notes of the conversion of the Nozick of 1974 into the arch communitarian of 1989, "in his libertarian incarnation he was radically minimal-statist, in his communitarian one he is radically maximal-statist." (de Jasay 1996, pp. 5–60).

By contrast, MacIntyre (1988) wants to have little to do with liberalism. He sees the object of modern man's quest for moral identity "in Thomism, a moral-cum-religious tradition that embodies objective virtues in a genuine community." Among sociologists, Bellah et al. (1986) argue that Americans "must return to those communal and religious traditions, the 'habits of the heart', that Tocqueville saw as the corrective to a debilitating individualism" (Himmelfarb 1996, p. 12).

By contrast, those on the conservative side of the ongoing American culture wars, instead of talking of "community" talk of "civil society." "Their intention is to 'empower' civil society—families, communities (in the plural), voluntary associations, churches—as a bulwark not only against the excessive individualism of liberalism, but also against an overweening state." But as with communitarians there are also differences among the proponents of civil society. "While libertarians are hostile to government on principle, most 'social conservatives' [whose leading advocate is William Bennett] are fearful only of big or bad government" (Himmelfarb 1996, p. 13). The social conservatives perhaps come closest to the classical liberal position.

28. Fawcett (2004), p. 23.

29. Arrow (2000), p. 3. Solow (2000) also asks pertinently: "Just what is social capital a stock of? Any stock of capital is an accumulation of past flows of investment, with past flows of depreciation netted out. What are those past investments in social capital? How could an accountant measure them and calculate them in principle? I am not worrying about where the numbers would come from, I am wondering about what instructions you would give a search party" (p. 7).

30. Thus, Etzioni (1988) states: "The more people accept the neoclassical paradigm as a guide for their behavior, the more the ability to sustain a market economy is undermined" (p. 251). While in their Communist Manifesto, Marx and Engels (1848) maintain: "What the bourgeoisie, therefore, produces above all are its own grave diggers" (p. 12).

31. Lane (2000), p. 327.

32. Frey and Stutzer (2002), p. 9.

33. Frey and Stutzer (2002) provide a judicious survey.

34. See Di Tella, MacCulloch, and Oswald (2001).

35. For a concise and incisive survey of contemporary welfare economics, including problems in deriving a social welfare function, see Little (2002).

36. Little (2002) notes dryly of social choice theory, "it has also spawned three Nobel Prices. Seldom have so many clever people spent so much time on a matter of so little importance" (p. 105, n. 3).

37. Cardinalization of utility depends upon making interpersonal comparisons. Broome (1991) provides an exhaustive discussion of how this could be done. He

himself does not believe that the assumptions required are persuasive. See Little (2002) for a lucid outline of the issues.

38. Hammond (1991), pp. 220–21. Also see Sen (1995).

39. Hirsch (1976), *The Social Limits to Growth*, Harvard University Press, Cambridge, MA.

40. Layard (1980); Frank (1999).

41. Layard (2004). The reviewer of this book in *The Economist* (Jan. 15, 2005, pp. 77–8) rightly noted: "If raising the level of happiness is to be the chief aim of government policy, as he argues it should, where then is the call to make divorce harder, given the pain that he says broken homes inflict on children? Further, where is his desire to compel the worship of a higher being, also on his list as source of happiness? Thankfully, both are absent, but he never mentions the obvious reason for why they are: namely, that most people value freedom as a greater good than enforced happiness. The pursuit of happiness, Lord Layard's book will convince most people, is a private matter."

42. Roemer (1982).

43. Lane (2000).

44. Smith (1759/1982), pp. 149–50. More recently Daniel Kahneman et al. (2004a) have used experimental evidence which reports mood changes throughout the day to assess happiness levels rather than through surveys like the "World Values Survey." They find that happiness is less determined by fundamental realities like being married or having a good job, than by the daily minutia of life—such as a good night's sleep and a short commute. Furthermore, a study by Jason Riis et al. (2005) by University of Michigan psychologists of dialysis patients found that they were just as happy as those without any major medical ailments. Similarly, a recent study of young cancer survivors (Shankar et al. 2005) found that they rated their childhoods as happy, as a healthy youngster. All this experimental evidence supports Adam Smith's contention in the quoted passage that people "tend to adapt to new life circumstances, staying neither very happy nor very sad for long, even in the face of life-changing events." (Victoria Griffith," Science Briefing," *Financial Times*, February 11, 2005. This article also provides web links to the above studies.)

45. Rajan and Zingales (2004), p. 72.

46. Ibid., p. 6. They note that: "a search fund is a pool of money to finance a search for companies that might be willing to be bought out. . . . Typically a recent graduate from a business or law school, with no money of his own, puts the fund together. The fund pays for the expenses of the search and some living expenses for the principal (the searching graduate). After identifying an appropriate target, the principal has to negotiate the purchase as well as arrange financing. In return for their initial investment in the pool, investors in the search fund get the right to invest in the acquisition at favorable terms. Once the target is acquired, the principal runs the firm for a few years and eventually sells it, pays off investors, and hopefully, keeps a sizeable fortune for himself" (p. 5).

47. Micklethwait and Wooldridge (2003), p. 12. They provide a lucid and concise history of the corporation.

48. Ibid., p. 13.

49. See Demsetz (1992).

50. See Demsetz (1992); and Lal and Myint (1996).

51. Ando (2000).

52. See Manne (1972, 2002); Barry (1998, 2001).

53. Manne (2002).

54. Demsetz (2003).

55. Henderson (2001).

56. Munk (1999), p. 34, cited in Henderson (2001).

57. The promotion of democracy by the American imperium is discussed in detail in my *In Praise of Empires*.

Chapter Eight: The Greens and Global Disorder

1. Henderson (2001).

2. An excellent account of these moral issues and the market is provided in Searle (1998).

3. de Tocqueville (1835/1968). He wrote: "In aristocratic nations secondary bodies form natural associations which hold abuses of power in check. In countries where such associations do not exist, if private people did not artificially and temporarily create something like them, I see no other dike to hold back tyranny of whatever sort, and a great nation might with impunity be oppressed by some tiny faction or by a single man" (vol. II, chap. 5).

4. See Bentley (1908); Truman (1953); and Latham (1952). While contemporary political pundits like Putnam (2000) bemoan the decline of these voluntary organizations as Americans are seen to be increasingly "bowling alone."

5. Olson (1965).

6. A more serious challenge to Olson's malign view of interest group activity has been provided by Gary Becker, who has sought to provide a rigorous formulation of a model of competition among pressure groups for political influence. He partially restores the more benign view of such participation of the political sociologists. But his arguments depend upon ignoring the "rent-seeking" costs associated with pressure group politics. See Lal (1996a/1999).

7. Schattschneider (1975), pp. 34–5.

8. Barfield (2001), p. 80.

9. These figures are based on an unpublished manuscript by Marguerite A. Peeters, "Hijacking Democracy: Global Consensus on Global Governance," American Enterprise Institute, Washington, DC, 2001; cited in Barfield (2001), p. 88.

10. Otto (1996), p. 110.

11. Peeters (2001), chap. 1, p. 23; cited in Barfield (2001), p. 78.

12. Barfield (2001), p. 79.

13. Peeters (2001), p. 34; cited in Barfield (2001), p. 80.

14. Kenneth Anderson (2000) notes: "When international NGOs assert that they are the voice of the world's citizens, the assertion makes no sense because the world is not a polity that has citizens—it has, to be sure, people, many of them with great needs—but to be a 'citizen' is to be part of a constituted polity, not just a supporter of an NGO and its agenda" (p. 108).

15. Martin Wolf, column in *Financial Times*, September 2, 1999, p. 12.

16. Shaffer (2001), pp. 66–7.

17. Burke (1774/1999).

18. The title of the book by Rauch (1994).

19. Zakaria (2003), p. 171. This book provides the best and most succinct account of the growth of illiberal democracy in the United States.

20. See Raustiala, "The Participatory Revolution," cited in Barfield (2001), p. 90.

21. Peeters (2001), chap. 1, p. 2.

22. See Beckerman (1995).

23. The final outcome of which was my book (Lal 1980a) on estimating these so-called "shadow prices" for India. Environmental economics properly conceived is nothing else but the proper application of the theory of cost-benefit analysis. In the 1970s a number of manuals were devised to provide rules for applying this form of applied welfare economics to developing countries. The most famous of these manuals, and the one I was associated with in my work in the 1970s, was Little-Mirrlees (1974). Surveying the use of cost-benefit analysis in aid institutions including the World Bank in 1990, Little and Mirrlees (1990) explicitly dealt with the question of sustainability. They rightly noted: "Sustainability has come to be used in recent years in connection with projects. This is more a buzz word—probably derived from the environmental lobby—than a genuine concept. It has no merit. Whether a project is sustainable (forever?—or just for a long time?) has nothing to do with whether it is desirable. If unsustainability were really regarded as a reason for rejecting a project, there would be no mining, and no industry. The world would be a very primitive place" (p. 365). Dasgupta and Maler (1994) rightly emphasize that environmental economics is nothing else but the proper application of cost-benefit analysis based on welfare economics. As they note, "most writings on sustainable development start from scratch and some proceed to get things hopelessly wrong. It would be difficult to find another field of research endeavor in the social sciences that has displayed such intellectual regress" (p. 12).

24. Solow (1974). All the rules for the optimal exploitation of exhaustible resources are developments of what is called "Hotelling's rule" (Hotelling 1931).

25. See Sugg and Kreuter (19940. The collection of essays in Morris (ed.) (2002) provides an excellent discussion on various issues which relate to "sustainable development."

26. See Buchanan and Stubblebine (1962). Pecuniary externalities occur when one individual's activity affects the financial circumstances of another. But this does not result in a misallocation of resources. Thus, suppose there is a cost-saving invention by one producer. He increases his output and reduces his price. Through market interdependence the profits of other producers are reduced. It is readily shown that the consumer gains and those of the cost-reducing producer are always greater than the losses of the inefficient producers. What is more, the cost-reducing producer must *not* take account of the losses of the inefficient producers, for if he did, he would restrict output and would be behaving as a quasi-monopolist; thus, the industry's output level would be suboptimal. Pecuniary externalities are thus synonymous with market interdependence and the price system. They must be Pareto-irrelevant, as they do not affect the Pareto-efficiency of the economy.

By contrast, technological externalities are interdependencies between economic agents that are *not* mediated through the market and hence *not* reflected in relative prices. A well-known example is the smoke emitted by a factory that raises the costs of a nearby laundry.

27. Thus, Schneider (1989) who, while recognizing the "uncertainties and caveats" surrounding the scientific evidence, nevertheless wants scientists to get involved in hyping the evidence because he states of his and other scientists' desire "as human being [to] want to leave the world a better place than they found it" (p. x).

28. Lal (1990c).

29. One example will have to suffice. In late 2002 two economists, my old colleague David Henderson at University College London, who was subsequently the chief economist at the OECD, and Ian Castles, the former head of Australia's Bureau of Statistics, produced a report which questioned the projections made by the IPCC. Their criticisms were wide ranging, but focused on the IPCC's forecasts of greenhouse emissions. They argued that the methods employed had given an upward bias to the projections. *The Economist* (February 15, 2003, in its "Economics Focus: Hot Potato," p. 84) picked this up and put their report on its website. This report was published in the journal *Energy and Environment*, vol. 14, no. 2–3 (2003). The IPCC responded in the same issue accusing Castle and Henderson of peddling "deplorable misinformation." Castle and Henderson in the subsequent issue of the journal (vol. 14, no. 4) showed that the IPCC response failed to answer their critique and provided new grounds for concern. One of the major points at issue is the IPCC's projections of growth rates in developing countries on which their projections of future global emissions are based. As *The Economist* (Nov. 8, 2003, in its "Economic Focus: Hot Potato" revisited, p. 96) noted of the Castle-Henderson response, the IPCC has implausibly assumed that "growth in poor countries will be so fast that by the end of the century Americans will be poorer on average than South Africans, Algerians, Argentines, Libyans, Turks, and North Koreans. Mr. Castle and Mr. Henderson can hardly be alone in finding this odd." It then goes on to comment on the closing of ranks amongst these environmental scientists when their lack of statistical and economic expertise is shown up. This is worth quoting in full: "The fact that the IPCC mobilized as many as 15 authors to supply its response is interesting. The panel's watchword is strength in numbers (lacking though it may be in strength at numbers). The exercise criticized by Mr. Castle and Mr. Henderson involved 53 authors, plus 89 expert reviewers and many others besides. Can so many experts get it wrong? The experts themselves may doubt it, but the answer is yes. The problem is that this horde of authorities is drawn from a narrow professional milieu. Economic and statistical expertise is not among their strengths. Making matters worse, the panel's approach lays great emphasis on peer review of submissions. When the peers in question are drawn from a restricted professional domain—whereas the issues under consideration make demands upon a wide range of professional skills—peer review is not a way to assure the highest standards of work by exposing research to skepticism. It is just the opposite: a kind of intellectual restrictive practice, which allows flawed or downright shoddy work to acquire a standing it does not deserve." And it is on the basis of this shoddy work by the IPCC that the signatories of the Kyoto Protocol are willing to stake "billions of dollars worth of global output" (ibid.).

30. See Lomberg (2001). The witch hunt by environmental scientists that this excellent and very comprehensive survey of all the evidence on numerous environmental issues evoked, is symptomatic of the religious nature of the green movement. See the website, which details the Danish Scientific Committee's charges against

Lomberg, his response which the *Scientific American* refused to publish, and the alternative independent group of scientists who have looked at all the evidence and absolved Lomberg, and supported his main conclusions.

31. Schneider (1989), p. 37.

32. Schelling (1992).

33. See Beckerman (1995).

34. See Nordhaus (1994).

35. Nordhaus (1994), p. 81.

36. See Nordhaus (1994), table 5.1, and p. 83. The impact on annualized value of consumption for the world in billions of dollars per year is 11 for the optimum; 10 for the 10-year delay; 0 for laissez faire; 224 for geo-engineering; and −283 for stabilizing emissions at 1990 levels; −501 for stabilization at 80% of 1990 emission levels; and −1639 for stabilizing CO_2 emissions to allow a maximum of 1.5 degrees C increase in temperature. These numbers can be compared to an annual consumption rate of approximately \$20,000 billion in the 1990–99 period of Nordhaus's model.

37. Simon (1996), p. xxxiii.

38. World Development Report 1992, World Bank (1992).

39. Lomberg (2001), p. 329.

40. Reynolds (1985).

41. Wrigley (1988).

42. See Illarionov (2004, 2004a). He argues that: "Kyoto's followers are already paying a heavy price. Since 1997, slower emissions growth in 17 pro-Kyoto's high income countries (the 15 pre-enlargement members of the EU, Canada and Japan) than in 11 non-Kyoto countries (including the U.S., Australia, and South Korea) has been associated with slower growth in GDP (1.9 percent annually against 3.3 percent) and a slower reduction in carbon intensity—the amount of carbon emitted per unit of GDP" (2004a). In Illarionov (2004) he details how the chief scientific advisor to the U.K. government Sir David King tried to hijack a conference on climate change organized by the Russian academy of sciences. Having failed to do so "when questions on professional topics were asked, and being unable to answer these questions, Mr. King and other members of the delegation turned to flight. . . . Mr. King in an unprecedented incident, cut short his answer to a question in mid-sentence, realizing he was unable to answer it, and left the seminar room. . . . In our opinion the reputation of British science, the reputation of the British government, and the reputation of the title "Sir" has sustained heavy damage" (p. 11).

43. Langewiesche (2000).

44. See E. M. Whelan (1985).

45. See Lal (2000b).

46. See www.malaria.org.

47. Cited in Tren and Bate, *When Politics Kills: The Political Economy of Malaria Control*, IEA, London.

48. Borlaug (2000).

49. Krattiger (2000).

50. Whelan (2000).

51. Potrykus (2000).

52. The following is based on Lal (1998).

Chapter Nine: Conclusions

1. See Lal (2003c) for a fuller discussion.

2. See Przeworski and Limomgi (1997) for a survey. The best of these statistical studies is by Helliwell (1992), and the most cogent critique of the econometrics involved is by Deaton and Miller (1995).

3. Lal and Myint (1996).

4. De Tocqueville (1856/1998).

5. D. Lal, "A Force to Lift the Curse of Natural Resources," *Financial Times*, October 3, 2003.

Bibliography

Acemoglu, D., S. Johnson, and J. A. Robinson (2001): "An African Success Story: Botswana," Working Paper 01–37, Dept. of Economics, MIT, Cambridge, Mass.

Aftalion, F. (1990): *The French Revolution—An Economic Interpretation.* Princeton University Press, Princeton, N.J.

Anderson, K. (2000): "After Seattle: Public International Organizations, Non-Governmental Organizations, and Democratic Sovereignty in an Era of Globalization: An Essay on Contested Legitimacy." Mimeo, Washington College of Law, American University, Washington, D.C., August.

Ando, A. (2000): "On the Japanese Economy and the Japanese National Accounts." NBER Working Paper No. 8033, National Bureau of Economic Research, Cambridge, Mass.

Arrow, K. (1974): *The Limits of Organization.* Norton, New York.

———. (2000): "Observations on Social Capital." In P. Dasgupta and I. Serageldin (eds.), *Social Capital.* World Bank, Washington, D.C.

Arrow, K., and F. Hahn (1971): *General Competitive Analysis.* Holden Day, San Francisco.

Baechler, J. (1975): *The Origins of Capitalism.* Blackwell, Oxford.

Bagehot, W. (1873): *Lombard Street.* William Clowes and Sons, London.

Bairoch, P. (1967): *Diagnostic de l'Evolution Economique du Tiers-Monde 1900–1966.* Gauthoers-Villars, Paris.

———. (1981): *Disparities in Economic Development Since the Industrial Revolution.* Macmillan, London.

———. (1993): *Economics and World History.* University of Chicago Press, Chicago.

Balassa, B. (1971): *The Structure of Protection in Developing Countries.* Johns Hopkins University Press, Baltimore.

———. (1982): *Development Strategies in Semi-Industrial Economies.* Johns Hopkins University Press, Baltimore.

Baldwin, R. E. (1969): "The Case Against Infant-Industry Tariff Protection." *Journal of Political Economy* 77 (May/June): 295–305.

Baldwin, R. E., and G. G. Cain (1997): "Shifts in U.S. Relative Wages: The Role of Trade, Technology, and Factor Endowments." *NBER Working Papers* No. 5934, NBER, Cambridge, Mass.

Bardhan, P. (1989): "The New Institutional Economics and Development Theory: A Brief Assessment." *World Development* 17 (9): 1389–95.

Barfield, C. E. (2001): *Free Trade, Sovereignty, Democracy: The Future of the World Trade Organization.* American Enterprise Institute, Washington, D.C.

Barry, B. (1978): *Sociologists, Economists and Democracy.* University of Chicago Press, Chicago.

Barry, N. (1998): *Business Ethics.* Macmillan, London.

Barry, N. (2001): "Ethics, Conventions and Capitalism." In B. Griffiths et al., *Capitalism, Morality and Markets.* Institute of Economic Affairs, London.

Basu, K. (1999): "Child Labor: Cause, Consequence, and Cure, With Remarks on International Labor Standards." *Journal of Economic Literature* 37 (September): 1083–1119.

Basu, S., and A. M. Taylor (1999): "Business Cycles in International Historical Perspective." *Journal of Economic Perspectives* 13 (2): 45–68.

Basu, K., and Z. Tzannatos (2003): "The Global Child Labor Problem: What Do We Know and What Can We Do?" *World Bank Economic Review* 17 (3): 147–73.

Bauer, P. (1971/1976): *Dissent on Development.* Harvard University Press, Cambridge, Mass.

Bauer, P. (2000): *From Subsistence to Exchange.* Princeton University Press, Princeton, N.J.

Baumol, W. J., J. Panzar, and R. Willig (1982): *Contestable Markets.* Harcourt Brace Jovanovich, New York.

Bayly, C. A. (1989): *Imperial Meridian.* Cambridge University Press, Cambridge.

Becker, G. (1983): "A Theory of Competition Among Pressure Groups for Political Influence." *Quarterly Journal of Economics* 98, 3 (August): 371–400.

———. (1988): "Public Policies, Pressure Groups, and Deadweight Costs." In G. Stigler, Charles A. Beard, and Mary R. Beard (ed.) (1927): *The Rise of American Civilization,* 2 vols., Macmillan, New York.

Beckerman, W. (1995): *Small Is Stupid: Blowing the Whistle on the Greens.* Duckworth, London.

Bellah, R. N., R. Madsen, W. M. Sullivan, A. Swindler, and S. M. Tipton (1986): *Habits of the Heart.* Harper and Row, New York.

Bentley, A. P. (1908): *The Process of Government.* University of Chicago Press, Chicago.

Bergsten, C. F. (1996): "The Dollar and the Euro." *Foreign Affairs* 76: 83–95.

Berkowitz, P. (2003): "The Demagoguery of Democratic Theory." *Critical Review* 15 (2): 123–45.

Berlin, I. (1969): "Two Concepts of Liberty" in his *Four Essays on Liberty,* Oxford University Press, Oxford.

Berlin, I. (1996): *The Sense of Reality.* Farrar, Strauss and Giroux, New York.

Berman, E., J. Boud, and Z. Griliches (1994): "Changes in the Demand for Skilled Labor Within U.S. Manufacturing: Evidence From the Annual Survey of Manufactures." *Quarterly Journal of Economics* 109 (May): 367–97.

Berman, H. (1983): *Law and Revolution.* Harvard University Press, Cambridge, Mass.

Bernanke, Ben S., and M. Gertler (1995): "Inside the Black Box: The Credit Channel of Monetary Policy Transmission." *Journal of Economic Perspectives* 9 (4): 27–48.

Bernardi, R. (1970): "The Economic Problems of the Roman Empire at the Time of Its Decline." In C. M. Cipolla (ed.), *The Economic Decline of Empires.* Methuen, London.

Bernhofen, D. M., and J. C. Brown (2000): "A Direct Test of the Theory of Comparative Advantage: The Case of Japan." Working Paper, Clark University, January.

Beteille, A. (1996): "Caste in Contemporary India." In C. J. Fuller (ed.), *Caste Today*. Oxford University Press, New Delhi.

Bevan, D. L., P. Collier, and J. W. Gunning (1989): *Peasants and Governments*. Clarendon Press, Oxford.

————. (1999): *The Political Economy of Poverty, Equity and Growth—Nigeria and Indonesia*. Oxford University Press, New York.

Bhagwati, J. (1979): *Anatomy and Consequences of Trade Control Regimes*. National Bureau of Economic Research, New York.

————. (1998): "The Capital Myth: The Difference Between Trade in Widgets and Trade in Dollars." *Foreign Affairs* 77: 7–12.

————. (1999): "Globalization: Who Gains, Who Loses?" In H. Siebert (ed.), *Globalization and Labor*, pp. 225–36. J.C.B. Mohr, Tubingen.

————. (ed.) (2002): *Going Alone*. MIT Press, Cambridge, Mass.

————. (2002a): *Free Trade Today*. Princeton University Press, Princeton, N.J.

Bhagwati, J., and R. E. Hudec (1996): *Fair Trade and Harmonization*, 2 vols. MIT Press, Cambridge, Mass.

Bhagwati, J., and M. Kosters (eds.) (1994): *Trade and Wages*. American Enterprise Institute, Washington, D.C.

Bhagwati, J., and V. K. Ramaswami (1963): "Domestic Distortions, Tariffs and the Theory of Optimum Subsidy." *Journal of Political Economy* 71: 44–50.

Bhagwati, J., and C. Rodriguez (1975): "Welfare Theoretical Analyses of the Brain Drain." *Journal of Development Economics* 2 (3): 195–221.

Bhagwati, J., and T. N. Srinivasan (1980): "Revenue Seeking: A Generalization of the Theory of Tariffs." *Journal of Political Economy* 88: 1069–87.

Bhalla, S. (2002): *Imagine There's No Country: Poverty, Inequality and Growth in the Age of Globalization*. Institute of International Economics, Washington, D.C.

Bhattacharya, D. (1979): *A Concise History of the Indian Economy, 1750–1950*, 2nd ed. Prentice Hall of India, New Delhi.

Binmore, K. (1990): *Essays in the Foundations of Game Theory*. Blackwell, Oxford.

————. (1994 and 1998): *Game Theory and the Social Contract, Vol. 1: Playing Fair; Vol. 2: Just Playing*. MIT Press, Cambridge, Mass.

Blaug, M. (1987): "Classical Economics." In Eatwell, Milgate, and Newman (eds.), *The New Palgrave—A Dictionary of Economics*, vol. 1. Macmillan, London.

Blustein, P. (2003): *The Chastening*. Public Affairs, New York.

Bogetic, Z. (2000): "Official Dollarization: Current Experiences and Issues." *Cato Journal* 20 (2): 179–213.

Boldrin, M., and D. Levine (2002): "The Case Against Intellectual Property." *American Economic Review* 92, 2 (May): 209–12.

Boone, P. (1994): "The Impact of Foreign Aid On Savings and Growth." Mimeo, London School of Economics, London.

Bordo, M. (2003): "Exchange Rate Choice in Historical Perspective." *NBER Working Papers* No. 9654, NBER, Cambridge, Mass.

Bordo, M., and M. Flandreau (2003): "Core, Periphery, Exchange Rate Regimes and Globalization." In Bordo, Taylor, and J.G. Williamson (eds.): *Globalization in Historical Perspective*. University of Chicago Press, Chicago.

Bordo, M. D., C. Goldin, and E. N. White (eds.) (1998): *The Defining Moment*. University of Chicago Press, Chicago.

Borjas, G. J., R. B. Freeman, and L. Katz (1997): " How Much Do Immigration and Trade Affect Labor Market Outcomes?" *Brookings Papers on Economic Activity 1*: 1–67.

Bork, R. P. (1996): *Slouching Towards Gomorrah*. Harper-Collins, New York.

Borlaug, N. E. (2000): "Ending World Hunger: The Promise of Bio-Technology and the Threat of Anti-science Zealotry." *Plant Physiology* 124: 487–90.

Bourguignon, F., and C. Morrisson (2002): "Inequality Among World Citizens: 1820–1992." *American Economic Review* 92, 4 (September): 727–41.

Bramwell, A. (1989): *Ecology in the 20th Century: A History*. Yale University Press, New Haven, Conn.

Brennan, G., and J. Buchanan (1980): *The Power to Tax*. Cambridge University Press, Cambridge.

Broome, J. (1991): *Weighing Goods*. Blackwell, Oxford.

Buchanan, J. M., and C. Stubblebine (1962): "Externality." *Economica* 29: 371–84.

Buchanan, J. M., and G. Tullock (1962): *The Calculus of Consent*. Michigan University Press, Ann Arbor.

Burke, E. (1774/1999): "Speech to the Electors of Bristol." In J. Payne (ed.), *Select Works of Edmund Burke*, vol. 4. Liberty Fund, Indianapolis.

Cagan, P. (1965): *Determinants and Effects of Changes in the Stock of Money, 1875–1960*. Norton, New York.

Cain, P. J. (1998): "Was It Worth Having? The British Empire, 1850–1950." *Revista de Historia Economica* 16: 351–76.

Cain, P. J., and A. G. Hopkins (2002): *British Imperialism 1688–2000*. Longman, London.

Calvo, G. A., and C. Reinhart (2002): "Fear of Floating." *Quarterly Journal of Economics* 117 (May): 379–408.

Cameron, R. (1993): *A Concise Economic History of the World*, 2nd ed. Oxford University Press, New York.

Cavalli-Sforza, L. L. (2000): *Genes, Peoples and Languages*. Farrar, Straus, and Giroux, New York.

Caves, R. E. (1996): *Multinational Enterprise amd Economic Analysis*, 2nd ed. Cambridge University Press, Cambridge.

Chang, F. M., J. R. Kidd, K. J. Livak, A. J. Pakstis, and K. K. Kidd (1996): "The World-wide Distribution of Allele Frequencies at the Human Dopamine D4 Receptor Locus." *Human Genetics* 98: 91–101.

Chen, C., M. Burton, E. Greenberger, and J. Dmitrieva (1999): "Population Migration and the Variations of Dopamine D4 Receptor (DRD4) Allele Frequencies Around the Globe." *Evolution and Human Behavior* 20: 309–24.

Chesnais, J.-C. (1987): *La Revanche du Tiers-Monde*. Laffont, Paris.

Cigno, A., F. C. Rosati, and L. Guarcello (2002): "Does Globalization Increase Child Labor?" *World Development* 30 (9): 1579–89.

Claire, G. (1977): *Freedom of Association and Economic Development*. ILO, Geneva.

Cline, W. P. (1984): *International Debt: Systematic Risk and Policy Response*. Institute of International Economics, Washington, D.C.

Clissold, T. (2004): *Mr. China*. Robinson, London.

Coase, R. H. (1937/1988): "The Nature of the Firm." *Economica* 4 (November 1937); reprinted in his *The Firm, the Market and the Law*. University of Chicago Press, Chicago, 1988.

Colambato, E., and J. Macey (1996): "The Decline of the Nation-State and Its Effects on Constitutional International Economic Law." *Cardozo Law Review* 18.

Colinvaux, P. (1983): *The Fate of Nations*. Penguin, London.

Colley, L. (1992): *Britons*, Yale University Press, New Haven, Conn.

Collier, P. et al. (1997): "Redesigning Conditionality." *World Development* 25 (9): 1399–1407.

Collier, P., and D. Dollar (2001): "Can the World Cut Poverty In Half? How Policy Reform and Effective Aid Can Meet International Development Goals." *World Development* 29 (11): 1787–1802.

Collier, P., and A. Hoeffler (1998): "On Economic Causes of Civil War." *Oxford Economic Papers* 50 (4): 563–73.

Collier, P., and D. Lal (1986): *Labour and Poverty in Kenya 1900–1980*. Clarendon Press, Oxford.

Conybeare, J.A.C. (2002): "Leadership By Example? Britain and the Free Trade Movement of the 19th Century." In Bhagwati (ed.), *Going Alone*. MIT Press, Cambridge, Mass.

Copans, J. (1980): "From Senegambia to Senegal: The Evolution of Peasantries." In M. A. Kelin (ed.), *Peasants in Africa*. Sage, Beverly Hills, Calif.

Corden, W. M. (1974/1997): *Trade Policy and Economic Welfare*. Clarendon Press, Oxford.

———. (1977/1986): *Inflation, Exchange Rates and the World Economy*. Clarendon Press, Oxford.

———. (2002): *Too Sensational: On the Choice of Exchange Rate Regimes*. MIT Press, Cambridge, Mass.

Crafts, N.F.R. (1985): *British Economic Growth During the Industrial Revolution*. Clarendon Press, Oxford.

Dasgupta, P. (1980): "Decentralization and Rights." *Economica* 47 (May): 107–23.

Dasgupta, P., and K. G. Maler (1994): "Poverty, Institutions and the Environmental-Resource Base." In J. Behrman and T. N. Srinivasan (eds.), *Handbook of Development Economics*, vol. 3, North Holland, Amsterdam.

Davis, D., and S. Harrell (eds.) (1993): *Chinese Families in the Post-Mao Era*. University of California Press, Berkeley.

Deaton, A., and R. Miller (1995): "International Commodity Prices, Macroeconomic Performance, and Politics in Sub-Saharan Africa." *Princeton Essays in International Finance* 79 (December), Princeton, N.J.

De Bary, W. T. (1998): *Asian Values and Human Rights*. Harvard University Press, Cambridge, Mass.

De Bary, W. T., and Tu Weiming (eds.) (1998): *Confucianism and Human Rights*. Columbia University Press, New York.

De Jasay, A. (1985): *The State*. Blackwell, Oxford.

———. (1996): *Before Resorting to Politics*, the Shaftsbury Papers 5, Edward Elgar, Cheltenham.

Delargy, P.J.R., and C. Goodhart (1999): *Financial Crises: Plus ca Change, Plus c'est Lameme Chose*. Special Paper No. 108, LSE Financial Markets Group, London School of Economics, London.

DeLong, J. Bradford (2000): "The Triumph of Monetarism?" *Journal of Economic Perspectives* 14 (1): 83–94.

Delumeau, J. (1990): *Sin and Fear*. St. Martins Press, New York.

De Melo, J. and D. G. Tarr (1992): *A General Equilibrium Analysis of U.S. trade policy*. MIT Press, Cambridge, Mass.

Demsetz, H. (1967): "Towards a Theory of Property Rights." *American Economic Review* 57 (2): 347–59.

———. (1969): "Information and Efficiency—Another Viewpoint." *Journal of Law and Economics* 12: 1–22.

———. (1989): "Two Systems of Belief About Monopoly" in his *Efficiency, Competition and Policy*, Blackwell, Oxford.

———. (1992): "Economic Development and the Corporate Control Problem." Mimeo, UCLA Department of Economics, May.

———. (1995): *The Economics of the Business Firm*. Cambridge Economic Press, Cambridge.

———. (2003): "Business Governance and the Institutions of Capitalism." Mimeo, UCLA Department of Economics, June.

Derringer, K., and L. Squire (1996): "A New Data Set for Measuring Income Inequality." *World Bank Economic Review* 10 (3): 565–92.

Desai, P. (2003): *Financial Crisis, Contagion and Containment*. Princeton University Press, Princeton, N.J.

De Tocqueville, A. (1835/1968): *Democracy in America*. Collins, London.

———. (1856/1998): *The Old Regime and the Revolution*. University of Chicago Press, Chicago.

Devlin, P. (1959): *The Enforcement of Morals*. Oxford University Press, London.

Dickson, B. J. (2003): *Red Capitalists in China*. Cambridge University Press, Cambridge.

Di Tella, R., R. J. MacCulloch, and A. J. Oswald (2001): "Preferences Over Inflation and Unemployment: Evidence From Surveys of Happiness." *American Economic Review* 91 (1): 335–41.

Dollar, D. and A. Kraay (2001): "Trade, Growth and Poverty." Mimeo, World Bank, Washington D.C.

Domar, E. (1970): "The Causes of Slavery or Serfdom: A Hypothesis." *Journal of Economic History* (March): 18–32.

Dooley, M. P., D. Folkerts-Landau, and P. Garber (2003): "An Essay on the Revised Bretton Woods System." *NBER Working Papers* No. 9971, Sept. 2003, NBER, Cambridge, Mass.

Dooley, M. P., D. Folkerts-Landau, and P. Garber (2004): "Direct Investment, Rising Real Wages and the Absorption of Excess Labor in the Periphery." *NBER Working Papers* No. 10626, July 2004, NBER, Cambridge, Mass.

Dorn, J. A., and A. J. Schwartz (eds.) (1987): *The Search for Stable Money*. University of Chicago Press, Chicago.

Douglas, M., and A. Wildavsky (1983): *Risk and Culture*. University of California Press, Berkeley.

Dowd, K. (1989): *The State and the Monetary System*. Phillip Allan, London.

Downs, A. (1957): *An Economic Theory of Democracy*. Harper Bros., New York.

Dumke, R. H. (1994): "German Unification in the 19th Century: The Political Economy of the Zolverin." *Discussion Beitrage D-87755*, Institut fur Volkswirtschaftslehre, Universitat der Bundeswehr Muchen (August).

Dumont, L. (1970): *Homo Hierarchicus*. Widenfeld and Nicholson, London.

———. (1986): *Essays on Individualism*. University of Chicago Press, Chicago.

Easterly, W. (2001): *The Elusive Quest for Growth*. MIT Press, Cambridge, Mass.

Eaton, J. M., M. Gersovitz, and J. Stiglitz (1986): "The Pure Theory of Country Risk." *European Economic Review* 30 (June): 481–513.

Edmonds, E., and N. Pavcnik (2001): "Does Globalization Increase Child Labour?" Mimeo, Dartmouth College.

Edwards, S. (1989): *Real Exchange Rates, Devaluation and Adjustment*. MIT Press, Cambridge, Mass.

———. (1999): "How Effective Are Capital Controls?" *Journal of Economic Perspectives* 13 (4): 65–84.

———. (2002): "The Great Exchange Rate Debate After Argentina." *NBER Working Paper* No. 9257, Oct. 2002, NBER, Cambridge, Mass.

———. (2004): "Thirty Years of Current Account Imbalances, Current Account Reversals and Sudden Stops." *NBER Working Papers* No. 10276, January 2004, NBER, Cambridge, Mass.

Ehrlich, P. (1968): *The Population Bomb*. Ballantine, Baltimore.

Eichengreen, B. (1989): "Hegemonic Stability Theories of the International Monetary System." In R. N. Cooper et al., *Can Nations Agree?* Brookings Institution, Washington, D.C.

———. (1992): *Golden Fetters: The Gold Standard and the Great Depression*. Oxford University Press, New York.

———. (1996): *Globalizing Capital*. Princeton University Press, Princeton, N.J.

———. (2002): *Financial Crises*. Oxford University Press, Oxford.

Eichengreen, B., and M. Bordo (2002): "Crises Now and Then: What Lessons From the Last Era of Financial Globalization?" *NBER Working Paper* No. 8716, NBER, Cambridge, Mass.

Eichengreen, B., and R. Hausmann (1999): "Exchange Rates and Financial Fragility." *NBER Working Papers*, No. 7418, Nov., NBER, Cambridge, Mass.

Eichengreen, B., R. Hausmann, and U. Panizza (2003): "Currency Mismatches, Debt Intolerance and Original Sin: Why They Are Not the Same and Why It Matters." *NBER Working Paper* No. 10036, NBER, Cambridge, Mass.

Eichengreen, B., and D. Leblang (2002): "Capital Account Liberalization and Growth: Was Mr. Mahathir Right?" *NBER Working Paper* No. 9427, NBER, Cambridge, Mass.

Engerman, S. L. (1983): "Contract Labor, Sugar and Technology in the 19th Century." *Journal of Economic History* 43: 635–59.

Engerman, S. L., and R. E. Gallman (eds.) (2000): *The Cambridge Economic History of the United States*. Cambridge University Press, Cambridge.

Engerman, S. L., and K. L. Sokoloff (1994): "Factor Endowments, Institutions and Differential Paths of Growth Among the New World Economies: A View From Economic Historians of the United States." *NBER Working Paper* Historical Paper No. 66, Cambridge, Mass.

Epstein, R. A. (2003): *Skepticism and Freedom: A Modern Case for Classical Liberalism*. University of Chicago Press, Chicago.

Epstein, R. A. (2004): *Free Markets Under Siege*. 23rd Wincott Lecture, Institute of Economic Affairs, London.

Estevadeordal, A., B. Frantz, and A. M. Taylor (2003): "The Rise and Fall of World Trade, 1870–1939." *Quarterly Journal of Economics* 118, 2 (May): 359–407.

Etherington, N. (1984): *Theories of Imperialism: War, Conquest and Capital*, Croom Helm, London.

Etzioni, A. (1988): *The Moral Dimension: Toward a New Economics*. Free Press, New York.

Evans, R. (1993): *Deng Xiaoping*. Hamish Hamilton, London.

Fawcett, E. (2004): "Witchcraft." *Times Literary Supplement*, Sept. 10, p. 23.

Feenstra, R. C. (1998): "Integration of Trade and Disintegration of Production in the Global Economy." *Journal of Economic Perspectives* 12 (4): 31–50.

Feldstein, M. (1997a): "The Political Economy of the European Economic and Monetary Union: Political Sources of an Economic Liability." *Journal of Economic Perspectives* 11: 23–42.

———. (2002): "Economic and Financial Crises in Emerging Economies." NBER *Working Paper* No. 8837, Nov., NBER, Cambridge, Mass.

———. (1997b): "EMU and International Conflict." *Foreign Affairs* 76: 60–73.

———. (2003): "Why Is Productivity Growing Faster?" *NBER* Working Paper No. 9530, Feb. 2003, Cambridge, Mass.

Fidler, S. (2001): "Who's Minding the Bank?" *Foreign Policy* Sept./Oct.

Findlay, R. (1996): "The Emergence of the World Economy." Dept. of Economics, Columbia University, Discussion Paper No. 9596-08, New York.

Findlay, R., and M. Lundahl (2003): "The First Globalization Episode: The Creation of the Mongol Empire, or the Economics of Chinggis Khan." Mimeo, Dept. of Economics, Columbia University, and Stockholm School of Economics.

Findlay, R., and S. Wellisz (eds.) (1993): *The Political Economy of Poverty, Equity and Growth—Five Small Open Economies*. Oxford University Press, New York.

Findlay, R., and J. Wilson (1987): "The Political Economy of Leviathan." In A. Razin and E. Sadka (eds.), *Economic Policy in Theory and Practice*. St. Martin's Press, New York.

Finer, S. E. (1997): *The History of Government*, 3 vols. Oxford University Press, Oxford.

Fischer, S. (1999): "On the Need for an International Lender of Last Resort." *Journal of Economic Perspectives* 13 (4): 85–104.

Flemming, J. S. (1982): "Comment on Minsky." In C. P. Kindleberger and J. P. Laffargue (eds.), *Financial Crises—Theory, History and Policy*. Cambridge University Press, Cambridge.

Fogel, F. W. (1989): *Without Consent or Contract*. Norton, New York.

Franco, P. (2004): *Michael Oakeshott—An Introduction*, Yale University Press, New Haven.

Francois, J. F., and L. M. Baughman (2001): "Cost to American Consuming Industries of Steel Quotas and Taxes." The Trade Partnership, Washington, D.C., April 30th.

Frank, R. H. (1999): *Luxury Fever: Why Money Fails to Satisfy in an Era of Excess*. Free Press, New York.

Freud, S. (1930/1969): *Civilization and Its Discontents*. Norton, New York.

Frey, B. (1997): "The Public Choice of International Organizations." In D. C. Mueller (ed.), *Public Choice—A Handbook*. Cambridge University Press, Cambridge.

Frey, B., and A. Stutzer (2002): *Happiness and Economics*. Princeton University Press, Princeton, N.J.

Freyer, T. A. (2000): "Business Law and American Economic History." In Engerman and Gallman (eds.) (2000), vol. 2. *The Cambridge Economic History of the United States*, Cambridge University Press, Cambridge.

Friedman, M. (1962): *Capitalism and Freedom*. University of Chicago Press, Chicago.

286

Friedman, M., and R. Friedman (1980): *Free to Choose*. Harcourt Brace Jovanovich, New York.

Friedman, M. and A. J. Schwartz (1963): *A Monetary History of the United States*. Princeton University Press, Princeton, N.J.

———. (1986): "Has Government Any Role in Money?" *Journal of Monetary Economics*, June.

Gallagher, J., and R. Robinson (1953): "The Imperialism of Free Trade." *Economic History Review* 6 (1): 1–15.

Gandhi, M. K. (1958–   ): *The Collected Works of Mahatma Gandhi*. Navjeevan Trust, Delhi.

Gauthier, D. (1986): *Morals by Agreement*. Clarendon Press, Oxford.

Gay, P. (2001): *Schnitzler's Century—The Making of Middleclass Culture 1815–1914*. Allen Lane, London.

Gellner, E. (1988): *Plough, Book and Sword—The Structure of Human History*. Collins Harvill, London.

———. (1993): *The Psychoanalytic Movement: The Cunning of Unreason*. Northwestern University Press, Evanston, Ill.

Ghosh, A. R., and J. D. Ostroy (1995): "The Current Account in Developing Countries: A Perspective from the Consumption-Smoothing Approach." *World Bank Economic Review* 9 (2): 305–33.

Gibbon, E. (1787/1985): *The Decline and Fall of the Roman Empire*. Penguin Classics, London.

Gillbert, P. J., and D. M. Newberry (1994): "The Dynamic Efficiency of a Regulatory Constitution." *Rand Journal of Economics* 25: 538–54.

Gilbert, C., A. Powell, and D. Vines (1999): "Positioning the World Bank." *The Economic Journal* 109 (459): F598–633.

Gilbert, C., and D. Vines (eds.) (1999): *The World Bank: Policies and Structure*. Cambridge University Press, Cambridge.

Goldsmith, J. (1994): *The Trap*. Macmillan, London.

Goldsmith, R.W. (1984): " An Estimate of the Size and Structure of the National Product of the Early Roman Empire." *Review of Income and Wealth* (September): 263–88.

Goldstein, M., and N. Lardy (2003): "A Modest Proposal for China's Renimbi." *Financial Times*, Aug. 26, 2003, p. 13.

———. (2005): "A Faulty Strategy Weakens China's Prospects." *Financial Times*, March 4, 2005, p. 13.

Goodhart, C.A.E. (1988): *The Evolution of Central Banking*. MIT Press, Cambridge, Mass.

Goody, J. (1983): *The Development of the Family and Marriage in Europe*. Cambridge University Press, Cambridge.

Gordon, R. (2003): "High Tech Innovation and Productivity Growth: Does Supply Create Its Own Demand?" *NBER* Working Paper 9437, Cambridge, Mass.

Goto, J. (1989): "The Multifiber Agreement and Its Effects on Developing Countries." *World Bank Research Observer* 4 (3): 203–27.

Gourevitch, P. A. (1993): "Democracy and Economic Policy: Elective Affinities and Circumstantial Conjunctures." *World Development* (August): 1271–80.

Graham, F. D. (1948): *The Theory of International Values*. Princeton University Press, Princeton, N.J.

Granville, B. (2003): "Strengthening the Link Between Debt Relief and Poverty Reduction: The HIPC Initiative." In V. K. Aggarwal and B. Granville (eds.): *Sovereign Debt: Origins, Crises and Restructuring*. Royal Institute of International Affairs, London.

Gray, J. (1983): *Mill on Liberty: A Defence*, Routledge, London.

Grecu, A. (2004): *Flat Tax—the British Case*. Adam Smith Institute, London.

Greenwald, B., and J. Stiglitz (1986): "Externalities in Economies with Imperfect Information and Incomplete Markets." *Quarterly Journal of Economics* 101: 229–64.

Greif, A. (1994): "Cultural Beliefs and the Organization of Society: A Historical and Theoretical Reflection on Collectivist and Individualist Societies." *Journal of Political Economy* 102 (5): 912–950.

Gunder Frank, Andre (1978): *World Accumulation, 1492–1789*. Monthly Review Press, New York.

———. (1998): *Reorient: Global Economy in the Asian Age*. University of California Press, Berkeley.

Gwartney, J., and R. Lawson (2003): *Economic Freedom of the World—2003 Annual Report*. The Fraser Institute, Vancouver.

Hacker, L. M. (1954): "The Anti-capitalist Bias of American Historians." In F. Hayek (ed.): *Capitalism and the Historians*. University of Chicago Press, Chicago.

Hahn, F. (1973): *On the Notion of Equilibrium in Economics*. Cambridge University Press, Cambridge.

———. (1984): "Reflections on the Invisible Hand." In his *Equilibrium and Macroeconomics*. Blackwell, Oxford.

Hall, R. E. (ed.) (1983): *Inflation*. University of Chicago Press, Chicago.

Hall, R., and A. Rabushka (1995): *The Flat Tax*, 2d ed. Hoover Institution, Stanford, Calif.

Hallpike, C. R. (1986): *The Principles of Social Evolution*. Clarendon Press, Oxford.

Hammond, P. (1991): "Interpersonal Comparisons of Utility: Why and How They Are and Should Be Made." In J. Elster and J. E. Romer (eds.): *Interpersonal Comparison of Well Being*, pp. 200–254. Cambridge University Press, Cambridge.

Hancock, G. (1989): *Lords of Poverty: The Power, Prestige, and Corruption of the International Aid Business*. Macmillan, London.

Hanke, S. H. and S.J.K. Walters (1997): "Economic Freedom, Prosperity and Equality: A Survey." *The Cato Journal* 17 (2): 117–46.

Hansen, J. E., and M. Sato (2001): "Trends of Measured Climate Forcing Agents." *Proceedings of the National Academy of Sciences* 98: 14778–83.

Harberger, A. C. (1972): *Project Evaluation*. University of Chicago Press, Chicago.

———. (ed.) (1984): *World Economic Growth*. ICS Press, San Francisco.

———. (1984a): "Reflections on the Present and Future Role of the World Bank." Report for World Bank, mimeo.

———. (1998): "A Vision of the Growth Process." *American Economic Review* 88 (1): 1–32.

Harrison, G. W., T. F. Rutherford, and D. G. Tarr (1996): "Quantifying the Uruguay Round." In W. Martin and L. A. Winters (eds.), *The Uruguay Round and Developing Countries*. Cambridge University Press, Cambridge.

Harrison, S. (1960): *India, The Most Dangerous Decades*. Oxford University Press, Madras.

288

Hart, H.L.A. (1955): "Are There Any Natural Rights." *Philosophical Review* 64; reprinted in A. Quinton (ed.) (1967): *Political Philosophy*. Oxford University Press, Oxford.

———. (1963): *Law, Liberty and Morality*. Oxford University Press, London.

Hayek. F. (1931): *Prices and Production*. Routledge, London.

———. (1941): *The Pure Theory of Capital*. Routledge, London.

———. (1944): *The Road to Serfdom*. Routledge, London.

———. (1954): *Capitalism and the Historians*. University of Chicago Press, Chicago.

———. (1960): *The Constitution of Liberty*. Routledge, London.

———. (1976): *Law, Legislation and Liberty*, vol. 2. Routledge, London.

———. (1976a): *Denationalization of Money*. Institute of Economic Affairs, London.

Headrick, D. R. (1979): "The Tools of Imperialism: Technology and the Expansion of European Colonial Empires in the Nineteenth Century." *Journal of Modern History* 51 (June): 231–63.

Hecksher, E. (1955): *Mercantilism*, 2 vols. Allen and Unwin, London.

Helliwell, J. F. (1992): "Empirical Linkages between Democracy and Economic Growth." *NBER Working Paper* No. 4066, May. Cambridge, Mass.

Henderson, P. D. (2001): *Misguided Virtue*. Institute of Economic Affairs, London.

———. (2000): "False Perspective: The UNDP View of the World." *World Economics* 1: 16–19.

Hicks, J. R. (1969): *A Theory of Economic History*. Clarendon Press, Oxford.

———. (1979): *Causality in Economics*. Blackwell, Oxford.

Himmelfarb, G. (1975): "The Conservative Imagination: Michael Oakeshott." *American Scholar* 44 (summer): 405–20.

Himmelfarb, G. (1994): *The Demoralization of Society*. Alfred A. Knopf, New York.

———. (1995): *On Looking Into the Abyss*. Viking, New York.

———. (1996): "The Unraveled Fabric—And How to Knit It Up: Mixed Motives Among the New Communitarians." *Times Literary Supplement*, May 17, pp. 12–13.

Hindley, B. (1994): *The Goldsmith Fallacy*, Rochester Paper 3, Trade Policy Unit, Centre for Policy Studies, London.

Hirshlerifer, J. (2001): The Dark Side of the Force: Economic Foundations of Conflict Theory. Cambridge University Press, Cambridge.

Holsey, C. M., and T. E. Borcherding (1997): "Why Does Government's Share of National Income Grow? An Assessment of the Recent Literature on the U.S. Experience." In D. C. Mueller (ed.): *Perspectives on Public Choice—A Handbook*. Cambridge University Press, Cambridge.

Hopkins, A. G. (1973): *An Economic History of West Africa*. Longman, London.

———. (1980): "Property Rights and Empire Building: Britain's Annexation of Lagos, 1861." *Journal of Economic History* 40: 777–98.

Hotelling, H. (1931): "The Economics of Exhaustible Resources." *Journal of Political Economy* 39: 137–75.

Houghton, J. (1994): "Global Warming—the Complete Briefing." Lion Hudson, Oxford.

Huang, Y. (2003): *Selling China: Foreign Direct Investment During the Reform Era*. Cambridge University Press, Cambridge.

Huber, J. R. (1971): "Effect on Prices of Japan's Entry Into World Commerce After 1858." *Journal of Political Economy* 79: 614–28.

Hufbauer, G., J. Schott, and K. Elliot (1990): *Economic Sanctions Reconsidered*. Institute of International Economics, Washington, D.C.

Hume, D. (1750/1975): *An Enquiry Concerning the Principles of Morals*. Oxford University Press, London.

———. (1740/1978): *A Treatise on Human Nature*. Clarendon Press, Oxford.

———. (1779/1948): *Dialogues Concerning Natural Religion*. Hafner Press, New York.

Huntington, S. P. (1993): "The Clash of Civilizations." *Foreign Affairs* 72 (3): 22–49.

Illarionov, A. (2004): "Russian Scientists Reassert Opposition to Kyoto Accord." *Environmental and Climate News* (September): 10–11.

Illarionov, A. (2004a): "Kyoto Protocol Is Bad News for Us All." *Financial Times*, Nov. 15, p. 19.

Irwin, D. A. (1988): "The Welfare Effects of British Free Trade: Debate and Evidence from the 1840's." *Journal of Political Economy* 96 (6): 1142–64.

———. (1996): *Against the Tide*. Princeton University Press, Princeton, N.J.

———. (2002): *Free Trade Under Fire*. Princeton University Press, Princeton, N.J.

———. (2002a): "Did Import Substitution Promote Growth in the Late Nineteenth Century?" *NBER Working Papers* No. 8751, February, NBER, Cambridge, Mass.

———. (2003): "The Optimal Tax on Antebellum U.S. Cotton Exports." *Journal of International Economics* 60, 2 (August): 275–91.

Jenkins, R. (1999): *Democratic Politics and Economic Reform in India*. Cambridge University Press, Cambridge.

Jenner, W.J.F. (1992): *The Tyranny of History*, Penguin, London.

Johnson, H. G. (1953–54/1958): "Optimum Tariffs and Retaliation." *Review of Economic Studies* 21(2) (55): 142–53, reprinted in his *International Trade and Economic Growth*, Allen and Unwin, London.

———. (1965): "Optimal Trade Intervention in the Presence of Distortions." In R. E. Baldwin et al., *Trade, Growth and the Balance of Payments*. Amsterdam: North-Holland.

Jones, E. L. (1981): *The European Miracle*. Cambridge University Press, Cambridge.

Jones, R., and S. Engerman (1996): "Trade, Technology and Wages: A Tale of Two Countries." *American Economic Review* 86 (2): 35–40.

Josephson, M. (1934): *The Robber Barons*. Harcourt, Brace, New York.

Judt, T. (1997): "The Social Question Redivivus." *Foreign Affairs* 76 (5): 95–117.

Kahneman, D., A. B. Krueger, D. A. Schkade, N. Schwartz, and A. A. Stone (2004): "Towards National Well Being Accounts." *American Economic Review* 94 (2): 429–34.

Kahneman, D. et al. (2004a): "A Survey Method for Characterizing Daily Life Experience: The Day Reconstruction Method." *Science* 306 (December 3): 1776–80.

Kanbur, R. (2001): "Economic Policy, Distribution and Poverty: The Nature of Disagreements." *World Development* 29 (4): 1083–94.

Kant, I. (1784–95/1983): *Perpetual Peace and Other Essays*. Hackett Publishing, Indianapolis.

Keatings, W. R. et al. (2000): "Heat Related Mortality in Warm and Cold Regions of Europe: Observational Study." *British Medical Journal* 32: 670–73.

Keesing, D. B., and M. Wolf (1980): *Textile Quotas Against Developing Countries*. Trade Policy Research Center, London.

Keightley, D. N. (1990): "Early Civilization in China: Reflections on How It Became Chinese." In P. S. Robb (ed.), *Heritage of China*. University of California Press, Berkeley.

Keohane, R. O. (1984): *After Hegemony*. Princeton University Press, Princeton, N.J.

Keynes, J. M. (1919/1971): *The Economic Consequences of the Peace*. Macmillan, London.

———. (1926): *The End of Laissez-Faire*. Hogarth Press, London.

Keynes, J. M. (1933/1972): *The Collected Writings of John Maynard Keynes (CW)*, vol 10: *Essays in Biography*. Macmillan, London.

———. (1936): *The General Theory of Employment, Interest and Money*. Macmillan, London.

Kindleberger, C. P. (1973): *The World in Depression, 1929–39*. University of California Press, Berkeley.

———. (1976): "Systems of International Organization." In D. Calleo (ed.), *Money and the Coming World Order*. New York University Press, New York.

———. (1978): *Mania, Panics and Crashes*. Basic Books, New York.

King, M. (1999): "The Evolving Role of Banks in International Capital Flows." In M. Feldstein (ed.), *International Capital Flows*. University of Chicago Press, Chicago.

Knock, T. J. (1992): *To End All Wars*. Princeton University Press, Princeton, N.J.

Kohli, A. (1990): *Democracy and Discontent*. Cambridge University Press, Cambridge.

———. (ed.) (2001): *The Success of India's Democracy*. Cambridge University Press, Cambridge.

Krattiger, A. F. (2000): "Food Biotechnology: Promising Havoc or Hope for the Poor?" *Proteus* 17:38.

Kreps, D. (1990): *Game Theory and Economic Modelling*. Clarendon Press, Oxford.

Krueger, A. O. (1974): "The Political Economy of the Rent-Seeking Society." *American Economic Review* 64: 291–303.

———. (1977): *Growth, Distortions and Patterns of Trade among Many Countries*. Princeton Studies in International Finance, no. 40, Princeton University, N.J.

———. (1978): *Liberalization Attempts and Consequences*. National Bureau of Economic Research, New York.

———. (1992): "The Effects of Regional Trading Blocs on World Trade." Paper presented at conference on "NAFTA, the Pacific and Australia/New Zealand," University of Texas at Austin.

———. (1995): *Trade Policies and Developing Nations*. Brookings Institution, Washington, D.C.

———. (ed.) (1996): *The Political Economy of American Trade Policy*. University of Chicago Press, Chicago.

———. (1998): "Whither the World Bank and IMF?" *Journal of Economic Literature* 36 (4): 1983–2020.

———. (1999): "Are Preferential Trading Arrangements Trade-Liberalizing or Protectionist." *Journal of Economic Perspectives* 13 (4): 105–24.

———. (1999a): "Free Trade Agreements as Protectionist Devices: Rules of Origin." In J. R. Melvin, J. C. Moore, and R. Reizman (eds.), *Trade, Theory and Econometrics*. Routledge, New York.

———. (2001): "International Financial Architecture for 2002: A New Approach to Sovereign Debt Restructuring." Mimeo, IMF, Washington, D.C.

Krugman, P. (1998): "Saving Asia: It's Time to Get Radical." *Fortune*, Sept. 7, pp. 74–80.

Kupperman, K. O. (1993): *Providence Island, 1630–1641: The Other Puritan Colony.* Cambridge University Press, Cambridge.

Laffont, J. J., and J. Tirole (1993): *A Theory of Incentives in Procurement and Regulation.* MIT Press, Cambridge, Mass.

Lake, D. A. (1993): "Leadership, Hegemony, and the International Economy: Naked Emperor or Tattered Monarch With Potential?" *International Studies Quarterly* 37: 459–89.

Lal, D. (1972): "The Foreign Exchange Bottleneck Revisited: A Geometric Note." *Economic Development and Cultural Change* 20 (4): 720–30.

———. (1976): "Agricultural Growth, Real Wages, and the Rural Poor in India." *Economic and Political Weekly* 26 (June): A47–A61.

———. (1978): *Poverty, Power and Prejudice.* Fabian Society, London; reprinted in Lal (1994).

———. (1980/1993): "A Liberal International Economic Order: The International Monetary System and Economic Development." *Princeton Essays in International Finance,* no. 139, October; reprinted in Lal (1993).

———. (1980a): *Prices for Planning.* Heinemann Educational Books, London.

———. (1981): *Resurrection of the Pauper Labor Argument,* Thames Essay No. 28, Trade Policy research Center, London; reprinted in Lal (1994).

———. (1983/1997/2002): *The Poverty of Development Economics.* Institute of Economic Affairs, London, 1st, 2nd, 3rd editions; U.S. editions, Harvard University Press, 1985; 2nd edition, MIT Press, Cambridge, Mass., 2000; Indian edition, Oxford University Press, New Delhi, 2000.

———. (1984): "The Political Economy of the Predatory State." DRD Discussion Paper No. 105, World Bank, Washington, D.C.

———. (1985): "Nationalism, Socialism and Planning: Influential Ideas in the South." *World Development* 13 (6): 749–59; reprinted in Lal (1993).

———. (1987): "The Political Economy of Economic Liberalization." *World Bank Economic Review* 1 (2): 273–99; reprinted in Lal (1993).

———. (1987a): "Markets, Mandarins and Mathematicians." *Cato Journal* 7 (1): 43–70; reprinted in Lal (1994).

———. (1987b): "Alternative Roads to Economic Integration: The Case for Currency Competition in European Integration." *Case Western Reserve Journal of International Law* 22 (2, 3): 299–310; reprinted in Lal (1994).

———. (1988/2004): *The Hindu Equilibrium, vol. 1.* Clarendon Press, Oxford; revised and abridged edition, Oxford University Press, Oxford.

———. (1990): "Manners, Morals and Materialism: Some Indian Perceptions of America and Great Britain." In L. and N. Glazer (eds.), *Conflicting Images: India and the United States.* Riverdale Publishing, Glenn Dale, Md.; reprinted in Lal (1994).

———. (1990a): *Fighting Fiscal Privilege.* Social Market Foundation, Paper no. 7, London; reprinted in Lal (1994).

———. (1990b): *Political Economy and Public Policy.* Occasional paper no. 19, International Center for Economic Growth, San Francisco; reprinted in Lal (1993).

———. (1990c): *The Limits of International Cooperation*. Twentieth Wincott Memorial Lecture, Occasional Paper no. 83, Institute of Economic Affairs, London.

———. (1992): "The Migration of Money: From a Libertarian Viewpoint." In B. Barry and R. E. Goodin (eds.), *Free Movement*, pp. 95–114. Simon & Schuster, London. Reprinted in Lal (1994).

———. (1993): *The Repressed Economy, Economists of the 20th Century*. Edward Elgar, Aldershot.

———. (1993a): "Does Openness Matter? How to Apprise the Evidence." In H. Siebert (ed.), *Growth in the World Economy*. J.C.B. Mohr, Tubingen; reprinted in Lal (1994).

———. (1994): *Against Dirigisme*. ICS Press, San Francisco.

———. (1995): "Policies for Economic Development: Why the Wheel Has Come Full Circle." *South African Journal of Economics* 63 (4): 489–517.

———. (1995a): *Poverty, Markets and Democracy*. The 1995 Nestle inaugural lecture on the Developing World, Nestle, U.K.

———. (1995b): "Eco-Fundamentalism." *International Affairs* 71: 515–28.

———. (1995c): "India and China—Contrasts in Economic Liberalization?" *World Development* 23 (9): 1475–94; reprinted in Lal (1999).

———. (1995d): "Notes on Money, Debt and Alternative Monetary Regimes for Brazil." *Revista de Economia Politica* 15, 4 (Oct.–Dec.): 99–111.

———. (1996): "Foreign Aid: An Idea Whose Time Has Gone." *Economic Affairs* (Autumn): 9–13.

———. (1996a/1999): "Participation, Markets and Democracy." In M. Lundahl and B. J. Nudulu (eds.), *New Directions in Development Economics*. Routledge, London; reprinted in Lal (1999a).

———. (1998): *Unintended Consequences*. MIT Press, Cambridge, Mass.

———. (1998a): "From Planning to Regulation: Towards a New Dirigisme?" *Cato Journal* 17 (2): 211–27; reprinted in Lal (1999a).

———. (1999): *EMU and Globalization*. Policy Series No. 17, Politeia, London.

———. (1999a): *Unfinished Business*. Oxford University Press, New Delhi.

———. (2000): "The Challenge of Globalization: There Is No Third Way." In I. Vasquez (ed.), *Global Fortune*. Cato Institute, Washington, D.C.

———. (2000a): "Does Modernization Require Westernization?" *The Independent Review* 5, 1 (Summer): 5–24.

———. (2000b): *Smoke Gets in Your Eyes: The Economic Welfare Effects of the World Bank-World Health Organization Global Crusade Against Tobacco*. FMF Monograph no. 26, Free Market Foundation, Sandton, South Africa.

———. (2000c): "Political Habits and the Political Economy of Economic Repression and Reform." *Cuadernos de Economia* 37 (112): 415–43.

———. (2002): "The New Cultural Imperialism: the Greens and Economic Development." *Humane Studies Review* 14 (3): 1–18.

———. (2003a): "Free Trade and Laissez Faire—Has the Wheel Come Full Circle?" *The World Economy* 26 (4): 471–82.

———. (2003b): "The Japanese Slump." In R. Pethig and M. Rauscher (eds.), *Challenges to the World Economy—A Festschrift for Horst Sieber*. Springer, Berlin.

———. (2003c): "Is Democracy Necessary for Development?" In S. Ramaswamy and J. W. Cason (eds.), *Development and Democracy*. University Press of New England, Lebanon, N.H.

————. (2003d): "Asia and Western Dominance—Retrospect and Prospect." *Journal of the Asia Pacific Economy* 8 (3): 283–99.

————. (2004): In *Defense of Empires*. The Wendt lecture, American Enterprise Institute, Washington, D.C.

————. (2004a): In *Praise of Empires—Globalization and Order*. Palgrave-Macmillan, New York.

————. (2004b): "India." In P. Bernholz and R. Vaubel (eds.), *Political Competition, Innovation and Growth in the History of Asian Civilizations*. Edward Elgar, Cheltenham.

Lal, D. and associates (1975): *Appraising Foreign Investment in Developing Countries*. Heinemann Educational Books, London.

Lal, D., S. Bery, and D. K. Pant (2003): "The Real Exchange Rate, Fiscal Deficits and Capital Flows: India 1981–2000." *Economic and Political Weekly* 38 (47): 4965–75.

Lal, D., H. Kim, G. Lu, and J. Prat (2003): "The Welfare Effects of Tobacco Taxation: Estimates for 5 Countries/Regions." *Journal des Economistes et des Etudes Humaines* 13 (1): 3–20.

Lal, D., R. Mohan, and I. Natarajan (2001): "Economic Reforms and Poverty Alleviation: A Tale of Two Surveys." *Economic and Political Weekly* 36 (12): 1017–28.

Lal, D., and H. Myint (1996): *The Political Economy of Poverty, Equity and Growth*. Clarendon Press, Oxford.

Lal, D., and I. Natarajan (2001): "The Virtuous Circle: Savings, Distribution and Growth Interactions in India." In D. Lal and R. Snape (eds.), *Trade, Development, and Political Economy: Essays in Honor of Anne O. Krueger*. Palgrave, Basingstoke.

Lal, D., and S. Rajapatirana (1987): "Foreign Trade Regimes and Economic Growth in Developing Countries." *World Bank Research Observer* 2 (2): 189–217; reprinted in Lal (1993).

Lal, D., and M. Fg. Scott (1990): *Public Policy and Economic Development: Essays in Honor of Ian Little*. Clarendon Press, Oxford.

Lal, D., and R. Snape (eds.): *Trade, Development and Political Economy: Essays in Honor of Anne O. Krueger*. Palgrave, Basingstoke.

Lal, D., and S. Wijnbergen (1985): "Government Deficits, the Real Interest Rate and LDC Debt: On Global Crowding Out." *European Economic Review* 29: 157–91. Reprinted in Lal (1993).

Lal, D., and M. Wolf (eds.) (1986): *Stagflation, Savings and the State*. Oxford University Press, New York.

Lall, S., and P. Streeten (1977): *Foreign Investment, Transnationals and Developing Countries*. Macmillan, London.

Lane, R. E. (2000): *The Loss of Happiness in Market Democracies*. Yale University Press, N.Y.

Langewiesche, W. (2000): "The Shipbreakers." *The Atlantic Monthly*, August.

Lardy, N. (2002): *Integrating China Into the World Economy*. Brookings Institution, Washington, D.C.

————. (2003): "Trade Liberalization and Its Role in Chinese Economic Growth." Mimeo, IMF-NCAER conference on "A Tale of Two Giants: India and China's Experience With Reform and Growth." New Delhi, November.

Latham, E. (1952): *The Group Basis of Politics*. Cornell University Press, Ithaca.

Lawrence, R., and M. Slaughter (1993): "International Trade and American Wages in the 1980s: Giant Sucking Sound or Small Hiccup?" *Brookings Papers on Economic Activity 2*, pp. 161–226.

Layard, R. (1980): "Human Satisfactions and Public Policy." *The Economic Journal* 96 (363): 737–50.

———. (2004): *Happiness: Lessons from a New Science*, Penguin Press, New York.

Leamer, E. (1996): "In Search of Stolper-Samuelson Effects on U.S. Wages." *NBER Working Paper*, no. 5427, NBER, Cambridge, Mass.

———. (1999): "Competition in Tradables as a Driving Force of Rising Income Inequality." In H. Siebert (ed.): *Globalization and Labor*. J.C.B. Mohr, Tubingen.

———. (2004): "Who's Afraid of Global Trade?" Mimeo, UCLA Anderson School of Management.

Levinson, A. (1996): "Environmental Regulations and Industry Location: International and Domestic Evidence." In Bhagwati and Hudec (eds.), *Fair Trade and Harmonaization*) vol.1, pp. 329–56. MIT Press, Cambridge, Mass.

Lewis, D. K. (1965): *Conventions—A Philosophical Study*. Harvard University Press, Cambridge, Mass.

Lewis, W. A. (1978): *Growth and Fluctuations 1870–1913*. George Allen and Unwin, London.

———. (1978a): *The Evolution of the International Economic Order*. Princeton University Press, Princeton, N.J.

Li, H., L. Squire, and H. Zou (1998): "Explaining International and Intertemporal Variations in Income Inequality." *Economic Journal* 108 (January): 93–134.

Lin, J. Y. (1990): "Collectivization and China's Agricultural Crisis in 1959–61." *Journal of Political Economy* 98 (6): 1228–52.

———. (2003): "Development Strategy, Viability and Economic Convergence." *Economic Development and Cultural Change* 51 (2): 277–308.

Lin, J.Y., F. Cai, and Z. Li (2003): *The China Miracle—Development Strategy and Economic Reforms*. Chinese University Press, Hong Kong.

Lindberg, M., and L. Squire (2003): "The Simultaneous Evolution of Growth and Inequality." World Bank working paper, World Bank, Washington, D.C.

Lindert, H. and J. G. Williamson (2003): "Does Globalization Make the World More Unequal." In M. Bordo, a. M. Taylor, and J. G. Williamson (eds.), *Globalization in Historical Perspective*. Chicago University Press, Chicago.

Lipsey, R. E. (2001): "Foreign Direct Investment and the Operations of Multinational Firms: Concepts, History and Data." *NBER Working Paper* No. 8665, NBER, Cambridge, Mass.

Lipson, C. (1985): *Standing Guard*. University of California Press, Berkeley.

Little, I.M.D. (1957): *A Critique of Welfare Economics*, 2nd ed. Clarendon Press, Oxford.

———. (1970–71): "Trade and Public Finance." *Indian Economic Review* 6: 119–32.

———. (1979): "Welfare Criteria, Distribution and Cost-Benefit Analysis." In M. J. Boskin (ed.), *Economics and Human Welfare*. Academic Press, New York; reprinted in Little (1999).

———. (1999): *Collections and Recollections*. Clarendon Press, Oxford.

———. (2002): *Ethics, Economics and Politics*. Oxford University Press, Oxford.

Little, I.M.D., and J. Clifford (1965): *International Aid*. Allen and Unwin, London.

Little, I.M.D., R. N. Cooper, W. M. Corden, and S. Rajapatirana (1993): *Boom, Crisis and Adjustment*. Oxford University Press, New York.

Little, I.M.D., and J. A. Mirrlees (1974): *Project Appraisal and Planning for Developing Countries*. Heinemann Educational Books, London.

———. (1990): "Project Appraisal and Planning Twenty Years On." *World Bank Annual Conference on Development Economics 1990* pp. 351–82.

Little, I.M.D., T. Scitovsky, and M. Fg. Scott (1970): *Industry and Trade in Some Developing Countries*. Oxford University Press, London.

Lluch, C. (1986): "ICOR's, Savings Rates and the Determinants of Public Expenditure in Developing Countries." In D. Lal and M. Wolf (eds.), *Stagflation and the State*. Oxford University Press, New York.

Lomberg, B. (2001): *The Skeptical Environmentalist*. Cambridge University Press, Cambridge.

MacIntyre, A. (1988): *Whose Justice? Which Rationality?* Duckworth, London.

———. (1990): "Individual and Social Morality in Japan and the United States: Rival Conceptions of the Self." *Philosophy East and West* 40 (4): 489–97.

Maddison, A. (1998): *Chinese Economic Performance in the Long Run*. OECD, Paris.

———. (2001): *The World Economy—A Millennial Perspective*. OECD, Paris.

———. (2003): *The World Economy—Historical Statistics*. OECD, Paris.

———. (2004): *Growth and Interaction in the World Economy: The Roots of Modernity*. The Wendt Lecture, American Enterprise Institute, Washington, D.C.

Magnet, M. (1993): *The Dream and the Nightmare: The Sixties Legacy of the Underclass*. Quill/Murrow, New York.

Makin, J. H. (1984): *The Global Debt Crisis*. Basic Books, New York.

Malcolm, N. (1995): "The Case Against Europe." *Foreign Affairs* 74 (2): 52–68.

Malinvaud, E. (1972): *Lectures on Microeconomic Theory*. North Holland, Amsterdam.

Mallaby, S. (2004): *The World's Banker*. Penguin Press, New York.

Manne, H. (1972): *The Modern Corporation and Social Responsibility*. American Enterprise Institute, Washington, D.C.

———. (2002): "Bring Back the Hostile Takeover." *Wall Street Journal*, June 26.

Marwick, A. (1998): *The Sixties*. Oxford University Press, Oxford.

Marx, K., and F. Engels (1848/1932): *Manifesto of the Communist Party*. International Publishers, New York.

Maskus, K. (2000): *Intellectual Property Rights in the Global Economy*. Institute of International Economics, Washington, D.C.

Matthews, R.C.O. (1986): "The Economics of Institutions and the Sources of Growth." *Economic Journal* 96 (December): 903–18.

Mayer, A. (1996): "Caste in an Indian Village: Change and Continuity 1954–1992." In C. J. Fuller (ed.), *Caste Today*. Oxford University Press, New Delhi.

McClelland, J. S. (1996): *A History of Western Political Thought*. Routledge, London.

McCloskey, D. (1980): "Magnanimous Albion, Free Trade and the British Income." *Explorations in Economic History* 17 (July): 303–20.

Meade, J. E. (1955): *Trade and Welfare*. Oxford University Press, London.

Meltzer, A. H. (1995): "Monetary, Credit (and other) Transmission Processes: A Monetarist Perspective." *Journal of Economic Perspectives* 9 (4): 49–72.

———. (2003): "Argentina 2002: A Case of Government Failure." *Cato Journal* 23 (1): 29–31.

Meltzer Commission (2000): *International Financial Institutions Advisory Commission: Report to Congress*; available online at http://www.house.gov/jec/imf/meltzer.htm.

Michaels, P. J. (2004): *Meltdown*. Cato Institute, Washington, D.C.

Michaels, P. J. et al. (2002): "Revised 21st Century Temperature Projections." *Climate Research* 23: 1–9.

Michaely, M., D. Papageorgiou, and A. Choksi (199i): *Liberalizing Foreign Trade, vol.7: Lessons of Experience From Developing Countries*. Basil Blackwell, Oxford.

Micklethwait, J., and A. Wooldridge (2003): *The Corporation*. Allen Lane, London.

———. (2004): *The Right Nation—Why America Is Different*. Allen Lane, London.

Mill, J. S. (1848/1970): *Principles of Political Economy*. Penguin, London.

———. (1859/1910): *On Liberty*. Everyman Library, London.

———. (1861/1910): *Representative Government*. Everyman Library, London.

———. (1874/ 1969): "Nature." In J. M. Robson (ed.), *Collected Works of John Stuart Mill*, vol. 10. University of Toronto Press, Toronto.

Minogue, K. (1963): *The Liberal Mind*. Liberty Fund, Indianapolis.

———. (1979): "The History of the Idea of Human Rights." In W. Laquer and R. Rubin (eds.), *The Human Rights Reader*. New American Library, New York.

———. (1993): *The Constitutional Mania*, Policy Study No. 134, Centre for Policy Studies, London.

———. (1995): *Politics*. Oxford University Press, Oxford.

Minsky, H. P. (1977): "A Theory of Systematic Fragility." In E. I. Altman and A.W. Sametz (eds.), *Financial Crisis*. Wiley, New York.

Morris, J. (ed.) (2002): *Sustainable Development*. Profile Books, London.

Morse, R. H. (1964): "The Heritage of Latin America." In L. Hartz (ed.), *The Founding of New Societies*. Harcourt, Brace and World, New York.

Mosley, P. (1987): *Overseas Aid*. Wheatsheaf, Brighton.

Mueller, D. C. (ed.) (1983): *The Political Economy of Growth*. Yale University Press. New Haven.

Munk, N. (1999): "How Levi's Trashed a Great American Brand." *Fortune*, April 1.

Murray, C. (1984): *Losing Ground*. Basic Books, New York.

Myint, H. (1948): *Theories of Welfare Economics*. Harvard University Press, Cambridge, Mass.

———. (1967): "The Inward and Outward-Looking Countries of Southeast Asia." *Malayan Economic Review* 12: 1–13.

———. (1987): "Neoclassical Development Analysis: Its Strengths and Weaknesses." In G. Meier (ed.), *Pioneers in Development*, 2nd series. Oxford University Press, New York.

Nehru, J. (1962): *An Autobiography*, Indian edition. Allied Publishers, New Delhi.

Newberry, D., and N. Stern (eds.) (1987): *The Theory of Taxation for Developing Countries*. Oxford University Press, New York.

Nietzsche, F. (1881/1982): *Daybreak: Thoughts on the Prejudices of Morality*. Cambridge University Press, Cambridge.

Nordhaus, D. (1994): *Managing the Global Commons*. MIT Press, Cambridge, Mass.

North, D. (1968): "Sources of Productivity Change in Ocean Shipping, 1600–1850." *Journal of Political Economy* 76 (5): 953–70.

North, D. (1990): *Institutions, Institutional Change and Economic Performance*. Cambridge University Press, Cambridge.

Nozick, R. (1974): *Anarchy, State, and Utopia*. Basil Blackwell, Oxford.

———. (1989): *The Examined Life—Philosophical Meditations*. Simon & Schuster, New York.

Nussbaum, M. (1992): "Virtue Revived." *Times Literary Supplement*, July 3, pp. 9–11.

Oakeshott, M. (1990): *Rationalism in Politics and Other Essays*, new and expanded ed. Liberty Fund, Indianapolis.

———. (1993): *Morality and Politics in Modern Europe*. Yale University Press, New Haven.

O'Brien, P. K. (1998): "Inseparable Connections: Trade, Economy, Fiscal State and the Expansion of Empire, 1688–1815." In P. J. Marshall (ed.), *The Oxford History of the British Empire, Vol. 2: The 18th Century*. Oxford University Press, Oxford.

Obstfeld, M., and K. Rogoff (1995): "The Mirage of Fixed Exchange Rates." *Journal of Economic Perspectives* 9 (4): 73–96.

———. (1996): *Foundations of International Macroeconomics*. MIT Press, Cambridge, Mass.

Obstfeld, M., and A. M. Taylor (2003): "Globalization and Capital Markets." In Bordo, Taylor, and Williamson (eds.), *Globalization in Historical Perspective*. University of Chicago Press, Chicago.

O'Leary, B. (2002): "In Praise of Empires Past." *New Left Review* 18 (Nov./Dec.): 106–30.

———. (2003): "Status Quo Patriotism." *New Left Review* 23 (Sept./Oct.): 100–104.

Oliver, R. (1999): *The African Experience*, rev. ed. Weidenfeld and Nicolson, London.

———. (ed.)(1976–84): *Cambridge History of Africa*, 8 vols. Cambridge University Press, Cambridge.

Olson, M. (1965): *The Logic of Collective Action*. Harvard University Press, Cambridge, Mass.

———. (2000): *Power and Prosperity*. Basic Books, New York.

O'Rourke, K. H. (2000): "Tariffs and Growth in the Late 19th Century." *The Economic Journal* 110 (463): 456–83.

O' Rourke, K. H., and J. G. Williamson (1999): *Globalization and History*. MIT Press, Cambridge, Mass.

Otto, D. (1996): "Non-Governmental Organizations in the United Nations: The Emerging Role of International Civil Society." *Human Rights Quarterly* 18 (1): 107–41.

Peeters, M. A. (2001): *Hijacking Democracy: Global Consensus on Global Governance*. Mimeo, American Enterprise Institute, Washington, D.C.

Phelps-Brown, H. (1983): *The Origins of Trade Union Power*. Clarendon Press, Oxford.

Plant, R. (1992): "Autonomy, Social Right and Distributive Justice." In J. Gray (ed.), *The Moral Foundations of Market Institutions*. IEA Health and Welfare Unit, London.

Pocock, J.G.A. (1975): "Early Modern Capitalism—The Augustan Perception." In E. Kamenka and R. S. Neale (eds.), *Feudalism, Capitalism and Beyond*. Arnold, London.

———. (1975a): *The Machiavellian Moment*. Princeton University Press, Princeton, N.J.

Polachek, S. W. (1992): "Conflict and Trade: An Economic Approach to Political International Interactions." In W. Isard and C. H. Anderton (eds.), *Economics of Arms Reduction and the Peace Process*, pp. 89–120. North Holland, Amsterdam.

Pollock, M. A., and G. C. Shaffer (eds.) (2001): *Transatlantic Governance in the Global Economy*. Rowman and Littlefield, Lanham, Md.

Pomeranz, K. (2000): *The Great Divergence*. Princeton University Press, Princeton, N.J.

Portes, R., and H. Rey (1998): "The Emergence of the Euro as an International Currency." *Economic Policy* 26: 307–43.

Potrykus, I. (2000): "The 'Golden Rice' Tale." *Agbioview*, October 23, archived at agbioview.listbot.com.

Prasad, E., K. Rogoff, S-J Wei, and M. Ayhan Kose (2003): *Effects of Financial Globalization on Developing Countries: Some Empirical Evidence*. IMF, Washington, D.C.

Prescott, E. (2002): "Prosperity and Depression." *American Economic Review* 92, 2 (May): 1–15.

Przeworski, A., and F. Limongi (1993): "Political Regimes and Economic Growth." *Journal of Economic Perspectives* 7 (3): 51–69.

Putnam, R. D. (1993): *Making Democracy Work*. Princeton University Press, Princeton, N.J.

———. (2000): *Bowling Alone*. Simon & Schuster, New York.

Rabushka, A. (2004): *The Flat Tax Idea Gains Momentum*. Hoover Institution, Stanford, Calif.

———. (2005): *The Flat Tax at Work in Russia: Year Four*. Hoover Institution, Stanford, Calif.

Rajan, R. G. and A. Subramanian (2005): "Aid and Growth: What Does the Cross-Country Evidence Really Show?" *NBER Working Paper* No. 11513, June 2005, NBER, Cambridge, Mass.

Rajan, R. G., and L. Zingales (2004): *Saving Capitalism from the Capitalists*. Random House Business Books, London.

Rancierre, R., A. Tornell, and F. Westerman (2003): "Crises and Growth: A Reevaluation." *NBER Working Papers* No. 10073, NBER, Cambridge, Mass.

Rauch, J. (1994): *Demosclerosis*. Random House, New York.

Raustiala, K. (1996): "Democracy, Sovereignty, and the Slow Pace of International Negotiations." *International Environmental Affairs* 8: 7–11.

Raustiala, K. (1997): "States, NGO's, and Environmental Institutions." *International Studies Quarterly* 20: 719–40.

Raustiala, K. (1997a): "The 'Participatory Revolution' in International Environmental Law." *Harvard Environmental Law Review* 21: 537–86.

Ray, R. K. (1979): *Industrialization in India—Growth and Conflict in the Private Sector 1914–47*. Oxford University Press, Delhi.

Reserve Bank of India (2004): *Report on Currency and Finance 2002–03*. Reserve Bank of India, Bombay.

Reynolds, L. G. (1985): *Economic Growth in the Third World*. Yale University Press, New Haven.

Riasanovsky, N. V. (1993): *A History of Russia*, 5th ed. Oxford University Press, New York.

Ricardo, D. (1821/1951): *On the Principles of Political Economy and Taxation*, 3rd ed. Cambridge University Press, Cambridge.

Riis, J., G. Lowenstein, J. Baron, C. Jepson, A. Fagerlin, and P. A. Ubel (2005): "Ignorance of Hedonic Adaptation to Hemo-dialysis: A Study Using Ecological Momentary Assessment." *Journal of Experimental Psychology: General* 134, 1 (February): 3–9.

Rimmer, D. (1992): *Ghana's Political Economy 1950–1990*. Pergamon Press, Oxford.

Robbins, L. (1952): *The Theory of Economic Policy in English Classical Political Economy*. Macmillan, London.

———. (1976): *Political Economy: Past and Present*. Macmillan, London.

Roberts, J. M. (1990): *The Penguin History of the World*. Penguin Books, London.

Rockoff, H. (1998): "By Way of Analogy: The Expansion of the Federal Government in the 1930's." In Bordo, Goldin and White (eds.), *The Defining Moment*. University of Chicago Press, Chicago.

Rodriguez, F., and D. Rodrik (1999): "Trade Policy and Economic Growth: A Skeptic's Guide to Cross-National Evidence." *NBER Working Paper* No. W7081, April.

Rodrik, D. (1995): "Why Is There Multilateral Lending?" Annual World Bank Conference on Development Economics, World Bank, Washington, D.C.

Roemer, J. E. (1982): *A General Theory of Exploitation and Class*. Harvard University Press, Cambridge, Mass.

Rogoff, K. (1998): "Blessing or Curse? Foreign and Underground Demand for Euro Notes." *Economic Policy* 26: 263–303.

———. (1999): "International Institutions for Reducing Global Financial Instability." *Journal of Economic Perspectives* 13 (4): 21–42.

Rogowski, R. (1989): *Commerce and Coalitions*. Princeton University Press, Princeton, N.J.

Romer, C. D. (1999): "Changes in Business Cycles: Evidence and Explanations." *Journal of Economic Perspectives* 13 (2): 23–44.

Rosemont Jr., H. (1998): "Human Rights: A Bill of Worries." In De Bary and Weiming (eds.), *Confucianism and Human Rights*. Columbia University Press, New York.

Ruggie, J. G. (1983): "International Regimes, Transactions and Change: Embedded Liberalism in the Post-war Economic Order." In Stephen D. Krasner (ed.), *International Regimes*, pp. 195–223. Cornell University Press, Ithaca, NY.

Sachs, J. D., and A. Warner (1995): "Economic Reforms and the Process of Global Integration." *Brookings Papers on Economic Activity* 1, pp. 1–118. Brookys Institute, Washington, D.C.

Sala-a-Martin, X. (2002): "The Disturbing 'Rise' of Global Income Inequality." *NBER Working Papers* No. 8904, NBER, Cambridge, Mass.

———. (2002a): "The World Distribution of Income (estimated from individual country distributions)." *NBER Working* Papers No. 8933, NBER, Cambridge, Mass.

Sally, R. (1998): *Classical Liberalism and International Economic Order*. Routledge, London.

Salter, W. E. (1959): "Internal and External Balance: The Role of Price and Expenditure Effects." *Economic Record* 35 (August): 226–38.

Samatar, A. I. (1999): *An African Miracle*. Heinemann, Portsmouth, N.H.

Sandel, M. J. (1996): *Democracy's Discontent*. Harvard University Press, Cambridge, Mass.

Saul, S. B. (1976): *The Myth of the Great Depression 1873–1896*. Macmillan, London.

Schatschneider, E. E. (1975): *The Semi-Sovereign People*. Hinsdale, Dryden, Ill.

Schelling, T. C. (1992): "Some Economics of Global Warming." *American Economic Review* 82 (1): 1–14.

Schneider, S. H. (1989): *Global Warming*. Sierra Club, San Francisco.

Schrag, P. (1999): *Paradise Lost: California's Experience, America's Future*. University of California Press, Berkeley.

Schumpeter, J. A. (1950): *Capitalism, Socialism and Democracy*. Harper and Row, New York.

———. (1954): *History of Economic Analysis*. Oxford University Press, Oxford.

———. (1955): *Imperialism and Social Classes*. Meridian, New York.

Schwartz, A. J. (1996): "Do Currency Boards Have a Future?" In G. E. Wood (ed.), *Explorations in Economic Liberalism—The Wincott Lectures*. Macmillan, London.

———. (2003): "Do Sovereign Debtors Need a Bankruptcy Law." *Cato Journal* 23 (1): 87–100.

———. (2003a): "Comment on Bordo and Flandreau." In Bordo, Taylor, and Williamson (eds.), *Globalization in Historical Perspective*. University of Chicago Press, Chicago.

Scott, M. Fg (1989): *A New View of Economic Growth*. Clarendon Press, Oxford.

Scruton, R. (2000): *WHO, What and Why?* Institute of Economic Affairs, London.

Searle, G. R. (1998): *Morality and the Market in Victorian Britan*. Clarendon Press, Oxford.

Selgin, G. A. (1988): *The Theory of Banking*. Rowan and Littlefield, Totowa, N.J.

Sen, A. K. (1983): "The Profit Motive." *Lloyds Bank Review*, January, pp. 1–20.

———. (1992): *Inequality Re-examined*. Clarendon Press, Oxford.

———. (1995): "Rationality and Social Choice." *American Economic Review* 85 (1): 1–24.

———. (1999): *Development and Freedom*. Oxford University Press, Oxford.

Servan-Schreiber, J.-J. (1968): *The American Challenge*. Hamish Hamilton, London.

Shaffer, G. C. (2001): "The World Trade Organization Under Challenge." *Harvard Environmental Law Review* 25: 9–13.

Shankar, S., L. Robison, M.E.M. Jenney, T. H. Rockwood, E. Wu, J. Feusner, D. Friedman, R. L. Kane, and S. Bhatia (2005): "Health-Related Quality of Life in Young Survivors of Childhood Cancer Using the Minneapolis—Manchester Quality of Life-Youth Forum." *Pediatrics*, 115, 2 (Feb. 14): 435–42.

Shiller, R. (2001): *Irrational Exuberance*. Broadway Books, New York.

Shleifer, A., and R. Vishny (1997): "The Limits to Arbitrage." *Journal of Finance* 52 (1): 35–56.

Simon, J. (1996): *The Ultimate Resource*. Princeton University Press, Princeton, N.J.

Skidelsky, R. (1983): *John Maynard Keynes*, vol. 1. Macmillan, London.

———. (2000): *John Maynard Keynes*, vol. 3. Macmillan, London.

Smith, A. (1759/1982): *The Theory of Moral Sentiments*. Liberty Fund, Indianapolis.

Snape, R. (1996): "Trade Discrimination? Yesterday's Problem?" *Economic Record* 72, 219 (December): 381–96.

Solomou, S. (1990): *Phases of Economic Growth 1850–1973: Kondratieff Waves and Kuznets Swings*. Cambridge University Press, Cambridge.

Solow, B. L. (1991): "Slavery and Colonization." In Solow (ed.), *Slavery and the Rise of the Atlantic Economies*. Cambridge University Press, Cambridge.

Solow, R. M. (1974): "The Economics of Resources or the Resources of Economics." *American Economic Review* 64 (2): 1–14.

———. (2000): "Notes on Social Capital and Economic Performance." In P. Dasgupta and I. Serageldin (eds.), *Social Capital*. World Bank, Washington, D.C.

Sowell, T. (1996): *Migrations and Cultures: A World View*. Basic Books, New York.

Srinivas, M. N. (1996): *Village, Caste, Gender and Method*. Oxford University Press, New Delhi.

Srinivasan, T. N. (1996): "The Generalized Theory of Distortions and Welfare Two Decades Later." In R. C. Feenstra et al. (eds.), *The Political Economy of Trade Policy*. MIT Press, Cambridge, Mass.

———. (2000): "The Washington Consensus a Decade Later: Ideology and the Art and Science of Policy Advice." *The World Bank Research Observer* 15 (2): 265–70.

Srinivasan, T. N., and J. Bhagwati (2001): "Outward Orientation and Development: Are the Revisionists Right?" In D. Lal and R. Snape (eds.), *Trade, Development and Political Economy*. Palgrave, Basingstoke.

Stigler, G. (1965/1986): "The Economist and the State." In K. R. Leube and T. G. Moore (eds.), *The Essence of Stigler*. Hoover Institution, Stanford, Calif.

———. (ed.) (1988): *Chicago Studies in Political Economy*. University of Chicago Press, Chicago.

Stiglitz, J. (1994): *Whither Socialism?* MIT Press, Cambridge, Mass.

———. (2002): *Globalization and Its Discontents*. Allen Lane, London.

Strachey, L. (1918/1971): *Eminent Victorians*. Penguin, Harmonsworth.

Sugden, R. (1986): *The Economics of Rights, Co-operation and Welfare*. Blackwell, Oxford.

———. (1998): "Conventions" in *The New Palgrave Dictionary of Economics and the Law*. Macmillan, Basingstoke.

———. (1993): "A Review of 'Inequality Re-examined' by Amartya Sen." *Journal of Economic Literature* 31, 4 (December): 1947–86.

Sugg, I., and U. Kreuter (1994): *Elephants and Ivory*. Institute of Economic Affairs, London.

Swan, T. W. (1963): "Longer-Run Problems of the Balance of Payments." In H. W. Arndt and W. M. Corden (eds.), *The Australian Economy—A Volume of Readings*. Cheshire, Melbourne.

Tanzi, V., and L. Schuknecht (2000): *Public Spending in the 20th Century*. Cambridge University Press, Cambridge.

Tawney, R. H. (1926/1990): *Religion and the Rise of Capitalism*. Penguin Books, London.

Taylor, A. M. (2002): "Globalization, Trade and Development: Some Lessons From History." *NBER Working Papers* No. 9326, November.

Taylor, C. (1974): "Socialism and Weltanschung." In L. Kolakowski and S. Hampshire (eds.), *The Socialist Idea—A Reappraisal*. Weidenfeld and Nicholson, London.

Taylor, J. (2002): "Sovereign Debt Restructuring: A U.S. Perspective." Mimeo, U.S. Dept. of Treasury, Washington, D.C.

———. (2003): "Increasing Economic Growth and Stability in Emerging Markets." *Cato Journal* 23 (1): 127–34.

Temin, P. (1976): *Did Monetary Forces Cause the Great Depression?* Norton, New York.

———. (2003): "Mediterranean Trade in Biblical Times." Paper for Hecksher Symposium, Stockholm School of Economics, 2003 (to be published in the conference volume).

de Tocqueville, A. (1835/1968): *Democracy in America*. Collins, London.

Tooby, J., and L. Cosmides (1989): "Evolutionary Psychology and the Generation of Culture, Part 1." *Ethology and Sociobiology* 10: 29–49.

Toulmin, S. (1990): *Cosmopolis*. University of Chicago Press, Chicago.

Tren, R., and R. Bate (2001): *When Politics Kills: The Political Economy of Malaria Control*. Institute of Economic Affairs, London.

Truman, D. B. (1953): *The Government Process*. Alfred A. Knopf, New York.

Tullock, G. (1967): "The Welfare Costs of Tariffs, Monopoly and Theft." *Western Economic Journal* 5: 224–32.

Tumlir, J. (1984): *Economic Policy as a Constitutional Problem*. Institute of Economic Affairs, London.

———. (1985): *Protectionism: Trade Policy in Democratic Societies*. American Enterprise Institute, Washington, D.C.

UK. HM. Treasury (2005): *Flat Taxes*, July 2005, UK Treasury website.

U.S. International Trade Commission (USITC) (1999): *The Economic Effects of Significant U.S. Import Restraints*. Publication 3201, USITC, Washington, D.C.

United Nations Population Division (2002): *World Population Prospects: The 2002 Revision*. United Nations, New York.

van Ark, B., et al. (2002): "Change Gears: Productivity, ICT and Services—Europe and the United States. "*Groningen Growth and Development Center*. Working Paper GD-60, Groningen.

Vargas Llosa, Mario (2000): "Liberalism in the New Millennium." In I. Vasquez (ed.), *Global Fortune*. Cato Institute, Washington, D.C.

Vaubel, R. (1977): "Free Currency Competition." *Weltwirtschaft Archiv* 113: 435–59.

———. (1984): "The Government's Money Monopoly: Externalities or Natural Monopoly?" *Kyklos* 37 (1): 27–58.

———. (1994): "The Political Economy of the IMF: A Public Choice Analysis." In D. Bandow and I. Vasquez (eds.), *Perpetuating Poverty: The World Bank, the IMF, and the Developing World*. Cato Institute, Washington, D.C.

———. (1996): "Bureaucracy at the World Bank and the IMF." *World Economy* 19 (2): 195–210.

Vietor, R.H.K. (2000): "Government Regulation of Business." In Engerman and Gallman (eds.) *The Cambridge Economic History of the Untied States*, vol. 3. Cambridge University Press, Cambridge.

Wade, R. H. (2001): "Making the World Development Report 2000: Attacking Poverty." *World Development* 29 (8): 1435–41.

Wallerstein, I. (1974–1988): *The Modern World System*, 3 vols. Academic Press, New York.

Wasserman, S. (1998): "Years of Hope, Days of Rage." *Los Angeles Times Book Review*, October 11, pp. 5–6.

Weber, M. (1920/1958): *The Protestant Ethic and the Spirit of Capitalism*. Charles Scribner's Sons, New York.

Webster, C. K. (1995): *Why Freud Was Wrong*. Harper Collins, London.

Whelan, E. M. (1993): *Toxic Terror—The Truth Behind the Cancer Scare*, 2d ed. Promethews Books, Buffalo, NY.

Whelan, E. (2000): "The Case for Genetically Modified Food." *Nutrinews*, archived at agbioview.listbot.com.

White, L. (1984): *Free Banking in Britain*. Cambridge University Press, Cambridge.

Whybrow, P. C. (2204): *American Mania*. Norton, New York.

Whyte, M. K. (1996): "The Chinese Family and Economic Development: Obstacle or Engine?" *Economic Development and Cultural Change* 45 (1): 1–30.

Williams, B. (1985): *Ethics and the Limits of Philosophy.* Fontana Paperbacks, Collins, London.

Williamson, J. (1990): "What Washington Means by Policy Reform." In J. Williamson (ed.): *Latin American Adjustment: How Much Has Happened?* Institute for International Economics, Washington, D.C.

———. (2000): "What Should the World Bank Think About the Washington Consensus." *World Bank Research Observer* 15 (2): 251–64.

Williamson, J. G. (1985): *Did British Capitalism Breed Inequality?* Allen and Unwin, Boston.

———. (1996): "Globalization, Convergence and History." *Journal of Economic History* 56 (June): 1–30.

———. (1998): "Globalization, Labor Markets and Policy Backlash in the Past." *Journal of Economic Perspectives* 12 (Fall): 51–72.

———. (2001): "Demographic Change, Economic Growth and Inequality." In N. Birdsall, A. C. Kelly, and S. W. Sinding (eds.), *Population Matters*, pp. 106–36. Oxford University Press, Oxford.

———. (2003): "Was It Stolper-Samuelson, Infant Industry or Something Else? World Tariffs 1789–1938." NBER Working Paper No. 9656, NBER, Cambridge, Mass.

Williamson, O. E. (1985): *The Economic Institutions of Capitalism.* Free Press, New York.

Wilson, J. D. (1996): "Capital Mobility and Environmental Standards: Is There a Theoretical Basis for a Race to the Bottom?" In Bhagwati and Hudec (eds.), *Fair Trade and Harmonization*, vol. 1, pp. 393–427. MIT Press, Cambridge, Mass.

Wolf, M. (1984): *Costs of Protecting Jobs in Textiles and Clothing.* Trade Policy Research Center, London.

———. (1994): *The Resistible Rise of Fortress Europe.* Rochester Paper No. 1, Trade Policy Unit, Center for Policy Studies, London.

———. (2001): "Infantile Leftist." *Prospect* 65 (July): 12–13.

Wood, A. (1995): "How Trade Hurt Unskilled Workers." *Journal of Economic Perspectives* 11: 57–80.

Wood, G. E. (2003): "Competition, Regulation and Financial Stability." In P. Booth and D. Currie (eds.), *The Regulation of Financial Markets.* Institute of Economic Affairs, London.

World Bank (1989): *Sub-Saharan Africa: From Crisis to Sustainable Growth.* World Bank, Washington, D.C.

World Bank (1992): *World Development Report 1992: Development and the Environment.* Oxford University Press, New York.

World Bank (2001): *World Development Report 2000/01: Attacking Poverty.* Oxford University Press, New York.

World Business Council (WBC) (2000): *Corporate Social Responsibility.* Geneva.

World Commission on Environment and Development (the 'Brundtland' report) (1987): *Our Common Future.* Oxford University Press, Oxford.

Wrigley, E. A. (1988): *Continuity, Chance and Change.* Cambridge University Press, Cambridge.

Wyatt-Walter, A. (1996): "Adam Smith and the Liberal Tradition in International Relations." *Review of International Studies* 22 (1).

Wynia, G. (1990): *The Politics of Latin American Development*. Cambridge University Press, Cambridge.

Wyplosz, C. (1997): "EMU: Why and How It Might Happen." *Journal of Economic Perspectives* 11 (4): 3–22.

Yan, Y. (2003): *Private Life Under Socialism*. Stanford University Press, Stanford, Calif.

Zakaria, F. (1997): "The Rise of Illiberal Democracies." *Foreign Affairs* 76 (6): 22–43.

———. (2003): *The Future of Freedom*. Norton, New York.

Zarnowitz, V. (1999): "Theory and History Behind Business Cycles: Are the 1990s the Onset of a Golden Age?" *Journal of Economic Perspectives* 13 (2): 69–90.

Index

Adam Smith Institute, 249n.35
Africa: colonialism, impact of, 35–36; polities of, 176–77
Agency for International Development (USAID), 223
agrarian civilizations: material and cosmological beliefs in, 154–55; merchant capitalists in, 2–5
agriculture: barriers to trade in, 70; privatization of in China, 167–69
Ahluwalia, Montek, 130
Amnesty International, 230
Anderson, Kenneth, 274n.14
Ando, Albert, 199
Anglo-Turkish convention (1838), 32
Annan, Kofi, 209
anti-dumping measures, 69–70
Aquinas, Saint Thomas, 267n.38
Argentina, 115
Aristotle, 122, 267n.38
Arrow, Kenneth, 191, 193
Arrow-Debreu theorems, 55
Asian model of development, 115–17
Attaturk, Kemal, 39, 165
Augustine (Archbishop of Canterbury), 156
Augustine of Hippo, Saint, 159–60, 267–68n.38

Baechler, Jean, 1–2
Bagehot, W., 123
Bairoch, Paul, 34–35, 241n.16
balance of payments adjustments, 97–100
Balassa, Bela, 237n.2

banks/banking system: Asian financial crises and, 115–16; blue-sky laws, 39, 42; debt crises and (see debt crises); deposit insurance, 259n.40; free banking and the stability of the money supply, 259–60n.43; the global financial infrastructure, 122–26; the gold standard and, 30–31; international capital flows (see international capital flows); OPEC surpluses and offshore branches of money center banks, 45–46. See also exchange rates; monetary policy/system
Barfield, Claud, 88
Barings Bank, 124
Basle Convention, 222
Basu, S., 107
Bauer, Peter Thomas, 142, 237n.2
Beard, Charles, 60
Becker, Gary, 274n.6
Bellah, Robert, 272n.27
Bennett, William, 272n.27
Bentham, Jeremy, 54
Bergsten, C. F., 257n.12
Berlin, Isaiah, 271n.19
Berman, Harold, 6, 270–71n.10
Bernanke, Ben S., 244n.56
Bevan, David, 111
Bhagwati, J., 63, 241n.16, 242n.20
Bhalla, Surjit, 128, 130–32, 134–37, 139, 263n.7
Bhartiya Janata Party, 165, 167, 174, 176, 231
bin Laden, Osama, 40
Biodiversity Convention, 225–27
Bismarck, Otto von, 51, 197, 232

307

state-owned enterprises (SOEs), 170–72
steam engine, 23
Stigler, George, 65
Stiglitz, Joseph, 55, 127, 131–32, 147, 149, 266n.43
Stokes, Eric, 228
Stolper, Wolfgang, 25
Strachey, Lytton, 163
Stutzer, A., 192
Subramanian, A., 144
Suez intervention of 1956, 40
Sugden, R., 270n.4
Summers, Lawrence, 147
supply-side economic policies, 46
sustainable development, 202, 211–14, 224. *See also* environment
Swan, T. W., 97
Sweden, 66
Swiss Federal Institute of Technology, 226
Switzerland, 66

Taiwan, 43
Tanzania, 111, 145
Tanzi, V., 251–52n.13, 251n.10
tariffs. *See* protectionist policies
Tawney, R. H., 1, 7, 166
taxation: of corporate dividends, 201–2; flat taxes, 248–49n.35; Tobin tax, 123; of trade (*see* protectionist policies)
Taylor, A. M., 107
Temin, P., 239n.12, 244n.56
Temple, Henry John, 126
terms of trade/optimal tariff argument for protection, 26, 30, 242n.19–20
textiles: labor and capital in production of, changes in related to the Industrial Revolution, 52–53; Multi Fiber Agreement (MFA), 69, 77
Thailand, 110
Thatcher, Margaret, 51, 66, 93
Third World: cultural nationalists' objections to globalization, 151 (*see also* morality); current development policies for, 42–43; debt crisis in, 114–15; economic development under Pax Britannia, 32–36; economic nationalism in following World War II, 40; foreign aid to, 139–49; modernization and Westernization, concerns regarding, 165–80; OPEC and current globalization for, 43–46
Tobin, James, 262n.61

Tobin tax, 123
Tocqueville, Alexis de, 18, 206, 233, 272n.27, 274n.3
Tornell, Aaron, 110, 258n.23
Torrens, Robert, 26, 30
Toulmin, Stephen, 228–30
township and village enterprises (TVEs), 169
trade: domestic distortions, theory of, 63–64; elementary theory of, 23–27, 240n.13; ethics in, rejection of, 80; free and economic liberalism (*see* free trade; liberal international economic orders); governmentally imposed restrictions on (*see* protectionist policies); international framework for under the current liberal international economic order, 41; labor standards and, 76–80; mercantilism, 20–22; most favored nation principle in treaties regarding, 28, 68, 71; preferential trading arrangements (*see* preferential trading arrangements); traded and nontraded goods, distinction between, 22–23; U.S. policies regarding (*see* trade policy of the United States)
trade bloc, 71
Trade Policy and Economic Welfare (Corden), 62–64, 91
trade policy of the United States: fair trade, argument for, 75–76; fast track authority in negotiating trade agreements, 68; labor market developments and, 80–83; movement from protectionism to free trade, 67–68; multilateral system of free trade, retreat from, 71–80; the new protectionism under GATT, 68–70; political history of, 28–29, 41, 67–68; reciprocity, belief in the principle of, 27, 32, 41, 68–69, 89–90; social and labor standards, argument for, 76–80; TRIPS agreement, 87–88
trade unions: development of British, 29, 53; the gold standard and rise of, 31
transactions costs, 152–53
transport costs, distinction between traded/nontraded goods created by, 22–23
treaties: fast track authority in negotiating, 68; most favored nation clauses in, 28, 68, 71. *See also* names of treaties
Treffler, Daniel, 70
TRIPS agreement, 87–88
Tumlir, Jan, 255n.69
TVEs. *See* township and village enterprises